Intelligent Tutoring Systems

Computers and People Series

Edited by
B. R. GAINES

The series is concerned with all aspects of man-computer relationships, including interaction, interfacing modelling and artificial intelligence. Books are interdisciplinary, communicating results derived in one area of study to workers in another. Applied, experimental, theoretical and tutorial studies are included.

Intelligent Tutoring Systems

edited by

D. SLEEMAN
University of Leeds, U.K.

and

J. S. BROWN
Cognitive and Instructional Sciences, Xerox PARC, U.S.A.

1982

ACADEMIC PRESS

A Subsidiary of Harcourt Brace Jovanovich, Publishers

London · New York
Paris · San Diego · San Francisco
São Paulo · Sydney · Tokyo · Toronto

ACADEMIC PRESS INC. (LONDON) LTD.
24/28 Oval Road
London NW1

United States Edition published by
ACADEMIC PRESS INC.
111 Fifth Avenue
New York, New York 10003

Second printing 1983

British Library Cataloguing in Publication Data

Intelligent tutoring systems.—(Computers and people)
1. Computer-assisted instruction
I. Sleeman, D.   II. Brown, J. S.   III. Series
371.3′9445   LB1028.5

ISBN 0-12-648680-8

Printed in Great Britain by
J. W. Arrowsmith Ltd, Bristol BS3 2NT

Contributors

J. S. BROWN
Cognitive and Instructional Sciences, Xerox PARC, Palo Alto, California 94305, U.S.A.

R. R. BURTON
Cognitive and Instructional Sciences, Xerox PARC, Palo Alto, California 94305, U.S.A.

W. J. CLANCEY
Computer Science Department, Stanford University, Stanford, California 94305, U.S.A.

A. COLLINS
Bolt Beranek and Newman, Inc., 50 Moulton Street, Cambridge, Massachusetts 02138, U.S.A.

M. R. GENESERETH
Computer Science Department, Stanford University, Stanford, California 94305, U.S.A.

J. DE KLEER
Cognitive and Instructional Sciences, Xerox PARC, Palo Alto, California 94305, U.S.A.

S. E. GOLDIN
Bolt Beranek and Newman, Inc., 50 Moulton Street, Cambridge, Massachusetts 02138, U.S.A.

I. P. GOLDSTEIN
Massachusetts Institute of Technology, Cambridge, Massachusetts 02139, U.S.A.

R. J. HENDLEY
Department of Computer Studies, The University, Leeds LS2 9JT, U.K.

R. KIMBALL
Cognitive and Instructional Sciences, Xerox PARC, Palo Alto, California 94305, U.S.A.

M. MATZ
Massachusetts Institute of Technology, Cambridge, Massachusetts 02139, U.S.A.

M. L. MILLER
Massachusetts Institute of Technology, Cambridge, Massachusetts 02139, U.S.A.

T. O'SHEA
Institute for Educational Technology, Open University, Walton Hall, Milton Keynes MK7 6AA, U.K.

D. SLEEMAN
Department of Computer Studies, The University, Leeds LS2 9JT, U.K.

A. STEVENS
Bolt Beranek and Newman, Inc., 50 Moulton Street, Cambridge, Massachusetts 02138, U.S.A.

Preface

Early CAI workers set themselves the task of producing teaching systems which could adapt to the needs of individual students. It is now generally agreed that this is a *very* difficult task, and one that will only be accomplished as a result of extensive research in both AI and Cognitive Science.

Many of the papers in this volume touch on one of the central issues, namely, *Student Modelling*. This volume reports on much of the progress made by the field of *Intelligent Tutoring Systems* to date, and highlights *some* of the challenges which remain to be tackled. Indeed, this is the first volume to be published in this area, although it does draw upon the special issue of the International Journal of Man-Machine Studies devoted to this topic, and we expect that it will be of interest to educators, educational technologists as well as to workers in the fields of AI and Cognitive Science.

February 1982

D. Sleeman
J. S. Brown

Chapters 1, 3, 4, 5, 6, 10, and 11 were first published as a special issue of the International Journal of Man-Machine Studies, January 1979, Volume 11.

Chapters 1, 3, 4, 5, 6, 10 and 13 were first published as a special issue of the
International Journal of Man-Machine Studies, January 1979, Volume 11

Contents

Part III
Artificial Intelligence Techniques

Introduction: Intelligent tutoring systems

The appearance of a collection of papers in any area gives the opportunity to reflect on the current state of research and practice, and indulge in some speculation about the future. We propose such an overview, in the hope that it will give some perspective to the field of Intelligent Tutoring Systems (often known as *Intelligent* Computer-Assisted Instruction, ICAI), particularly for those who may not be fully aware of recent activities.

The precursor to Intelligent Tutoring Systems was *generative* CAI, an enterprise with a relatively long history for a computer-related field. During the mid-60's, Uhr and his collaborators implemented a series of systems which generated problems in arithmetic and in vocabulary-recall (Uhr, 1969). Subsequently, a number of systems were devised to provide drill and practice in arithmetic, and to select problems at a level of difficulty appropriate to the student's overall performance (Suppes, 1967; Woods & Hartley, 1971). For obvious reasons, such systems have been called "adaptive" and their sophistication lay in the task-selection algorithms. In these systems, models of the student were based more on parametric summaries of behavior than explict representations of his knowledge. Because of the inherent simplicity of the task domain, this technique was sufficiently robust that the systems could function effectively for real instructional uses. In fact, both the Stanford and the Leeds systems have been used extensively and regularly in teaching for over a decade.

There is no sharp boundary between adaptive instructional systems and those generally falling under the rubric of ITS. Indeed, one of the original goals for ITS was to extend the domain of applicability, the power, and the accuracy, of adaptive systems. Doing so involves more than just examining the student's answers. To optimize long-term learning gains, evaluative experiments are necessary to determine the circumstances in which help should be given, and, for example, whether the student or the program should choose the level of difficulty of the next problem (Hartley and Sleeman, 1973). The intention of O'Shea's System (O'Shea, 1981) was for the system *itself* to perform sensible experiments which would lead to an improved teaching strategy for a particular group of students. In Kimball's system (Kimball, 1981), advice was given to a student based on the quality of his solution method rather than the correctness of his answer.

In the last five years researchers have focussed on supportive learning environments intended to facilitate *learning-by-doing:* transforming factual knowledge into experiential knowledge. These systems attempt to combine the problem-solving experience and motivation of 'discovery' learning with the effective guidance of tutorial interactions. These two objectives are often in conflict since, to tutor well, the system must constrain the student's instructional paths and exercises to those whose answers and likely mistakes can be completely

1

specified ahead of time. To overcome these limitations, the system must have its *own* problem-solving expertise, its own diagnostic or student modelling capabilities and its own explanatory capabilities. In order to orchestrate these reasoning capabilities it must also have explicit control or tutorial strategies specifying *when* to interrupt a student's problem-solving activity, *what* to say and *how* best to say it; all in order to provide the student with instructionally effective advice. Without such intelligent guidance, the student is liable to struggle uselessly with a conceptual roadblock that he is ill-equipped to handle, or to gloss over other situations that could have high instructional impact given his current state of knowledge.† But by augmenting open-ended, problem-solving environments with the above kind of tutorial intelligence, it becomes possible to transform a student's conceptual flounderings and misconceptions into profound and efficient learning experiences -- ones rooted in his own actions and hypotheses. In brief, the augmentation of environments with intelligent tutoring enables more students' misconceptions to be transformed into constructive learning experiences.

From another perspective, these systems can be seen as explorations into how the dramatic advances in computer technology can be used to produce new kinds of learning environments. Those paradigms for using computers in education which were based on scarce computational resources probably can not be extended to effectively utilize the computation-rich world of tomorrow's technologies. Falling hardware costs, together with evolving theories of the cognitive sciences, offer many new ways to exploit computation and knowledge in the educational arena; ITS is exploring some of these. This is not to say that CAI will not play a role; Indeed, it as well as many other intriguing choices are being made more easily **possible by the advent of inexpensive microcomputers.**

Intelligent tutorial systems take the form of computer-based 1) problem-solving monitors, 2) coaches, 3) laboratory instructors and 4) consultants. They exist primarily as experimental vehicles on a variety of domains:

1. Symbolic integration (Kimball, 1981).

2. Electronic troubleshooting, the various SOPHIE systems (Brown, Burton & deKleer, 1981).

3. Axiomatically-based mathematics, the EXCHECK system (Smith et al, 1975)

4. Interpretation of NMR spectra, the PSM-NMR system (Sleeman and Hendley, 1981).

† Some floundering can be vitally important. The crucial meta-skill of knowing when one's floundering is useless can only be discovered by trial and error. The subtlety of separating potentially productive exploration from useless wanderings only points to the challenges of constructing sensitive and well-motivated tutorial principles.

5.   Medical diagnosis, the GUIDON system (Clancey, 1981).

6.   Informal gaming environments: the West system (Burton & Brown, 1981) and the WUMPUS system (Goldstein, 1981).

7.   Program-plan debugging, the SPADE system (Miller, 1981).

8.   A Consultancy System for users of MACSYMA, an Algebraic manipulation system (Genesereth, 1981).

Each of these has tended to emphasize some aspects of an overall coaching systems and neglect others. Thus it is not surprising that the designers of these systems are dissatisfied with their system's overall performance. The following are some of the acknowledged shortcomings:

1.   The instructional material produced in response to a student's query or mistake is often at the wrong level of detail, as the system assumes too much or too little student knowledge.

2.   The system assumes a particular conceptualization of the domain, thereby coercing a student's performance into its own conceptual framework. None of these systems can discover, and work within, the student's own (idiosyncratic) conceptualization to diagnose his "mind bugs" within that framework.

3.   The tutoring and critiquing strategies used by these systems are excessively ad hoc reflecting *unprincipled* intuitions about how to control their behavior. Discovering consistent principles would be facilitated by constructing better theories of learning and mislearning -- a task requiring detailed psychological theories of knowledge representation and belief revision.

4.   User interaction is still too restrictive, limiting the student's expressiveness and thereby limiting the ability of the tutor's diagnostic mechanisms).

The above dissatisfactions are highly interrelated but do suggest a framework within which to view ITS-related activities: (1) those performing detailed (protocol) analyses of the learning, mislearning and teaching processes, (2) those developing theoretical constructs for use within ITSs that may also be psychologically insightful, and (3) those developing artificial intelligence (AI) techniques that utilize such theoretical constructs to enhance the functionality, robustness and responsiveness of ITSs. Within this framework, the papers in this book can be seen as laying the groundwork for continuing investigation.[†]

Stevens, Collins & Goldin (1981) report a detailed analysis of student protocols to determine the misconceptions and alternative conceptions which students appear to have in their causal models of meteorology. By choosing the domain of algebra, a

---

[†] Indeed the contents of this volume have been organized to a first approximation using this schema together with the more detailed subdivisions of AI techniques given below. Many of the papers make contributions to more than one category.

considerably simpler knowledge base. Matz (1981) has developed one of the first detailed psychological models of *why* a student *might* form certain misconceptions or bugs. Her theory provides a cornerstone for building flexible diagnostic systems and, more immediately, it suggests that a Coach must pay attention to the sequence of worked examples and encountered problem states from which the student is apt to abstract (invent) functional invariances. This suggests that no matter how carefully an instructional designer plans a sequence of examples, he can never know all the intermediate steps and abstracted structure that a student will generate while solving an exercise. Indeed, the student may well produce illegal steps in his solution and from these invent illegal algebraic principles.

In terms of theoretical constructs, Goldstein (1981), Burton and Brown (1981), Burton (1981), and Sleeman (1981) suggest new constructs for representing explicitly the state of knowledge in a student. Goldstein (1981) introduces the suggestive metaphor of an *overlay* model, that is, a student model which is, basically, a subset of an articulate model of an expert's knowledge base. Burton and Brown (1981) advance the conceptual notion of a *differential* model that abstracts how the student's behavior is critically different from that of an expert. Sleeman and Hendley (1981) use a comparison algorithm, which compares the Formal Language statements extracted from the user's explanation with those produced by the domain-algorithm, that similarly creates a data-structure which highlights how the user's and the expert's actions differ. Whereas the overlay and differential constructs represent a student's knowledge as a subset of the expert's skill, other constructs are needed to facilitate representing mislearned sub-skills that are not primarily subsets of the correctly learned skills. This issue is addressed by Burton (1981) in his DEBUGGY system, which uses a *perturbation* construct to represent a student's misconceptions as variants of the fine grain procedural structure of the correct skill. Sleeman (1981) represents domain knowledge as rules and then captures potential errors as variants of those rules (*mal-rules*).

Many of the papers contained in this book also involve substantial AI research. That new AI techniques have been evolved is not surprising given the particular demands of ITS; that systems give a reasonably *fast* response, be *robust* and be able to cope with *noisy, inconsistent* and *incomplete* responses/information.

We wish to single out three sets of issues that may be of special interest to AI researchers: †

1. Implementation of friendly interfaces and conversational systems.
2. The contribution of the student-modelling work to techniques for induction.
3. Special-purpose inference/deduction techniques.

---

†A fourth issue not discussed in this book is reasoning with incomplete and inconsistent databases. Interested readers are referred to Collins et al (1975) and Chisholm and Sleeman (1979) for an ITS-related discussion of this topic.

1. Habitable (Friendly) Natural Language Systems

The majority of early natural language parsers were syntactically oriented. They assigned each word of the sentence to one or more syntactic categories and derived a structural description of the input sentence which, among other things, standardized it for later semantic processing. Although syntactic interpretation is generally needed in order to handle the full range of linguistic utterances, especially complex quantification, certain limited domains of inquiry can be handled robustly and efficiently by formalizing the semantic structure of the domain directly as a grammar in its own right. Burton explored this avenue extensively in SOPHIE (Burton, 1976; Brown, Burton & deKleer, 1981). In this system a "fuzzy" semantically-driven parser was used: fuzzy, in that unknown words could be skipped once the parser had located a substantial part of a semantic entity, and semantically-driven, in that it searched for and recognized semantic entities like the concept of *measurement* rather than syntactic entities such as nouns. A critical aspect of this work is its modelling of the problem-solving discourse in order to handle a user's deletions, ellipses and pronouns. The deletions and pronouns have variable meaning depending on the context created by the preceding dialogue. The technique for handling this class of linguistic phenomena employs a relatively simple *meaning representation* produced by the semantic grammar. It represents the context-sensitive concepts of the utterance as uninstantiated items which are then interpreted in the context of the discourse model.

The semantic grammar technique has also been used in ACE (Sleeman & Hendley, 1981) to analyze complex and lengthy explanations of students' solutions to sub-problems. Student explanations are typically inconsistent and, even more troublesomely, incomplete. Explanations are characteristically composed of a series of arguments; ACE must realize that a new argument has been encountered even though the current argument is incomplete. Subsequently, ACE provides default values for the missing items of the incomplete argument. ACE thus addresses many of the same issues as GUS (Bobrow et al, 1977) and effectively uses a frame-based representation for its domain-knowledge.

If a conversational system is to manage realistic dialogues it must have some representation of the user's conceptualization of the domain. Without such a model the system may provide comment at the wrong level of detail or mistake the user's current focus of attention. Some teaching systems use these models to guide the selection of the teaching tasks; these same models can also be used to influence the dialogue as Clancey (1981) has demonstrated in his GUIDON system.

2. Student Modelling and Concept Formulation

Many of the systems presented here attempt to induce a model of the student from his observable behavior. Algorithms for producing such models need to address the following challenging issues: "credit" allotment; combinatorial explosion when inducing compound concepts out of primitives; and discounting noisy data.

The assignment-of-credit problem concerns determining how to rationally allocate blame (i.e., credit for having caused the failure) when more than one elementary step is necessary of success. This problem is, when there is failure on a task that requires multiple skills, which skill (or skills) doesn't the student know. An analogous problem is allocating credit for success between methods when there is more than one potentially successful method. In both Burton and Brown (1981) and Goldstein (1981) the blame aspect of the problem arises when trying to determine why a student did NOT make a better move.†

Combinatorial explosion underlying the construction of student models or, equivalently, the formation of theories about a student's knowledge base, arises from attempts to use a generative mechanism to explain students' behavior as a collection of primitive actions, plans or rules. Without a generative capability, the ability of the system to model complex (correct or aberrant) behavior is severely limited. In Sleeman's system, LMS, the student is modelled as a collection of primitive rules and mal-rules and in Burton's, DEBUGGY, as a collection of primitive bugs. In LMS, the search space is formulated so that each set of problems presented to the student focusses on a particular rule. This technique drastically reduces the number of hypotheses that must be considered. In DEBUGGY, heuristics are employed to limit the size of the search space and to guide the search through the reduced space. Both papers discuss the assumptions their systems make about the genetic structure of the skill being diagnosed, about the design of the diagnostic test and about which skills interact with other skills, thereby sometimes masking them.

Another aspect of concept formation arises in "bridging" the gap between the manifest steps of a student's solution. This can involve the rather simple case of conjecturing intermediate steps that were performed in the student's head but not written down or it can involve discovering the underlying motives or plans that eventually led to the student producing the observed sequence of steps. Substantial tutorial leverage can be obtained from discovering the user's underlying plan, as demonstrated by Genesereth (1981). In his system the set of possible plans is generated by a model of a naive user which consists of a collection of plan fragments (some of which may be incorrect). This system uses a combination of bottom-up and top-down processing heuristics to limit the set of actual plans explored.

†This diagnostic task is quite different from determining why a student made an error. When the student does something that is incorrect, the system has what the student did as a good clue. But, in the case of omission, the system can not tell, whether the student does not know a required skill or if he has the skill but does not know where to use it.

Current techniques for inducing student's plans are both brittle (the opposite of robust) and combinatorially explosive. Miller (1981), in his SPADE system, has explored a way of circumventing the combinatorial search for such plans: he provides students with a special purpose editor that enables them to *specify* their plans for solving their problems.

The modelling process must also involve techniques for handling noisy data since student's mistakes come not only from systematic misunderstanding but also from fatigue and cognitive overload. Such mistakes will often mask out those errors that have a systematic explanation unless the diagnostic process has some model that explicitly accounts for the noise. Handling this problem has turned out to be extraordinarily important in using an ITS with students in a realistic, classroom setting. This issue is explored in DEBUGGY (Burton, 1981); *non-systematic* mistakes are inferred by means of a technique called coercion. Coercion perturbs its current best model of the student's systematic misconceptions in accordance with its model of noise. LMS (Sleeman, 1981) deals with this issue more "conventionally" by using a statistical evaluation of the hypothesis' strength (cf. Meta-DENDRAL (Buchanan, 1974)).

3. Special-Purpose Deduction Techniques

Deducing the answer to a student's question, evaluating his hypothesis and, in general, providing him insightful feedback does little good if the student constantly finds himself waiting for the system to respond. Consequently, ITSs designed to run field experiments must stri ve for a certain level of efficiency. Of course, achieving efficiency at the cost of loosing robustness is hardly going to render these systems more useful. Furthermore, increasing efficiency by simply relying on coding tricks may be useful for particular systems, but does not advance our understanding about how to build future ITSs. This brings us to the topic of special-purpose inference techniques that are both robust and conceptually efficient.

This issue has been a subject of study in the various versions of SOPHIE (Brown, Burton & deKleer, 1981). SOPHIE I and II explore the uses of an example-driven inference scheme built on top of a general-purpose simulator. Unlike classical deduction schemes that require a proof to be completed before any conclusion is drawn, this inference scheme enables intermediate results to be used by the tutoring sub-system while the inference engine is still in the process of completing its "proof." In this manner, a student can often receive some useful information concerning the validity of his hypothesis quickly and can process that while the tutor deduces additional information. This technique decomposes inference into two processes. The first uses a rather simple logic to derive potentially useful/interesting examples. The examples are then passed to the other process (e.g., simulator) that derives the implications of each candidate example. Each scheme is tuned for its particular task in terms of both its logical calculus and its knowledge base.

SOPHIE III explores quite a different class of inference schemes. Its electronics expert combines a general-purpose constraint propagation scheme with a circuit-specific reasoner, the latter's knowledge being encoded in a structure that reflects a given circuit's hierarchically composed modules. By orchestrating the interactions of the propagation scheme with circuit-specific rules, it is possible to minimize the number of rules needed for capturing any one circuit while maintaining the overall efficiency and robustness of the system. SOPHIE III's general purpose troubleshooting expertise is achieved in a surprisingly simple way by extending the critical role of assumptions used in its electronics expert module. The electronics expert is solely concerned with making predictions about the outcome of new hypothetical measurements from evidence already provided it. It meticulously records the justifications for these predictions and all the assumptions underlying them (i.e., that the components upon which the predictions are based are indeed functioning as specified). The troubleshooting expert then compares these predictions with observations to determine which assumptions are violated, or substantiated, thereby isolating the fault.

CONCLUSIONS

ITS has clearly abandoned one of CAI's early objectives, namely that of providing total courses, and has concentrated on building systems which provide supportive environments for more limited topics. If ITSs are to have any practical importance, the subject areas need to be chosen with comsiderable care as each system represents a major investment of resources. The ITSs reviewed above are set in the following subject areas:

> Place value arithmetic
> Solving simple algebraic equations
> Non-deterministic (or backtracking) problem solving
> Debugging (of electronic circuits and program/plans)
> Medical Diagnosis.

We would suggest that each of these topics essentially represents an educational "watershed" in that if any of these skills are not acquired, further progress is greatly inhibited. Basic arithmetic is an obvious example. Similarly, the solution of algebraic equations is central to much of physics and chemistry. Non-deterministic algorithms cause great difficulties when they are first encountered in mathematics or in science, as the student has often "decided" that problems in these domains always have a closed or algorithmic solution. We are thus suggesting that the subject areas have been well chosen, and that access to such systems in the classroom would do much to remove some current "bottlenecks."

Most of the efforts during the last few years focused on building experimental ITSs. They were designed with future technology in mind so it is not surprising to find that these systems require substantial resources on large-scale computers (e.g., PDP-10s) to run. But there has always been the nagging question of when such systems would become cost effective? An indirect way of answering that question is to observe that things are getting better. As this book underwent final editing, an extended version of the INTERLISP programming environment, the language in which many of the systems described in this book are written, has been made available on a personal machine (Burton et al, 1980) and three of the systems -- GUIDON, WEST, DEBUGGY -- made fully operational on it.† We hope this enables a new kind of investigation, one concerning the *formative* evaluation of ITSs. In order for this research to progress, we need to know not just whether a prototype ITS is effective, but rather, in what ways it is effective and why, and in what ways it is *ineffective* and why. Hopefully, both the cognitive and knowledge-engineering techniques underlying ITSs will provide a framework for understanding and expressing why a given feature is, or is not, useful and thus will enable formative evaluations to be precise without having to be statistical.

In addition to expecting more ambitious and generalizable ITSs to emerge in the next few years, we also expect to see a shift of emphasis into both the cognitive and sociological aspects of these new kinds of learning environments. In particular, a great deal of the knowledge and problem-solving skills that are communicated by human coaches or laboratory instructors are done so implicitly. Much of what constitutes domain-specific problem-solving expertise has never been articulated. It resides in the heads of tutors, getting there through experience, abstracted but not necessarily accessible in an articulatable form. Since a computer-based coach has limited opportunities to learn experientially, at least in the foreseeable future, its designers must make this knowledge explicit. Likewise, in the arena of tutorial strategies, much remains to be discovered and made explicit. We hope that educational theorists will find the explicit formulation of tutoring, explanation and diagnostic processes inherent in intelligent tutoring systems a test bed for developing more precise theories of teaching and learning.

Since the learning paradigm enabled by ITSs stresses activity-based learning, it is very unlikely that the computer-based tutor will be able to handle all situations that will arise. Structuring the learning enviroment to encourage individual members to help each other could provide a congenial and effective backup for these systems. It may turn out that the helpful nature of the ITS, encourages this type of peer aid by providing an example of friendly behavior, thus breaking the competitive or "test taking" mentality. Unfortunately, we know little about how to structure formal learning environments in ways that encourage the kinds of cooperation often found in naturalistic learning situations.

We expect to see an increasing amount of attention paid to the various aspects of student modelling and diagnosis, but progress will be slow because the motivations and plans underlying a person's behavior when attempting to solve a non-trivial problem are indeed complex. In return, the payoff should be high with ramifications extending beyond ITSs into the area of diagnostic testing. It is our

† A further system, LMS, is in the process of being transferred to a micro-based system.

hope that these advances will lead to screening and diagnostic systems that can test students in more holistic and meaningful tasks, (as opposed, to the strictly sequenced tasks which current systems use to separate out sub-skills).

The achievements of ITSs to date provide some basis for optimism and point out the value of investigating formal, but non-toy, problems in the context of real-world tasks. By so doing, the resultant systems should be of interest to AI practitioners, cognitive and educational theorists, and users alike!

The following have provided insightful reviews for some of the papers appearing in this volume: Bruce Buchanan, Jaime Carbonell, Ian Chisholm, Bill Clancey, J.R. Hartley, Austin Henderson, Mark Miller, Tim O'Shea, N.S. Sridharan and Richard Young.

References

BOBROW, D. G., KAPLAN, R. M., KAY, M. *et al.* (1977). GUS, a frame-driven dialog system. *Artificial Intelligence*, **8** (2), 155–173.
BROWN, J. S., BURTON, R. R. & DeKLEER, J. (1981). Pedagogical, natural language and knowledge engineering techniques in SOPHIE I, II and III. Chapter 11 in this volume.
BUCHANAN, B. G. (1974). Scientific theory formation by computer. *Proceeding of the NATO Advanced Study Institute on Computer Oriented Learning Processes.*
BURTON, R. R. (1976). *Semantic Grammar: an Engineering Technique for Constructing Natural Language Understanding Systems.* Bolt Beranek and Newman, Inc., ICAI Report 3.
BURTON, R. R. (1981). Diagnosing bugs in simple procedural skills. Chapter 8 in this volume.
BURTON, R. R. & BROWN, J. S. (1981). An investigation of computer coaching for informal learning activities. Chapter 4 in this volume.
BURTON, R. R. *et al.* (1980). *Paper on Interlisp-D.* Xerox Cognitive and Instructional Sciences Report 5 (SSL-80-4). Palo Alto Research Center.
CHISHOLM, I. H. & SLEEMAN, D. H. (1979). An aide for theory formation. In *Expert Systems in the micro-electronic Age* (D. Michie, ed.), pp. 202–212. EUP, Edinburgh.
CLANCEY, W. J. (1981). Tutoring rules for guiding a case method dialogue. Chapter 10 in this volume.
COLLINS, A., WARNOCK, E. H., AIELLO, N. & MILLER, M. L. (1975). Reasoning from incomplete knowledge. In *Representation and Understanding: Studies in Cognitive Science* (D. Bobrow and A. Collins, eds), pp. 383–415. Academic Press, New York.
GENERESETH, M. R. (1981). The role of plans in intelligent tutoring systems. Chapter 7 in this volume.
GOLDSTEIN, I. P. (1981). The genetic graph: a representation for the evolution of procedural knowledge. Chapter 3 in this volume.
HARTLEY, J. R. & SLEEMAN, D. H. (1973). Towards intelligent teaching systems. *International Journal of Man-Machine Studies,* **5**, 215–236.
KIMBALL, R. A. (1981). A self-adapting, self-improving tutor for symbolic integration. Chapter 12 in this volume.
MATZ, M. (1981). Towards a generative theory of high school algebra errors. Chapter 2 in this volume.
MILLER, M. L. (1981). A structured planning and debugging environment for elementary programming. Chapter 6 in this volume.
O'SHEA, T. (1981). A self-improving quadratic tutor. Chapter 13 in this volume.
SLEEMAN, D. H. (1981). Assessing aspects of competence in basic algebra. Chapter 9 in this volume.

SLEEMAN, D. H. & HENDLEY, R. J. (1981). ACE: A system which analyses complex explanations. Chapter 5 in this volume.

SMITH, R. L., GRAVES, H., BLAINE, L. H. & MARINOV, V. G. (1975). Computer-assisted axiomatic mathematics: informal rigor. In *Computer Education* (O. Lecarne and R. Lewis, eds). North Holland, Amsterdam.

STEVENS, A., COLLINS, A. & GOLDIN, S. E. (1981). Misconceptions in student's understanding. Chapter 1 in this volume.

SUPPES, P. (1967). Some theoretical models for mathematics learning. *Journal of Research and Development in Education*, **1**, 5–22.

UHR, L. (1969). Teaching machine programs that generate problems as a function of interaction with students. *Proceedings of the 24th National Conference*, pp. 125–134.

WOODS, P. & HARTLEY, J. R. (1971). Some learning models for arithmetic tasks and their use in computer-based learning. *British Journal of Educational Psychology*, **41** (1), 35–48.

1. Misconceptions in students' understanding

ALBERT STEVENS, ALLAN COLLINS AND SARAH E. GOLDIN

Bolt, Beranek & Newman, Inc., Cambridge, Mass. 02138, U.S.A.

Tutorial dialogues can be analyzed as an interaction in which a tutor "debugs" a student's knowledge representation by diagnosing and correcting conceptual misunderstandings. In this paper, we outline some tentative steps toward a theory which describes tutorial interactions. We outline the goal structure of a tutor, describe types of conceptual bugs that students have in their understanding of physical processes and discuss some of the representational viewpoints necessary to diagnose and correct these bugs.

Introduction

The concerns of this paper had their roots in our attempts to build an intelligent computer-aided instructional (ICAI) system to tutor students about physical processes. Our approach has been to work out a theory based on analyses of tutoring dialogues and experiments and then build a system based on that theory. This methodology places additional constraints on the possible forms our models can take. Not only must the theory describe the actual performance of human tutors, it must also be practical, in terms of possible implementation.

Grounding our work in the concrete problems of system-building has led us to consider several issues that might not have been obvious given some other paradigm. By far the most important issue we have been forced to confront is the overwhelmingly central role of detailed, domain-specific knowledge in governing almost every aspect of the tutorial process. An essential premise of any ICAI system is that the system itself must incorporate some knowledge of the domain to be taught, if only to monitor the student's progress toward instructional goals. We have found, however, that the nature of stored knowledge determines not only the content of a tutorial interaction, but also the goal structure that governs the tutor's selection of examples, questions and statements at different points in the dialogue, the types of misconceptions that students have and the way that tutors diagnose and correct these misconceptions based on student errors.

In much of psychology, there has been a bias toward emphasizing highly general, domain-independent mechanisms that are supposedly central to the instructional process. Our work demonstrates that such a perspective is incomplete without a detailed consideration of domain-specific knowledge, its representation and its interaction with more general aspects of cognition.

We have two goals in this paper. First, we would like to discuss some of the issues that have been raised in our attempts to build a knowledge-driven ICAI tutor. The first section will include a brief description of the current tutorial system, focusing on the kind of knowledge it incorporates and the reasons why the current knowledge base is inadequate. We will introduce the notion of multiple viewpoints in knowledge, a concept that we hope will provide solutions to some of the current system's problems.

This research was sponsored by the Personnel and Training Research programs, Psychological Division, Office of Naval Research, under contract no. N00014-76C-0083, contract authority identification No. NR 154-379.

Our second goal is to demonstrate how the tutor's knowledge of his domain determines the goal structure of the dialogue and the process of "debugging"—i.e. error diagnosis and correction. We will use examples from human dialogues and experiments to illustrate these points, attempting to make concrete some of the general issues raised in the first section.

Knowledge-driven CAI: what kind of knowledge is necessary?

SCRIPT-BASED KNOWLEDGE

The first version of our system, called the WHY system, can carry on a simple teaching dialogue about the causes of rainfall. The aim of WHY is to develop in the student a "causal model" of the mechanisms underlying the wet type of climate that prevails in Oregon or Ireland. We have come to use the term "causal model" operationally, to summarize the student's ability to answer questions, give explanations and make predictions about the causal relations involved in producing heavy rainfall. In the original formulation of the WHY system, however, the meaning of causal model was exemplified in the basic knowledge structure of the system, a script-like sequence of events representing the different temporal or causal steps in processes that affect rainfall.

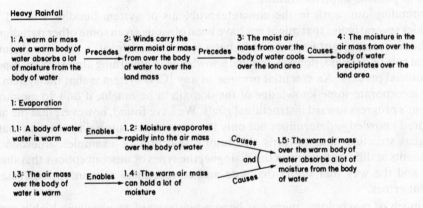

FIG. 1. The WHY system script for heavy rainfall and the subscript for evaporation.

The flavor of the original WHY knowledge structure can be seen by examining Fig. 1. This figure illustrates in informal notation the top-level script for heavy rainfall, which consists of four steps: Evaporation, Movement of the air mass, Cooling and Precipitation. The subscript for the first step is also shown, consisting of a more detailed breakdown of the steps involved in evaporation.

The structures we term "scripts" do not correspond exactly to the structures usually designated by this label (Schank & Abelson, 1977). However, they do share certain important features with the Schank & Abelson formulation.

(1) They are generic knowledge structures representing information about classes of phenomena.

(2) They represent a partially-ordered sequence of events, linked by temporal or causal connectors.

(3) They have a hierarchically-embedded structure, with subscripts expanding on the content of major script events.

(4) They have a set of roles (e.g. AIR-MASS, BODY-OF-WATER) that will be bound to particular geographic or meteorological entities when the script is applied to a particular case (e.g. Ireland).

In summary, one possible way of describing the causes of heavy rainfall is to view the phenomenon as a temporally-ordered linear sequence of events. This is the notion embodied in the WHY system.

In practice, this knowledge structure turns out to be inadequate. The WHY system can ask questions about places where heavy rainfall occurs, diagnose missing steps in the student's knowledge, and inform the student about the correct steps. It is sensitive to some student errors. However, it typically misses the cause of these errors, correcting the surface error but failing to diagnose the underlying misconception that the error reflects. Also, there are many important aspects of physical processes and many important ways of describing physical processes that the WHY system fails to use.

The types of misconceptions in a student's knowledge that a system can diagnose are heavily dependent on the knowledge represented in the system. The script structures in the WHY system are able to represent misconceptions that result because of missing substeps or extra substeps in the various scripts. However, these are only two of several types of misconceptions that occur. (We will discuss others below.)

The problems of failing to discuss important aspects of physical processes and failing to use important ways of describing physical processes arise because the script–subscript structure is limited in the types of knowledge it can represent. We believe that representing knowledge about physical processes requires multiple "representational viewpoints". Our script structures provide one of these, the viewpoint of a sequence of temporally-ordered processes, some causally related to others, and some subprocesses of others. This representational viewpoint is important, but equally important is the "functional viewpoint", which emphasizes the functional relationships among the attributes of the various objects involved in different processes.

A REPRESENTATION OF FUNCTIONAL RELATIONSHIPS

A functional perspective is necessary to account for statements and questions in the dialogues that do not fit into a step-sequence format, e.g. "Does the temperature of water affect evaporation?" or "What happens to the temperature of the air as it rises?" We have developed a representational format for this type of knowledge. The basic unit of our representation for functional relationships is a description of some process such as cooling or evaporation. An example is shown in Fig. 2. This represents the process of evaporation as it occurs in the rainfall domain. Its parts are as follows.

(1) A set of ACTORS, each with a ROLE in the overall process. For example, the ocean often plays the role of MOISTURE SOURCE.

(2) A set of FACTORS which affect the process. The factors are all attributes of various actors. For example, the temperature of the moisture source is a factor in evaporation.

EVAPORATION

Actors
Source: Large-body-of-water
Destination: Air-mass

Factors
Temperature(Source)
Temperature(Destination)
Proximity(Source, Destination)

Functional-relationship
Positive(Temperature(Source))
Positive(Temperature(Destination))
Positive(Proximity(Source, Destination))

Result
Increase(Humidity(Destination))

Fig. 2. A functional representation for evaporation.

(3) A description of the RESULT of the process. The result is always a change in the value of some factor. For example, the result of evaporation is to increase the humidity of the destination air mass.

(4) A description of the FUNCTIONAL RELATIONSHIP that holds among the factors and the result. We believe that there is room for complexity and subtlety in the description of functional relations (e.g. including threshold concepts, discontinuities, etc.), but we currently use a simple descriptive scheme that allows only positive and inverse relationships. For example, in evaporation there is a positive relation between the temperature of the moisture source and the resulting humidity of the air mass.

This representation is general in two ways. It can be partially specified by assigning values to the actor attributes. For example, representing an instance of a large amount of evaporation requires assigning the value "WARM" to the temperature of the source and destination and a value like "ADJACENT" to the proximity relationship. Inference rules that make use of the information about relevant attributes and functional relationships can be constructed to check (at some level of approximation) if the assigned values of factors and results are consistent—for example, whether warm water temperature is consistent with high humidity. Brown, Burton & Zdybel (1973) using finite state automata have implemented a system that can make such inferences.

The second way that this representation can be further specified is by instantiating the actors. For example, in the case of rainfall over Ireland, the source is the Gulf Stream. All the process information regarding functional relationships and properties can then be inherited by the particular case.

A functional perspective differs from the scriptal view in several ways. First of all, it is non-linear and interactive rather than ordered and sequential. Positive or inverse functional relations "work" in either direction, whereas "increase" and "decrease" would be encoded as different events in a script representation. Secondly, causal relations are implicit and indefinite in the functional view, rather than explicitly stated as in the scriptal structure. Saying that air humidity is positively related to air temperature suggests some causal relation, but does not spell out which factor is primary.

On the other hand, both types of knowledge structure are generic; both can be instantiated. Also, both perspectives can be used to generate inferences. In general, the two viewpoints both represent "causal models" of the domain, but with differing emphases that affect their respective utilities for different tasks. One can make an analogy to the contrast between an analysis of variance and a correlational analysis of a set of data. Both methods describe the same results; their conclusions will overlap, but they emphasize different features of the data.

Knowledge as a determinant of tutorial interactions

One of the major constraints on a theory of tutoring is that it adequately describe the structure of tutorial dialogues. We have found that the "semantics" of the rainfall domain—the major components of knowledge and the way those components are related—strongly influence the "syntax" of the tutorial interaction—what questions are asked and in what sequence. Moreover, there is evidence for both scriptal and functional viewpoints controlling the dialogue structure. The scriptal organization seems to govern the sequencing of major topics, while a functional perspective describes the dominant features of the interaction microstructure.

Our analyses of tutorial dialogues reveal a general structure that follows from the script structure of the knowledge base. Tutors discuss topics in a rational order, typically following discussion of one process with discussion of a temporally or causally adjacent process, or with a discussion of component subprocesses. The basics of the scriptally-oriented goal structure have been described in detail in Stevens & Collins (1977). In brief, the script of heavy rainfall provides a set of instructional objectives for the tutor. First, each step in the top-level sequence will be queried. Missing or erroneous steps will usually cause the tutor to shift the level of analysis down one level, to the relevant subscript, in order to find the source of and correct the error. If a student understands all the major steps in the script, the tutor may move to the subscript level and examine the knowledge in greater depth, or may propose a specific case and ask the student to apply the general schema to this new instance.

This global, script-based structure can be seen in the dialogue excerpt in Fig. 3. The tutor begins by discussing the climate and water temperature around Oregon, eliciting the Evaporation event (exchanges 7 to 10). The next sequence of exchanges (11 to 13) articulates the movement of moist air over the land. The answer to question 13 mentions the Condensation stage. Since a step has been left out (Cooling), the tutor backs up and establishes the goal of eliciting that step from the student (14). The student does provide the missing step, but in order to make sure of this apparent understanding, the tutor drops down into the Cooling subscript (15–19). Here, indeed, he discovers several errors, which he works to correct (20–21). Then he commences a similar pattern of questioning about the case of Ireland. This sequence also follows the basic script structure, with the pattern EVAPORATION ⇒ CONDENSATION ⇒ backup to COOLING (up to question 30).

Thus a scriptal knowledge structure seems to describe some of the major organizational features of our tutorial dialogues. However, close examination of the interaction reveals that the tutor probes the student about many different aspects of the knowledge. When the student makes an error, the tutor will sometimes correct it immediately, but in many cases will ask other questions until the misconception underlying the error is

(7) Tutor: Do you know what the climate is like in Washington and Oregon?
Student: Is it cold?
(8) Tutor: No, it is rather mild. Can you guess about the rainfall there?
Student: Normal I guess
(9) Tutor: Well, the Japan current which starts in the south-eastern Pacific, flows along the coast of Japan and across the North Pacific ending up off the coast of Washington and Oregon. How do you think that current affects the climate there?
Student: It's probably rainy
(10) Tutor: It is indeed very wet, there are rain forests in both Washington and Oregon. What does that tell you about the temperature of the Japan current?
Student: It's warm
(11) Tutor: Right. Where do you think the wind blows in that area?
Student: Towards Wash. and Oregon
(12) Tutor: From where?
Student: From the sea
(13) Tutor: Right again. What do you think happens to the moist air blown over Washington and Oregon by those winds?
Student: It condenses and it rains
(14) Tutor: Yes, why?
Student: Because the moist air cools and the clouds can't hold the water so it rains
(15) Tutor: Ok, what causes the moist air to cool?
Student: It cools when the wind blows it and it lowers from the sky
(16) Tutor: What happens to the temperature of moist air when it rises?
Student: It gets warm
(17) Tutor: No. Warm air rises, but as it rises it cools off. Do you think the mountains in Washington and Oregon have anything to do with cooling the moist air blowing in off the coast?
Student: Yes
(18) Tutor: How?
Student: As it rises, or even if it doesn't rise, the cold mountains could cool it off
(19) Tutor: No, contact with a cold object does not provide enough cooling to an air mass to cause rain. Rainfall is almost always the result of cooling due to rising air. How do you think the mountains might affect the rising of the moist air from over the ocean?
Student: I'm not sure
(20) Tutor: When the air is blown against the mountains it has to rise to get over them. As it rises it cools and rainfall occurs. Can you guess what the average rainfall is like on the other side of the mountains?
Student: It's probably heavy
(21) Tutor: No, almost all the moisture condenses out on the ocean side of the mountains, then once the air has passed over the mountains it settles back down in altitude and warms up so there is very little rainfall. In fact the climate east of the Rockies is very dry. Do you see the relationship between the mountains in Washington and Oregon and the cold air mass that sits over Ireland most of the time?
Student: I think so
(22) Tutor: What do you think it is?
Student: The cold air mass stays low, and warm enough so it doesn't rain
(23) Tutor: Let's review why it rains in Ireland. Where does the moist air come from there?
Student: From the Gulf Stream
(24) Tutor: Right. Now what happens when that warm moist air from over the Gulf Stream is blown over Ireland?
Student: It condenses
(25) Right, but why?
Student: Because the air rises and cools
(26) Tutor: Right again, now can you tell me what causes the air to rise over Ireland?
Student: The wind?
(27) Tutor: The wind moves the air, but that is not what causes it to rise. Do you think the cold air mass that is usually sitting over Ireland might be important?
Student: If it just sits there it is
(28) Tutor: What happens when the warmer moist air is blown in off the water and hits the stationary cold air mass?
Student: It makes it rise

FIG. 3. A dialogue segment from a teaching session between a human teacher and a student.

(29) Tutor: Right, why?
Student: Because warm air rises and when this warm air rises with the cool air on top of it, then the air will cool and it will rain
(30) Tutor: Almost. The warm air rises over the cool air the same way that the warm air in Washington and Oregon rises over the mountains. That is because they are in the way of where the warm air is being blown by the wind. Now do you see why the mountains and the cold air mass serve the same function in the two different places?
Student: Yes
(31) Tutor: Good. Let's look briefly at the Amazon jungle region. Can you guess whether the climate is dry or wet there?
Student: Wet
(32) Tutor: Yes. The moisture is blown in from over the ocean by the prevailing wind. Do you have any idea what might cause the air to rise and cool in that area?
Student: The trees?
(33) Tutor: No. Do you know or can you guess what geographical feature marks the western boundary of the Amazon jungle?
Student: The Andes Mountains
(34) Tutor: Right, what effect do you suppose they might have on the rainfall in the jungle region?
Student: They'd make the air have to go over the mountains, so it would rain in the jungle

FIG. 3—continued.

isolated. Some of this dialogue microstructure seems to be governed by a functional perspective like that described earlier, which suggests possible sources of error in the student's functional model.

Examples of questions driven by a functional perspective can be seen in the dialogue excerpt in Fig. 3, in questions 16 through 29. Examples from other dialogues are shown in Table 1. In each case, the question or statement refers to one of the specific aspects of the functional representation described earlier. A cursory examination of our dialogues suggests that a large percentage of tutors' statements and questions fall into these categories. For example, in a representative dialogue, which consisted of 41 exchanges, four of the tutor's statements were about attributes of actors, four were about the results of processes and seven were about functional relationships. This accounting includes 15 of the tutor's statements. Of the remaining 26, eight are references to prior, intermediate or subsequent processes at a level of abstraction that can be handled by script structures. The remainder, which we do not have good ideas about, include references to the spatial structures of the processes, descriptions of physical principles and explication of a metaphor.

TABLE 1

Example statements for each part of the representation

Factors (Attributes of Actors)
"Do you think the amount of moisture in the air affects the amount of rainfall?"
"Does the temperature of water affect evaporation?"

Results of Processes
"Condensation is the process by which moisture in the air becomes liquid water again."
"Evaporation is the process by which water in the ocean becomes moisture in the air."

Functional Relations
"What happens to the temperature of the air as it rises?"
"Do you remember how temperature affects evaporation?"

Tutors discuss far more than the causal and temporal linkages between steps in a script structure. They probe and discuss information about attributes of the actors that are important, the results of processes and the form of the relationships that hold between the attributes of actors and the results of processes.

The use of "debugging" knowledge

TYPES OF BUGS IN UNDERSTANDING RAINFALL

Our analyses of dialogues show that tutors spend a good part of their time diagnosing conceptual bugs from errors manifested in the dialogue. We believe that much of the teacher's skill as a debugger depends on knowledge about the types of conceptual bugs students are likely to have, the manifestations of these bugs, and methods for correcting them. It is thus clear that an important component of any teaching system is a method for representing, diagnosing and correcting bugs.

To examine the types of bugs that occur in students' understanding of rainfall, we compiled a systematic test about the causes of heavy rainfall by generating questions for all major script nodes in the current WHY knowledge base. These questions were presented to subjects in a questionnaire headed by a context-setting paragraph, which explained that all questions referred to areas of the world with habitually heavy rainfall. Some typical questions from the test are:

"How is the moisture content of the air related to heavy rainfall?"
"What role does rising air play in causing rainfall?"
"What causes evaporation?"

Instructions emphasized that even if the subjects felt they did not know an answer, they should try to answer the question nevertheless. We adopted these instructions because we found that the typical response from a subject confronted with this test was "I don't know anything about rainfall." Subsequent probing revealed that often they knew a good deal more than they thought.

This experiment provided us with a substantial body of data on errors and misconceptions. In order to analyze the responses in detail, we tabulated all incorrect answers under the appropriate questions and then tried to identify a basic set of conceptual bugs and to classify errors according to this set. Our analysis revealed two points of major interest.

(1) A particular conceptual bug is often shared by many students.
(2) A particular conceptual bug is often manifested in many different surface forms.

For example, a bug we call the Cooling-by-contact bug is very common, occurring for 6 of our 8 subjects. Some verbatim examples of manifestations of this bug are:

(1) "Cold air masses cool warm air masses when they collide."
(2) "Winds cause air to cool."
(3) "Mountains cause condensation because cold land touching warm air causes condensation."
(4) "Cold fronts, wind, snow and rain cause air to cool."
(5) "Cold air masses cool the clouds so the rain falls."

TABLE 2
The set of observed misconceptions

Misconception	Number of Subjects	Example
(1) Cooling-by-contact	6	"Mountains cause condensation because cold land touching air causes condensation."
(2) Heating-by-radiation	6	"The sun warms the air."
(3) Small-moisture-source	5	"A 12 by 12 by 10 foot pond is enough to cause rainfall."
(4) Rising-causes-increased-pressure	3	"Rising air makes the moist air rise, pressure increases . . ."
(5) Absorption-by-expansion	3	". . . decrease in pressure causes water molecules to expand, causes evaporation."
(6) Heating-by-contact	3	". . . land warms the air at night."
(7) Squeezing-causes-condensation	2	"Putting pressure on air masses causes condensation."
(8) Temperature-of-water-irrelevant-for-evaporation	2	"Temperature of water is unrelated to evaporation."
(9) Temperature-differential-causes-evaporation	2	"Air has to be cooler than the body of water for evaporation to occur."
(10) Insufficient-warming-of-water	2	"A current can be warm because it comes from a warm source of water— for example, a lake which is warm."
(11) Heating-causes-condensation	1	"Air warming up causes rainfall."
(12) Winds-cause-pressure-increases	1	"Winds are forceful and cause various air pressures."
(13) Cooling-causes-evaporation	1	"When a body of water is cold, it evaporates."
(14) Rising-results-in-pressure-equalization	1	"Air that is warmer is expanded and has less pressure. It rises until its pressure is equal to surrounding air."
(15) Cooling-causes-air-to-rise	1	"Cooling causes air to rise."
(16) Evaporation-causes-air-to-rise	1	"Evaporation causes air to rise."

None of the above types of cooling are of any consequence in causing heavy rainfall. The type of cooling necessary occurs when an air mass is forced to rise, resulting in expansion and energy loss.

We identified a total of 16 common bugs in this experiment. They are shown in order of frequency in Table 2. Using these 16 bugs we were able to account for 58% of the answers originally judged to be incorrect or omitted. (By ignoring omissions, we can account for 72%.) This is a conservative estimate. For many of the remaining errors and omissions, one can make plausible arguments that one of these bugs could lead to that error. Many statements that we did not account for were factual errors, for example, "Heavy rainfall occurs only in warm areas." Others were naming errors, for example, "When water evaporates, it turns to steam."

Many of the bugs we observed are specific to the domain of rainfall. This should be neither surprising nor disturbing. A good teacher must possess knowledge of the types of misconceptions that arise in the domain being taught. It is likely that there are other bugs that occur in students' knowledge about rainfall, which we have not detected, but it would surprise us if this number is unreasonably large.

Clearly, the common elements of these errors are quite abstract; diagnosing bugs cannot possibly depend on identification of key words or other superficial features. The tutor must have pre-stored generic knowledge structures and procedures for mapping these surface errors onto the deep level representation. This is obviously not a simple problem.

Bugs can show up in all parts of the functional representation. The Cooling-by-contact bug is represented as a transformation on the correct role of the object or as a difference in the attribute of the object that is believed to be relevant. The Heating-causes-condensation bug is represented as a change in the direction of a functional relationship. The Small-moisture-source bug is represented as a substitution of an incorrect actor in the Moisture source role. Once again, it is clear; if we are to understand the tutorial skills of diagnosis and correction, we must have a highly specified representation for common misconceptions.

WHERE DO BUGS COME FROM?

Having looked at the bugs we have isolated, we now believe that they are still relatively shallow, reflecting even deeper levels of misconceptions in knowledge. The major reason for believing this is that bugs themselves seem to form patterns. The patterns seem best explained as the result of deeper problems in the student's knowledge. Sometimes these deeper problems are due to the application of an incorrect metaphor in understanding a process; other times the patterns reflect incorrect or missing general relationships between processes, like the notion of inverse process, or the idea of positive feedback.

An example of a pattern that reflects an incorrect application of a metaphor is the "sponge pattern". It includes at least two bugs: the Absorption-by-expansion bug and the Squeezing-causes-condensation bug. In effect, the student views the air mass as a giant sponge, expanding to absorb moisture and later having it squeezed out. Tutors typically deal with this deep-level misconception by using a "container" analogy for the air mass, identifying the capacity of the container with air temperature rather than volume.

A second type of pattern is that which arises because of missing generalizations about process relationships. For example, the pattern which includes the Heating-causes-condensation bug but which also includes the correct functional relationship between heating and evaporation seems to reflect the student's lack of understanding that condensation and evaporation are inverse processes. Tutors deal with this bug by informing the student that the two processes are inverses and explaining the sense in which this is so.

As noted above, these processes of understanding draw on a large set of real-world knowledge that students have built up over their lifetime. The bugs often seem to depend on the student's failure to understand some deep physical principles that support the correct model. In order for tutors to deal with conceptual bugs, they must recognize this mode of understanding and attempt to discover what models the student applies to understand the processes being taught.

Remaining problems and possibilities

In the previous sections, we outlined some tentative steps toward solving the problems of goal structure, representing misconceptions, and providing the additional representational viewpoint of a set of functionally related processes. We believe that the heart of these problems lies in the representation of knowledge. Our tentative steps toward representing knowledge and misconceptions about physical processes extend the script-like representation we have been using, but we believe we are still just scratching the surface.

Adding just one viewpoint has given us more windows into problems that were opaque using our previous scriptal knowledge structure. Even more important, the general notion of alternative perspectives adds new dimensions to the solution domain. The multiple-viewpoint framework allows us to conceptualize the whole question of knowledge-driven CAI in a new way, in terms of how knowledge should be partitioned among different viewpoints. In the remainder of this paper, we will point out a few of the issues that now seem critical.

INTERACTING BUGS

In most cases, a single bug accounts for each error, but there are cases where bugs interact to produce a single surface error. Brown & Burton (1978) have shown that in arithmetic, students often have a set of bugs that interact to produce non-obvious patterns of errors. The observations from our experiment suggest that similar things may happen in the rainfall domain. For example, one subject said in response to a question about the role of cold air masses:

"Cold air masses hitting warm air masses cause condensation."

Since she mentioned contact and not rising, the most straightforward diagnosis from this statement is that she has a Cooling-by-contact bug. However, the problem really seems to be due to two interacting bugs: Heating-by-contact and Heating-causes-condensation. Two of this student's responses to other questions were:

"Air warming up causes rainfall."
"Tropical winds warm air."

Thus her description of condensation caused by cold air masses hitting warm air masses is most likely due to these bugs' interaction to produce a model in which cold air is warmed by contact with the warm air (Heating-by-contact bug) and then this warming produces rainfall (Heating-causes-condensation bug).

The existence of interactions implies that the mapping from errors to bugs is not one to one. We suspect that there are many cases where the relationship between a set of errors and the underlying bugs may be quite subtle. The existence of non-obvious interactions may account for our inability to classify many of the errors we observed.

The "metaphor problem" described above may also be relevant to the relationship of errors to conceptual problems. Configurations of surface errors may result from some sort of schematic model of rainfall based on real world experience. One such model that occurs fairly frequently could be called the "Collision schema." The student somehow believes that warm, moist air colliding with cold air causes turbulence and hence produces storms and rainfall. Intermediate steps in this model may not be made explicit. This basic scriptal structure seems to derive from some vague knowledge that rainstorms often occur when there is a meeting of warm and cold fronts. The schema is likely to be associated not only with scriptal bugs, but also with functional errors such as Cooling-by-contact or Winds-cause-pressure-increases. One could of course describe the performance of such a student by listing all the bugs that tend to co-occur in this case. However, a more powerful solution to this problem would be to enable the tutoring system to abstract the general concept of collision underlying these errors, to recognize the inappropriateness of the analogy, and to correct both latent and manifest bugs all at once by replacing this incorrect model with a more appropriate one.

OTHER REPRESENTATIONAL VIEWPOINTS

The existence of bug patterns implies that there are still other representational viewpoints necessary to deal completely with physical processes. The analogical use of the "sponge" concept suggests that a complete analysis will require techniques for representing and modifying models drawn from other domains. The process-relationship example implies that the representation of general process relationships like "inverse processes," "feedback systems" and "cyclical process" will need to be included. There seem to be multiple ways of describing what appears to be essentially the same information, emphasizing different aspects of that knowledge. For example, there is the energy viewpoint, from which various processes appear to add or remove type of energy from different actors. There is the change-of-state viewpoint, from which various actors appear to change form and location as time progresses. Spatial relationships must also be included eventually, perhaps producing a perspective in which the processes in causing rainfall appear as various trajectories across a mental map.

The availability of multiple viewpoints raises the possibility that some errors may turn out to reflect the fact that some perspective is missing in the student's knowledge. Alternatively, some bugs might be described as a failure to integrate several different viewpoints, a failure to recognize contradictions between two different perspectives or to update one viewpoint when relevant changes are made in another.

Multiple representational viewpoints complicate tremendously our task of building a system to carry on reasonable tutorial interactions. Nevertheless, the step from a unitary to a multi-dimensional representation for instructional knowledge is a necessary one. Exploring a single new perspective, that of functional relationships, has proved fruitful. We believe that defining additional viewpoints will provide new insights into the nature of tutorial skill.

References

BROWN, J. S. & BURTON, R. R. (1978). Diagnostic models for procedural bugs in basic mathematical skills. *Cognitive Science*, **2**, 155–192.
BROWN, J. S., BURTON, R. & ZYDBEL, F. (1973). A model-driven question answering system for mixed-initiative computer-assisted instruction. *IEEE Transactions on Systems, Man and Cybernetics*, **3**, 248–257.
SCHANK, R. & ABELSON, R. (1977). *Scripts, Plans, Goals and Understanding*. Hillsdale, N.J.: Erlbaum Associates.
STEVENS, A. & COLLINS, A. (1977). The goal structure of a socratic tutor. In *Proceedings of the Association for Computing Machinery Annual Conference*. (Also available as *BBN Report No. 3518* from Bolt Beranek and Newman Inc., Cambridge, Mass., 02138).

2. Towards a process model for high school algebra errors

M. MATZ

M.I.T.

This paper develops a unifying account for some observed systematic errors in a subdomain of mathematics—high school algebra problem solving. It proposes that errors are the results of reasonable, although unsuccessful, attempts to adapt previously acquired knowledge to a new situation. This proposal idealizes an individual's problem solving behavior as a process employing two components. The first component, the knowledge presumed to precede a new problem, usually takes the form of a rule a student has extracted from a prototype or obtained directly from a textbook. These are referred to as the base rules. The second component consists of a handful of extrapolation techniques that specify ways to bridge the gap between known rules and unfamiliar problems. These extrapolation techniques project what is known, either by figuring out a way to view an unfamiliar problem as a kind of familiar one, or by revising a known rule so that it is applicable in the new situation. Many common errors are shown to reflect either unmade developmental changes or an incorrect choice of an (otherwise correct) extrapolation technique. A third class of errors, processing errors, is described briefly.

1. Introduction

People are able to solve mathematical problems they have never seen before, ranging from simple homework exercises to novel and complex variants. What makes this aspect of human problem solving significant is the striking uniformity of the answers produced—both correct and incorrect. Naive problem-solvers tend to make the same mistakes, and even the occasional mistakes made by adept problem-solvers are typically uniform. Given that we are not taught incorrect answers nor solution procedures for every problem encountered, this regularity demands an explanation, a theory of mathematical competence. Such a theory would explain how new rules are constructed from familiar knowledge, or more particularly, how existing rules are extended (successfully or unsuccessfully) to handle a wider range of inputs. This inquiry employs two classic methods for probing the content and mechanisms underlying a competence: analysing the errors people make in its use and studying its acquisition. With this evidence we can begin to piece together a theory of algebraic competence in much the same manner as linguistic researchers have formulated a theory of linguistic competence by using grammaticality judgments and considerations of children's acquisition of language.

Specifically, this research develops a unifying account for some observed systematic errors in a subdomain of mathematics—high school algebra problem solving. It proposes that errors here are the results of reasonable, though unsuccessful, attempts

This report describes research done at the Artificial Intelligence Laboratory of the Massachusetts Institute of Technology. Support for the laboratory's artificial intelligence research is provided in part by the Advanced Research Projects Agency of the Department of Defense under Office of Naval Research contract N00014-75-C-0643 and in part by National Science Foundation Grant MCS77-04828.

25

to adapt previously acquired knowledge to a new situation. This account idealizes an individual's problem-solving behavior as a process employing two components. The first component is a collection of *base rules*. These rules incorporate the knowledge presumed to precede a new problem. They are rules that a student has extracted from a prototype or gotten directly from a textbook. For the most part, these are basic rules (such as the distributive law) that form the conventional textbook content of algebra. The second component consists of a handful of *extrapolation techniques* that specify ways to bridge the gap between known rules and unfamiliar problems. These extrapolation techniques project what is known either by viewing an unfamiliar problem as a kind of familiar one, or by revising a known rule so that it is applicable in the new situation. Many common errors are shown to arise from one of two processes:

* inappropriate use of a known rule *as is* in a new situation
* incorrect adaptation of a known rule to solve a new problem.

These processes are termed "reasonable" because often (1) the rule that serves as the basis for extrapolation works correctly for problems that are nearly isomorphic variations of the prototype from which it was drawn, or because (2) the extrapolation techniques that specify ways to adapt or extend base rules are often useful techniques that apply correctly in many other situations. The problem thus lies not in an extrapolation technique, but in the student's misguided belief in (or failure to evaluate) the appropriateness of using that technique in the particular situation at hand.

This reliance on errors as the central evidence for a model of algebraic competence deserves some justification. In developing a model of a skill, like speaking a language or solving algebra problems, people fluent at that skill can easily overlook both its subtle and obvious aspects. Errors, as reflections of students' misconceptions and missing conceptions, call attention to the tacit knowledge that fluent problem-solvers automatically apply. They show up by contrast essential pieces of a model, such as constraints on the applicability of extrapolation techniques. Other errors indicate that the considerations for determining legal decompositions of a problem into subproblems must also be made explicit. In addition to highlighting facets of the knowledge underlying a skill, errors can also provide evidence for possible processing-oriented decompositions of procedures. When a person's attempt to carry out some procedure breaks down or is only partially executed, the resultant error can indicate intermediate stages of the execution of that process, suggesting a particular decomposition of the solution process.

Besides analysing errors, we can also learn about the nature of algebraic competence by studying its development, a backdrop that provides the base knowledge on which the extrapolation techniques operate. One of the advantages of considering high school algebra problem solving is that to a large extent the base knowledge is well-specified; students bring to their study of algebra a prior knowledge of arithmetic. The developmental approach says that we can better understand their behavior by closely analysing the changes that need to be made in the transition from arithmetic through algebra. When students fail to make one of these changes conventionally, they are forced to make do with what they already know in a new situation where it is inadequate or inappropriate. Thus by studying the conceptual changes that need to be made in learning algebra, we can predict that errors are likely to be made whenever a new problem to be solved requires a mastery of one of the new concepts. Furthermore, we can also predict the nature of the errors that are likely to occur since the incorrect answer will be based on the old conception.

In short, the primary intent of this paper is to show how a number of common high school algebra errors can be viewed as the result of a systematic adaptation of previously acquired knowledge using a small number of extrapolation techniques. This perspective divides many of the commonly observed errors into three categories:

(1) errors generated by an incorrect choice of an extrapolation technique
(2) errors reflecting an impoverished (but correct) base knowledge
(3) errors arising during the execution of a procedure

The following sections of this paper discuss each of these in turn.† Section 2 focusses on two elementary extrapolation techniques, generalization and linear decomposition, whose misuse produces a number of diverse errors. Section 3 examines the conceptual transition from arithmetic to algebra in order to highlight a developmental coherency underlying errors in the second category above. And section 4 shifts attention from the knowledge employed to the problem-solving process itself.

The scope of this work is illustrated by the table in Appendix A that lists the errors that are discussed.‡ All of these errors were actually produced by people. They were culled from tutoring experiences, from tests given to both high school and remedial college classes, and from protocols gathered by Davis *et al.* (1978). However, these data are used suggestively, not statistically. To explain why particular errors are likely, I simply needed to identify the common errors and misconceptions that did occur; rough judgements of frequency sufficed. Because of the informal nature of the study, the data throughout the paper are collectively referred to as the *observed errors*; specific sources are not cited.

Finally, although the content of this paper benefitted from partial computer implementations as a rough test for the adequacy of various rules for reproducing errors, the computer implementation will not be discussed. Much work remains to assemble these observations and explanations into a full computational model; only some of the observations about the conceptual transitions from arithmetic to algebra have been incorporated computationally. However, this project has been primarily an exploratory study to test the viability of a generative/developmental approach. The most solid results are interspersed throughout in the analyses of each of the observed errors.

2. Extrapolation

In solving a new problem, there are two possible ways to proceed. If a student already has an applicable rule, an answer can be constructed by directly executing that rule. But if none of the student's current rules applies as is, the student is forced to find some way to bridge the gap between known rules and unfamiliar problems. This is a more

† This kind of conceptual error taxonomy has its precedent in the work of Donaldson (1963). Donaldson classified the errors arising in a set of reasoning tasks as being either *structural* (failure to appreciate relationships in the problem or to grasp some principle essential for its solution), *arbitrary* (lack of loyalty to the givens of the problem under the influence of previous experiences), or *executive* (errors that arise not from failure to understand how the problem should be tackled, but in some failure in actually carrying out the manipulations required).

‡ Errors that are not discussed in this paper are covered in Matz (1980).

indirect (and creative) route to producing an answer since the student has to figure out first how to adapt an old rule or how to view a new problem as a variant of some familiar one. In short, the student must extrapolate. This section centers on two of the most frequently used and misused extrapolation techniques, linearity and generalization. But before describing these specific extrapolation techniques, let me briefly discuss one factor that influences the way students extrapolate: varying conceptions about what it means for a rule to apply to a problem.

2.1. APPLYING A RULE

When students first learn high school algebra rules, rule patterns can usually be placed in a 1–1 correspondence with problems. Each single literal in a pattern maps to a single literal in the algebraic expression of the problem to be solved, a situation that can also be described as a "top-level" match since the rule pattern can be projected onto the object as a whole. A top-level match is a more precise way of stating that a rule *fits* a situation. As the algebraic expressions in question become more complex, there are more literals in a problem than in the relevant rule pattern. To handle this situation one can either give up literal-for-literal matches or give up top-level-only matching. An insistence on literal-for-literal matches constrains one to view algebra rules strictly as a matter of *pattern-replacement* rather than as *schemas* which act more like procedures for constructing a replacement. The distinction between these two ways of interpreting rules reflects whether patterns are considered as *character-strings* or as *expression trees* and often separates experienced problem-solvers from novices. More sophisticated problem-solvers view patterns as descriptions of expression trees and match pattern literals to subexpressions, e.g. substituting "$(3+X)$" for "X" in some pattern. This is still a kind of top-level match since the rule pattern is again projected onto the object as a whole. In contrast, novices view patterns as descriptions of character strings. Rather than compromising literal-for-literal correspondences, they no longer confine themselves to top-level matches, but use embedded matches as well. This means that if the pattern of a rule matches a subexpression of an algebraic expression or equation, the result is then formed by replacing the matched subexpression with the result specified by the rule in the original expression, all other parts remaining the same (the other parts are carried along as is). For example, a novice applies the cancellation rule $AX/A = X$ to every literal instance of it in an expression (as indicated below), producing the following error:

$$\frac{\boxed{AX} + \boxed{BY}}{\boxed{X} + \boxed{Y}} \Rightarrow A + B$$

For some students, embedded matching provides a way to handle larger, more complex expressions while continuing to use only simple literal-for-literal matching of rule patterns and algebraic expressions.† But as the examples in the next two sections demonstrate, it is this naive perception of rule patterns as character strings that underlies many of the misguided extrapolations.

---

† The "literal-for-literal" matching strategy also encompasses matches of a pattern like AX with an instance like $2AX$, i.e. a "literal-for-compound-literal" match where a compound literal is a concatenation of two or more literals.

2.2. LINEARITY

"Linearity" describes a way of working with a decomposable object by treating each of its parts independently: an operator is employed *linearly* when the final result of applying it to an object is gotten by applying the operator to each subpart and then straightforwardly combining the partial results. The assumption of linearity is quite natural for many students since much of their previous experience is compatible with a linearity hypothesis. For example the immense number of occasions that students add and use the distributive law in arithmetic is very likely to reinforce the acceptance of linearity. This trend continues with early algebra problems since these often involve either arithmetic (linear) procedures applied to symbolic values instead of numbers, or combining like terms, also a term-by-term, linear-like process.

Errors that reflect hidden or unrecognized linear assumptions can be categorized according to the phase in the problem-solving process in which the linearity assumption figures, i.e. whether it extends the applicability of an existing rule or guides the abstraction of a rule from a solved sample problem. This section looks at the first category. These linear extrapolation errors are in turn subdivided into *generalized distribution* errors and *repeated application* errors according to whether the operator used in solving a problem is internal or external to the expression being operated on.

Throughout the discussion, the symbol "$\Rightarrow$" will denote an invalid equality statement.

2.2.1. Linearity errors: generalized distribution

One of the largest and most frequently occurring class of errors are the linear decomposition errors, typified by: $\sqrt{(A+B)} \Rightarrow \sqrt{A} + \sqrt{B}$. In general, these errors result

TABLE 1

Generalized distribution

Correct

$$A(B+C) = AB + AC$$

$$A(B-C) = AB - AC$$

$$\frac{1}{A}(B+C) = \frac{1}{A}(B) + \frac{1}{A}(C) \quad \text{equivalently,} \quad \frac{B+C}{A} = \frac{B}{A} + \frac{C}{A}$$

$$(AB)^2 = A^2 B^2 \quad \text{more generally,} \quad (AB)^n = A^n B^n$$

$$\sqrt{(AB)} = \sqrt{A} * \sqrt{B} \quad \text{more generally,} \quad (AB)^{1/n} = (A)^{1/n} (B)^{1/n}$$

Incorrect

$$\sqrt{(A+B)} \Rightarrow \sqrt{A} + \sqrt{B}$$

$$(A+B)^2 \Rightarrow A^2 + B^2$$

$$A(BC) \Rightarrow AB * AC$$

$$\frac{A}{B+C} \Rightarrow \frac{A}{B} + \frac{A}{C}$$

$$2^{a+b} \Rightarrow 2^a + 2^b$$

$$2^{ab} \Rightarrow 2^a 2^b$$

when a composite algebraic expression is linearly decomposed by distributing its top-most or dominant operator across an expression's parts. The operator being distributed appears in the expression itself. Linear decompositions are at times correct and at other times not, as Table 1 illustrates.

All of the errors in the second part of the table appeared in the collected data. We can account for all of the correct and incorrect examples above with the following schemas (see Table 2):

For one binary operator ($\triangle$) and one unary operator ($\square$):

$$\text{SCH1:} \quad \square(X \triangle Y) \Rightarrow \square X \triangle \square Y$$

For two binary operators:

$$\text{SCH2:} \quad (X \square Y) \triangle Z \Rightarrow (X \square Z) \triangle (Y \square Z)$$

$$\text{SCH3:} \quad X \square (Y \triangle Z) \Rightarrow (X \square Y) \triangle (X \square Z)$$

TABLE 2

	$\square$ OPR	$\triangle$ OPR	Result
SCH3:	times[1]	plus	$A(B + C) = AB + AC$
SCH1:	square root	times	$\sqrt{(AB)} = \sqrt{A} * \sqrt{B}$
SCH1:	square root	plus	$\sqrt{(A + B)} \Rightarrow \sqrt{A} + \sqrt{B}$
$X \square Y$ is the base; Z is the exponent			
SCH2:	times	exponentiate	$(AB)^n = A^n B^n$
X is the base; $Y \triangle Z$ is the exponent			
SCH3:	exponentiate	times	$2^{ab} \Rightarrow 2^a 2^b$

[1] Since the multiplication in the distributive law is written implicitly using concatentation rather than explicitly with the binary operator "$*$", the distributive law may look more like an instance of SCH1 than SCH3. Using SCH1 would require the $\square$ operator to be "$*A$", as if SCH3 had been curried once to yield SCH1.

These schemas would be triggered in the course of solving algebra problems of the type "Simplify" or "Solve for X" in order to achieve goals like "decompose-expression" or "isolate-X". According to a premise of this explanation, abstractions like the two schemas above must come from somewhere; they are grounded in some familiar prototype. Very likely they result from a generalization of the distributive law. One plausible way this might happen is as follows. A student exposed to both:

$$A(B + C) = AB + AC \quad \text{and} \quad A(B - C) = AB - AC$$

might easily be led to believe that *any* operator could serve as the middle operator. And if generalizing over operators worked for the middle operator, why not for the distributed (dominant) operator as well, especially since the student may recall seeing problems where the same dominant operator was, in fact, distributed (e.g. square root, exponentiation). In other words, based on a recollection that a generalized version of distribution once worked correctly for some operators other than plus and times, the student follows that course again, invoking distributivity with the operator in the current situation. Of course this derivation should not be taken to imply that students necessarily perform exactly this sequence of mental steps. However, whatever sequence they do perform has effectively the same outcome as the schemas above.†

The pair of examples dealing with the square root operator,

$$\sqrt{(AB)} = \sqrt{A} * \sqrt{B} \quad \text{and} \quad \sqrt{(A+B)} \Rightarrow \sqrt{A} + \sqrt{B}$$

and with exponentiation,

$$(AB)^n = A^n B^n \quad \text{and} \quad 2^{ab} \Rightarrow 2^a 2^b$$

highlight the fact that an operator in and of itself should not be tagged as "distributable" or "non-distributable". The characterization of a distributable operator must talk about the distributable operator *with respect to the other operator involved in the action.* For instance, the square root operator distributes over the times operator, but it does not distribute over the plus operator. Apparently, even adept problem-solvers can temporarily forget this distinction and tag the square root operator as non-distributable or exponentiation as distributable since they occasionally have to substitute in numbers to reassure themselves that:

$$\sqrt{(AB)} = \sqrt{A} * \sqrt{B} \quad \text{and} \quad 2^{ab} \neq 2^a 2^b$$

2.2.2. Linearity errors: repeated application

Often a new problem differs from a prototype by having more terms than the prototype. When the extra terms all have the same form as the term(s) in the prototype, a common extrapolation strategy is simply to iterate the operator or rule used in the prototype over the extra terms. If the extra terms are not in the same form as the term(s) in the prototype, some students attempt to apply the rule just to the terms that do match, leaving the extra terms as is, i.e. they apply the rule selectively as an embedded rather than a top-level match. In both these cases the operator or rule that is applied repeatedly is not syntactically contained in the expression being operated on (as was the case for the generalized distribution errors), but instead is one that the student copied from a prototype. A linearity assumption lurks behind this presumption that an operator can be applied independently to the terms in an expression.

The next set of examples epitomizes this use of an iterated operator strategy. When people solve equations incorrectly involving a sum of fractions where the variable to

---

† There is an equally plausible alternative derivation for one error that appeared in the table,

$$\frac{A}{B+C} \Rightarrow \frac{A}{B} + \frac{A}{C}$$

This fraction error can be constructed by reversing the roles of the numerator and denominator in the following correct rule for decomposing a fraction:

$$\frac{B+C}{A} \Rightarrow \frac{B}{A} + \frac{C}{A}$$

In other words, the incorrect rule is a symmetric analogue of the correct rule which can be formed by flipping the fractions in the correct rule. This might happen if a student sees no reason to treat the denominator of a fraction any differently than the numerator.

Although I do not discuss symmetry in this paper, I believe that it should be included in the collection of extrapolation techniques that people often employ.

be solved for occurs in one of the denominators, they are likely to take the reciprocal of each of the fractions in the sum. The example excerpts below illustrate.

$$\text{Solve for } X: \quad \frac{1}{3} = \frac{1}{X} + \frac{1}{7}$$

$$3 = X + 7$$

$$\text{Solve for } R: \quad \frac{1}{R} = \frac{1}{R_1} + \frac{1}{R_2} + \frac{1}{R_3}$$

$$R = R_1 + R_2 + R_3$$

Again, in keeping with the premises of this account, the urge to take the reciprocal must have its grounds in some correctly-working prototype. Problems of the form

$$\text{Solve for } X: \quad \frac{1}{X} = \frac{1}{2}$$

$$X = 2$$

provide such a basis for a student's extrapolation, but a rather shaky one since a reciprocal interpretation is inaccurate here. This "reciprocal" error actually involves two errors, (1) a misinterpretation of the prototype and (2) a false extrapolation assumption that the reciprocal operator of the prototype could be iterated to handle the extra terms in the new situation. The misinterpretation of the prototype is covered in detail in Matz (1980).

Cancellation errors also fit neatly into this theoretical framework. Errors of the form

$$\frac{AX + BY}{X + Y} \Rightarrow A + B$$

can be reproduced using the extrapolation-by-iteration strategy. Here the (iterated) base rule is probably

$$\frac{AX}{X} \Rightarrow A$$

According to this account, students notice two instances of the base rule in the new problem above, AX/X and BY/Y. This leads them to decompose linearly the expression, cancel iteratively, and then simply compose the partial results. However, not all cancellation problems can be handled so neatly or comprehensively by iteration. The symmetry of this particular example and the unambiguous partial results trivialize the processes of decomposing and then recomposing the partial answers. For more ragged problems, the way partial answers are composed into a final answer (superficially) appears more ad hoc: sometimes signs (particularly minus signs) are ignored, cancelled literals are variously treated as 0 or 1, and not all the partial answers always figure in the final answer. But these variations can also be accounted for in a rule-governed manner. We can posit a small number of "well-formed answer" rules that govern the composition of the partial results and interact to reproduce a large range of erroneous surface behavior (see Matz, 1980). The point is that the core phenomena, the commonly observed cancellation errors, can be viewed as attempts to extrapolate by iterating the standard rule over the terms of a fraction of polynomials.

Then, by overlaying well-formed answer rules† on top of this basic process, we can account for a wide range of surface behavior with a small number of context-sensitive interacting rules. This interaction of extrapolation techniques with well-formed answer rules can also account for an individual student's seemingly contradictory behavior.

Both the reciprocal and the cancellation errors could have been avoided if the problem-solver had modified the situation to fit the rule instead of extending the rule's applicability by iterating it. For the reciprocal error, the new problem could be put in the form of a familiar one (a fraction equalling another fraction) by first finding a common denominator and then collecting the sum of fractions into a single fraction. Likewise if the student first factored out a common term in the cancellation problems, the familiar rule could have been projected onto the transformed new problem. Failure to find a common term should be taken to imply that the familiar rule cannot be applied, and not that some other way should be found to use the rule. However, it is beyond the scope of this account to explain why some people, and not others, choose the right path.

To sum up, the reciprocal errors, cancellation errors and generalized distribution errors all seem to indicate that students do not realize that not all operators or procedures behave like the linear ones they are most familiar with. This is to be expected. Besides its contribution here to a conceptual system for classifying errors, linearity has always been one of the fundamental ideas of both scientific and strategic problem-solving. Thus, although linear assumptions are at times inappropriate, we cannot say that linear extrapolation techniques are inherently incorrect. Rather, their validity depends on the particular context in which they are employed. Their misuse stems both from not recognizing that such an assumption has been made, and from an inadequate knowledge of semantic constraints.

2.3. GENERALIZATION

The second major extrapolation technique, generalization, bridges the gap between known rules and unfamiliar problems by revising a known rule to accommodate particular operators and numbers that appear in a new situation. This kind of revision process figured in the formulation of the generalized distribution schemas above. But the need in algebra to generalize over numbers arises much more frequently than that of generalizing over operators, an unsurprising observation since algebra itself can be regarded as generalized arithmetic. Generalization enables the formulation of a general rule from a sample problem based on the assumption that particular numbers in sample problems are incidental rather than essential. This assumption is nearly always valid, but there is a classic exception. In the solution of a problem like:

$$(X-3)(X-4)=0$$

$$(X-3)=0 \quad \text{or} \quad (X-4)=0$$

$$X=3 \quad \text{or} \quad X=4$$

† Well-formed answer rules serve as critics that embody a student's expectations about the form of answers. These are called into action after a student has executed a procedure. Skilled problem-solvers also seem to have answer critics. However, their rules supplement rather than substitute for semantic (checking) knowledge. For example, experts have expectations about the order of magnitude of an answer and the number of expected solutions to an equation.

although the 3 and 4 are not critical to the procedure itself, the 0 is. Students who fail to realize the critical nature of the 0 treat it just as they do the other numbers in the prototype and construct a rule like:

$$(X - A)(X - B) = K$$

$$(X - A) = K \quad \text{or} \quad (X - B) = K$$

$$X = \text{Solve} \, [(X - A) = K] \quad \text{or} \quad X = \text{Solve} \, [(X - B) = K]$$

This rule works fortuitously as long as the right-hand sides of subsequent problems are equal to zero. Later a teacher may solve a problem of the form:

$$(X - 5)(X - 7) = 3$$

Even if students see the new preliminary steps the teacher performs to transform this problem into one where the zero product rule can be applied,† they may remember only that problems of this form can be solved. Given a similar homework problem, students once again utilize their "constant-product rule" to produce solutions of the form:

$$(X - 5)(X - 7) = 3$$

$$(X - 5) = 3 \quad \text{or} \quad (X - 7) = 3$$

$$X = 8 \quad \text{or} \quad X = 10$$

Since the initial "constant-product rule" exactly covers the new situation as well, the student is not even confronted with a thought-provoking discrepancy between rule and problem.

This scenario recalls the distinction between the course of extrapolation taken by adept problem-solvers and that taken by naive problem-solvers apparent in the earlier reciprocal and cancellation error scenarios. Adept problem-solvers try to rewrite (i.e. preprocess) a new problem so that it can match a relevant rule whereas naive students tend to revise a relevant rule or apply it repeatedly.

Because students are so accustomed to generalizing over numbers, one can predict that errors will be made for any type of problem whose specific numerical values are critical. In the type of problem above, students completely miss the fact that the 0 is critical. The rule they appear to have extracted from the sample problem has slots designated to be filled by arbitrary numbers. However, specific numbers in rules are not always considered to be arbitrary. In the context of the collection of rules concerning the identities for addition and multiplication the numbers 0 and 1 are probably recognized as being special:

$$A * 1 = A \quad \text{and} \quad A + 0 = A$$

However, over time these two rules may get merged into one overly general rule (again △ denotes an unspecified operator):

$$A \triangle \langle \text{special number} \rangle = A$$

But then this more abstract rule could be accidentally triggered when a student saw

† $X^2 - 12X + 35 = 3$; $X^2 - 12X + 32 = 0$; $(X - 8)(X - 4) = 0$ etc.

"$A*0$", thus accounting for the error,

$$A*0 \Rightarrow A$$

Furthermore, a student could have both the correct rule for multiplying by zero, $A*0 = 0$, as well as the generalized identity rule above. The presence of *two* rules whose patterns match "$A*0$" could explain why an individual student seems to randomly produce correct and incorrect behavior.

Similarly, if the notion of an additive inverse and a multiplicative inverse get lumped together, the correct rule,

$$A+(-A) = 0$$

might be generalized as,

$$A \triangle \langle A \text{ inverse} \rangle \Rightarrow 0$$

This overly general rule could be responsible for the observed error,†

$$A * \frac{1}{A} \Rightarrow 0$$

2.4. CONCLUSIONS

This section has proposed that some of the most commonly observed algebra errors result from using extrapolation techniques to extend rules in prototype problems. But this style of error analysis has implications beyond merely accounting for specific data. It provides an explanation that goes beyond a restatement of the observed facts, correct and incorrect answers, by addressing one of the fundamental characteristics of mathematical competence, the ability to construct new solution procedures.

Although the derivations in this section plausibly describe how particular prototype problems are extended, more work remains to model completely the process of extrapolation. First, the assessment of the differences between a prototype problem or a base rule and a new problem needs to be formalized. This assessment provides the motivation and information for actually selecting an extrapolation technique. Second, a complete model needs to incorporate criteria for evaluating the legality of an extrapolation. Criteria for legal extrapolations would embody some of the deductive structure of high school algebra, for example, the justifications that explain why the zero-product method of solving a quadratic equation works or why the reciprocal interpretation succeeds for simple problems. These same criteria would provide information for determining whether the particular operators and numbers of a

† Alternatively, if a student forgot the correct multiplicative inverse rule the student might try to reconstruct it from a possibly impoverished notion of "inverse" as something that "undoes" an operation just performed, leaving nothing. This also yields the incorrect inverse rule above. But these generalized inverse rule derivations do not seem to be as compelling as the one for the generalized identity rule because the two correct inverse rules are not as syntactically similar as the two correct identity rules. Again, if this error had instead appeared in the context of a group of cancellation problems, a more likely explanation than the generalized inverse rule account is one that was mentioned earlier: $A/A \Rightarrow 0$ because "after you cancel, there is nothing left".

prototype are essential or incidental, influencing the selection or rejection of particular extrapolation techniques.

Finally, since extrapolation techniques figure prominently in an account of novel problem-solving behavior, we should in some way justify the choice of those used here. Why favor linearity over non-linearity? To begin with a simple pragmatic justification, these extrapolation techniques cover the data at hand. They are descriptively adequate in that we can use them to account for common errors. But in addition to their purely descriptive value, there are important theoretical grounds for their selection: these techniques are methods that generally work well for students in prior mathematical experience. Both linearity and generalization have this characteristic; they are useful, often encountered techniques that apply correctly in many situations. For example, the generalization rule that replaces specific numbers with arbitrary ones in example problems (under the assumption that the specific number is incidental rather than critical) plays an essential role in one's ability to learn from examples. Without it we could not form a general rule from specific problems.

Likewise, students gain repeated practice with linear procedures in arithmetic and early algebra when adding, using the distributive law, and combining like terms. As it turns out, this criterion of "working well in the past" is not only the most straightforward, but also is perhaps the only logically justifiable criterion for the selection of useful projection techniques (Goodman, 1977).

In summary, my answer to the question "why these extrapolation techniques and not others" is that these techniques (1) bridge the differences between new and old problems; (2) are familiar to students; and (3) have proved successful in many past situations. In turn, since extrapolation techniques specify how to use old rules to construct answers for new situations, the particular collection of extrapolation techniques functionally determines the set of possible generable answers. Thus the "naturally selected" repertoire of extrapolation techniques is responsible for why certain errors and not others are commonly observed.

3. Conceptual changes

Analysing the conceptual changes involved in moving from arithmetic to algebra contributes both to a theory of errors and to the development of a computational model of algebraic competence. First, just to develop a model of a competence one needs to know what skills and concepts comprise it. One of the classic ways to uncover internal structure is to look at what develops, the ontogeny of a competence. Secondly, any implementation that purports to be a model of how people learn algebra must be powerful enough actually to achieve a mature competence (it must be able to solve more than trivial problems), yet not so powerful as to presuppose knowledge that could not itself be learned. Thirdly, one of the claims mentioned in the introduction was that when students fail to make conceptual changes conventionally, they are forced to make do with what they already know in a new situation where their knowledge is inadequate or inappropriate. By describing necessary conceptual changes one can predict both that errors will occur and what those errors are likely to be.

The major conceptual changes in learning high school algebra center around what distinguishes algebra from arithmetic: the nature of symbolic values, the expanded interpretations for the equal sign, and an altered style of problem-solving. This section covers each of these changes separately along with its associated errors. A brief description of a third class of errors, processing errors, is also included.

3.1. SYMBOLIC VALUES

Algebra was created as an abstraction of arithmetic so that equations could be solved once for all numbers, and so that general statements could be made about various processes that yield the same result. The critical transition step was the introduction of the concept of a symbolic value, a device permitting one to denote and manipulate abstractions. One of the initial tasks for students learning algebra is to make the connection between algebraic and arithmetic objects. This involves first recognizing that letters have referents (that they are abstractions of something and not just arbitrary entities) and next figuring out how to operate with abstractions and to denote and interpret results.

For students who initially fail to realize that a letter represents a number, operating with a letter seems totally underconstrained. Such students commonly respond that "you can't multiply by X, you don't know what X is". The *name-process* convention (Davis, 1978) extends the arithmetic notion about "doing" an operation like multiplication by specifying how to denote a result. Since symbolic values are in a sense placeholders, any operation with a symbolic value as an argument cannot be evaluated to the point of achieving a numerical answer. Instead the procedure call is left as a name for the potential result of the process; the result of multiplying 2 by X is $2X$. In order to work with symbolic values students need to accept the concept of and notation for these suspended operations. Accepting this concept means relaxing arithmetic expectations about well-formed answers, namely that an answer is a number.

Both the name-process convention and the realization that variables represent numbers link the syntactic manipulation of character strings to the semantic interpretation of symbolic expressions. This enables the transfer of arithmetic knowledge about standard operations and correct arithmetic facts to algebra. Without this link, students can neither compute with symbolic values nor verify results. They forget whether $0*A$ equals 0 or A and so treat both 0 and 1 indiscriminately as identities regardless of the particular operation involved. They fail to realize that one could arithmetically carry out symbolic operations by using an arbitrary referent for the symbolic value, that instantiation and evaluation turn algebraic statements into arithmetic ones, reducing the verification of the legality of an algebraic transformation to checking the arithmetic truth of an instantiation. This sort of knowledge is part of an informal understanding of the way a logical theory and a model are related.

3.2. NOTATION

Notational ambiguity and duality in algebra further obscure the link between symbolic evaluation and numerical evaluation. Syntactically similar expressions differ semantically because the equals sign, concatenation, plus and minus have multiple meanings which are distinguished only by parsing rules and context. Difficulties with the dual usage of plus and minus both as binary operators and as signs (unary operators) are primarily carry-overs from arithmetic; they are not introduced by any new algebraic ideas. But for concatenation and especially the equals sign, the addition of alternate interpretations coincides with the arithmetic–algebra transition, giving rise to a characteristic collection of errors.

In arithmetic, concatenation is used in place-value notation and also in the notation for mixed fractions where it denotes implicit addition:

$$43$$

$$4\,3/4$$

Then in algebra it denotes symbolic multiplication:

$$XY$$

$$3X$$

and often both in one expression:

$$43X$$

A developmental theory predicts that errors will occur in using concatenated strings because some students will continue to use the previous (arithmetic) interpretation. Data support this prediction. Typical errors are:

concluding that $4X = 46$ given that $X = 6$

(using the place-value interpretation of concatenation)

or that $XY = -8$ given that $X = -3$ and $Y = -5$

(using the implicit addition interpretation of concatenation)

Although seemingly minor, notational changes like the interpretation of concatenation illustrate that algebra is not the straightforward generalization of arithmetic we believe it to be.

Other commonly-made errors also reflect either conceptual or perceptual developmental problems. As Davis (1978) points out, when students are first exposed to multiplication, they often continue to add. Later, they occasionally multiply instead of exponentiate, e.g. $(-1)^3 = -3$. In every case observed by Davis and his co-workers, the error implied that the student continued to use a previously learned binary operator.

Before turning to equality, let me make one final comment on symbolic values. One subtle and complicating feature about the abstract character of symbolic values is that the precise nature of the abstraction varies. Symbolic values may be constrained, unconstrained, or constant, and may assume a set of values or a single value. Lumping together symbolic constants, parameters, unknowns, arbitrary symbolic values, and pattern variables as simply "variables" draws attention only to a single common feature—their abstractness. Such an overly general concept of a variable blurs distinctions that affect how that entity is manipulated; it obscures restrictions about exactly how and where the value it refers to varies, whether from one specific problem to the next or within a single problem. Activities such as simplifying expressions, solving equations and pattern-matching treat these varieties of variables in subtly different ways.

A good illustration of how the nature of a symbolic value varies can be drawn by presenting a series of problems ordered as they would appear in a typical algebra course. The earliest algebra problems, like "evaluate $7+X$ when X is 6", specify a single value for a symbolic value so that an algebra problem trivially maps to an arithmetic one. In these exercises the referent of a symbolic value is fixed for a given problem. Later, in problems about simplifying expressions, the symbolic value acts as a prototypical domain element, capable of taking on *any* numerical value. To verify that a proposed simplification is equivalent to the initial expression the student must choose an instantiation and realize that the choice is arbitrary (aside from special cases like 0 or 1). The interpretation of a symbolic value changes again with the shift from expression to equation-oriented contexts, from prototype to "unknown", from standing for *any* or all numbers to standing for a *particular* value or restricted set of values. One more shift occurs when parameters are introduced: now there are seemingly two unknowns, the solution to the equation and the parameters. Students become confused about which of the two to solve for; they often solve for the parameter in terms of the unknown. Parameters also unsettle a student's recently formed standards for judging when an answer has been obtained (whether an expression can be evaluated further) since answers can still involve symbolic values, e.g. "the distance is $3t$". Similarly, when problems with two unknowns and two equations are assigned, some students solve for one unknown in terms of the other, an error reminiscent both of the parameter problem and of solving for a single unknown in terms of itself. The difficulty stems from confusion about the dependency relationship between multiple occurrences of the unknown in an equation in one variable, and between the two unknowns in a system of two equations and two unknowns. Once recognized, conceptual subtleties like these seem transparent and thus insignificant. But for naive students, they are significant and they accumulate, making algebra progressively more formidable.

3.3. EQUALITY

The maturation of the concept of equality is one of the most critical and subtle conceptual changes involved in learning high school algebra. Unlike the situation with symbolic values, this change clearly involves extending an existing concept rather than acquiring a completely new one, especially since arithmetic equality statements and algebraic equations share the same notation. This means that before students can begin to learn the new use of the equals sign they must first realize that there is something new to learn, that algebraic equations cannot be dealt with simply as arithmetic equality statements with letters instead of numbers. This section outlines some of the adjustments students must make.

In arithmetic the equals sign is predominantly used to connect a problem with its *numerical* result, as a relation between a "procedure call" and the result of its execution. It is also used (although somewhat less frequently) to connect two processes that yield the same result, e.g. $2*3 = 3+3$, or a process with the sequence of intermediate steps leading to a final result, e.g. $2(6-4) = 2*2 = 4$. These chains of equalities will be referred to as *reductions*. Each link in the chain is some simplification or change in form of its predecessor. Both process-result equality statements and reductions are tautologies or universally true statements. Tautologies comprise the arithmetic uses of equality. But algebraic equality, in addition to tautologies, also includes the use of the equals sign to express *constraints*, e.g. $3X + 3 = 2X + 7$ is true only when $X = 4$. Unlike tautologies, constraint equations are not universally true statements; the equals sign in an equation does *not* connect equivalent expressions. Instead the left- and right-hand side expressions are two distinct descriptions, neither of which is really a property of the unknown, *but their equality constrains the unknown*. Given an equation, the task of solving it is a matter of determining the restrictions (the values of the unknown) that make the equation true.† Thus tautologies and contraint equations differ with respect to the domain over which they are true.

Besides their semantic differences, constraint equations and the subsequent equations generated in solving them (the steps of a solution) abide by different graphical conventions. By "graphical conventions" I mean the information implicitly conveyed by the layout on paper of the steps of a solution, be it a chain of reductions or a sequence of equations. Graphical conventions tell where corresponding expressions are located, i.e. where the "before" expression is in relation to the "after" expression or, equivalently, the direction and location of the implicit transformations from line to line. With process-result statements, the transformation usually takes place from the left-hand side to the right-hand side; in the students' vernacular, the left-hand side "goes to" or "turns into" the right-hand side. Similarly, with reductions like:

$$(X-3)(X+4) = X(X+4)+(-3)(X+4)$$
$$= X*X+4X+(-3)X_1+(-3)4$$
$$= X^2+4X-3X-12$$
$$= X^2+X-12$$

or

$$(X-3)(X+4) = X(X+4)+(-3)(X+4) = X^2+4X-3X-12 = X^2+X-12$$

a chain is created by starting with one algebraic object and successively operating on it until some result is attained, e.g. the expression is in its "simplest" form. Since transformations (or the execution of the process inherently specified by the expression) proceed uniformly in one direction, we "read" these chains of equalities top to bottom in a *single* column or left to right *across* a line. Furthermore, in chains of reductions equality is preserved among the *entire* collection of left- and right-hand sides; any two expressions are equal.

By contrast, in solving equations execution proceeds downward in two columns. And instead of successively transforming a single expression, it is a *relationship* (the equation) that is transformed by applying the same operation to both sides. (Operations applied to both sides will be referred to as deductions to collectively distinguish them from reductions.) Although deductions do not preserve the equality of corresponding sides of consecutive lines, they do preserve the value of the unknown. For example,

Solve: $\dfrac{3}{X} = \dfrac{6}{3X+1}$ (consecutive corresponding sides are not equal)

$X(3X+1)\dfrac{3}{X} = X(3X+1)\dfrac{6}{3X+1}$ (consecutive corresponding sides are equal)

$9X+3 = 6X$

etc.

---

† For students who fail to realize that the solution to a constraint equation is that value that makes it an identity, the act of *checking* is meaningless. They do not see how an obvious statement like "6 = 6" validates a solution.

With simple equations like $2X = 1$, it is easy to read the restriction (the solution) from the description. For more difficult equations, we express the constraint in successively simpler forms by means of both reductions and deductions. Reformulating the constraint effectively decouples the sides of the constraint equation so that the unknown can be easily "read off" it, e.g. $X = 4$.† In the solutions to equations, there are three relationships (as opposed to only one for reductions) to consider to figure out what was done in a sample problem: the relationship between consecutive left-hand sides, between consecutive right-hand sides, and between consecutive lines. Students have literally to read between the lines in order to determine:

(1) the *nature* of each transformation;
(2) the *relationship* between two transformations that yield respectively the next consecutive left- and right-hand sides; and
(3) the *equality or inequality* of consecutive corresponding sides, a judgment based on the determination of (1).

Consequently, working with equations requires facility both in interpreting the equals sign when it appears explicitly and in recognizing equivalent expressions when it does not. This is especially critical since most solutions to sample problems intermix deductions and reductions throughout a solution process and even within a single line by compressing several steps into one. This packs more (and varied) information between the lines of a solution, complicating the analysis task.‡

So far, I have pointed out that algebraic equality subsumes arithmetic equality and incorporates as well a new sense of equality, constraint equations. However, in making the transition from arithmetic to algebra, students begin by working just with algebraic tautologies. Here, the sense of equality is the same as in arithmetic, the only new twist concerns the introduction of variables and the evaluation of expressions involving them (ref. the "name-process" problem mentioned earlier). Real conceptual change is required only when constraint equations appear. Unfortunately, a cursory comparison of the new kind of equality statements with the old ones (chains of reductions) does not obviously suggest the distinction between them or even that there is something new to be learned. Thus the syntactic similarity between two semantically different statements like:

$$4X + 12 = 4(X + 3) \quad \text{and} \quad 3X + 3 = 2X + 7$$

---

† Students who fail to realize (1) that multiple occurrences of the unknown symbolic value are mutually constrained or (2) that the goal of the solution is a decoupled expression, tend to solve for "X" in terms of itself, e.g. $X = (4Z + X^2)/7$.

‡ One aspect of a transformation that is difficult to infer from a sample problem is the *scope* of that transformation. For instance, from a sample solution to an equation of the form:

$$AX = C$$

$$X = C/A$$

the student may correctly note that *both sides* must be divided, but incorrectly infer the scope of the necessary division. Based on this misinterpretation, the student produces errors such as:

$$AX + B = C$$

$$X + B = C/A$$

Here the student considers that dividing a single term constitutes dividing the "side". But if the student happens to isolate the X by first getting rid of the B, the error-prone rule works fortuitously.

presents a serious obstacle: some students are often still working under the preconception that each individual line is a tautology, a habit that leads them to "read" *across* each line of the solution. As a result they expect that some transformation has turned the expression on the left side of the equals sign into the expression on the right-hand side. This expectation leads to total confusion, especially in problems where the student is asked to fill in the justifications for the steps of a proof. Supposedly, facility with the theorems and axioms promotes an understanding of the nature of a "legal" step. But those students who fail to recognize that a change in "reading styles" is required cannot even locate where, in a sequence of equations, the axioms have been applied. Misled by their previous experience with the equals sign, they attempt in vain to find an axiom that matches across each individual *line* of a solution.

To conclude, let me comment on the homework exercises that are intended to effect the transition between the tautological and constraint uses of the equals sign. When constraint equations are first introduced, most of the equations used as samples and for homework are very simple, so simple that they can delay important conceptual and perceptual changes while encouraging misconceptions. Consider the following examples:

$$(1) \quad X - 5 = 17$$

$$(2) \quad 2X + 3 = 3X$$

$$(3) \quad 3X + 2 = 11$$

Although these really are equations, they are easily perceived as familiar process-result problems. Some students solve these trivial equations by inspection. In (2) for instance, one student used the following argument:

You want to make the two sides the same. So the difference between $2X$ and $3X$ is an X. The 3 has to make up for the difference, so X is 3.

Other students begin to develop a pattern-matching approach (Lewis, 1979). Their line of reasoning (roughly) tries to determine a factorization of the right-hand side which looks like the left-hand side, e.g. in problem (3), 11 is $3*3 + 2$, so X must be 3. As the problems get more difficult, the success rate of the method rapidly diminishes, as the following scenario indicates:

$$\text{Solve for } X: \quad \frac{X+1}{X+4} = \frac{5}{6}$$

The "process-result" oriented students want to answer that X must be both 4 and 2 since:

$$\frac{X+1}{X+4} = \frac{4+1}{2+4} = \frac{5}{6}$$

Notice also that this solution employs a linear planning strategy like those discussed in the previous section. Here the student sets up independent subgoals to achieve the desired end: (1) solve the equation formed by setting the numerators equal and (2) solve the equation formed by setting the denominators equal.

The intent of these examples is not to prove that clever guessing is a short-lived approach. Rather, they illustrate that the conceptual and perceptual changes required for more difficult equation solving are not necessarily promoted by initial training problems. Those problems do not clearly illustrate that statements with equals signs can be reversed (the process on the right and the result on the left) or even that they can have multiple and distinct operations on both sides.† Moreover, because those "equations" can still be viewed as familiar process-result statements, they fail to elicit the real change—the underlying idea of a constraint.

4. The changing nature of problem solving

Working arithmetic problems means executing algorithms. Once students know the arithmetic facts and rules for combining intermediate results like carries and partial sums, the first, next, and last steps, the operands, and the number of iterations of an operation are all clearly specified by the problem and its corresponding algorithm. In contrast, adjusting to algebra involves having to compose a plan for solving a problem as well as carry it out, additional steps that often lead to processing errors. This section contrasts these activities with arithmetic problem solving and describes two sorts of processing errors, *planning* errors and *execution* errors. Execution errors carry additional interest in that even skilled problem solvers are at times susceptible to them.

4.1. PLANNING AND PLANNING ERRORS

Algebraic problem directives, like "factor" or "solve", describe only the features of a desired result and not, as in arithmetic, a single method to execute. The first hurdle is knowing exactly what the goal is, i.e. correctly inferring the features of the desired result from the instruction and sample problems. For example, if the goal is to factor the expression:

$$X^2 + 5/6X + 1/6$$

then

$$X(X + 5/6) + 1/6$$

is not an appropriate result; "factor" means rewrite the entire expression as a product, and not simply factor part of it. Some students quickly learn the form of the goal, e.g. an answer template like $(X \pm A)(X \pm B)$, long before they figure out the styles of reasoning to attain it. Likewise, those students who solve for X in terms of itself have assimilated an overly general interpretation of the answer template "$X = \ldots$". For both "factor" and "solve" the features of the goal are fixed, but for "simplify", the attributes of the goal state are more volatile. Aesthetic convention usually decrees that one fraction is simpler than two (even if the common denominator is complex) and prefers the factored form to the expanded polynomial.

Having identified the proper goal, the reasoning process to achieve it can take a number of forms, including strategies such as means-ends analysis‡ or constraint

† For a study of how the transition from process-result views of equality to constraint equations could be carefully taught see (Kieran, 1979).

‡ For instance, in solving an equation the steps to be carried out are selected by a kind of means-ends analysis: operations on equations like division and subtraction are associated with the particular goal that they advance, such as isolating the unknown.

propagation. These different styles of reasoning make algebra problem solving a much more flexible activity than rote execution of arithmetic algorithms. In part this added flexibility (alternative strategies and non-rigid order of execution) derives from the abstract nature of algebra: abstraction allows a richer set of descriptions for objects, especially since objects can be named by the processes that generate them. Most algebraic "answers" still reflect the operations that are composed to generate them. Consequently a process that could have yielded an algebraic "result" can often be reconstructed. In contrast, a numerical result of an arithmetic problem retains no trace of the particular process that led to it. Since a numerical result is not uniquely invertible, the original process cannot be recovered. Thus the inherent unidirectionality of arithmetic equality statements constrains the analysis and execution of arithmetic problems to proceed in a forward direction. On the other hand, algebraic equalities have a bi-directional nature: they indicate one process when read left to right and a cognitively different process when read in the reverse direction (Kaput, 1978). For example, the following line represents the factoring process

$$X^2 + 5X + 6 \Rightarrow (X+2)(X+3)$$

while

$$(X+2)(X+3) \Rightarrow X^2 + 5X + 6$$

represents the multiplication process. In other words, even though equality (in both domains) is *mathematically* symmetrical, *cognitively* and *pragmatically* it is not. And in algebra, but not necessarily in arithmetic, an equality statement usually has a meaningful interpretation in both directions. This duality enables new styles of reasoning to be employed in solving problems. For example, to fill in the answer template for the binomial factors of a quadratic, $(X \pm A)(X \pm B)$, one analyses various factorizations of the quadratic's constant term. Potential factorizations of the constant term are constrained in that their sum must be the coefficient of the cross-product (linear) term. This style of reasoning operates backwards from the answer template, relying on the bi-directional view of the equals sign to connect the process of factoring with the process of expanding (or multiplying out.) The bi-directionality of algebraic processes injects a flexibility into algebraic problem-solving which, in the eyes of some students, makes the activity more complicated.

Along with the introduction of goal oriented problem-solving, planning also introduces the need to recognize progress towards and the attainment of goals. This is especially critical since plans are often pieced together on the fly: the next step in a plan is at times determined only after seeing the results of a previous step and re-assessing the distance between that step and the goal. When students do not assess whether a rule gets them closer towards a goal, they execute steps that are obviously *applicable*, but not *productive*; their work has an aimless character. For instance, immediately after multiplying through by a common denominator some students cancel, leaving themselves back at the original point and casting about for another step to try, as in the following protocol excerpt:

$$\frac{3X}{X+3} + \frac{Y}{X-7} = 11$$

$$\frac{3X(X-7)+Y(X+3)}{(X+3)(X-7)}=11$$

$$\frac{3X(X-7)}{(X+3)(X-7)}+\frac{Y(X+3)}{(X+3)(X-7)}=11$$

Determining whether the goal of an algebra problem has been attained also involves some thought. In *arithmetic* a numerical result signals the completion of a problem and success. But in *algebra* indicators of progress are more complex: a student must sometimes judge whether an expression can be evaluated further. Moreover, a failure while executing a procedure forces a departure from the simple execution of algorithms into a more strategic mode; a student is forced to decide what other goal (if any) to resume or pursue. When a local failure is wrongly assessed as a global failure, like the failure of a particular procedure to produce a desired result, some students quit instead of looking for another approach. Similarly, when perspectives are at too low a level, students can lose sight of the problem-solving repertoire, locking themselves into one approach. For example, after finding binomial factorizations for a series of quadratics, some are unable to recognize a case where all the terms have a common factor. But if directed *specifically* to a common factor problem, they handle it easily.

To summarize, algebra is marked by a planning-style of problem-solving that reflects the richness of its conceptual structure. Protocols suggest that students can often deal successfully with sub-components of algebra problem-solving, but at the same time lack the perspective or ability to integrate these into a workable plan.

4.2. PROCESSING ERRORS

In contrast to the errors discussed so far, the next class of errors can be considered to be *execution* errors rather than *conceptual* errors. Although the distinction is not an exact one, it is meant to capture the difference between errors that reflect slips of performance rather than real misunderstandings. Even so, the study of these errors is still useful; we can often draw inferences both about probable modularizations of particular procedures that students use to solve problems and about the activity of a hypothesized "executive" that controls their application.

When a person's attempt to carry out some procedure breaks down, the resultant error can indicate intermediate results of that process, suggesting how particular procedures are actually decomposed into subprocedures. The reason for inferring a particular modularization rather than some other is that another structuring would have different subparts and thus different intermediate results at the interfaces of those subparts. An exemplar of this category of processing errors is a common error in high school algebra, dubbed the "Lost Common Denominator" bug. This bug produces traces such as:

$$\text{Solve for } X: \qquad \frac{5}{2-X}+\frac{5}{2+X}=4$$

$$5(2+X)+5(2-X)=4$$

The excerpt appears as if the student applied the transformation,

$$\frac{A}{B}+\frac{C}{D}\Rightarrow AD+BC$$

to the left-hand side.† Since this error is one to which both competent and naive problem solvers are susceptible, its explanation tests the adequacy of a single theory to provide a coherent view of a range of problem-solving abilities.

Let me sketch one plausible way the bug may be generated. The first subgoal is to simplify the left-hand side by eliminating the fractions. One method cross-multiplies the two fractions to normalize the numerators with respect to the common denominator, the product of the original denominators. In anticipation of the next step, multiplying by the common denominator to eliminate the fraction, only the normalized numerators are written. But in the process of getting the numerators correctly normalized, one can inadvertently "forget" to complete the anticipated action, and so fail to multiply the right-hand side by the common denominator. This produces the second line in the excerpt above. For comparison's sake, let me outline another procedure that usually yields the *correct* next step. Instead of cross-multiplying to normalize the two numerators with respect to the common denominator, the alternative method B serially multiplies each term on both sides of the equation by the common denominator. In this case, a cancel immediately follows the multiply for each fraction, the intermediate step again is unwritten, but the correct answer results.

Although subtle, the distinction—one of process, not effect—is significant. The cross-multiplication version is probably the error-prone one.‡ This version seems to consist of a main procedure that multiplies the equation by the common denominator and a call to a subprocedure that returns the normalized numerators for the two fractions, and that, as a side effect, sets the common denominator; the subprocedure computes the normalized numerators by cross-multiplying the two fractions. In generating this error the student seems to have forgotten to return from the execution of the subroutine to finish the calling procedure. Very likely the tendency to treat the subprocedure as if it were the entire procedure stems from its similarity to another complete procedure, solving an equation of two fractions by cross-multiplication.

In general, one might expect partially executed procedures§ to be the evidence left behind when subgoal bookkeeping gets even slightly complicated.

The next example illustrates another kind of processing error, one that seems to suggest that students monitor the process of executing a plan and "adjust" as it is being executed.

$$\text{Solve for } X: \quad \frac{1}{X} + \frac{1}{X^2} = \frac{3}{X^2} + 6X^2$$

$$X + 1 = 3 + 6X^2$$

---

† The name "Lost Common Denominator" bug is retained just for consistency with previous papers and is not meant to exclude descriptions of other processes which would produce the same trace.

‡ The error $(A/B) + (C/D) = AD + BC$ is avoided when the complexity of the task is reduced with a simplified version of essentially the same problem, i.e. the task of adding two fractions with unlike denominators. This seems to support the conclusion that the error is not conceptual, but rather caused by the complexity of subgoal bookkeeping, i.e. a processing error.

§ Errors of the form $2(X+3) \Rightarrow 2X + 3$ are commonly considered to be a kind of partial execution error. An alternative account for them posits that they are not partial execution errors, but are instigated by their lyrical similarity to the phrase $AX + B$. $2(X+3)$ is read as $2X+3$ because concatenation has no verbal utterance the way times,*, does. This lyrical interposition hypothesis is like the visual similarity account for the Lost Common Denominator error above—procedures that are perceptually similar get confused.

Lewis (1980) has found that this mistake is made by adept problem solvers as well as naive students. In the protocol above the student has started to multiply sequentially the terms on both sides of the equation by the common denominator, X^2, but has neglected to also multiply the last term, $6X^2$, by X^2. This error suggests that procedures may be annotated with a description of their purpose or the goal they achieve, e.g. multiplying by a common denominator "clears the denominator". This annotation is then checked locally to determine whether the procedure is relevant before it is applied to an expression. If the procedure is not considered to be relevant to a particular subexpression, a sort of "local execution monitor" overrides the global planner that originally ordered the execution of that procedure. In the example above, since $6X^2$ has no denominator, multiplication by X^2 is omitted.

Categorizing an error like the one above as a processing error seems quite useful since it allows us to account for day-to-day fluctuations in behavior as well as for errors made by competent problem solvers. However, it remains a rather weak explanatory category since it would be quite difficult to establish rigorously the psychological validity of any detailed processing explanation.

5. Conclusions

The aim of this paper has been to provide an account for the striking uniformity of errors students make in solving algebra problems. The systematic nature of common errors is explained here by a process-oriented theory that views errors as the results of reasonable, though unsuccessful, attempts to adapt previously acquired knowledge to new situations. The advantages of this approach are twofold. First, it facilitates a unified account of both correct and incorrect algebra problem-solving since the process of extrapolation and a common set of extrapolation techniques underlie the production of diverse errors as well as correct answers. Additional support for this view comes from the fundamental role that the two major extrapolation techniques, linearity and generalization, have played in other accounts of human problem-solving skills, most notably in Sussman (1973) and Goldstein (1976). The second contribution of this approach is that it explains students' recent problem-solving behavior in terms of their previous learning and problem-solving experiences by taking into account the sequential ordering of topics, sample problems, and homework exercises in an algebra course. Thus it tries to develop a model of a student's ability that is coherent over time.

Why does this process-oriented explanation for the observed regularity of errors succeed? One property of anything systematic is that it has systematic errors. Thus the results of this study fall out of the application of a computational metaphor to algebraic problem-solving. If we assume that students methodically attempt to apply what they know, then accounting for their answers becomes a matter of identifying (1) what knowledge it is that they know and deem relevant to a particular problem, and (2) what rules govern the application of that knowledge. In adopting such a view of incorrect problem-solving, this work builds on ideas advanced by the BUGGY research project (Brown and Burton, 1978). The BUGGY research group developed a computational model that accounted for the systematic nature of mathematical errors. By substituting one or more buggy subprocedures for their correct counterparts, they reproduced observed subtraction errors and thus demonstrated that students' errors could be explained as the surface manifestation of consistently used incorrect procedures. The analysis of the systematic errors in high school algebra problem-solving presented here shares the underlying theoretical premise of the BUGGY project (in part because the work was begun in collaboration with the members of that group), but it has a different focus. Rather than simply account for the kinds of errors that appear in terms of buggy perturbations of a correct procedure, this work has also proposed how buggy algebra procedures themselves might have been created.

Evaluated strictly as a unifying explanation for high school algebra errors, the analysis presented here is significantly different from most previous studies. Most existing taxonomies of high school algebra errors usually group errors as arithmetical or algebraic, and then further divide the algebraic errors according to problem types, e.g. cancellation errors, collecting-like-term errors, equation errors. By contrast, I have proposed a conceptual system for classifying high school algebra errors that elicits the common misconceptions that lie behind the errors and that suggests why some errors (and not others) are likely to occur. Approximately 30 common errors have been analysed and woven together in this context, including errors committed by adept problem-solvers.

What I have also hoped to point out in this paper is that even though mathematical knowledge has an established notation in terms of axiomatic-deductive frameworks, those formalisms alone do not make a working problem-solver nor do they capture the knowledge of mathematics underlying human competence. Perhaps the greatest short-coming of this work is that it omits a complete specification for a computational model. But in a way this simply reflects a corresponding lack in our theories about algebraic competence. Computational models can only be as strong as the theoretical base on which they stand, and this work is no exception. At times the scope of this project has been a hinderance, but as Minsky (1977) writes:

> Minds are complex, intricate systems that evolve through elaborate developmental processes. To describe one, even at a single moment of that history, must be very difficult. On the surface, one might suppose it even harder to describe its whole developmental history. Shouldn't we content ourselves with trying to describe just the "final performance?" We think just the contrary. Only a good theory of the principles of the mind's development can yield a manageable theory of how it finally comes to work.

In a similar spirit, one might also suggest that only a good model of student problem-solving behavior can lead to a successful ICAI system for that skill.

References

BROWN, J. S. & BURTON, R. (1978). Diagnostic models for procedural bugs in basic mathematical skills. *Cognitive Science*, **2**, 155–192.

BROWN, J. S., BURTON, R., MILLER, M., DeKLEER, J., PURCELL, S., HAUSMANN, C. & BOBROW, R. (1975). *Steps Toward A Theoretical Foundation For Complex, Knowledge-Based C AI.* Bolt, Beranek, and Newman, Inc., Report 3135 (ICAI Report 2).

BROWN, J. S., BURTON, R., HAUSMANN, C., GOLDSTEIN, I., HUGGINS, B. & MILLER, M. (1977). *Aspects of a Theory for Automated Student Modelling.* Bolt, Beranek, and Newman, Inc., Report 3549 (ICAI Report 4).

DAVIS, R. & HENKIN, L. (1978). Aspects of mathematics learning that should be the subject of testing. Presented at the NIE conference on Testing and Education, August 1978.

DAVIS, R., JOCKUSCH, E. & McKNIGHT, C. (1978). Cognitive processes in learning algebra. *Journal of Children's Mathematical Behavior*, **2**, No. 1.

DONALDSON, M. (1963). *A Study of Childrens Thinking.* Tavistock Publications, London.

GOLDSTEIN, I. (1976). *Planning Paradigms—Knowledge for Organizing Models Into Programs*. MIT AI Working Paper 123.

GOODMAN, N. (1977). *Fact, Forecast, and Fiction*. Hackett Press.

KAPUT, J. (1978). Mathematics and learning: epistemological considerations. Presented at the Amherst conference on Cognitive Process Instruction, August 1978.

KIERAN, C. (1979). *Constructing Meaning For The Concept Of Equation*. M.S. paper, Mathematics Department, Concordia University, Canada.

KIERAN, C. (1980). Constructing meaning for the concept of equation. Paper presented at the American Education Research Association meeting, April 1980.

LEWIS, C. (1979). Paper presented at the Conference on Cognitive Processes in Algebra, University of Pittsburgh, July 1979.

LEWIS, C. (1980). Paper presented at the American Education Research Association meeting, April 1980.

MATZ, M. (1980). Towards a computational theory of algebraic competence. *Journal of Mathematical Behavior*, **3**.

MINSKY, M. (1977). *Plain Talk About Neurodevelopmental Epistemology*. MIT AI Memo 430.

SUSSMAN, G. (1973). *A Computational Model of Skill Acquisition*. MIT AI TR297.

Appendix A: the data of algebra errors

evaluate $4X$ when $X = 6$:

$$46$$
$$46X$$

evaluate XY when $X = -3$ and $Y = -5$

$$-8$$

evaluating $2(-3)$ as -1 and $(-1)^3$ as -3

parsing $3r^2$ as $3 + r^2$ or as $(3r)^2$

simplifying $3 + 23(S - 4)$ to $26(S - 4)$

simplifying $3XY + 4XZ$ to $7XYZ$

claiming one can't multiply by X because "you don't know what X is"

$$\frac{2X}{2X} \Rightarrow 0$$

$$A\frac{1}{A} \Rightarrow 0$$

$$0 * A \Rightarrow A$$

$$\sqrt{(A + B)} \Rightarrow \sqrt{A} + \sqrt{B}$$

$$(A + B)^2 \Rightarrow A^2 + B^2$$

$$A(BC) \Rightarrow AB * AC$$

$$\frac{A}{B + C} \Rightarrow \frac{A}{B} + \frac{A}{C}$$

$$\frac{A + B}{C + D} \Rightarrow \frac{A}{C} + \frac{B}{D}$$

$$2^{a+b} \Rightarrow 2^a + 2^b$$

$$2^{ab} \Rightarrow 2^a 2^b$$

Simplify:

$$\frac{AX+BY}{X+Y} \Rightarrow A+B$$

$$\frac{X}{2X+Y} \Rightarrow \frac{1}{2+Y}$$

$$\frac{X+3Z}{2X+Y} \Rightarrow \frac{3Z}{2+Y}$$

$$\frac{X-3}{2X} \Rightarrow \frac{-3}{2}$$

$$\frac{X^2+2XY+Y^2}{X^2-Y^2} \Rightarrow 2XY$$

partial distribution: $2(X+3) \Rightarrow 2X+3$
$$-(3X-W) \Rightarrow -3X-W$$

$$(AX+B)(CX+D) \Rightarrow ACX^2+BD$$

solving for "X" in terms of itself, e.g. $X = \dfrac{(4Z+X^2)}{7}$

Solve for X: $\dfrac{X+1}{X+4} = \dfrac{5}{6}$
$$X = 4, 2$$

Solve for X: $2X+5 = 11$
$$X+5 = \tfrac{11}{2}$$

Solve for X: $3X+5 = Y+3$
$$X+5 = Y$$

Solve for R: $\dfrac{1}{R} = \dfrac{1}{R_1} + \dfrac{1}{R_2} + \dfrac{1}{R_3}$
$$R = R_1 + R_2 + R_3$$

Solve for X: $\dfrac{1}{X} + \dfrac{1}{X^2} = \dfrac{3}{X^2} + 6X^2$
$$X + 1 = 3 + 6X^2$$

factoring $X^2 + \tfrac{5}{6}X + \tfrac{1}{6}$ as $X(X + \tfrac{5}{6}) + \tfrac{1}{6}$

Solve for X: $(X-5)(X-7) = 3$
$$(X-5) = 3 \text{ or } (X-7) = 3$$
$$X = 8 \text{ or } X = 10$$

Solve for X: $\dfrac{5}{2-X} + \dfrac{5}{2+X} = 4$
$$5(2+X) + 5(2-X) = 4$$

3. The genetic graph: a representation for the evolution of procedural knowledge†‡

IRA P. GOLDSTEIN

Xerox Palo Alto Research, 3333 Coyote Hill Road, Palo Alto, CA 94304, U.S.A.

I shall describe a model of the evolution of rule-structured knowledge that serves as a cornerstone of our development of computer-based coaches. The key idea is a graph structure whose nodes represent rules, and whose links represent various evolutionary relationships such as generalization, correction, and refinement. I shall define this graph and describe a student simulation testbed which we are using to analyze different genetic graph formulations of the reasoning skills required to play an elementary mathematical game.

Keywords: information processing psychology, learning, knowledge representation, CAI, ICAI, AI.

1. Introduction

1.1. A LEARNER-BASED PARADIGM FOR AICAI IS EVOLVING

The 1970's have seen the evolution of a new generation of computer-aided instructional programs based on the inclusion of AI-based expertise within the CAI system. These systems surmount the restrictive nature of older script-based CAI by supplying "reactive" learning environments which can analyze a wide range of student responses by means of an embedded domain-expert. Examples are AICAI tutors for geography (Carbonell, 1970), electronics (Brown, Burton & Zdybel, 1973), set theory (Smith *et al.*, 1975), Nuclear Magnetic Resonance spectroscopy (Sleeman, 1975), and mathematical games (Burton & Brown, 1976; Goldstein & Carr, 1977).

However, while the inclusion of domain expertise is an advance over earlier script-based CAI, the tutoring theory embedded within these benchmark programs for conveying this expertise is elementary. In particular, they approach teaching from a *subset* viewpoint: expertise consists of a set of facts or rules. The student's knowledge is modelled as a subset of this knowledge. Tutoring consists of encouraging the growth of this subset, generally by intervening in situations where a missing fact or rule is the critical ingredient needed to reach the correct answer.

This is, of course, a simplification of the teaching process. It has allowed research to focus on the critical task of representing expertise. But the subset viewpoint fails to represent the fashion in which the new knowledge evolves from old by such processes as analogy, generalization, debugging and refinement.

† This research was supported under NSF grant SED77-19279 and conducted at the Artificial Intelligence Laboratory, Massachusetts Institute of Technology.

‡ This paper has evolved from many fruitful conversations with members of the Cognitive Computing Group at the MIT AI Lab (in particular Greg Clemenson, Mark Miller, Sandy Schoichet, Bob Sjoberg, Bill Swartout, Barbara White, Kurt van Lehn, Bruce Roberts, Jim Stansfield and Steve Rosenberg) and with members of the ICAI group at Bolt, Beranek and Newman (in particular John Seely Brown and Dick Burton).

This paper explores the *genetic graph* as a framework for representing procedural knowledge from an evolutionary viewpoint,† thereby contributing to the movement of AICAI from an *expert-based* to a *learner-based* paradigm.‡ After introducing our experimental domain, the mathematical game Wumpus, and describing an expert-

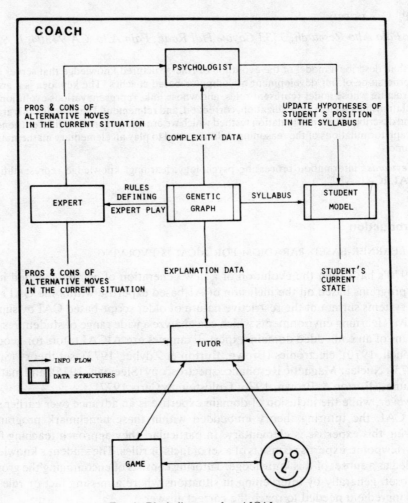

FIG. 1. Block diagram of an AICAI tutor.

† A potential confusion in terminology may occur here. The term "genetic" is often equated with heredity. However, I use it here in its older sense, namely, the *genetic method* is the study of the origins and development of a phenomena. This paper is an exercise in Genetic Epistemology, the study of the origin and development of knowledge. This enterprise has been articulately advocated by Piaget (1971), who considers it the foundation on which psychology should be based.

‡ There are other dimensions to this paradigm shift that include: (1) more sophisticated modelling of the student's knowledge and learning style (Burton & Brown, 1976; Brown, Burton & Larkin, 1977; Carr & Goldstein, 1977), (2) widening the communication channel from student to teacher via natural language interfaces (Burton & Brown, 1977), and (3) developing a theory of teaching skills (Collins, Warnock & Passafiume, 1975).

based coach which we have implemented, I define the genetic graph and describe how it can improve the range of tutoring advice that the AICAI system can provide and the accuracy of the model that the system builds of the learner. Fig. 1 illustrates its central role.

I then discuss in greater detail the model of the learner implicit in the genetic graph. By articulating this model, I am able to suggest a measure of *learning complexity* in terms of the topological properties of the graph. I conclude with a suggestion for reformulating traditional Piagetian notions of accommodation, assimilation and equilibration in terms of our procedural epistemology.

While I shall describe a student simulation testbed which we have implemented to test various genetic graph formulations, this paper is largely exploratory. Its purpose is to serve as a critique of existing expert-based AICAI systems, in particular our Wumpus coach, and a proposal for an improved "learner-based" design.

1.2. A GRAPH REPRESENTATION OF THE SYLLABUS HAS ROOTS IN AICAI RESEARCH

Scholar (Carbonell, 1970), the earliest of the AICAI tutors, employed a graph (semantic net) representation for declarative facts about geography. The graph, however, encoded only domain specific relationships; it did not embody a series of progressively more refined levels of geography knowledge linked by various evolutionary relationships.†

SOPHIE-1 (Brown *et al.*, 1973), the next major AICAI milestone, was an expert-based system for the more complex domain of electronic troubleshooting. SOPHIE-1 compared a student's troubleshooting hypotheses for an electronic circuit with that of its embedded expert and offered advice when the student's analysis went astray. It employed a procedural rather than a network representation for its electronics knowledge, but this representation was largely a black box. SOPHIE-1 did not have access to a detailed, modular, human-oriented representation of troubleshooting skills. Nor did it have a representation for the genesis of these skills.

SOPHIE-2, now under development, will incorporate a modular, anthropomorphic representation for the expert's knowledge (De Kleer, 1976). This structured expertise serves as a better foundation for expert-based tutoring, but still is not a model of how the student evolved to that level of competence.

BUGGY (Brown *et al.*, 1977), a program for building procedural models of a student's arithmetic skills, does incorporate both a graph representation for the basic skills and some evolutionary relationships. The basic skill representation is a graph with links representing the skill/subskill relationships. The evolutionary component consists of "deviation" links to "buggy" versions of the various skills.

BIP-II (Westcourt, Beard & Gould, 1977), a tutor for programming skills, again employs a network for the basic skill representation, but embodies a different set of evolutionary relationships. There are links for representing analogy, generalization, specialization, prerequisite and relative difficulty relations. The BIP-II skill network, however, does not include deviation links nor define an operational expert for the

---

† Scholar might be extended in this fashion, especially if employed with younger children whose theory of the world may not already be stabilized in the expert form embodied by Scholar.

programming domain. Rather it employs author-supplied exercises attached to the relevant skills in the network.†

The genetic graph is a descendant of these network representations. Its nodes are the procedural skills of players of varying proficiency and its links include the analogy, specialization, generalization and prerequisite relations of BIP-II and the deviation relationships of BUGGY.‡

2. Wumpus serves as an experimental domain

Designing coaches for the maze exploration game, Wumpus (Yob, 1975) has proven to be a profitable experimental domain because the game exercises basic skills in logic and probability.§ This section defines our version of the game‖ and describes two expert-based coaches which have been previously implemented for it. The next section formulates an evolutionary epistemology of the knowledge required for skilled play, providing the basis for an improved "learner-based" design.

2.1. DEFINITION OF THE WUMPUS GAME

The player is initially placed somewhere in a warren of caves with the goal of slaying the Wumpus. The difficulty in finding the beast arises from the existence of dangers in the warren—bats, pits and the Wumpus itself. Pits and the Wumpus are fatal; bats move the player to a random cave elsewhere in the warren. But the player can infer the probable location of dangers from warnings he receives. The Wumpus can be sensed two caves away, pits and bats one cave away. Victory results from shooting an arrow into the Wumpus's lair; defeat if the arrows are fruitlessly exhausted.

Becoming skilled poses a non-trivial learning experience for most children and adults:¶ locating multiple dangers in a randomly connected warren of 20 or more caves can be complex. Hence, the game provides a useful problem domain for developing a theory of the evolution of procedural skills.

2.2. WUMPUS AICAI TUTORS

In 1976, we developed WUSOR-I (Stansfield, Carr & Goldstein, 1976), an expert-based coach. Skilled play was analyzed in terms of rules such as these:

---

† Malt (Koffman & Blount, 1975), a tutor for machine language programming, does include an "expert" for problems composed from a limited set of skills and solved in a tutor-prescribed order. However, MALT's syllabus of skills are related only by the probability with which MALT includes them in a system-generated problem, and not by any evolutionary links. Hence, MALT does not have BIP's ability to choose a problem based on its evolutionary relationship to the student's current knowledge state.

‡ The skill nodes themselves, corresponding to rules of the form: "if C1 & C2 & ..., do A1 & A2 & ...", could be expanded into more primitive networks of conditions and conjunction nodes similar to those employed in BUGGY and BIP-II, but I do not discuss that extension in this paper. Instead, I concentrate on describing the evolutionary relationships between skills.

§ Our group is also exploring evolutionary epistemologies for other domains ranging from elementary programming to airplane flying.

‖ Yob's original game was played on the graph of a dodecahedron. Our version is a generalization involving a variable maze geometry, a variable number of dangers, and a variable warning distance for each danger.

¶ By non-trivial, I mean that the experience is on the order of hours rather than minutes and that some players (given no coaching) fail to acquire certain skills after many hours of play. This is based on informal observations of over 30 players ranging in age from grade school children to adults.

Positive Evidence: A warning implies that a danger is in a neighboring cave.
Elimination: If a cave has a warning and all but one of its neighbors are known to be safe, then the danger is in the remaining neighbor.
Multiple Evidence: Multiple warnings increase the likelihood that a given cave contains a danger.

Below is an interaction with the WUSOR-I coach which illustrates the fashion in which the coach explains a rule if its employment would result in a better move than the one chosen by the student. The student's responses are indented and underlined.

You are at cave 15 with neighbors 4, 14 and 0. Brrr! There is a draft. You are near a pit. What now?

    <u>1>4</u>

You are at cave 4 with neighbors 15, 14 and 2. Brrr! There is a draft. Squeak! A bat is near. (The game state is shown in Fig. 2.) What now?

    <u>2>14</u>

(E1) Mary, it isn't necessary to take such large risks with pits. There is multiple evidence of a pit in cave 14 which makes it quite likely that cave 14 contains a pit. It is less likely that cave 0 contains a pit. Hence, we might want to explore cave 0 instead. Do you want to take back your move?

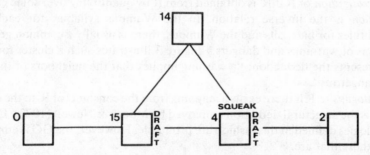

FIG. 2. The Wumpus game state after two moves.

WUSOR-I was insensitive to the relative difficulty of the various Wumpus skills. In 1977, we took our first step toward an evolutionary epistemology with WUSOR-II (Carr, 1977), wherein the rule set was divided into five phases representing increasing skill at the task:

Phase 1: Rules for visited, unvisited and fringe caves.
Phase 2: Rules for possibly dangerous, definitely dangerous and safe caves.
Phase 3: Rules for single versus multiply dangerous caves.
Phase 4: Rules for "possibility sets", i.e. keeping track of the sources of dangers.
Phase 5: Rules for numerical evidence.

The tutor did not describe the rule of a particular level of play until it believed the student was familiar with the rules of the preceding levels.†

† (Carr & Goldstein, 1977) describes the mechanisms by which it estimated the student's position in the syllabus.

These phases constituted a coarse genetic epistemology, better than the completely unordered approach of WUSOR-I, but still far from a detailed platform on which to build new knowledge from old in the student's mind. WUSOR-III, now being implemented, addresses this limitation. It has evolved from WUSOR-II by defining a set of symbolic links between rules that characterize such relationships as analogy, refinement, correction, and generalization.† The result is that the "syllabus" of the coach has evolved from an unordered skill set to a *genetic graph* of skills linked by their evolutionary relationships.

3. The genetic graph formalizes the syllabus

The "genetic graph" (GG) formalizes the evolution of procedural rules by representing the rules as nodes and their interrelationships as links. In this section I discuss four of these relationships—generalization/specialization, analogy, deviation/correction and simplification/refinement—and provide examples of their occurrence in the Wumpus syllabus. I also describe a student simulation testbed which we have implemented to explore the consequences of different rule formulations. In the next section, I consider what kinds of knowledge are not properly represented by a graph of rules, and propose appropriate extensions.

3.1. GENETIC LINKS SPECIFY EVOLUTIONARY RELATIONSHIPS BETWEEN RULES

R' is a *generalization* of R if R' is obtained from R by quantifying over some constant.‡ *Specialization* is the inverse relation. In the Wumpus syllabus, for each trio of specialized rules for bats, pits and the Wumpus, there is usually a common generalization in terms of warnings and dangers.§ Figure 3 illustrates such a cluster for rule 2.2 which represents the deduction: "a warning implies that the neighbors of the current cave are dangerous".

R' is *analogous* to R if there exists a mapping from the constants of R' to the constants of R. This is the structural definition employed by Moore & Newell (1973). Of course, not all analogies defined in this fashion are profitable. However, the GG is employed to represent those that are.

Figure 3 illustrates analogy links between the specialization trio of R2.2 For example, mapping SQUEAK to DRAFT and B+ (the set of caves risking BATS) to P+ (the sets of caves risking PITS) defines the analogy mapping between R2.2B and R2.2P. The similar nature of dangers makes clusters of this kind (one generalization and three specializations all connected by analogy links) common in the Wumpus world. As we shall discuss in section 5, identifying such densely linked clusters provides teaching leverage by providing multiple methods of explanation (one per link) for each constituent rule.

---

† It was also necessary to increase the grain of the rules. WUSOR-II rules were too coarse and hence obscured certain evolutionary relationships.

‡ This is a standard predicate calculus definition, applied here to quantifying over formulas representing rules rather than logical statements.

§ In one version of Wumpus, the wumpus warning propagates only one cave. In this case, bats, pits and the wumpus are exactly analogous. In more complex versions, the Wumpus is no longer exactly analogous. Hence, the analogies to bats and pit rules are in fact restricted cases or outright deviations. We represent this in the GG explicitly, thereby giving the coach an expectation for the traps the student will encounter.

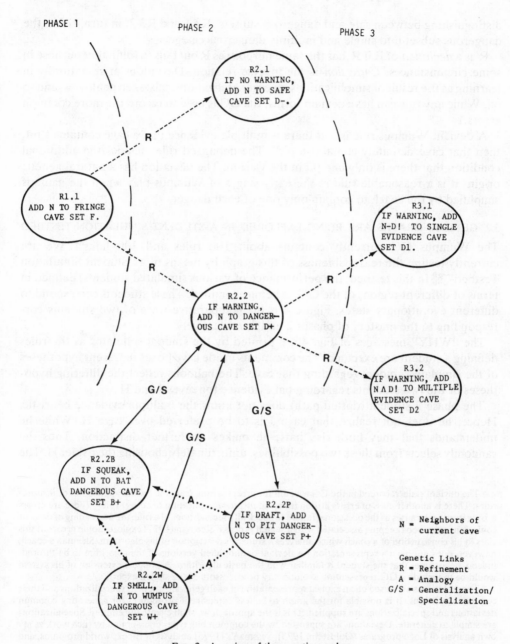

FIG. 3. A region of the genetic graph.

R' is a *refinement* of R if R' manipulates a subset of the data manipulated by R on the basis of some specialized properties. *Simplification* is the inverse relation. This relation represents the evolution of a rule to take account of a finer set of distinctions. The Wumpus syllabus contains five major refinements corresponding to the five WUSOR-II phases. Figure 3 illustrates the refinement of the rule R1.1 through phases 1, 2 and 3. R2.1 and R2.2, for example, refine R1's treatment of the fringe caves by distinguishing between safe and dangerous subsets. R3.1 and R3.2, in turn, refine the dangerous subset into single and multiply dangerous categories.

R' is a *deviation* of R if R' has the same purpose as R but fails to fulfill that purpose in some circumstances. *Correction* is the inverse relation. Deviations arise naturally in learning as the result of simplifications, overgeneralizations, mistaken analogies, and so on. While any rule can have deviant forms, the GG is used to record the more common errors.†

A deviant Wumpus rule is: "If there is multiple evidence that a cave contains a pit, then that cave definitely contains a pit". The debugged rule includes the additional condition that there is only *one* pit in the warren. The deviation has a natural genetic origin: it is a reasonable rule in the early stages of Wumpus play when the game is simplified by the coach to contain only one of each danger.

3.2. GENETIC GRAPHS ARE BEING EXPLORED IN A STUDENT SIMULATION TESTBED

The Wumpus GG currently contains about 100 rules and 300 links.‡ We are currently testing the reasonableness of this graph by means of a "Student Simulation Testbed".§|| In this testbed, the performance of various simulated students, defined in terms of different regions of the GG, is being examined. These students correspond to different evolutionary states. Figure 4 is the comparative trace of two students corresponding to the mastery of phases 2 and 3, respectively.

The "WHY" messages of Fig. 4 are printed by the student simulator as the rules defining a student are executed. The comments inside cave boxes represent hypotheses of the simulated student regarding that cave. The balloons reflect the differing hypotheses of the two students regarding bat evidence for caves J and H.

The phase 2 student (dotted path) does not know the multiple evidence heuristic. Hence, he does not realize that cave J is to be preferred over cave H. While he understands that they both risk bats, he makes no further distinction. Thus, he randomly selects from these two possibilities, unfortunately choosing the riskier H. The

---

† The deviant skills recorded in the GG account for errors arising from the *correct* application of *incorrect* rules. There is another class of errors arising from the *incorrect* application of *correct* rules. These are errors arising from such causes as the occasional failure to check all preconditions of a rule, the misreading of data, or confusion in the bookkeeping associated with a search process. Sleeman (1977) explores some errors of this class in his construction of a coach which analyzes a student's description of his algorithm. Sleeman's coach, however, does not have a representation for deviant or simplified versions of the algorithm to be tutored: indeed, he assumes that the student is familiar with the basic algorithm. A possible extension of his system would be to include a GG representing evolutionary predecessors of the skilled expert.

‡ These statistics are based on an explicit representation of each generalization, its specializations and their common deviations. It is possible for the graph to be less extensive if procedures for generating common deviations and specializations are supplied. This is the approach we shall eventually employ. Specializations are simple to generate. Deviations are suggested by the common bug types enumerated by such work as my own analysis of Logo programs (Goldstein, 1975), Sussman's (1975) analysis of Blocks world programs, and Stevens & Collin's (1977) study of bugs in causal reasoning; or they can be induced, for simple cases, by analyzing the student's performance (Self, 1974; Goldstein, 1975, Brown & Burton, 1977). However, my current research strategy has been to make the graph explicit, in order to understand its form. The next stage will include the extension to expanding the graph dynamically.

§ The testbed serves other purposes as well. Simulated students can be used to test the modelling and tutoring of teaching systems (Carr, 1977; Self, 1977; Wescourt *et al.*, 1977). They can also serve as models of real students, and hence can yield insight for a human teacher observing their performance (Brown *et al.*, 1977; Goldstein & Grimson, 1977).

|| Following this testing period, WUSOR-II will be converted to incorporate the GG. The expected improvement in modelling and tutoring is the subject of sections 5 and 6.

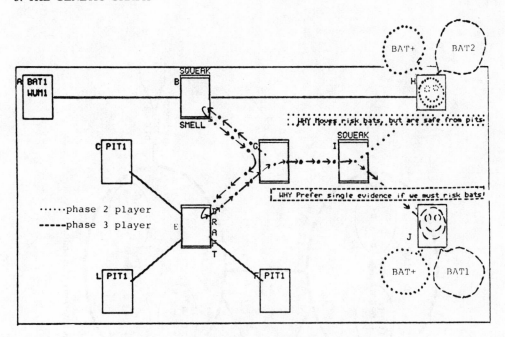

FIG. 4. Divergent behavior of two simulated students.

phase 3 student (dashed path) recognizes multiple (BAT2) evidence as more risky than single (BAT1) evidence and therefore selects the safer cave J.

Figure 4 is a composite of the graphic output for the two students. The testbed only executes a single student at a time. It does not generate balloons nor place the "WHY" messages on the Warren itself.

Expert-based CAI allows only for the definition of "simulated students" formed from subsets of the expert's skills. The power of the GG to broaden the tutor's understanding of the task is evident from the testbed: the GG permits not only the creation of subset students, but also students formed from specializations, deviations and simplifications of the expert's rules.

Nevertheless, it must be stressed that the evolutionary relations discussed here remain both underspecified and incomplete. There are many kinds of analogies, generalizations, and corrections. There are also other kinds of evolutionary processes for acquiring knowledge: learning by being told, learning by induction from past examples, and learning by deduction from old rules. The next chapter explores one of the directions in which the GG must be extended to be an adequate representation for the evolution of a student's knowledge.

4. Extensions to the genetic graph

The preceding section defined a set of genetic relationships between individual rules. In this section, we extend the genetic graph to incorporate genetic relationships between groups of rules and between rules and the declarative facts that explain and justify their behavior.

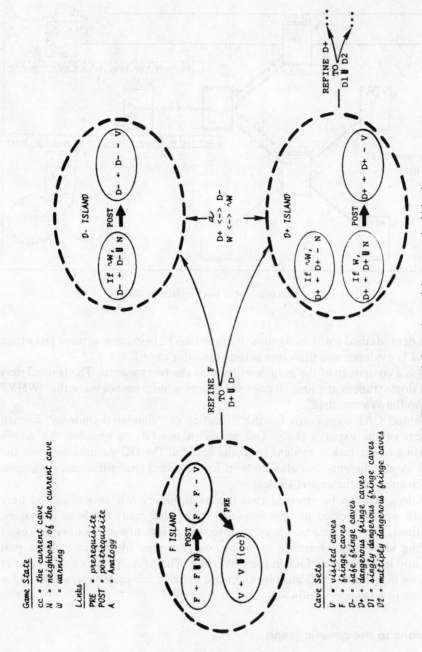

Fig. 5. The extended genetic graph is a network of islands.

4.1. THE EXTENDED GG GROUPS RELATED KNOWLEDGE INTO ISLANDS

Our first order theory of a GG has the limitation that rules which are closely related and generally learned as a group are not so represented. To address this limitation, rules are grouped into *islands*. A natural criterion for forming islands is to group rules that have the same goal. For Wumpus, this translates into grouping rules which manipulate the same kind of evidence. This is illustrated in Fig. 5.

For example, the D+ island contains the rules which manipulate D+, the set of possibly dangerous caves. One rule subtracts the neighbors of the current cave from D+ if there is no warning. The complementary rule is also present: it adds to D+ the neighbor set if there is a warning. The third rule in the D+ island subtracts the visited caves from D+. It insures that D+ contains only fringe caves. (A postrequisite planning link exists between these last two rules which is explained later in this section.)

Islands allow the coach to tutor the student in terms of an overall concept for a group of rules and to model the student in terms of his possession of the conceptual base underlying a rule set. Just as an analogy between two rules can be explained, so too can an analogy between two islands of rules. Figure 5 illustrates this with an analogy link between the safe and dangerous islands.

The acquisition of a group of skills is a natural learning episode since acquiring the island is a local task—the rules all follow from a single concept. But moving to the next island requires a new conceptual base. To explore this movement, the simulated student testbed allows macro instructions which add entire islands of rules to the simulated student being constructed:

> (Define__student 5 (island F) (island D−) (island D+))
    Student 5 defined.   ; *This is the phase 2 player of Fig. 4.*
> (Define__student 6 (student 5) (island D1) (island D2))
    Student 6 defined.   ; *This is the phase 3 player of Fig. 4.*

4.2. THE EXTENDED GG REPRESENTS THE JUSTIFICATIONS OF RULES

The GG as a representation of knowledge is still incomplete. Rules by themselves do not describe the declarative knowledge that explains and justifies their behavior. For Wumpus, this declarative knowledge includes the definition of the evidence sets and axiomatic statements of their properties. Figure 6 shows the declarative facts listed below linked to the various groups of rules whose behavior they justify.

The fringe F is the union of D+ and D− (the safe caves).
A warning implies that some of the neighbors of the current cave are members of D+.
D− and D+ are disjoint.

The GG employed in the student simulation testbed has not yet been augmented in this fashion.

This extension will be important because of the possibility that the same evolutionary relationships linking procedural rules can play a role linking declarative statements. One logistic statement can be a generalization of another, or analogous under some mapping of constants, or a refinement. With such an extended GG, the coach could tutor both procedural and declarative knowledge, obtaining leverage by moving between the two in the light of the student's current difficulties.

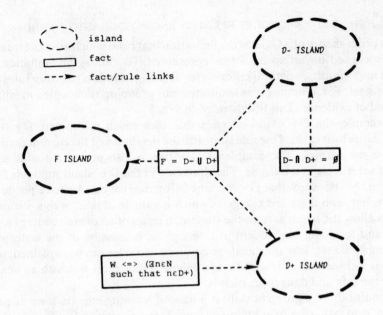

Cave Sets

F = fringe caves
D- = safe fringe caves
D+ = dangerous fringe caves
∅ = null set
N = neighbors of the current cave

FIG. 6. Islands of rules have declarative foundations.

4.3. THE EXTENDED GG REPRESENTS PLANNING KNOWLEDGE

Not all knowledge about rules describes their evolutionary relationships. Since sets of rules form problem solving programs for the task, we should expect, as with all programs, that knowledge about their order of application must be represented. There is no difficulty in extending the GG to represent this knowledge. It is only necessary to define the appropriate links. For this reason, prerequisite and postrequisite relations are defined.† Figure 5 illustrates various planning relations. For example, a postrequisite link insures that the D+ rule "If there is a warning, add the neighbors to D+" is followed by the rule "Subtract the visited cave set from D+." This second rule is needed since some of the neighbors added to D+ may have been already visited, and hence are safe.†

   † An alternative is to supply meta-rules that specify the order of application. This is a useful approach when the goal is an expert program, but it is not sufficient for the tutoring context. A meta-rule that specifies that a trio of rules be executed in the order R1, R2, R3 does not tell the tutor whether this is the only order or merely one among a set of possible orders. The tutor must know if it is to respond appropriately to the student's idiosyncratic approach. The planning links provide only the basic ordering constraints. Sacerdoti (1975) makes a similar argument for planning networks to facilitate self-debugging on the part of a problem solving system.

   ‡ A single rule could have been written: "If there is a warning, add N-V to D+", but breaking this procedure into two rules allows a finer grain of modelling and tutoring. The coach must be able to identify the deviant simplification of adding the neighbors without pruning the caves already visited. Thus as a general philosophy, rules are broken into small chunks with planning knowledge made explicit via links between rules.

Thus, the extended GG incorporates planning knowledge. As with any addition of knowledge, it supplies tutoring leverage. The coach can now expect that for certain rules, the student's difficulty may lie not in knowing the rules, but in understanding their order. The consequences of such confusion can be explored in the student simulation testbed. Below is illustrated a situation where the student has apparently forgotten to execute a postrequisite rule and shows the advice the new GG-based coach might offer in such situations.

The following interaction with the Wumpus game was obtained from a version that allows the player to record his or her hypotheses on the display screen. The player's responses are underlined. The final tutorial intervention (in italics) is a hypothetical one by the GG-based coach now under construction.
We are now in cave D. The neighbors are caves C, G, and B. What now?
>B
We are now in cave B. The neighbors are caves F, D, and A. What a stench! The Wumpus must be in one of the neighboring caves. Squeak! I hear bats. They must be in one of the neighboring caves. What now?
>X+   ;*This command marks caves that may contain a danger.*
  Which danger (Bats, Pits or Wumpus)? BW. Which caves? AFD
  ;*The result is that the display screen shows a warren in which BAT+ and WUM+ markers appear in the designated caves. (Fig. 7 is a snapshot of the display in this state.)*

What now?

>C

Ira, you have correctly recorded that caves A, F and D risk bats based on the squeak in cave B. However, you have moved to cave C without concluding that cave D is safe. You know cave D is safe because you have visted there. You might want to record this knowledge to avoid confusion.

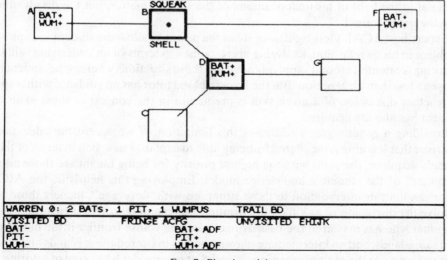

FIG. 7. Planning advice.

4.4. THE EXTENDED GG IS A NETWORK OF ISLANDS

In conclusion, the extended genetic graph is not different in kind from the basic genetic graph. It remains a graph of knowledge nodes linked by various genetic relationships. Its increased power derives from a hierarchical structure of grouped rules (islands), an extension of individual nodes from representing only rules to representing both rules and facts, and an augmentation of the link set to include control knowledge.

Implicit in this structure is the following view of learning: new rules are constructed from old in terms of processes corresponding to the individual links. However, the graph does not describe a unique evolutionary path. One learner may rapidly acquire a generalization, another may first build several specializations before constructing the generalization, while a third may never acquire the generalization. Hence, the tutor should encourage this idiosyncratic construction of new knowledge by giving advice appropriate to the learner's current knowledge state (position in the graph) and particular style of learning (preference for particular links). The redesign of the Wumpus coach to employ the guidance of the GG to more closely approximate this ideal tutoring behavior is the subject of the next two sections.

5. The genetic graph is a basis for tutoring

The GG guides the Tutor component of an AICAI system in two ways. First, it suggests which skills to discuss with the student, namely those at the frontier of the student's position in the graph. Second, once a skill is chosen for discussion, the GG supplies guidance for explaining that skill in more than one way by means of relating it to its evolutionary predecessors.

5.1. THE GENETIC GRAPH SUGGESTS THE TUTORING TOPIC

In script-based CAI, the order in which topics are introduced is predefined. The student proceeds to the next author-supplied question after he has successfully answered the current query. This has the advantage that the author can control the introduction of material in the light of his understanding of the subject matter, but the disadvantage that the order is rigid.

Expert-based CAI is less rigid since it has the power to allow the student to explore a problem in his own fashion, analyzing his responses in terms of an underlying skill set. Tutoring is oriented around supplying advice in those situations wherein the student has chosen a less than ideal option. But the Expert-based tutor has no guidance with respect to whether discussion of a given skill is premature in the context of those skills the student has already acquired.

Providing a genetic graph addresses this limitation. If we accept the educational heuristic that learning is facilitated by being able to explain a new skill in terms of those already acquired, the skills with the highest priority for being taught are those on the "frontier" of the student's knowledge model. Employing this heuristic, the AICAI tutor can limit its intervention to those situations with "leverage", namely those that involve the discussion of a skill on the frontier. For example, consider two students: a beginner who has mastered the basic fringe rules and whose frontier is the dangerous and safe islands, and an intermediate player who has mastered these islands and whose frontier is now at the multiple evidence island. Let us consider what kind of tutoring the

AICAI coach should offer if the player moves to cave 14 in the scenario game of Fig. 2. Recall that 14 is a bad choice because the existence of double evidence makes it likely that a fatal pit is there. For the intermediate student, the tutor would intervene—there is leverage to describe the double evidence heuristic in terms of its evolutionary predecessors; for the beginner, the tutor would not—there are no available genetic links with which to build an explanation.

The GG does not solve the "choice of topic" problem. It offers the frontier as a preferred subset, but the Tutor must still choose among this subset or possibly decide to reject it entirely.† To make this decision, the Tutor must apply general teaching heuristics ("Vary the topic discussed!") and student specific strategies ("Maximize the opportunity for 'discovery learning'; that is, do not discuss any topic at all when the student's progress through the syllabus is proceeding at a satisfactory rate!"). The role of the GG in this context is simply to make available to these teaching heuristics the epistemological relations between the skills of the syllabus.

5.2. THE GENETIC GRAPH SUPPLIES MULTIPLE EXPLANATIONS

Once a topic is selected, the ability to explain that topic in more than one way is an important tutoring technique. Script-based CAI achieved this explanatory power by supplying "author" languages in which clever explanations could be written by teachers. Expert-based CAI, by eliminating scripts, lost this power. But in return it acquired the ability to respond to a larger number of situations, albeit by means of a restricted number of machine-generated explanation types. Genetic AICAI retains the Expert-based CAI ability to respond to a large number of situations, but adds the capability to explain a particular skill in diverse ways. This capability derives from the ability to explain a new rule in terms of its genetic links. For each link type, the tutor is provided with an explanation strategy. For example, Fig. 8 shows three variations on a WUSOR-II explanation generated by explaining the "avoid multiply dangerous situations" rule in terms of its evolutionary relatives. (The basic WUSOR-II explanation is the one we examined earlier for the poor move to cave 14 in the game state of Fig. 2.)

As with the selection of the rule to be discussed, the choice of explanation for that rule is not determined by the GG. That choice depends on general teaching heuristics (such as "Vary your explanation!") and student specific criteria (such as "Avoid strategies which have been consistently unsuccessful in the past!"). The role of the GG, however, is to increase the available choices on which these selectional heuristics operate.

---

† There are alternatives to frontier tutoring. A teacher could seek to explain the syllabus as a whole to give the student perspective. Then later the teacher could return to a given subset of the syllabus and refine the student's knowledge. Norman refers to this approach as Web tutoring (Norman, Gentner & Stevens, 1976). It is more useful however for a syllabus of facts than one of procedural skills. The reason is that skills have prerequisite relations that prevent advanced skills from being used before simpler ones are acquired. Static facts don't generally have such a rigid ordering. Thus our skill tutors usually do not employ the Web technique.

Nevertheless, it is possible to explain a skill whose evolutionary predecessors have not been acquired by constructing a long explanation *ab initio*. The frontier heuristic biases the system against such an approach, but the Tutor may be required to employ it in some situations (the frontier skills have already been explained many times and the student appears to need some perspective on the syllabus) and for some kinds of syllabi (the skills are largely independent of one another).

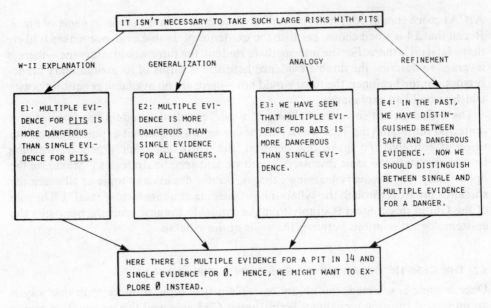

FIG. 8. Variations on an explanation.

5.3. TUTORING USING AN EXTENDED SYLLABUS REPRESENTATION

The range of tutoring strategies is increased further by employing the extended syllabus described in the previous section. Examine again Fig. 5. The islands of rules for dangerous and safe caves are linked by a "bridge analogy", a generalization of the analogy linking the individual rules. By tutoring the bridge analogy, explanatory leverage is gained by providing support for an entire group of rules in a single explanation.

Similarly, a declarative foundation provides another opportunity for generating support for an entire set of rules. Here the common link is from a set of declarative facts to the island of rules they imply. For example, the tutor, using the declarative foundation, might discuss the general importance of the concept of multiple evidence rather than the specific rules employed to maintain the single and multiple evidence sets. Again, the tutoring hypothesis is that by discussing the declarative foundation, the student will deduce a group of related rules on his own. It is therefore a potentially powerful tutoring strategy.

5.4. THE GENETIC GRAPH DOES NOT SOLVE THE TUTORING PROBLEM

Tutoring is a complex task for AI-based CAI systems that do not have access to author-supplied scripts. The system must decide (1) whether to invervene, (2) what topic to discuss, and (3) how much to say about that topic.† The GG does not decide these questions. However, it does serve, first, to constrain the set of topics by defining a

---

† See Collins *et al.* (1975) for a study of Socratic intervention strategies.

frontier, and, second, to extend the variety of explanations available for discussing the topic of choice.

6. The genetic graph is a basis for modelling

To offer appropriate tutorial advice, a teacher must accurately model the student. The GG facilitates the modelling process in an AICAI tutor in three ways. First, the nodes of the graph provide a more refined structure for a model of the student's knowledge state than the skill sets of subset AICAI systems. Second, the organization of the graph provides a metric regarding which skills the student can be expected to acquire next. Third, the links of the graph provide a complementary structure for a model of the student's learning behavior.

6.1. THE STUDENT KNOWLEDGE MODEL OVERLAYS THE NODES OF THE GENETIC GRAPH

Script-based CAI systems build student knowledge models by maintaining statistics on the correctness of the student's answers. The validity of such models is severely limited by the restricted capability of the script to judge correctness, having only a list of expected responses on which to judge the answer.

Expert-based CAI systems escape the limitation of the script by constructing their student knowledge model from hypotheses regarding which skills of the *embedded expert* the student is believed to possess. I have termed such models "overlays" (Goldstein & Carr, 1977) to emphasize that their structure is derived from the structure of the underlying expert system.

As an example of the improvement of expert-based modelling over scripts, consider Wumpus. The embedded expert of the WUSOR-II coach can evaluate any game state that arises. The number of such states, given an arbitrary number of caves, of dangers in these caves, and of student paths through the resulting maze, is enormous. Scripts of correct answers are clearly out of the question.

But expert-based models have a fundamental limitation. They fail to consider that the novice student may not be employing a subset of the expert's skills, but rather using simplifications, deviations, and other evolutionary predecessors of those skills.† Given our GG, the extension is clear. The student's knowledge model will be constructed as an overlay, not on the final set of skills, but on the GG itself.

6.2. THE GENETIC GRAPH GUIDES THE CONSTRUCTION OF THE MODEL

Given the form of the model as attributing regions of the GG to the student, it is now appropriate to examine how the model is induced. I shall describe the basic method employed by expert-based CAI programs, and then construct an improvement based on the learning metric implied by distance between skills in the GG.

Expert-based CAI constructs the student knowledge model by hypothesizing that a student does not possess a skill if the student's answer for a given situation is worse than

---

† In certain situations, there is a rationale for expert-based models. The "expert" may be one selected to be only minimally in front of the student. Or the task may be sufficiently restricted that novices are generally subsets of the expert's skills. Or the skills themselves may be broken into small "micro-skills" so that modelling in terms of the presence and absence of these micro skills is reasonable. Indeed, the Genetic AICAI system reduces to the expert case if the GG does not in fact contain other than a single subset of skills. Thus, the expert-based CAI system can be profitably viewed as a simplification of the Genetic AICAI system.

the answer the expert could deduce based on that skill.†‡ To illustrate this, consider again the scenario of Fig. 2. If the student chooses cave 14, which is more dangerous than its fellows by the multiple evidence skill, WUSOR-II increases the weight of its hypothesis that the student does not possess this skill.§

This method of comparing embedded expertise to student performance remains basic to the Genetic AICAI system, but is improved as follows: the GG is viewed as defining a number of "players" of increasing power, corresponding to intermediate skill plateaus in the graph. For Wumpus, there are five such players defined in terms of the five phases of Wumpus skill:

> *Phase 1: rules for visited, unvisited and fringe caves.*
> *Phase 2: rules for possibly dangerous, definitely dangerous and safe caves.*
> *Phase 3: rules for single versus multiply dangerous caves.*
> *Phase 4: rules for "possibility sets", i.e. keeping track of the sources of dangers.*
> *Phase 5: rules for numerical evidence.*

Each of these "players" examines the student's move and proposes which skills the student appears to be employing. These hypotheses are attached to nodes of the GG. The overall belief that the student possesses a given skill is a summation over the hypotheses of the individual players.

If it were the case that the student might possess skills from anywhere in the GG with equal probability, then all of these players would have equal weight when formulating the overall hypothesis. But, the GG embodies a theory of the evolution of the learner's knowledge. This theory is just that knowledge evolves along genetic links—from simplification to elaboration, deviation to correction, abstraction to refinement, specialization to generalization. For that reason, the hypotheses generated by advanced players further and further away from the current plateau are assigned less and less weight.

The result is a desirable conservatism in the modelling process. This is reasonable, since it accords with the common sense educational heuristic that a radical improvement in the play of a student is more likely due to luck than a discontinuous jump in his skills. By the same token, a radical deficiency in a particular move is more probably due to carelessness than a discontinuous jump to some earlier knowledge state.

This conservatism does not prevent the AICAI coach from ever believing in discontinuous jumps in the student's knowledge. Those players based on skills far from the student's current position in the graph are given some weight. Hence, the coach will eventually accept a radical change in the student's knowledge. But the conservatism is

---

† And contrariwise, if the student chooses the expert's choice, then the coach hypothesizes that the student is familiar with those skills the expert employed to determine that the move chosen was best.

‡ In fact, the process of modelling is more subtle than this. For each situation analyzed, the raw data is recorded as increments to two variables associated with each skill: APPROPRIATE which records how many times the Expert believed the skill was appropriate and USED which records how many times the player was believed to have employed the rule in appropriate situations. Their ratio forms the FREQUENCY of use of the skill. The AICAI tutor acts as though the student knows the rule when this ratio exceeds a threshold. The complexities in maintaining such a model are discussed in Carr & Goldstein (1977).

§ This simple modelling method is improved by the capability in some AICAI programs to take account of the student's background, and in some situations, to ask the student explicitly why he chose a certain option. These improvements are orthogonal to the improvement the GG allows in the fundamental method. They are discussed in Carr & Goldstein (1977).

important: without it, the coach has no capability at all to observe the lucky guess or occasional careless move. Hence, the metric on learning defined by the GG supplies a stability missing in expert-based CAI systems.

6.3. THE STUDENT LEARNING MODEL OVERLAYS THE LINKS OF THE GENETIC GRAPH

There is still a third dividend to the GG: its links provide the structure for a learning model. In the previous section, we discussed the coach's ability to explain a rule in multiple ways based on the various genetic links associated with that rule. Now given a knowledge model, the coach is in a position to observe the effect of a given explanation type. It can determine whether the student employs the skill in subsequent play. If a given explanation strategy consistently leads to skill acquisition, it is reasonable to believe that this explanation strategy is a successful one for the particular student. If not, then the opposite hypothesis can be induced, i.e. that the explanation strategy is not a successful teaching strategy for the particular student. Thus, a *learning overlay* can be generated over the set of genetic links that maintains a record of the effectiveness of the explanation strategy associated with that link type.

The use of such a model is straightforward: it serves to personalize the choice of explanation strategy for a particular student by selecting from those that have proven successful in the past.

6.4. THE GENETIC GRAPH DOES NOT SOLVE THE MODELLING PROBLEM

Constructing a model of the student's knowledge and learning attributes is a complex task for a human teacher to perform. It is certainly the most difficult activity of an AICAI tutor. The genetic graph provides a framework for this modelling. The student's knowledge is described in terms of the nodes of the graph; his learning behavior in terms of the links; his progress in terms of paths in the graph. It provides a more powerful foundation for modelling than either a script of correct answers or a set of expert skills.

Nevertheless, the GG does not solve the modelling problem. While the process of constructing a model gains guidance from the graph, it remains complex. No particular answer by the student is certain evidence. He may have misunderstood the question, or lost interest in formulating an answer, or changed his goals entirely. The coach, given its inability to observe the student's facial expressions, understand his language, or indeed even know whether he is at the console thinking or simply taking a stroll, is at a severe disadvantage compared to a human teacher. And modelling the student is among the most difficult tasks for skilled human teachers. I term this the "bandwidth problem". No matter how excellent the GG is as a representation of the knowledge being acquired, modelling is dependent on observing this acquisition. Hence, methods for increasing the bandwidth with which the computer coach can observe the student are an important supplement to the GG in model building.† The virtue of the GG is simply to provide a target data structure for the evidence gathered by this increased bandwidth.

---

† For Wumpus, we are currently exploring several kinds of "assistant programs" that serve to increase the bandwidth with which the Coach can observe the student. One assistant offers the display screen as an interactive medium to replace the pencil and paper the student uses to draw the warren and record his hypotheses. In this fashion, the coach can observe that part of the student's intermediate reasoning that is overt. It is our expectation that this graphic assistance will make a major improvement in the accuracy of the Coach's model.

There is another deeper limitation to the modelling paradigm offered here. While it is true that one can only model what one understands, it is not true that one must represent the syllabus in such an explicit form. A human teacher can be expected to grow his understanding of the task in response to observing the student's behavior. For the more general situation of tutoring in large open-ended worlds, this is necessary; however, it involves the incorporation of a learning capacity into the coach, a non-trivial though important function. The next section discusses a preliminary formulation of the learning theory that would be required.

7. The genetic graph is a basis for learning

Implicit in the genetic graph is a theory of learning. This section explores this theory and considers its implications for the design of computer coaches. The model of the student suggested by the genetic graph is shown in Fig. 9. The processes of the student are

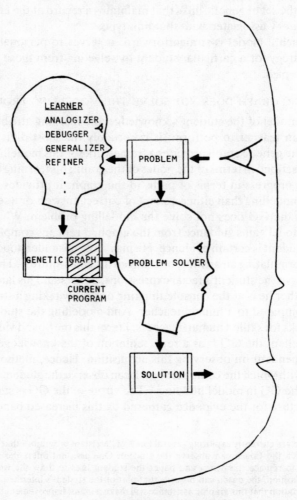

FIG. 9. Homunculus model of the student.

divided into two homunculi†—a problem solving specialist and a learning specialist—
with the graph serving as the student's basic memory structure for procedural knowledge. The problem solving homunculus applies the program defined by the frontier of
his genetic graph to the current task. The learning homunculus extends the genetic
graph in response to new tasks, tutorial advice and observed difficulties of the current
program.

The learning homunculus consists of a set of strategies corresponding to the various
links of the graph. Its task is to build new rules, leaving behind—as a record of its
operation—links which connect the new rules to their evolutionary predecessors. The
links are labelled with the learning strategy responsible for the construction.‡§

The genetic graph offers only a structure for a learning theory. It suggests that the
learning processes consist of procedures which generate the various links, but it does
not describe the details of these processes. It does not enumerate what criteria are used
to form analogies, recognize deviations, induce generalizations or construct conceptual
refinements.‖

However, this structure is of use, for it focusses our attention on issues involving the
interaction of the teaching and learning processes. Four of these issues which I discuss
below are: (1) the student as an active agent, (2) a genetic graph for learning, (3) a theory
of belief, and (4) the topology of the graph as a measure of learning complexity.

7.1. THE STUDENT IS AN ACTIVE AGENT

The model of the student presented above emphasizes the viewpoint that the student is
an active agent, engaged in a constructive process of generating new knowledge. From
this perspective, the tutor's objective is to encourage this process in the student. This
reminds us that the current activity of most AICAI tutors—intervening and supplying a
complete explanation—is only one end of the spectrum of tutoring activity. At the other
end of the spectrum is "tutoring without talking", that is saying nothing at all, but
instead altering the problem domain in order to facilitate the learning process.¶

There are as well a range of intermediate interventions between these two extremes.
An example is that the tutor could suggest that a rule exists that could be applied in the
current situation which is analogous to some already acquired rules, but not specifying
the new rule or stating the analogy. The next generation of AICAI tutors should be able

---

† I use the term "homunculus" to emphasize that the learning and problem solving components are
envisioned to be machines of exactly the same power. Their only difference lies in their programs.

‡ The links are left behind because they themselves can serve as input to the learning strategies. The
existence of a profitable analogy can suggest that more analogies "of an analogous kind" are possible. For
example, an analogy between the rules of bats and pits can suggest a similar analogy between bats and wumpii.
It may not be exact, but the suggestion offers a direction for the learning homunculus to explore.

§ It is of course a simplification to believe that the entire genetic graph remains available to the learner. In
fact, there must be a process of forgetting. This process must exist partly to avoid an indefinitely growing use of
space and partly to eliminate outdated knowledge that would serve only to misguide the learning processes. A
theory of forgetting is crucial to an overall theory of learning and of teaching, but goes beyond the scope of this
paper.

‖ Enumerating such criteria has been the focus of much work in AI, including Winston (1975), Evans
(1968), Moore & Newell (1973) and Richard Brown (1977) on analogy; and Sussman (1975), Goldstein
(1975), and Sacerdoti (1975) on debugging.

¶ "Tutoring without talking" is exemplified by one option WUSOR-II can exercise. It can alter the
complexity of the Wumpus game by varying the number of dangers, the propagation distances of their
warnings, the number of arrows, and the geometric complexity of the warren. WUSOR-II does this in
accordance with its estimate of the student's current level of skill.

to supply advice across this spectrum, altering the nature and extent of their intervention in relation to the current state of the student model.

7.2. A GENETIC GRAPH FOR LEARNING SKILLS IS POSSIBLE

Dividing the student into a Learning Homunculus and a Problem Solving Homunculus raises the question of whether the skills of the Learning Homunculus can themselves be represented as a genetic graph. If there are a collection of rules that define the processes of analogy, generalization, debugging and refinement which are themselves related by genetic links, then explicating this graph becomes an important AI/Psychology goal.

A competing hypothesis is that the learning processes are not related one to another, nor do they have simplifications from which they evolve. They are only an unstructured collection of heuristics, acquired in an isolated fashion. I believe this unlikely, but it may not be simple to explicate a genetic graph for learning.

Constructing a genetic graph for learning skills whose links are again the analogy, generalization and other genetic relationships discussed earlier suggests that still a third L^2 homunculus is not necessary to oversee the acquisition of learning skills. Rather, since the links are the same ones as occur in the domain graph, the Learning Homunculus is potentially able to operate on its own genetic graph. Thus the recursion of homunculi is terminated. If this is so, it would be an important result both for Artificial Intelligence and for psychology, namely that a single learning theory is sufficient for both domain knowledge acquisition and a recursive improvement in the system's own learning capacities.

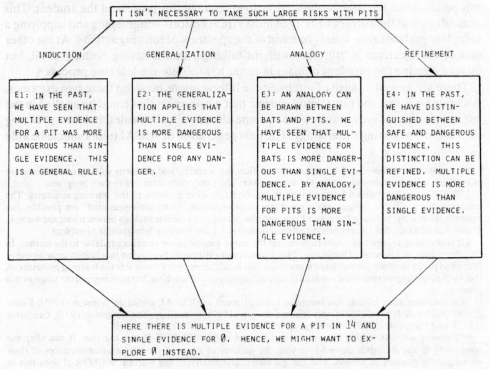

FIG. 10. Learning oriented explanations.

Naturally for the process to begin, there must be some learning strategies that are innate. Establishing from an AI standpoint which strategies are sufficient to generate the remainder then becomes an important research question.

Given a detailed account of the learning processes themselves, the possibility arises that the Coach might be able to tutor these very skills. As Fig. 10 illustrates, its tutoring could be oriented towards pointing out the relevant genetic strategies for constructing new rules. This will be an important direction for future research, since tutoring the skills of any particular domain is less important than tutoring the processes by which these skills are acquired.

7.3. A BELIEF MEASURE CAN BE DEFINED ON THE GENETIC GRAPH

Presenting both a Learning Homunculus and a Problem Solving Homunculus focusses our attention on the relation between the two: in particular, it raises the question of when a new rule added to the genetic graph becomes a part of the problem solver's program. It is a simplification to speak of the program of the Problem Solving Homunculus being the frontier of the genetic graph. A new rule may represent a misunderstanding, may not be an improvement, or may be as yet incomplete. Hence, some inertia is desirable in a dynamic learning system, if it is not to oscillate wildly or degrade its performance by accepting premature modifications.

This corresponds, perhaps, to the psychological observation that a student does not always employ a skill which has just been explained. While the student may be able to repeat the explanation, and even describe implications of the new knowledge, he may not actually use the skill when solving problems. Teachers recognize this property of students and employ the heuristic of supplying further examples and different kinds of explanations.†

A formal representation for this learning conservatism can be added to our learning model by introducing a belief measure. We can restrict a skill on the frontier from being employed by the problem solving homunculus until "belief" in this new piece of knowledge exceeds some threshold, where "belief" is a function of the number, kinds and recency of explanations and examples that have been provided. In terms of our genetic graph representation, we can say that a new rule is not employed until its linkage into the genetic graph is sufficiently strong, i.e. belief in the rule, defined in terms of the number and kinds of links that attach the rule to the existing graph, exceeds some threshold.‡

Such a metric can improve the tutor's expectations about the student's use of a rule following its introduction. The Psychologist module maintains a record of its estimate of the student's belief in a rule in terms of the types of explanations provided, their recency, and their number. When belief is below some threshold, the tutor can expect that more explanations will be needed and that the student will be able to describe the rule when queried, but probably not employ it.§

† Authors of script-based CAI systems can incorporate this educational heuristic by supplying multiple exercises and explanations. But the scripts do not provide a theory of where such additional advice will be needed.

‡ This is a first order theory. The linkage strength depends as well on the number of situations in which the rule has been explained, the time since these links were constructed, etc. However, this first order theory is sufficient to define some interesting learning complexity criteria which I discuss in the next section, and imply some procedural consequences for the Tutor.

§ This threshold can be dynamically adjusted on the basis of the student's performance.

Given this refined model, we can undertake a fine grained analysis of belief criteria in learners. For example, some students, many examples of a few links may engender stronger belief than single examples of many links. By examination of the student's performance with respect to the occurrence of such bonds, we can explore the trade-offs between diversity, repetition and recency. There is also the corresponding AI question of which belief metrics result in a reasonable learning rate, which lead to instability, and which are too conservative.

7.4. THE GENETIC GRAPH TOPOLOGY PROVIDES A LEARNING COMPLEXITY MEASURE

Focussing on the genetic graph as a record of the learning process suggests a relationship between various topologies of the graph and learning complexity. The utility of this characterization is that it provides guidance to the Tutor regarding which areas of the syllabus require more attention and to the Psychologist with respect to which skills the student can be expected to have difficulty with.†

From a learning viewpoint, the complete genetic graph of the tutor is a roadmap. It describes various paths the student's learning process might take. If the tutor's graph shows that a given rule has many links, then the expectation is that the student will have little difficulty in acquiring that rule himself. There are many opportunities for him to do so. But if another rule has but one link to the other rules, or indeed none, then here is a topology that suggests the need for tutoring advice.

For example, Fig. 3 showed a cluster of rules densely connected by generalization and analogy links. Our belief metric suggests that such clusters are easier to acquire than sparsely connected regions of the graph. The procedural import of graph density is to cause the Tutor to expect that repetition will be little needed in dense regions but strongly demanded in sparse areas.‡

Thus, topologies of the syllabus suggest a theory of learning complexity. Experiments are needed to determine if this is borne out. But if so, it is an important theoretical idea for education, independent of the use of computers.§

---

† Traditional epistemology discusses validity, not complexity. This is because complexity is not well-defined except in relation to a particular learning theory. Traditional epistemology did not have such a theory. We are developing a theory of knowledge that is not independent of the "knower".

‡ Recall that in our discussion of the genetic graph and its relation to the Psychologist, I introduced a learning complexity metric. This metric was employed to make the Psychologist conservative in its belief that the student's behavior had exhibited a particular skill when that skill was far from the frontier of the student's current knowledge state. Formally this took the form that the K model "appropriate" and "used" parameters are altered proportional to how far the skill is from the student's current knowledge frontier.

The learning complexity implied by the belief metric for certain syllabus topologies suggests a refinement of this complexity metric, namely that sparsely connected nodes should be expected to be more difficult to acquire then densely connected ones, if at the same distance from the knowledge frontier. In particular, with respect to skills on the frontier, the Psychologist should be conservative in believing that a student has acquired a particular skill when that skill is weakly linked to the student's knowledge frontier.

§ It is conceivable that formal analysis of a syllabus with a genetic graph may serve a useful educational function by predicting the learning complexity of the material. If the graph is largely a chain of rules, we can expect difficulty in convincing the student to employ these skills. Their support will rest entirely on repetition of a single explanatory method. On the other hand, if the GG contains many islands, bridges, and clusters, then we can expect that little tutoring may be required due to the rich interconnectedness of knowledge in this domain.

The validity of the formal analysis is not yet established. But its importance is clear. Education rests on at best a pop epistemology. Philosophic epistemology is too removed from learning. If our analysis provides a middle ground, rigorous, objective and concise but still about the learner's relation to knowledge and not some abstract definition of truth, then we have made progress in developing a theory of education.

7.5. DESIGNING SIMULATED STUDENTS IS A RESEARCH METHODOLOGY

We intend to explore the many issues raised here by extending our "student simulation testbed" to include computer students which learn. Such students can be used to explore the effect of different belief metrics on stability and of different learning strategies on the growth of the graph.

Ultimately, embedding a learning capacity in the coach can have an important consequence for the genetic graph itself. It can eliminate the requirement that the AICAI tutor have a complete graph to teach. The graph can be incomplete but grown by the embedded learning program when needed.

7.6. THE GENETIC GRAPH IS NOT A COMPLETE THEORY OF LEARNING

While the issues raised in this section are provocative, the genetic graph is by no means a complete theory of learning. Hard questions remain to be studied: When should a learning strategy be applied? How are profitable analogies, generalizations and refinements detected? What are the criteria for forgetting? Furthermore, there is an enormous amount of experimental exploration that must be done. But I believe it is clear that AICAI programs will gain increased leverage by embodying an explicit theory of the learner.

8. Conclusions

My interest in the evolution of a learner's knowledge was inspired by Piaget, who often speaks of himself as a *genetic epistemologist*. He characterizes the fundamental problem of genetic epistemology as: "*the explanation of the construction of novelties in the development of knowledge*". This paper has explored the construction of new knowledge in terms of a genetic graph. As a test of the effectiveness of this theory, I have described a design by which the graph can improve the tutoring and modelling of AICAI systems. I have also described a complementary design for a set of computer-based learning programs, in which the genetic processes form a separate expert operating on the learner's genetic graph.

Our next step will be to complete the implementation of an AICAI tutor based on the genetic graph approach, and experiment with the resulting system. I have little doubt that the genetic graph will increase the effectiveness of this tutor over a comparable Expert-based system. More interesting will be the fine-grained analysis of learning that such a system makes possible. We will employ it to explore such Piagetian questions as the following.

(a) Are there "stages" in the acquisition of these genetic processes as evidenced by certain explanation strategies proving unuseable for populations of different age and background?

(b) Does tutoring "procedural assimilation" prove easier than tutoring "procedural accommodation", where the former is defined in terms of the acquisition of additional procedures implementing a known concept, that is intra-island rules linked by generalization, specialization, analogy and correction links; while the latter represents the acquisition of a new concept and the associated growth of a new island of rules?†

(c) Do islands define stable knowledge plateaus, providing a lind of "equilibration"?

While I do not know the answers to these questions, I believe this paper demonstrates that the formal study of learning and teaching required by AICAI research is a powerful methodology for studying fundamental questions in cognitive psychology and artificial intelligence.

References

BROWN, R. (1977). Use of analogy to achieve new expertise. *MIT AI Technical Report 403*, April.

BROWN, J. S. & BURTON, R. (1977). Diagnostic models for procedural bugs in basic mathematical skills, *ICAI No. 10*. Bolt, Beranek and Newman, August.

BROWN, J. S., BURTON, R. & LARKIN, K. (1977). Representing and using procedural bugs for educational purposes. *Proceedings of 1977 Annual Conference, Association for Computing Machinery*, Seattle, October, pp. 247–255.

BROWN, J. S., BURTON, R. & ZDYBEL, F. (1973). A model-driven question-answering system for mixed-initiative Computer-Assisted Instruction. *IEEE Transactions on Systems, Man and Cybernetics*, **SMC-3**(3), 248–257.

BURTON, R. & BROWN, J. S. (1976). A tutoring and student modelling paradigm for gaming environments. In COLEMAN, R & LORTON. P. JR., Eds, *Computer Science and Education*, *ACM SIGCSE Bulletin*, **8**(1), 236–246.

BURTON, R. & BROWN, J. S. (1977). Semantic grammar: a technique for constructing natural language interfaces to instructional systems. *BBN Report No. 3587, ICAI Report No. 5*, May.

CARBONELL, J. (1970). AI in CAI: an Artificial-Intelligence approach to Computer-Assisted Instruction. *IEEE Transactions on Man–Machine Systems*, **MMS-11**(4), December.

CARR, B. & GOLDSTEIN, I. (1977). Overlays: a theory of modelling for Computer Aided Instruction. *MIT AI Memo 406 Memo 40)*, February.

CARR, B. (1977). II: A computer aided instruction program with student modelling capabilities. *MIT AI Memo 417 (LOGO Memo 45)*, May.

COLLINS, A., WARNOCK, E. & PASSAFIUME, J. (1975). Analysis and synthesis of tutorial dialogues. In BOWER, G., Ed., *The Psychology of Learning and Motivation*, Vol. 9. New York: Academic Press.

DE KLEER, J. (1976). Local methods for localizing faults in electronic circuits. *MIT AI Memo 394*, November.

EVANS, T. (1968). A program for the solution of geometric-analogy intelligence test questions. In MINSKY, M., Ed., *Semantic Information Processing*. Cambridge, MA: The MIT Press, pp. 271–353.

GOLDSTEIN, I. (1975). Summary of MYCROFT: a system for understanding simple picture programs. *Artificial Intelligence Journal*, **6**(3), Fall.

GOLDSTEIN, I. & CARR, B. (1977). The computer as coach: an athletic paradigm for intellectual education. *Proceedings of 1977 Annual Conference, Association for Computing Machinery*, Seattle, October, pp. 227–233.

GOLDSTEIN, I. & GRIMSON, E. (1977). Annotated production systems: a model for skill acquisition. *MIT AI Memo 407 (LOGO Memo 44)*, February.

---

† For Piaget, "accommodation" for situations where the learner builds new structures to handle a task; "assimilation" involves situations where the adaptation of old structures proves sufficient. My definitions of procedural assimilation and procedural accommodation are intended to provide a loose analogy, wherein new structures correspond to new islands. I employ this analogy only to indicate that our procedural approach allows the exploration of precise definitions for the notions of local and global changes to a knowledge structure. Whether a more precise match of computational and Piagetian terminology is possible (or fruitful) remains to be seen.

KOFFMAN, E. & BLOUNT, S. (1975). Artificial Intelligence and automatic programming in CAI. *Artificial Intelligence*, **6**, 215–234.

MOORE, J. & NEWELL, A. (1977). How can MERLIN understand? In GREGG, L. Ed., *Knowledge and Cognition*. Potomac, MD: Lawrence Erlbaum Associates.

NORMAN, D. (1976). *Studies of Learning and Self-Contained Educational Systems, 1973–1976*. University of California at San Diego, Center for Human Information Processing, *Report No. 7601*, March.

NORMAN, D., GENTNER, D. & STEVENS, A. (1976). Comments on learning: schemata and memory representation. In KLAHR, D., Ed., *Cognition and Instruction*. Hillsdale, N.J.: Erlbaum Associates.

PIAGET (1971). *Genetic Epistemology* (trans. E. Duckworth). New York: W. W. Norton.

SACERDOTI, E. (1975). The non-linear nature of plans. *Proceedings of the Fourth International Joint Conference on Artificial Intelligence*, Tbilisi, Georgia, U.S.S.R., pp. 206–218.

SELF, J. (1974). Student models in Computer-Aided Instruction. *International Journal of Man–Machine Studies*, **6**, 261–276.

SELF, J. (1977). Concept teaching. *Artificial Intelligence Journal*, **9**(2), 197–221.

SLEEMAN, D. (1975). A problem-solving monitor for a deductive reasoning task. *International Journal of Man–Machine Studies*, **7**, 183–211.

SLEEMAN, D. (1977). A system which allows students to explore algorithms. *Proceedings of the Fifth International Joint Conference on Artificial Intelligence*, August, pp. 780–786.

SMITH, R. L., GRAVES, H., BLAINE, L. H. & MARINOV, V. G. (1975). Computer-assisted axiomatic mathematics: information rigor. In LECAREME, O. & LEWIS, R., Eds, *Computers in Education Part I: IFIP*. Amsterdam: North Holland.

STANSFIELD, J., CARR, B. & GOLDSTEIN, I. (1976). Wumpus advisor I: a first implementation of a program that tutors logical and probabilistic reasoning skills. *MIT AI Laboratory Memo No. 381*, September.

STEVENS, A. & COLLINS, A. (1977). The goal structure of a Socratic tutor. *Proceedings of 1977 Annual Conference, Association for Computing Machinery*, Seattle, October, pp. 256–263.

SUSSMAN, G. (1975). *A Computational Model of Skill Acquisition*. New York: American Elsevier.

WESTCOURT, K., BEARD, M. & GOULD, L. (1977). Knowledge-based adaptive curriculum sequencing for CAI: application of a network representation. *Proceedings of 1977 Annual Conference, Association for Computing Machinery*, October, pp. 234–240.

WINSTON, P. (1975). Learning structural descriptions from examples. In WINSTON, P., Ed., *The Psychology of Computer Vision*. New York: McGraw-Hill, pp. 157–209.

YOB, G. (1975). Hunt the Wumpus. *Creative Computing*, September/October, 51–54.

4. An investigation of computer coaching for informal learning activities

RICHARD R. BURTON AND JOHN SEELY BROWN

Bolt Beranek and Newman, Inc., 50 Moulton Street, Cambridge, Mass. 02138, U.S.A.

Computer-based tutoring/coaching systems have the promise of enhancing the educational value of gaming environments by guiding a student's discovery learning. This paper provides an in-depth view of (i) the philosophy behind such systems, (ii) the kinds of diagnostic modeling strategies required to infer a student's shortcomings from observing his behavior and (iii) the range of explicit tutorial strategies needed for directing the Tutor to say the right thing at the right time. Examples of these issues are drawn for a computer-based coaching system for a simple game–How the West was Won. Our intention in writing this paper is to make explicit the vast amounts of tutorial knowledge required to construct a coaching system that is robust, friendly and intelligent enough to survive in home or classroom use. During the past three years, we have witnessed how subtle the computer-based coaching problem really is. We hope this paper conveys some of these subtleties—many of which continue to resist general solution.

Introduction

The revolution in personal computing will bring with it extensive use of complex games. Students will play computer-based games during much of their free time. These activities can provide rich, *informal* environments for learning. Games provide an enticing problem-solving environment that a student explores at will, free to create his own ideas of underlying structure and to invent his own strategies for utilizing his understanding of this structure. Properly constructed games can lead to the formation of strategies and knowledge structures that have general usefulness in other domains as well. However, a major stumbling block to the effective educational use of unstructured gaming or open-ended problem-solving environments is the amount of tutorial resources that are often required (i) to keep the student from forming grossly incorrect models of the underlying structure of the game/environment, (ii) to help him see the limits of his strategies, and (iii) to help him discover the causes of manifested errors.

One of the prerequisites for a productive informal learning environment is that it be made enticing to the student by enabling him to control it. The student must have the freedom to make decisions (incorrect as well as correct ones) and observe their results. While a student's incorrect decisions sometimes lead to erroneous results that he can immediately detect, they often produce symptoms that are beyond his ability to recognize. For an informal environment to be fully effective as a learning activity, it often must be augmented by tutorial guidance that recognizes and explains weaknesses in the student's decisions or suggests ideas when the student appears to have none. This is a significant challenge requiring many of the skills analogous to those of a coach or

† This research was supported, in part, by the Advanced Research Projects Agency, Air Force Human Resources Laboratory, Army Research Institute for Behavioral and Social Sciences, and Navy Personnel Research and Development Center under Contract No. MDA903-76-C-0108.

79

laboratory instructor. The tutor or coach† must be perceptive enough to make relevant comments but not so intrusive as to destroy the fun inherent in the game. This paper presents one such coaching system (named WEST) built around the game "How the West was Won." The system is examined as an instance of a general paradigm, called "Issues and Examples," for building such systems. Aspects of the system are examined to discover the limitations of the central paradigm and to characterize a wide variety of tutorial strategies that must be included to create a successful coaching system.

COACHING INSTUCTIONAL SYSTEMS

The pedagogical motivation underlying much of our coaching research can be characterized as "guided discovery learning." It assumes a *constructivist* position, in which the student constructs his new knowledge from his existing knowledge. In this theory, the notion of misconception or "bug" plays a central role. Ideally, a student's bug will cause an erroneous result that he will notice. If the student has enough information to determine what caused the error and can correct it, then the bug is referred to as *constructive*. If, however, the student does not have sufficient information to change his behavior as a result of the perceived error, the bug is termed *non-constructive*. One of the most important aspects of a learning environment is the degree to which the mistakes that a student makes are constructive. (See Fischer, Brown & Burton, 1978 for further discussion.) From this point of view, one of the major tasks of a Coach is to give the student additional information in order to transform non-constructive bugs into constructive ones. An additional task for the Coach, in dealing with bugs that do not have easily observable manifestations, is to point out that something can be improved.‡

A subtle requirement of this theory is that the Coach does not interfere too much. While the student is making mistakes in the environment he is also experiencing the idea of learning from his mistakes and discovering the means to recover from his mistakes. If the Coach immediately points out the student's errors, there is a real danger that the student will never develop the necessary skills for examining his own behavior and looking for the causes of his own mistakes.

There are two major but related problems that must be solved by a computer Coach. They are:

(1) when to interrupt the student's problem solving activity, and
(2) what to say once it has been interrupted.

In general, solutions to these problems require techniques for determining what the student knows (procedures for constructing a diagnostic model) as well as explicit tutoring principles about interrupting and advising. These, in turn, require a theory of how a student forms abstractions, how he learns, and when he is apt to be most receptive to advice. Unfortunately, few, if any, existing psychological theories are precise enough to suggest anything more than caution. The requirements that evolve from designing coaching systems should provide useful goals or forcing functions for future cognitive

† This usage of the term "coach" was originated by Goldstein (1977). We originally conceived of the West tutorial resource as a congenial "tutor" but the images evoked by the term "tutor" have proven to be inappropriate. In this paper we shall use "coach" to emphasize the informal nature of the learning situation.
‡ In a recent paper on the educational implications of Piaget's psychological theory, Groen has identified similar requirements. "A child will learn only if he extends the range of hypotheses he can generate and modifies or eliminates the transformations that lead to false ones. Thus, it is part of the teacher's task to ensure that the child is aware of anomalies and counter-examples that result from his activities" (Groen, 1978).

theories. In addition, the coaching systems themselves should be good test environments for such theories.

DIAGNOSTIC MODELING

Since the student is primarily engaged in a gaming or problem-solving activity, any explicit diagnosing of a student's strengths and weaknesses must be unobtrusive or subservient to his main activity. This means that the diagnostic component cannot use prestored tests or pose a lot of diagnostic questions to the student. Instead, the computer coach must restrict itself mainly to inferring a student's shortcomings from whatever he does in the context of playing the game or solving the problem. This can be a difficult problem. Just because a student does not use a certain skill while playing a game does not mean that he does not know that skill. For example, an opponent may never have created a situation that required him to invoke it. Although this point seems quite obvious, it poses a serious diagnostic problem. The absence of a manifested skill carries diagnostic value if and only if an expert in an equivalent situation would have used that skill. Hence, apart from the outright errors, the main window a computer-based Coach has to a student's misconceptions is through a "differential" modeling technique that compares what the student is doing with what the expert would be doing in his place. (See Sleeman & Hendley's article in this issue for further discussions on this point.) This "difference" must provide hypotheses about what the student does not know or has not yet mastered.

The process of constructing a differential model requires two tasks—both of which use a computer-based Expert,[†] but for different purposes. The first task is evaluating the quality of the student's current action or "move" in relationship to the set of possible alternative moves that an Expert might have made in the exact same circumstances. The second task is determining the underlying skills that went into the selection and composition of the student's move as well as each of the "better" moves of the Expert. In order to accomplish the first task, the Expert need only use the *result* of its knowledge and reasoning strategies, which is in the form of better moves. However, for the second task, it has to consider the "pieces" of knowledge involved in selecting and generating the better moves, since the absence of one of these pieces of knowledge might explain why the student failed to make a better move.

FORMS OF DOMAIN EXPERTISE FOR COACHING

The representation of domain expertise in a computer can be in one of two forms. One form is as a "glass-box" or articulate model (Goldstein & Papert, 1977). The model is referred to as "articulate" because each problem-solving decision it makes can, in principle, be explained in terms that match (at some level of abstraction) those of a human problem-solver.[‡] In contrast to the articulate Expert is the "black-box" Expert, which has data structures and processing algorithms that do not mimic those used by human beings. For example, the circuit simulator underlying SOPHIE-1 (Brown & Burton, 1975) is a black-box Expert, and is used only to check the consistency of student's hypotheses and answer some of his questions. Its mechanisms are never revealed to the student since they are certainly not the mechanisms the student is expected to acquire.

† From here on, the term Expert will be used to refer to the simulation of an expert player in the computer.
‡ The BUGGY (Brown & Burton, 1978), WUMPUS (See Goldstein's article in this issue), and GUIDON (see Clancey's article in this issue) systems are based on articulate experts, as are many production rule based experts.

Within the framework of the diagnostic problems faced by the computer Coach, the glass-box Expert seems to be the most useful since it can be used both for the evaluation process (by generating optimal moves) and for determining the skills underlying those moves. Skill determination is achieved by looking at the Expert's problem-solving trace for generating a given move and noting the skills that it used. The glass-box Expert is also useful in the evaluation task because it can generate the space of alternative "better" moves and hence determine the rank ordering of the given move. Note, however, that since the evaluation process involves determining the complete range of alternative behaviors, it requires substantially more computation and robustness than simply assessing the skills underlying any one particular move.

Since the implementation of a black-box Expert is not constrained by human-like algorithms, it potentially can be considerably more efficient and, therefore, more useful for evaluation of a student's move. However, the skills it uses to generate an optimal move are not analogous to the student's, so it can not be directly used for the skill determination task. This raises the possibility of combining an efficient and robust black-box Expert for evaluation with a less efficient glass-box Expert for skill determination.

Computational efficiency is not the only reason for developing the interplay of these two forms of expertise. The black-box Expert used for evaluation need only be augmented with those *incomplete* pieces of an articulate Expert which are needed to detect critical or tutorable *features* of the answers produced by the black-box Expert. The glass-box Expert need not be able to produce the complete solution itself. It needs only to work backwards from the solution to determine the "important" (tutorial) features of the solution. This realization opens up the possibility of constructing coaching systems for domains for which we do not have complete glass-box expertise.

It is possible that a lot of informal learning occurs through the combination of tacit expertise (in the form of a black-box) with incomplete but articulate pieces of a glass-box Expert. For example, no one has a complete, articulate theory on how to play expert chess. Although there are some excellent chess machines, they rely on non-human strategies for achieving their expertise, that is, they are black-box experts. There are also handbooks of chess principles which reflect pieces of articulate knowledge about opening moves, end game tactics, etc. A chess Coaching system could take advantage of the black-box Expert to identify critical moves and use incomplete but articulate knowledge to partially explain why the move was critical and how it might have been detected. People appear to learn natural language through a similar interaction. A complete, articulate theory of English does not exist. People do, however, manage to become fluent in English by receiving feedback from many "black-box experts"—other people who speak it. To help in the critiquing task, there are incomplete articulate pieces of knowledge, such as subject–verb agreement. That is, in addition to getting black-box feedback of the form "that's not grammatical," which could mean almost anything, people also get glass-box rules such as "Don't say 'they is,' say 'they are,' because you must have subject-verb agreement."†

† In this case, it might seem that the black-box Expert plays no significant role since the pieces of articulate knowledge used to critique the sentence could also be used to perform the role of the black-box; namely, reject the sentence as being ungrammatical. However, the black-box Expert also uses tacit knowledge to analyze the sentence in order to isolate structural elements (e.g. nouns, verbs) which are required for the articulate mini-theories or principles. We all know the subject-verb agreement rule and are very skilled at recognizing nouns in sentences, but very few of us can articulate a precise definition of a noun.

The modeling technique discussed in this paper employs a black-box Expert in conjunction with a set of local glass-box Experts. Briefly, the black-box Expert is used to determine the range of possible moves the student could have made, and the glass-box chunks of expertise determine possible causes for the less than optimal behavior of the student. As such, we hope this technique might also be useful in providing insights into how to transform various black-box Experts that currently exist (such as the symbolic integration capabilities of MACSYMA) into interesting, educational systems.†

TUTORING BY ISSUE AND EXAMPLE—A GENERAL PARADIGM

To be played well, any game complex enough to be interesting requires many different skills. From the point of view of a Coach, this is an important fact because it means that when a student does not perform well in a particular situation, it is not necessarily clear what skill he is lacking. The difficulty of determining which skill is being misused is increased by the fact that much of the evidence that the Coach has is indirect. That is, the Coach only knows that the student did *not* make a better move. From this negative information, he must determine why not, i.e. the move itself does not manifest a symptom or an error but the *absence* of another move does. (Contrast this with the subtlely different situation confronting BUGGY in which a bug in a kid's subtraction procedure will have symptoms explicitly contained in the BUGGY answer.)

OVERVIEW

The paradigm of "Issues and Examples" was developed to focus a coaching system on relevant portions of student behavior and to provide an overall coherence (goal) to the Coach's comments. The important aspects of the domain—that is, the skills and concepts the student is expected to master—are identified as a collection of "Issues". The Issues determine what parts of the student's behavior are monitored by the Coach. Each Issue represents an articulate mini-theory (a piece of a glass-box Expert) concerning the structure of the domain. It is characterized by two procedures. The first watches the student's behavior for evidence that the student does or does not use its particular concept or skill. As such, it is called an Issue Recognizer. The Recognizers are used to construct a "model" of the student's behavior. The second procedure of an Issue knows how to use various parts of the student model to decide if the student is "weak" in that Issue. It is called an Issue Evaluator. Thus each Issue has associated with it both a Recognizer and an Evaluator as procedural specialists.

At any point in the game, the hypotheses concerning the weaknesses of the student can be determined by running all of the Issue Evaluators on the model. When the student makes a "poor" move, his weaknesses are compared with the Issues necessary to make better moves in order to try to account for why he did not make a better move. That is, the Coach looks for an Issue in which the student is lacking and which is required for the Expert's better moves. Once an Issue has been determined, the Coach can present an explanation of that Issue together with a better move that illustrates the Issue. In this way, the student can see the usefulness of the Issue at a time when he will

---

† The technique might also be useful when there exists a complete glass-box Expert that can not do the problem in "all" ways. For these domains it cannot be assumed that the student is in fact working the same way as the expert.

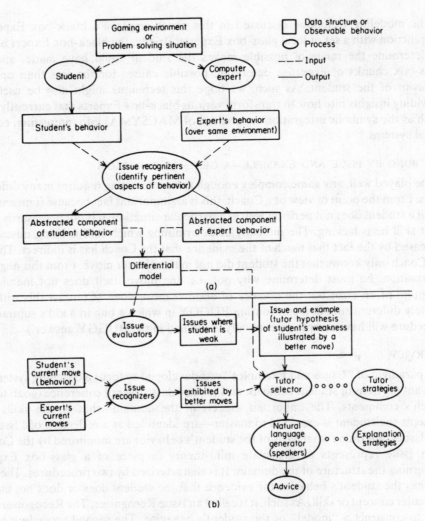

FIG. 1. Information flow diagram of modeller/tutor.

be most receptive to the idea presented—immediately after he has attempted a problem whose solution requires the Issue.

Figure 1 is a diagram of the modeling/tutorial process underlying the Issues and Examples paradigm. Figure 1(a) presents the process of constructing a model of the student's behavior. The model is a summary of the student's performance while solving a series of problems (in this case, moves in a game). Each time the student makes a move, the important aspects of his behavior (the Issues) are abstracted by the Recognizers. This abstracting is also done over the behavior of a computer-based Expert in the *same* environment by the *same* recognizers. The two abstractions are compared to provide a *differential model* of the student's behavior, which indicates those Issues on which the student is weak. We reiterate that without the Expert it is not possible to determine whether the student is weak in some skill, or whether the skill has not been used because the need for it has arisen infrequently in the student's experience.

Figure 1(b) presents the top level of the Coaching process. When the student makes a less than optimal move (as determined by comparing his move with that of the Expert), the Coach uses the Evaluation component of each Issue to create a list of Issues on which the student is weak. With the Expert's list of better moves, the Coach invokes the Issue Recognizers to determine which issues are illustrated by better moves. From these two lists (the "weak" Issues and the "better move" Issues), the Coach selects an Issue and a good move that illustrates it, (i.e. creates an example of it) and decides on the basis of other tutoring principles whether or not to interrupt.† If the Coach decides to interrupt, the selected Issue and Example are then passed to the explanation generators, which produce the feedback to the student.

The gaming situation

"How the West was Won" (WEST) is a computer board game that was originally designed at Project PLATO‡ to give students drill and practice in arithmetic. The board (see Fig. 2) is 70 spaces long. In a turn, each player receives three numbers (from spinners), which must be used in an arithmetic expression (using the operations addition, subtraction, multiplication, and division as well as parentheses) with the constraint that no operator or number can be used more than once. The value of the expression is the number of spaces the student is moved along the board. The object of the game is to be the first player to land exactly on 70. To make the student's task more complicated than just making the biggest number, there are several kinds of special moves. Towns occur every ten spaces. If you land on one, you advance to the next one, There are also shortcuts. If you land on one of these, you advance to the other end of the shortcut.§ And if you land on the space your opponent is occupying, he is bumped back two towns, unless he is on a town. The spinner values in WEST are kept small, so that special moves will often be better (get one further ahead) than making the biggest number.‖

Figure 2 shows a board situation that illustrates some of the complexities of tutoring, even in this simple game. The student is at 38, his opponent is at 39,¶ and with his spinners (2, 1, 2), the student makes the expression $2 + 1 \times 2$, resulting in a move of 4. Consider the alternative moves the student could have made: he could have moved 1 and bumped his opponent; he could have moved 2 and landed on a town; he could have moved 6 and taken a shortcut. What possible reasons may underlie this suboptimal move?

---

† If there are no Issues in common between the two lists, the reason for the student's problem lies outside of the collection of Issues, and the Coach says nothing.

‡ The PLATO game was designed by Bonnie Anderson in Dr Robert Davis's Elementary Mathematic Project (Dugdale & Kibbey, 1977).

§ In Fig. 2, Spaces 5, 25 and 44 are the beginning of shortcuts.

‖ The rules assumed in this paper are the ones used on the PLATO system as of 1975. Our Coach system, WEST, allows the student to change many of the rules. For example, the board length, the distance between towns, the location and number of shortcuts, and the set of legal arithmetic operations can all be changed and the Coach will continue to work. In addition, the number of spinners can be changed, but we have not built an Expert for such. Changing the rules gives students the opportunity to see the relationship between the rules and the "feeling" of the game.

¶ WEST is typically used by one student playing against the computer's Expert. It is also possible for two students to play against each other, in which case differential models are constructed for each student, thereby enabling coaching for both players.

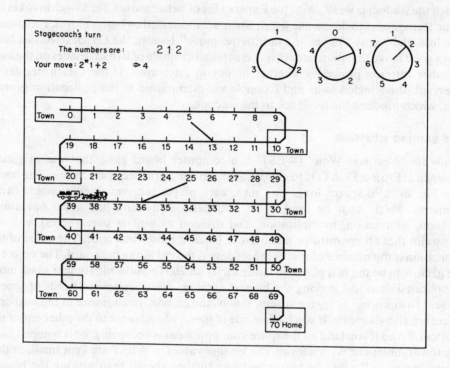

FIG. 2.

THE ISSUES IN WEST

In the Issues and Examples paradigm, the Issues embody the important concepts underlying a student's behavior and define the space of concepts the Coach can address. In WEST, there are three levels of Issues that a coach can focus on. At the lowest level are the basic mathematical skills that the student is practicing. In the current system these include the use of PARENTHESES, the use of various arithmetic operations such as SUBTRACTION and DIVISION, and the form of the student's move as an expression (PATTERN).

The second level concerns the skills needed to play WEST. The Issues at this level are: the special moves of BUMP, TOWN and SHORTCUT; the direction of a move (for example, both FORWARD and BACKWARD are legal); and the development of a STRATEGY for choosing a move, such as maximizing the distnace you are ahead of your opponent.

At the third level are the general skills of game-playing. One such general skill is the strategy of watching your opponent in order to learn from his moves. Another is the effect that different rules of the game have on determining the best strategy.†

---

† At present the Coaching system does not address these directly.

Each of these Issues is represented in two parts: a Recognizer and an Evaluator. The Recognizers are data-driven from the local context of the student's and the Expert's moves. The Evaluators are goal directed (what are the student's weaknesses?). The Issue Recognizers of WEST are straightforward, but are, nevertheless, more complex than simple pattern matchers. For example, the Recognizer for the PAREN-THESIS Issue must determine not only whether or not parentheses are present in the student's move (a lexical check of the expression underlying his move) but also whether they were necessary(which requires parsing the expression) or if they were necessary in the optimal move (which requires parsing the expert's behavior).

For the situation shown in Fig. 2, the following Issues are involved in better moves: Moving 1 entails knowing about the BUMP rule and using SUBTRACTION or DIVISION.† Moving 2 entails DIVISION, knowing about TOWNS, and knowing that the *order* of numbers in the expression does not have to be the same as the spinners. Moving 6 entails PARENTHESES and knowing about SHORTCUTS.

THE MODEL IN WEST

Figure 3 shows some of the fields of a student model created by the differential modeler. The fields it shows include patterns of moves used by the student, special moves, parenthesis usage, and strategy considerations. The columns headed by "MISS" or "MISSED" are places where the Expert would have used the skill but the student did not. They are indications of potential weaknesses. The student shown in Fig. 3 appears to be weak in the Issues PARENTHESIS and BUMP.

TUTORIAL CONSIDERATIONS

Even when relevant Issues and Examples have been identified, it may be inappropriate to tutor. This is determined by invoking various tutoring strategies. One example is the

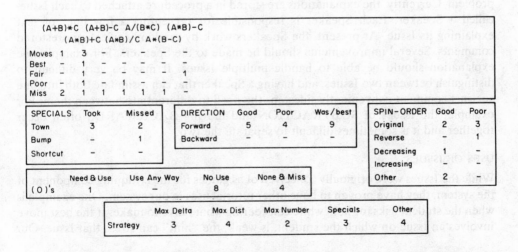

FIG. 3. Student model.

† The student could, of course, move 1 without being aware that it will lead to a bump. One ramification of inadvertent moves is that the Model will contain some "noise". Noise will be discussed in the section on Modeling Methodology.

decision about which of the competing Issues to choose. If there are two Issues, both applicable to a certain situation, which should be picked? This is one of the places where a "syllabus" (Goldstein, 1977) might be useful to provide relative orderings of importance or prerequisite links over the space of Issues. However, the Issues in WEST are sufficiently independent that there is little need to consider the prerequisite structure. Instead, additional tutoring principles must be invoked to decide which one of the set of applicable Issues should be used.

We have experimented with two alternative principles for guiding this decision thus far. The first is the *Focus* strategy, which ensures that if everything else is equal, the Issue chosen is that which was most recently discussed; that is, have the Coach hammer away on a particular Issue until it is mastered. The alternative principle is the *Breadth* strategy, which ensures that if everything else is equal, an Issue is selected that has not recently been discussed. This strategy minimizes the chance that a student gets bored by hearing too much about one Issue. A simple agenda mechanism enables either a pure Breadth or Focus strategy.† The default is the Breadth strategy, because it prevents one of two interdependent Issues from blocking the other. Strategies for manipulating the agenda mechanism provide only one source of guidance for the tutor. Additional tutoring principles will be examined in the next main section.

EXPLANATION

Once the decision has been made to tutor on a particular Issue with a particular Example, the Coach still has to decide how to express the Issue to the student. This is the explanation problem. It is in general very difficult. In addition to saying the things the student does not know, conversational postulates dictate that things the student knows already should *not* be said. (See Clancey's article for more of a discussion on this point.) In designing WEST, we have concentrated on the student modeling task and the task of determining when to break in, and have progressed very little on the explanation problem. Currently, the explanations are stored in a procedure attached to each Issue, called a Speaker. Each Speaker is responsible for presenting a few lines of text explaining its Issue. At present, the Speakers work by randomly selecting prestored comments. Several improvements should be made to the Speakers. For example, the explanation should be able to handle multiple Issues. It may be very difficult to distinguish between two Issues, and having a Speaker that can assimilate both into one succinct comment conveniently sidesteps the need to differentiate between them. For example, the Issues of SUBTRACTION and moving BACKWARDS often occur together and it is sometimes difficult to separate the two.

USES OF ISSUES

While the Issues were originally conceived of as guides for the critiquing component of the system, they have proven to have other tutorial uses in our system. One example is when the student asks for help while considering what move to make. If the best move involves an Issue on which the student, is weak, the "hint" can stress that Issue. Our

_____

† The agenda mechanism is implemented as a priority list, along with procedures for reordering it. When two Issues are possible, the one that occurs first on the list is chosen. The "focus" strategy moves a selected Issue to the front of the list, making it more likely to be chosen again, and the "breadth" strategy moves the selected issue further down the list. Since this list can be partitioned into sublists, it is straightforward to have one strategy manipulate the sublists and another to manipulate the elements within a sublist.

motivation here is that the Issue may be the critical piece of information to enable the student to see how he could make the good move, and hence the hint should put emphasis on it.

Issues are also useful in determining when to give the student *positive encouragement*, thus keeping him from viewing the Coach as being only critical. Our current Encouragement strategy directs the Coach to congratulate the student on his good move whenever it is the optimal move that demonstrates an Issue on which the student is weak. However, as we explain next, no one strategy determines what the Coach will do because different strategies may set up competing goals.

Pedagogical strategies

There are many principles that spell the difference between success and disaster in a computer-based gaming-plus-coaching environment for informal learning. Over the last few years, we have had a chance to experiment with WEST and modify it in response to various subtle and not-so-subtle difficulties that we have encountered. In this section we will discuss some of the principles that we found important to embed in our system and identify those which have general applicability to informal learning situations. For the purposes of our discussion, we will distinguish two types of principles—those for structuring the gaming environment itself and those for guiding the Coach within the environment. Although much of what we have discovered concerns explicit learning environments, we believe that many of these principles are also of importance in designing other "friendly" man–machine systems where the feel or ambiance of the total environment (including peripheral assistance or tutoring) is crucial.

PHILOSOPHY

Before discussing these principles, let us briefly summarize the philosophical under-pinnings of coaching environments. In these environments it is best for the student to discover for himself as much of the structure of a situation as possible.† Every time the Coach tells the student something, it is robbing him of the opportunity to discover it for himself. Many human tutors interrupt far too often, generally because of a lack of time or patience, and they may be preventing the development in their students of important cognitive skills—the cognitive skills that allow students to detect and use their own errors.

However, there are times when interference with the student's discovery process is called for. In gaming situations, an untutored (unwatched) student may fixate on a subset of the available moves and hence miss the potential richness of the game. In WEST, for example, a student may adopt the strategy of adding the first two spinners and multiplying the result by the third spinner, $(A+B)*C$. Since the third spinner tends to be largest, this strategy is close to the strategy of multiplying the largest number by the sum of the other two numbers (which produces the largest possible result). A student can remain at this plateau indefinitely without perceiving the failings of his strategy. But notice how much of the structure of the game is being missed. The student is unaware of special moves, such as bumps, and therefore of such questions as, "Is it

† This is not to say that structured material (e.g. textbooks) should not have a role in formal education or that guided discovery learning is the only way to learn!

better to send my opponent back 14 or get 9 ahead of him?" Since his strategy does not require searching to determine a move, the student misses the whole notion of strategy as a method for deciding between alternative moves. From the point of view of practicing arithmetic, he is performing one calculation per move instead of the dozens of mental calculations he would have to perform to answer questions such as, "What numbers can I form with these spinners?" or "Can I make a 15 with 9, 10, and 6?" By interjecting comments and suggesting better moves, a Coach can greatly expand the student's involvement in the environment.

The top-level goal driving the Coach is to ensure that its comments are both *relevant* and *memorable*. The Issues and Examples tutoring strategy provides a framework for meeting these two constraints. The Issues are used in the diagnostic process to identify at any particular moment what is relevant. The Examples provide *concrete instances* of these abstract concepts. Providing both the description of the generic Issue (a concept) as well as a concrete example of it increases the chance that the student will integrate this piece of tutorial commentary into his knowledge.

The Issue that is raised must be one in which the student is, in fact, having a problem, lest the advice be ignored or meet with hostility.

> Principle 1: Before giving advice, be sure the Issue used is one in which the student is weak.

The primary ramification of this principle is in how the Evaluators use the student model. As will be discussed in the next section, there is "noise" inherent in the model. The Evaluators for each Issue must allow for this and be "conservative". Another ramification of this principle is that the system should be cautious when tutoring an Issue that the student has recently been advised on.

Even if the diagnostic process can guarantee the weakness of an Issue at a given moment, the absence of a *good* Example of that Issue should prevent the Coach from breaking in. Thus one of the tutoring principles for enhancing a student's likeliness to remember what is said is to determine what a "good example" is:

> Principle 2: When illustrating an Issue, only use an Example (an alternative move) in which the result or outcome of that move is dramatically superior to the move made by the student.

Another basic principle that increases the chance of remembering the criticism of the Coach is to have the student episodically encode the example.

> Principle 3: After giving the student advice, permit him to incorporate the Issue immediately by allowing him to repeat his turn.

This principle not only provides him with the opportunity to observe the results of making a new move based on this Issue but is also apt to decrease his antagonism to the advice.

The final principle of this category presupposes that the student is a bit competitive and that he is less receptive to advice when he is about to lose (even if he incorporated the advice when repeating his turn).

> Principle 4: If a student is about to lose interrupt and tutor him only with moves that will keep him from losing.

INTEREST

In an informal learning situation, the student's interest stems primarily from the situation itself. A student plays a game because he enjoys it. Hence, one of the most important constraints of the Coach is not to destroy the student's inherent interest in the game by butting in too often. It would be much easier to implement a Coach that broke in whenever the student made a suboptimal move and told the student the better move. But faced with such a tutoring strategy, the student would quickly lose all interest in playing the game—especially if he were a poor player who could profit from judicious advice. Below are some of the principles incorporated into WEST to prevent it from being oppressive. The first two principles are the most obvious:

> Principle 5: Do not tutor on two consecutive moves, no matter what.
> Principle 6: Do not tutor before the student has a chance to discover the game for himself.

When a new student first sits down to play the game or when a student who has not played in a while returns to the game, he will take some time to familiarize himself with its mechanics. He will be using cognitive resources to figure out, for example, how to type in an expression. It is unreasonable to expect him to perform at his best when it comes to actually choosing a move before he feels fairly comfortable with the mechanics of the game.

> Principle 7: Do not provide only criticism when the Tutor breaks in! If the student makes an exceptional move, identify why it is good and congratulate him.

In WEST this is done whenever a FAIR player makes an optimal move or whenever a player makes an optimal move that uses an Issue in which he is weak. Note the various uses of the Expert just to carry out this one principle.

This next principle has appeared before in a slightly different form.

> Principle 8: After giving advice to the student, offer him a chance to retake his turn, but do not force him to.

If the student can use the Tutor's advice to improve his position in the game, he may be more attentive, but he should be given a chance to refuse to retake his turn, since he may consider a retake to be a subtle form of cheating.†

INCREASING THE CHANCES OF LEARNING

The next two principles were designed to increase the chances of learning from the gaming environment independent of the Coach's comments on the progress of the game.

> Principle 9: Always have the Computer Expert play an optimal game.

The student should be able to observe and learn from the best possible play of his opponent (typically the computer). One of the best metaskills that a student can learn from WEST (or any game) is to watch what your opponent is doing, especially if you are losing. To maximize the chance of the student seeing the value of this heuristic, he

---

† If WEST is being used in the mode where two students are playing against each other, the ability to retake turns after advice is turned off.

should always have a chance to observe expert play. Also, if the student realizes that the computer is not playing the best possible game, he may feel that he is being played down to and consequently lose interest in playing.

Principle 10: If the student asks for help, provide several levels of hints.

In WEST there are four levels of help. The first request for help causes the Coach to look at the student model for his current weaknesses. If a weakness is found in a skill that is required for an optimal move at this point in the game, the student is told to consider that Issue. For example, if the student is weak on the PARENTHESES issue and the optimal move for this turn requires parentheses, the student will be told "Why don't you try to use parentheses to change the order in which operations are done." The second request for help on the same move provides the student with the set of possible outcomes. For the third request, the Coach will select the outcome that it considers best. The fourth request causes the Coach to give the student an arithmetic expression that brings about the best outcome. Thus, the four successive levels of hints are based on the following rules:

Hint 1: Isolate a weakness and directly address that weakness.
Hint 2 (what): Delineate what the space of possible moves is at this point in the game.
Hint 3 (why): Select the optimal move and tell him why it's optimal.
Hint 4 (how): Describe how to make that optimal move.

ENVIRONMENTAL CONSIDERATIONS

While most of the interest in a gaming environment is derived from the game itself, many things can be done to the environment to make it more interesting. Graphics is a prime example. Playing against the computer is another. (Many CAI games have survived solely on the basis of these two considerations.) In this section we discuss some more subtle considerations that WEST employs. The next principle attempts to keep the student from getting discouraged.

Principle 11: If the student is losing consistently, adjust the level of play.

Notice that this principle conflicts with an earlier principle of always having the computer play an optimal game so that the student will have a model of expert play. For games in which there are several levels of structure to the play, such as chess, it may be better for the student to have a role model (hence opponent) which is only slightly above his level. This will tend to keep the games close while still providing examples of better moves. Our solution of this conflict is to give the computer bad spinners when it is ahead by an amount that varies with the quality of the player.

Principle 12: If the student makes a potentially careless error, be forgiving. But provide explicit commentary in case it was not just careless.

The system should be friendly about a student's error that may be from misinterpreting the rules of the game or from mistyping a move. On such errors, the system should not only allow the student to correct his mistake but, if a general rule of the game has been violated, it should draw attention to the rule and provide specific instances of it that are legal. For example, the WEST system has compiled into it diagnostic routines for many typical errors that a student is apt to make (such as precedence errors in arithmetic and giving as the value of his expression the end position of the move).

Although the twelve principles listed here are compiled into our system, it is our hope that at some future time these principles can be directly interpreted from a declarative representation of them. Such a representation could provide a *meta-environment* in which student teachers could modify and extend the rules and witness the effects on students. (See O'Shea's article in this issue for a further discussion on this point.) In WEST, a small advance along this dimension has been made by enabling the Coach to articulate all the pros and cons of what it should do next. Of course, the Coach's cogitation is not part of what a player sees as he is playing the game but instead is displayed on a second "screen". This trace of the Coach's behavior provides a graphic illustration of how many of the above principles interact to produce some very subtle tutorial behavior.

Analysis of modeling methodology

Thus far we have provided a glimpse into the underlying principles of our Coaching system as well as a simplified description of how a differential diagnostic model can be inferred from a student's behavior. It should now be clear how important the diagnostic model is to the successful execution of the top-level Issues and Examples Coaching paradigm. Consequently, we feel it is important to examine some of the limitations and underlying problems of this scheme that have not yet been discussed. We will begin with a more formal examination of the modeling process.

The inputs to the Modeler are the student's move and the set of better moves that the student could have made. Each of these moves has associated with it a set of requisite "Issues," which must be employed (in some manner) to obtain that move. For example, if the move M was to go back 2 spaces to land on a shortcut, the Issues of SHORTCUT, SUBTRACTION and BACKWARD are all required. From the student move, the Modeler can infer that the student knows the Issues needed for that move.†

What can be gleaned from knowing the set of *better moves* that the student did *not* take? In general, for each better move M, we only know that at least *one* of the set of Issues required for M was not employed and therefore reflects a potential weakness on the part of the student. But how do we know which of these Issues blocked the student from making that move? This is what we refer to as the "apportionment of blame/credit" problem: How should the Modeler apportion blame among the requisite Issues for the student's failure to discover a move?

Our solution in WEST has been to apportion blame more or less equally among all of the Issues required for the missed better moves.‡ One effect of this decision is the

---

† Even this cannot be inferred if there is more than one way to derive the move and the "Issues" deal with derivational rules. In WEST, the Issues are all things that uniquely underlie or are manifest in a move.

‡ In case the Modeler has more than one move that is better than the one the student made, it would be possible to find the intersection of the Issues required for each move. Unfortunately, the student is, in general, weak on more than one Issue, so this intersection will often be empty, meaning that at least two of the better moves were blocked for independent reasons. Since the evaluators have to work with noise in any case, we did not include this noise reduction heuristic. It has not proven to be a difficulty. The Coach does use this strategy when selecting an Issue to tutor. If one Issue is needed for all better moves, it is selected as the one most likely to have been missed.

introduction of incorrect information or "noise" into the model. That is, blame will almost certainly be apportioned to Issues that are in fact understood.

Having to overcome this source of noise is an excellent example of how diagnosing a student in a problem-solving situation in which the student is in total *control* is inherently more problematic than the standard mixed-initiative instructional system. In mixed-initiative systems, the Modeler can always construct a differential hypothesis from this source of ambiguity, pose a task to the student, and see what he does. Because it can create a sequence of such tasks, each one eliminating contending hypotheses, the Modeler can converge on the actual afflicting weaknesses. However, such intrusions by the Modeler into the gaming or problem-solving matrix could destroy the concentration and goal directedness of the student—creating an antidote potentially more destructive than the *raison-d'être* for a student model in the first place.

The simplified view of a student's move as a set of issues that somehow underlies the generation of the move suggests several other areas of concern in the modeling process. Since the system does not have a complete glass-box Expert, (does not account for the *entire* process that a person would use to derive the move) the set of Issues does not necessarily account for everything required to derive the move. This opens up the possibility that the underlying reason the student didn't make a move may not be one of the known Issues at all, but might instead be some other skill that has not been articulated as an Issue.† Any incompleteness in the set of Issues results in more noise in the differential student model.

An additional source of noise in the model is that students are seldom completely consistent. They often forget to use techniques that they know or get tired and accept a move that is easy to generate.

Another source of noise is learning. As the student plays the game, we hope he will be acquiring new skills that previously would have shown up as weaknesses. Even after a student learns an Issue, his model will continue to show the weakness that has accumulated over time. Ideally, the old pieces of the model should decay with time. Unfortunately, the costs involved in this computation are prohibitive. To avoid this failing of the model, the WEST Coach removes from consideration any Issues that the student has used recently (in the last three moves).

To combat the noise which arises in the model, the Evaluator for each Issue is implemented as a separate procedure. This allows individual tuning of the Evaluators in response to perceived failings. In WEST, the Evaluators use a comparison of the "taken fields" of the model with the "missed fields." The comparison percentages are adjusted to be high enough to yield conservative Evaluators. This alleviates the problems that might be caused by noise for less conservative techniques. Some coaching opportunities may be missed but eventually if the student has a problem addressed by an Issue a pattern will emerge.

STRATEGIES VERSUS ISSUES

In the scheme discussed above, the Expert is used to create a list of better moves, and then the Modeler diagnoses the student's weakness on the assumption that he did not make any of these better moves because he had not mastered one of the requisite skills

---

† If the Coach does not have an Issue, it will not break in, because the student's weakness may be beyond its scope. For this reason, the Issues define the space of weaknesses the Coach will try to correct.

or Issues underlying them. But what happens if the student is employing a strategy different from the Expert's? In such cases, the reason a student did not make a particular better move might simply be that he did not *want* to make it. According to his strategy, his move was the best one possible.

In order to cope with this problem, the Modeler must be able to detect when the student is using some other strategy and to characterize precisely what this other strategy is. If an executable description of the alternative strategy can be formed, then the Expert can be modified to use the new strategy. The Modeler can then reconstruct the differential student model on the basis of the modified Expert in order to separate out what Issues (as opposed to strategies) the student is weak on. Each of these tasks has its own complications. Let us proceed in this discussion under the simplifying assumption that the student maintains a consistent strategy and a consistent set of weaknesses during the period over which the model is being created.†

DIAGNOSING THE EXISTENCE OF A POSSIBLE ALTERNATIVE STRATEGY

If a modeling scheme looks at only one move of a student, it is impossible for it to determine whether the student's failure to make another move stemmed from a lack of a given skill or from harboring a suboptimal strategy.‡ However, from a *sequence* of student moves it may be possible to make such a separation. This results from the assumption that the student's strategy remains the same over the sequence of moves, whereas the Issues are likely to change from one move to the next.

The technique for detecting when a student is using a strategy different from the Expert's involves the amount of "tear" in the student model. Briefly, tear is a measure of the consistency of use of Issues. Tear starts to develop when several issues begin to reflect both a substantial amount of use when they should not have been used and non-use when they should have been. If tear in a model gets large enough, the Modeler is willing to expend some effort in conjecturing alternative strategies that the student might be using. Any alternative strategies can then be tested by re-running the Modeler over the student's past moves and comparing his behavior to that of the Expert using the conjectured strategy. If the resulting model has substantially less tear, then the conjectured strategy is taken to be a more accurate approximation of the student's strategy and is used to form the differential model. If the resulting model is not substantially more consistent, then this alternative strategy is rejected and other conjectures are tried until all reasonable conjectures are tested. Of course, for this classical "generate and test" heuristic to work, not only must the Modeler be able to generate reasonable alternative strategies, but the Expert also must be able to simulate the strategies (the conjectures must be runnable by the Expert) in order to be able to reconstruct and test the resulting student model.

CONJECTURING ALTERNATIVE STRATEGIES

Conjecturing alternative strategies is extremely difficult unless one has a sufficiently closed world that the set of possible strategies can be characterized. This

---

† A typical period is usually one session of play, consisting of a couple of games. Longer periods require a partitioning or layering of the model to capture the change or growth of a student's knowledge.

‡ Here again, we continue with the assumption that the Modeler is a watcher and not a manipulator of the environment and hence cannot interrupt the activity and pose its own task.

characterization can take the form of either a generative mechanism (e.g. a grammar) that synthesizes the alternative strategies (Miller & Goldstein, 1977, and also see Miller's article in this issue), or an explicit enumeration of possible alternative strategies. The world of WEST is sufficiently closed and small enough that the latter technique appears to work.

WEST's alternative strategies fall into two categories—those that are suboptimal because of a "mind bug" about the structure of the game and those that reflect an alteration in the spirit or rules of the game. An example of a "mind bug" would occur when a student always tries to move as far ahead as is possible given the particular spinner values—a nearly optimal strategy but one that overlooks the potential value of bumping your opponent. An example of an alteration of the spirit of the game occurs when the student is obsessed with bumping his opponent (e.g. because of the pretty graphics effect) and will always bump whenever a chance arises. Another example that reflects the subtlety of this category is the student who becomes fixated on getting the Coach to "speak" or interact with him. This student no longer cares about winning the game but instead becomes involved in psyching out the actual teaching strategies embedded in the system—an extremely interesting "meta-game". It should be remembered that the Coach is very conservative and will not break into the student's game unless there is a consistent pattern of poor behavior that the Coach can address. If the student is doing something completely "off the wall" it is unlikely that the Coach will break in.

Once a grammar or an explicit list of alternative strategies is created, one may determine the set of alternative strategies that a player may be using by creating a "handle" or feature recognizer (similar to an issue recognizer) for each strategy (or grammar rule).† Then, as the Modeler is accruing evidence for perceived student weaknesses on Issues, it can also be accruing evidence on possible alternative strategies by seeing which strategy features are present in each move. These features act solely as a heuristic. They are seldom unique to a given strategy, as several alternative strategies are likely to be consistent with any one move. For example, the strategy of making a maximal number might produce the same move as the strategy of maximizing the distance ahead of your opponent.

In summary, these strategy features provide *local* evidence about what alternative strategies the student may be using. A strategy for which there is local evidence is then used by the Modeler to construct a new hypothetical differential model. This new model provides a *global* check on the strategy by determining how much the tear of the differential model has been reduced.

In order to test the diagnostic sensitivity of this technique to distinguish actual student weaknesses from alternative student strategies, we have constructed various automated students (an idea proposed in Goldstein, 1977) that play with specific weaknesses *and* simultaneously with alternative strategies. These tests indicate that the technique just described is effective for WEST. We fully recognize the limited nature of this problem for the WEST "world" and are cautious in our belief that these techniques will suffice for more complex worlds.

---

† Such feature recognizers can be quite complex and often require properties of the space of possible moves instead of just the given student move. For example, one feature might concern whether the move involved the maximum *possible* number given the particular spinners.

Experiences with WEST

The basic Coaching system was completed in Spring of 1975 (Burton & Brown, 1976). At that time, we ran an informal experiment with 18 student teachers, in which each one used the system for at least one hour. Afterward, each was asked to complete a questionnaire about the Coach's performance. All but one had received advice from the Coach. Nine of the teachers commented favorably about the Coach's advice. Two others disagreed; one said that the Coach was offering a strategy that he did not feel he should follow because it would leave him "vulnerable to attack," an element of strategy not known to the Expert. Eight of ten subjects found the comments helpful in learning a better way to play the game and, most important, nine out of ten felt that the *Coach manifested a good understanding of their weaknesses*! One subject commented, "I misunderstood a rule; the computer picked it up in the second game."

WEST has also been used in elementary school classrooms. In a controlled experiment, the coached version of WEST was compared to an uncoached version. Table 1 gives the distribution of move patterns for the coached and uncoached groups. The

TABLE 1

Comparison between coached and uncoached groups of the percentage of times each move pattern was used when it was the best move

Pattern	Coached group (%)†	Control group (%)†
$(A+B)-C$	72	74
$(A*B)+C$	57	58
$(A*B)-C$	41	46
$(A+B)*C$	65	44
$A-(B+C)$	13	29
$A*(B-C)$	32	22
$(A*B)/C$	23	9
$A/(B-C)$	25	0
$A-(B/C)$	14	0
$(A/B)-C$	14	0
$(A-B)/C$	14	0
$A-(B*C)$	13	0
$(A+B)/C$	0	0
$A/(B*C)$	0	0
$A/(B+C)$	0	0
$A+(B/C)$	0	0

Special moves

Control group (%)†		Coached group (%)†	
TOWN:	72	TOWN:	79
BUMP:	18	BUMP:	54
SHORTCUT:	41	SHORTCUT:	54

† % of time pattern was taken and was best.

coached students showed a considerably greater variety of patterns, indicating that they had acquired many of the more subtle patterns and had not fallen permanently into "ruts" that prevented them from seeing the relatively rare occasions when such moves were important. Probably the most surprising result from this experiment was that the students in the coached group enjoyed playing the game considerably more than the uncoached group. This finding was especially significant, because one of our greatest fears had been that our coaching principles were sufficiently ill-developed that either the Coach would interrupt too often, destroying the inherent enjoyment of the game or too seldom, failing to get students out of ruts. We have not yet had the opportunity to explore why, in fact, students seem to prefer the game with the Coach. One interesting hypothesis is that the students using the Coaching version were actually engaged in a meta-game of "psyching out" the Coach to get it to speak. If this rather romantic hypothesis turns out to be valid, it would open a new arena for conveying some of the very important survival principles for formal education.

References

BROWN, J. S. & BURTON, R. R. (1975). Multiple representations of knowledge for tutorial reasoning. In BOBROW, D. & COLLINS, A. Eds, *Representation and Understanding: Studies in Cognitive Science.* New York: Academic Press.

BROWN, J. S. & BURTON, R. R. (1978). Diagnostic models for procedural bugs in basic mathematical skills. *Cognitive Science*, **2**, 155–192.

BURTON, R. R. & BROWN, J. S. (1976). A tutoring and student modeling paradigm for gaming environments. In *Proceedings for the Symposium on Computer Science and Education*, February.

CARR, B. & GOLDSTEIN, I. (1977). Overlays: A theory of modeling for computer aided instruction. *Artificial Intelligence Memo 406.* Massachusetts Institute of Technology, Cambridge, Massachusetts.

CLANCEY, W. (1979). Tutoring rules for guiding a case method dialogue. *International Journal of Man–Machine Studies*, **11**, 25–49.

DUGDALE, S. & KIBBEY, D. (1977). *Elementary Mathematics with PLATO.* Urbana, Ill.: University of Illinois (Computer-based Education Research Laboratory), July.

FISCHER, G., BROWN, J. S. & BURTON, R. R. (1978). Aspects of a theory of simplification, debugging, and coaching. In *Proceedings of the Second Annual Conference of Canadian Society for Computational Studies of Intelligence*, July.

GOLDSTEIN, I. P. (1977). The computer as coach: an athletic paradigm for intellectual education. *Artificial Intelligence Memo 389.* Massachusetts Institute of Technology, Cambridge, Massachusetts.

GOLDSTEIN, I. P. (1979). The genetic graph: a representation for the evolution of procedural knowledge. *International Journal of Man–Machine Studies*, **11**, 51–77.

GOLDSTEIN, I. & PAPERT, S. (1977). Artificial Intelligence, language, and the study of knowledge. *Cognitive Science*, **1**, (1), 1–21.

GROEN, G. J. (1978). The theoretical ideas of Piaget and educational practice. To appear in SUPPES, P. Ed., *Impact of Research on Education: Some Case Studies.* Washington, D.C.: National Academy of Education.

MILLER, M. L. (1979). A structured planning and debugging environment for elementary programming. *International Journal of Man–Machine Studies*, **11**, 79–95.

MILLER, M. L. & GOLDSTEIN, I. (1977). Problem solving grammars as formal tools for Intelligent CAI. In *Proceedings of Association of Computing Machinery.*

O'SHEA, T. (1979). A self-improving quadratic tutor. *International Journal of Man–Machine Studies*, **11**, 97–124.

SLEEMAN, D. H. & HENDLEY, R. J. ACE: a system which Analyses Complex Explanations. *International Journal of Man–Machine Studies*, **11**, 125–144.

5. ACE: A system which Analyses Complex Explanations

D. H. Sleeman and R. J. Hendley

Department of Computer Studies, The University of Leeds, U.K.

This paper discusses a Problem Solving Monitor which has been implemented to provide a supportive environment for students solving a non-deterministic task, the interpretation of nuclear magnetic resonance spectra. In particular, this paper discusses the facility which allows the student to give an explanation in Natural Language and which comments on this. The explanations considered here are complex as they involve a series of arguments, which in turn consist of a series of facts and a deduction. The protocols which were collected from various student problem solving sessions are analysed in some detail and the inconsistent and incomplete nature of the dialogues is stressed. A system which is able to cope with these deficient dialogues is presented.

1. Introduction

We have implemented a system which provides a supportive problem solving environment. The system assumes that the user 'knows' the relevant algorithm, but may need some help with solving a particular problem. In general, the system observes the student's behaviour, and makes observations or gives advice only when asked—and so we call these systems Problem Solving Monitors, PSMs. The particular task with which the PSM works has been outlined in greater detail in Sleeman (1975). In this context it is sufficient to say that it is a domain in which the task involves the solution of N sub-problems, and one in which back-tracking is often involved. (That is, in order to solve a particular sub-problem one may have to make an arbitrary decision and only after several further sub-problems have been solved, will it be clear whether or not the original choice was correct). The PSM then offers the following facilities:

  (i) tells the student whether or not his solution to a sub-problem is correct;
 (ii) the HELP mode indicates the solution(s) to the next sub-problem;
(iii) the EXPLAIN mode (only available after an incorrect ASSERTION) explains why the *last* ASSERTION was incorrect;
(iv) the FSR (Following Students Reasoning) mode asks the student to give an EXPLANATION, in Natural Language, of an aspect of his ASSERTION and then comments on this EXPLANATION.

As mentioned earlier the objective of the PSM is to help the student understand an algorithm so that he can successfully apply it to a range of problems. Both the HELP and EXPLAIN modes attempt to achieve this by showing the user what the *system* would do in the various situations. The FSR mode attempts to achieve the objective more directly. There is evidence (Pask, 1975) that this approach, which requires more involvement on the behalf of the student, is likely to be educationally more valuable. We were also attracted to this mode because of the challenges which it posed to Artificial Intelligence/Computer Science.

As indicated above the PSM has access to an algorithm which is able to solve the domain's problem and indeed the information which the PSM gives for each of the modes is based on the steps which the algorithm would perform in solving the same sub-problem. (We shall refer to this information as the algorithm's TRACE.)

The algorithm which the current PSM discusses is the interpretation of Nuclear Magnetic Resonance spectra, given the molecular formula and the spectrum itself. As we have noted earlier such interpretations involve the solution of N sub-problems namely the specification of each of the groups in the molecule—this process frequently involves back-tracking. To date, the FSR facility is able to discuss three aspects of the algorithm:

(i) the SPLITTING of the peak (we shall refer to this as FSR-SPL);
(ii) the SELECTION (ELIMINATION) of groups (referred to as FSR-EL);
(iii) the solution to a sub-problem (referred to as FSR-CHN, i.e. a discussion of the CHAINs of ASSERTIONs).

The complexity of the explanations involved are such that (iii) $\gg$ (ii) > (i). In an earlier paper (Sleeman & Hendley, 1978) we discuss the first two aspects and we shall discuss the more complex third aspect here—more from the point of view of analysing complex dialogues than from the standpoint of a sophisticated CAI system. With this in mind we shall review the nature of the explanations encountered.

1.1. FORM OF ARGUMENTS ENCOUNTERED

In the case of the SPLITTING of the peak and the SELECTION of a group, we express the form of the anticipated EXPLANATIONs as:

$\langle$EXPLANATION$\rangle$ ::= $\langle$ARGUMENT$\rangle$! $\langle$EXPLANATION$\rangle$
$\langle$ARGUMENT$\rangle$

$\langle$ARGUMENT$\rangle$ ::= $\langle$FACT-LIST$\rangle$ $\langle$DEDUCTION$\rangle$!
$\langle$DEDUCTION$\rangle$ $\langle$FACT–LIST$\rangle$

$\langle$FACT-LIST$\rangle$ ::= $\langle$FACT$\rangle$! $\langle$FACT-LIST$\rangle$ $\langle$FACT$\rangle$

where DEDUCTIONs and FACTs, are referred to collectively as ARGUMENT-COMPONENTs, and could have the following form:

[$\langle$TYPEINDICANT$\rangle$] $\langle$SUBJECT$\rangle$ [$\langle$RELATION$\rangle$] [$\langle$VALUE$\rangle$] !
[$\langle$TYPEINDICANT$\rangle$] [$\langle$VALUE$\rangle$] [$\langle$RELATION$\rangle$] $\langle$SUBJECT$\rangle$

where the classes in parentheses are optional. If the TYPEINDICANT is omitted then it has to be inferred from the context—indicants for DEDUCTIONs encountered in these dialogues include: "so" "therefore" "thus" and "then".

The form of possible EXPLANATIONs given by this grammar include:

(i) a series of FACT-DEDUCTION pairs;
(ii) a series of DEDUCTION-FACT pairs;
(iii) a series of FACTs followed by a single DEDUCTION;
(iv) a DEDUCTION followed by a series of FACTs.

In (i) and (ii) above, the order of the FACT-DEDUCTION or DEDUCTION-FACT pairs, is arbitrary, except that the last pair must relate to the DEDUCTION of the whole EXPLANATION, and, in (iii) and (iv), the order of the FACTs is quite arbitrary. In all instances, individual FACTs may be omitted, in which case the actual value is assumed. Besides accommodating the above, the system also points out incorrect FACTs and inconsistent DEDUCTIONs.

This same grammar is also able to accommodate the EXPLANATIONs which occur in the FSR-CHN mode. We shall now look at these EXPLANATIONs in some more detail.

1.2. EXPLANATIONS ENCOUNTERED BY THE FSR-CHN MODE

Figure 1 gives a fairly typical set of EXPLANATIONs which were encountered in this domain. These EXPLANATIONs were collected by modifying the original PSM such that it requested an EXPLANATION of the User's ASSERTION *before* it informed the User whether or not his ASSERTION was acceptable. Most of these EXPLANA-TIONs are for one particular molecule and we will interpret these EXPLANATIONs in terms of the Problem Solution Graph (PSG) given in Fig. 2.

Whilst we are analysing the protocols in terms of the PSG we shall also point out the types of errors/shortcomings which we noted.

The majority of these arguments will be drawn from the molecule $CH_3 CH_2 CO CH_3$ which in our notation has the spectrum $((3\ 2)\ (3\ 0)\ (2\ 3))$. Most of the reasoning dialogues given are applicable to the situation when two groups have been asserted, namely the CH_3 and CH_2 groups.

1. Complete explanation
"The next group could be the ether group with a corresponding null peak, followed by a methyl group with an area of 3 and a null splitting, but this is not possible because an atom would remain. However, if the next group was the ketone group with again a null peak, followed by a methyl group with an area of 3 and a null splitting, then this would be fine."

2. Inconsistent (errorful) arguments
"The next group should be the ketone group with a null peak followed by the methyl group and the $(4\ 0)$ peak. This is fine."

3. Incomplete arguments
(a) Incompletely specified DEDUCTION (failure messages).
   "Well suppose the next group is ether with a null peak—this is not possible. So let's suppose that the next group is a ketone with a null peak followed by a methyl group and the peak $(3\ 0)$, then that would be fine,"
(b) Partial Arguments.
   (i) Groups only are mentioned.
   "If the next group is an ether group, followed with a methyl group then this would not be possible because an atom would remain. However, if the next group was a ketone followed by a methyl group that would be fine."
   (ii) Argument based on peak values, i.e. groups are omitted.
   "We know that the next peak has to be null and so the following peak will have a zero splitting—there is such a peak it is the $(3\ 0)$ and so the corresponding group will be methyl and this is fine."
(c) Complete FACTs are sometimes omitted in second and subsequent ARGUMENTs. [Here we are discussing the *same* molecule, but only the *first* assertion has been made.]
   (i) "If the next group was CH2 with the $(2\ 3)$ peak and if this were followed by the ether group with the null peak and a methyl group with the $(3\ 0)$ peak then this would leave an atom over. However, if the next group was the ketone group with the null peak and this was followed with the methyl group and the $(3\ 0)$ peak this would be fine."
   (ii) Complete FACTs omitted *and* only partial assertions given.
   "If the next group was CH2 and if this was followed by the ether group and then by the methyl group this would leave an atom over. However, if the next group was ketone, followed by the methyl group then this would be fine."

4. Arguments which include global assertions about the domain
(This example is *not* based on this molecule.)
   "Well, as we have a Nitrogen atom and more than 2 hydrogens remaining in the molecular formula and $(2\ 0)$ remains in the spectrum. I guess that these correspond to the NH_2 group and so it is *not* possible to suggest the $(2\ 0)$ peak here."

FIG. 1. Protocols for the FSR-CHN mode.

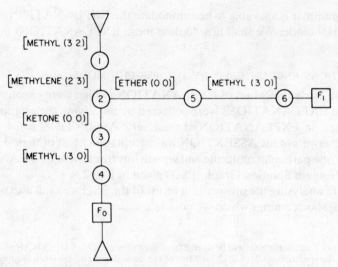

FIG. 2. Problem solution graph for the simpler problem. Node *i* is reached when assertion *i* is made.

Correct EXPLANATION

This EXPLANATION composes of 2 ARGUMENTs: ARGUMENT 1 being ASSERTIONs 5 and 6 followed by Failure 1 and ARGUMENT 2 being ASSERTIONs 3 and 4 and Failure 0 (i.e. success). This EXPLANATION is also complete—in that all ARGUMENT paths have been explored.

Inconsistent (errorful) ARGUMENTs

This EXPLANATION comprises of a single ARGUMENT. The first ASSERTION being 3 and the second ASSERTION is not found on the PSG and hence is not legal. (This ASSERTION attempts to use a resource, the (4 0) peak which is not available.) Note also that the EXPLANATION does not include the alternative possible solution path (i.e. ASSERTIONs 5, 6 and F1).

Incomplete ARGUMENTs

There are a number of cases to be considered here as the protocols show.
- (a) The DEDUCTION is unspecified—or only partially specified. In the first ARGUMENT F1 is not fully specified.
- (b) FACTs (ASSERTIONs) only partially specified.
  - (i) Groups only mentioned—i.e. peaks omitted.
    In all the ASSERTIONs quoted, i.e. 5 and 6, and 3 and 4 the peak information is consistently omitted.
  - (ii) Peaks only mentioned—i.e. groups omitted.
    In this ARGUMENT only the peak associated with ASSERTION 3 is mentioned and this information is used to deduce the peak for ASSERTION 4 (in this case, the associated group is also quoted).
- (c) Several FACTs (ASSERTIONs) are omitted from the second ARGUMENT.
  - (i) That is instead of giving a complete ARGUMENT only the components which differ from the earlier one are given. One can explain this protocol if one supposes that the User gives the first ARGUMENT in full, realizes that it

leads to a failure condition and then backtracks to the last node at which an arbitrary selection was made and further arbitrarily selects a different solution to the sub-problem (if one exists) and continues from that point. (In this instance quoting ASSERTIONs 3 and 4 and F0).

(ii) The second EXPLANATION given here also indicates that the User is *backtracking* but we also note that he is consistently giving partial ARGUMENTs i.e. information about peaks is omitted in all cases.

Use of a "Global" ASSERTION to guide the current ASSERTION

In this EXPLANATION the User asserted something which he believed to be true about the problem and then used this to eliminate a possible solution to the current sub-problem.

In this domain the FACTs and the DEDUCTIONs *do* have different forms. These forms can be summarized as:

$$\langle FACT \rangle ::= [\langle TYPEINDICANT \rangle] [\langle GROUP \rangle] \langle PEAK \rangle \;!$$
$$[\langle TYPEINDICANT \rangle] [\langle PEAK \rangle] \langle GROUP \rangle$$

and

$$\langle DEDUCTION \rangle ::= [\langle TYPEINDICANT \rangle] \langle SUCCESS\text{-}INDICANT \rangle \;!$$
$$[\langle TYPEINDICANT \rangle] \langle FAILUREINDICANT \rangle$$

where again the brackets indicate that the class may be omitted.

In this domain indicants which introduce FACTs are for instance "if" and "because" and indicants which introduce the DEDUCTIONs are "therefore", "so" and frequently "and" (see Fig. 1). ("and" for instance is also used as a normal connector, which has led to problems with the segmentation of EXPLANATIONs into their appropriate components).

One further point which needs making about the EXPLANATIONs which are encountered in the various domains, is that although the formulation we wrote for the FSR-SPL and FSR-EL grammar allowed for EXPLANATIONs with multiple ARGUMENTs and for ARGUMENTs with multiple FACTs and for multiple DEDUCTIONs many of these more complex EXPLANATIONs did *not* occur. In the case of the FSR-SPL mode there were at most 2 FACTs and a single DEDUCTION (using a fairly obvious notation: F1F2D or DF1F2). In the same notation an ARGUMENT for the FSR-EL mode can have *one* of the following forms:

$$\begin{array}{llll}
F_iD_i & F_jD_j & \ldots & F_nD_n \\
D_kF_k & D_sF_s & \ldots & D_nF_n \\
F_i & & \ldots & F_nD_n \\
D_n & F_k & \ldots & F_n
\end{array}$$

Whereas the EXPLANATIONs encountered in the FSR-CHN mode often contain several ARGUMENTs, which in turn contain a series of FACTs and one or more DEDUCTIONs. Using a similar notation, a *single* EXPLANATION here can have the form:

$$\begin{array}{lllll}
F_{11} & F_{12} & \ldots & F_{1a} & D_1 \\
F_{21} & F_{22} & \ldots & F_{2b} & D_2 \\
\vdots & \vdots & & \vdots & \vdots \\
F_{n1} & F_{n2} & \ldots & F_{ng} & D_n
\end{array}$$

Note too that the molecule which we have used to illustrate this mode is a relatively simple one. We shall later discuss a larger problem which will illustrate these features more fully.

2. The systems design

Figure 3 shows effectively the same protocols being run on the system as were shown in Fig. 1. Each piece of this dialogue is introduced by a cross-reference to the

```
**!
//CALL TO SYSTEM, SELECTION OF PROBLEM
CALL PSM
INPUT PROBLEM NUMBER:2
THE MOLECULAR FORMULA IS
(C 4 H 8 O)
IN OUR NOTATION THE SPECTRUM OF YOUR MOLECULE IS
((3 2) (3 0) (2 3))
$
//ASSERTION FOR THE FIRST SUB-PROBLEM
HEAD CH3 [3 2]
PARSES TO:((H) (C H 3) (3 2))
CORRECT
$
REASON
PARSES TO:(REASON)


//DIALOGUE 3.C1
PLEASE INPUT YOUR STMTS
:IF THE NEXT GROUP WAS CH2 WITH THE [2 3] PEAK AND IF THIS WERE FOLLOWED
BY THE ETHER GROUP WITH THE NULL PEAK AND A METHYL GROUP WITH THE [3 0]
PEAK THEN THIS WOULD LEAVE AN ATOM OVER
// THE 'MEANING' EXTRACTED FROM THE STUDENTS ARGUMENT
   THE NEXT GROUP IS (C H 2) WITH A PEAK (2 3).
   THE NEXT GROUP IS (O) WITH A PEAK (0 0).
   THE NEXT GROUP IS (C H 3) WITH A PEAK (3 0).
   THIS TERMINATES THE CHAIN PREMATURELY.
IS THIS WHAT YOU INTENDED?   :YES
PLEASE INPUT YOUR STMTS
:HOWEVER IF THE NEXT GROUP WAS THE KETONE GROUP WITH A NULL PEAK AND
THIS WAS FOLLOWED BY THE METHYL GROUP WITH THE [3 0] PEAK THEN THIS
WOULD BE FINE
// THE 'MEANING' EXTRACTED FROM THE STUDENT'S ARGUMENT.
   THE NEXT GROUP IS (C O) WITH A PEAK (0 0).
   THE NEXT GROUP IS (C H 3) WITH A PEAK (3 0).
   THIS IS THE SOLUTION.
IS THIS WHAT YOU INTENDED?   :YES
PLEASE INPUT YOUR STMTS
:ARGUMENT COMPLETED

WE ARE NOW CONSIDERING:
   THE NEXT GROUP IS (C H 2) WITH A PEAK (2 3).
   THE NEXT GROUP IS (O) WITH A PEAK (0 0).
   THE NEXT GROUP IS (C H 3) WITH A PEAK (3 0).
   THIS TERMINATES THE CHAIN PREMATURELY.
THIS ARGUMENT IS COMPLETELY CORRECT
WE ARE NOW CONSIDERING:
   THE NEXT GROUP IS (C H 2) WITH A PEAK (2 3).
   THE NEXT GROUP IS (C O) WITH A PEAK (0 0).
```

FIG. 3. System protocol for many of the explanations given in Fig. 1. User responses are underlined and the cross-references are to dialogues given in Fig. 1.

```
THE NEXT GROUP IS (C H 3) WITH A PEAK (3 0).
THIS IS THE SOLUTION.
AN ARG WHICH WE HAVE RECONSTRUCTED FROM THE PARTIAL ONE YOU GAVE
IS THAT WHAT YOU INTENDED?:YES
THIS ARGUMENT IS COMPLETELY CORRECT
DO YOU WISH TO SEE THE REASONING CHAINS WHICH YOU DID NOT EXPLORE:NO
DO YOU WISH TO CONTINUE:NO



$
//ASSERTION FOR SECOND SUB-PROBLEM
JOIN CH2 (2 3)
PARSES TO:((J) (C H 2) (2 3))
CORRECT
$
REASON
PARSES TO:(REASON)




//DIALOGUE 1
PLEASE INPUT YOUR STMTS
:THE NEXT GROUP COULD BE THE ETHER GROUP WITH A CORRESPONDING NULL  PEAK
FOLLOWED  BY  A  METHYL  GROUP WITH AN AREA OF 3 AND 0 SPLITTING HOWEVER
THIS IS NOT POSSIBLE BECAUSE AN ATOM WOULD REMAIN
// THE 'MEANING' EXTRACTED FROM THE STUDENT'S ARGUMENT.
  THE NEXT GROUP IS (O) WITH A PEAK (0 0).
  THE NEXT GROUP IS (C H 3) WITH A PEAK (3 0).
  THIS TERMINATES THE CHAIN PREMATURELY.
IS THIS WHAT YOU INTENDED?  :YES
PLEASE INPUT YOUR STMTS
:HOWEVER IF THE NEXT GROUP WAS THE KETONE GROUP WITH AGAIN A  NULL  PEAK
FOLLOWED  BY  A METHYL GROUP WITH A SPLITTING OF 0 AND AN AREA OF 3 THEN
THIS WOULD BE FINE
// THE 'MEANING' EXTRACTED FROM THE STUDENT'S ARGUMENT.
  THE NEXT GROUP IS (C O) WITH A PEAK (0 0).
  THE NEXT GROUP IS (C H 3) WITH A PEAK (3 0).
  THIS IS THE SOLUTION.
IS THIS WHAT YOU INTENDED?  :YES
PLEASE INPUT YOUR STMTS
:ARGUMENT COMPLETE




WE ARE NOW CONSIDERING:
  THE NEXT GROUP IS (O) WITH A PEAK (0 0).
  THE NEXT GROUP IS (C H 3) WITH A PEAK (3 0).
  THIS TERMINATES THE CHAIN PREMATURELY.
THIS ARGUMENT IS COMPLETELY CORRECT
WE ARE NOW CONSIDERING:
  THE NEXT GROUP IS (C O) WITH A PEAK (0 0).
  THE NEXT GROUP IS (C H 3) WITH A PEAK (3 0).
  THIS IS THE SOLUTION.
THIS ARGUMENT IS COMPLETELY CORRECT
DO YOU WISH TO SEE THE REASONING CHAINS WHICH YOU DID NOT EXPLORE:NO
DO YOU WISH TO CONTINUE:YES
```

FIG. 3—*cont.*

```
// DIALOGUE 2

PLEASE INPUT YOUR STMTS
:THE NEXT GROUP SHOULD BE KETONE WITH A NULL PEAK FOLLOWED BY  A  METHYL
GROUP AND THE (4 0) PEAK WHICH GIVES THE SOLUTION
// THE 'MEANING' EXTRACTED FROM THE STUDENT'S ARGUMENT.
 THE GROUP IS (C O) WITH A PEAK (0 0).
 THE NEXT GROUP IS (C H 5) WITH A PEAK (4 0).
 THIS IS THE SOLUTION.
IS THIS WHAT YOU INTENDED?  :YES
PLEASE INPUT YOUR STMTS
:ARGUMENT COMPLETE




WE ARE NOW CONSIDERING:
 THE NEXT GROUP IS (C O) WITH A PEAK (0 0).
 THE NEXT GROUP IS (C H 3) WITH A PEAK (4 0).
 THIS IS THE SOLUTION.
YOUR ARG. WAS NOT FOUND IN THOSE RETURNED BY THE ALG. -
 WE SHALL NOW ANALYSE IT IN MORE DETAIL
THE ASSERTION:
 THE NEXT GROUP IS (C O) WITH A PEAK (0 0).
IS FINE
THE ASSERTION:
 THE NEXT GROUP IS (C H 3) WITH A PEAK (4 0).
WAS WRONG FOR THE FOLLOWING REASON
PEAK IS NOT IN SPECTRUM STILL TO BE EXPLAINED
DO YOU WISH TO SEE THE REASONING CHAINS WHICH YOU DID NOT EXPLORE:NO
DO YOU WISH TO CONTINUE:YES




// DIALOGUE 3A + B
PLEASE INPUT YOUR STMTS
:THE NEXT GROUP COULD BE EITHER WITH A NULL PEAK BUT THIS IS  IMPOSSIBLE
SO  THE  NEXT  GROUP  IS  A KETONE WITH A NULL PEAK FOLLOWED BY A METHYL
GROUP AND THE (3 0) PEAK THEN THAT WOULD BE FINE
// THE 'MEANING' EXTRACTED FROM THE STUDENT'S ARGUMENT.
 THE NEXT GROUP IS (O) WITH A PEAK (0 0).
 IMPOSSIBLE TO FORM FURTHER GROUPS.
 THE NEXT GROUP IS (C O) WITH A PEAK (0 0).
 THE NEXT GROUP IS (C H 3) WITH A PEAK (3 0).
 THIS IS THE SOLUTION.
IS THIS WHAT YOU INTENDED?  :YES
PLEASE INPUT YOUR STMTS
:IF THE NEXT GROUP IS AN EITHER GROUP FOLLOWED BY  A  METHYL  GROUP  THEN
THIS WOULD NOT BE POSSIBLE BECAUSE AN ATOM WOULD REMAIN
// THE 'MEANING' EXTRACTED FROM THE STUDENT'S ARGUMENT.
 THE NEXT GROUP IS (O) WITH A PEAK (U U).
 TE NEXT GROUP IS (C H 5) WITH A PEAK (U U).
 THIS TERMINATES THE CHAIN PREMATURELY.
IS THIS WHAT YOU INTENDED?  :YES
PLEASE INPUT YOUR STMTS
:HOWEVER IF THE NEXT GROUP WAS A KETONE FOLLOWED BY A METHYL GROUP  THEN
THAT WOULD BE FINE
// THE 'MEANING' EXTRACTED FROM THE STUDENT'S ARGUMENT.
 THE NEXT GROUP IS (C O) WITH A PEAK (U U).
 THE NEXT GROUP IS (C H 3) WITH A PEAK (U U).
 THIS IS THE SOLUTION.
```

FIG. 3—cont.

```
IS THIS WHAT YOU INTENDED?   :YES
PLEASE INPUT YOUR STMTS
:ARGUMENT COMPLETE

WE ARE NOW CONSIDERING:
  THE NEXT GROUP IS (O) WITH A PEAK (O O).
  IMPOSSIBLE TO FORM FURTHER GROUPS.
ARG. OK AS FAR AS IT GOES
-BUT INCOMPLETE AND AN INCORRECT REASON GIVEN
WE ARE NOW CONSIDERING:
  THE NEXT GROUP IS (C O) WITH A PEAK (O O).
  THE NEXT GROUP IS (C H 3) WITH A PEAK (3 O).
  THIS IS THE SOLUTION.
THIS ARGUMENT IS COMPLETELY CORRECT
WE ARE NOW CONSIDERING:
  THE NEXT GROUP IS (O) WITH A PEAK (U U).
  THE NEXT GROUP IS (C H 3) WITH A PEAK (U U).
  THIS TERMINATES THE CHAIN PREMATURELY.
UNSPECIFIED ITEM IN ARGUMENT
  THE NEXT GROUP IS (O) WITH A PEAK (U U).
WHICH WE HAVE NOTED BUT WILL ACCEPT
UNSPECIFIED ITEM IN ARGUMENT
  THE NEXT GROUP IS (C H 3) WITH A PEAK (U U).
WHICH WE HAVE NOTED BUT WILL ACCEPT
THIS ARGUMENT IS COMPLETELY CORRECT
WE ARE NOW CONSIDERING:
  THE NEXT GROUP IS (C O) WITH A PEAK (U U).
  THE NEXT GROUP IS (C H 3) WITH A PEAK (U U).
  THIS IS THE SOLUTION.
UNSPECIFIED ITEM IN ARGUMENT
  THE NEXT GROUP IS (C O) WITH A PEAK (U U).
WHICH WE HAVE NOTED BUT WILL ACCEPT
UNSPECIFIED ITEM IN ARGUMENT
  THE NEXT GROUP IS (C H 3) WITH A PEAK (U U).
WHICH WE HAVE NOTED BUT WILL ACCEPT
THIS ARGUMENT IS COMPLETELY CORRECT
DO YOU WISH TO SEE THE REASONING CHAINS WHICH YOU DID NOT EXPLORE:NO
DO YOU WISH TO CONTINUE:NO

$
STOP
PARSES TO:(STOP)
ANOTHER PROBLEM?:NO
**!
```

FIG 3—cont.

corresponding dialogue in Fig. 1. As this represents the *complete* systems protocol there are a few additional interactions which are concerned with making ASSERTIONs and leaving the system—these are however clearly commented. Note that it is *not* possible at present to deal with ARGUMENTs which contain Global ASSERTIONs. This point will be discussed in some further detail in section 2.4. We shall now consider the components of the current system in some greater detail.

2.1. AN OUTLINE SPECIFICATION OF HOW THE FSR MODES OPERATE

Figure 4 shows schematically how the FSR modes operate. The student is asked for an EXPLANATION of his ASSERTION, or part of the ASSERTION, and gives that EXPLANATION in Natural Language, NLst. The Natural Language interface abstracts, from this, the Formal Language statements, FLst. Similarly, the domain

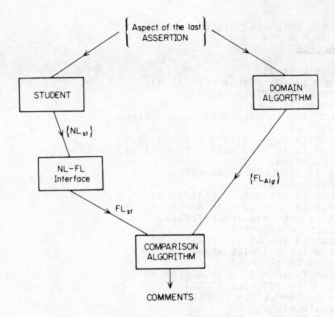

FIG. 4. Shows schematically how the FSR modes operate.

algorithm works the same problem in a special mode which returns a TRACE which contains the statements FLalg. The two sets of FL statements, i.e. the TRACEs, are compared by means of the domain specific Comparison Algorithm which returns a series of comments on the User's EXPLANATION. In the next two sections we shall describe in some more detail the Comparison Algorithm and the NL-FL interface.

2.2. THE COMPARISON ALGORITHM

The TRACE returned by the algorithm essentially will contain all possible solution paths. Thus, in the case of the molecule which we have been considering, given that the first 2 ASSERTIONs have been made, the TRACE would be:

((ASSERTION5 ASSERTION6 F1)
(ASSERTION3 ASSERTION4 F0))

The Comparison Algorithm consists of 3 stages: stage2 is only entered if a match is not found at stage1, similarly stage3 is only entered if stage2 fails. The stages are as follows.

(i) Look for the FLst in the TRACE returned by the algorithm. FACTs which match except for having a group or a peak unspecified are accepted (but noted by the system). Similarly, the algorithm accepts incompletely specified DEDUCTIONs (failure messages) and reports incorrect ones.†

(ii) Hypothesize possible EXPLANATIONs assuming that the student may have omitted some of the FACTs which he considered to be redundant as common with his

---

† These comments are currently embedded in the program; the Comparison Algorithm could profitably be restructured so as to be driven by a series of condition-action rules.

previous ARGUMENT. Thus the algorithm initially hypothesizes the ARGUMENT

$$(CONS\ (CAR\ PREVIOUS\text{-}ARG)\ CURRENT\text{-}ARG)$$

If this ARGUMENT is not found in the TRACE, the algorithm forms a second ARGUMENT using the first 2 ASSERTIONs from the PREVIOUS-ARGUMENT. This process is continued until a match is found or until the PREVIOUS-ARGUMENT is exhausted. If the algorithm finds an acceptable ARGUMENT, the system asks the student whether or not this is what he had intended, if it is, a detailed comparison is performed by stage 1 of this algorithm. If the reconstructed argument is not acceptable, then the search is continued.

As the matching of ARGUMENTs (in this case the hypothesized ARGUMENT and an ARGUMENT returned by the TRACE) is still performed by the algorithm outlined in (i), an ASSERTION will be acceptable even if the failure message or the groups or the peaks are only partially specified. The Problem Solution Graph for a more complex molecule is given in Fig. 5. Figure 6 shows the systems protocol for someone exploring the various EXPLANATIONs:

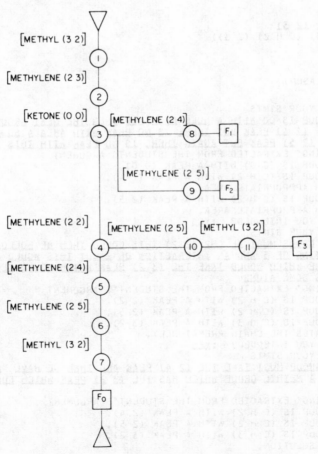

FIG. 5. Problem solution graph for the larger problem.

EXPLANATION1 is ASSERTION3, ASSERTION8 and FAILURE2
   and ASSERTION9 and FAILURE2

EXPLANATION2 is ASSERTION4, ASSERTION10, ASSERTION11 and
   FAILURE3

EXPLANATION3 is ASSERTION5, ASSERTION6, ASSERTION7 and
   FAILURE0

That is, in the second ARGUMENT of EXPLANATION1, ASSERTION3 has been omitted. Similarly ASSERTION3 is assumed in EXPLANATION2 and in

```
**!
CALL PSM
INPUT PROBLEM NUMBER:9
THE MOLECULAR FORMULA IS
(C 7 H 14 0)
IN OUR NOTATION THE SPECTRUM OF YOUR MOLECULE IS
((6 2) (2 5) (2 4) (2 3) (2 2))
$
THE HEAD IS CH3 (3 2)
PARSES TO:((H) (C H 3) (3 2))
CORRECT
$
THEN JOIN CH2 (2 3)
PARSES TO:((J) (C H 2) (2 3))
CORRECT
$
REASON
PARSES TO:(REASON)


PLEASE INPUT YOUR STMTS
:THE NEXT GROUP IS CO WITH A NULL PEAK AND THEN THE NEXT GROUP COULD  BE
CH2  WITH  A  (2 4) PEAK BUT THERE IS NO PEAK WITH AREA 4 SO IT COULD BE
CH2 WITH THE (2 5) PEAK BUT AGAIN THERE IS NO PEAK WITH THIS AREA
// THE 'MEANING' EXTRACTED FROM THE STUDENTS ARGUMENT
  THE NEXT GROUP IS (C 0) WITH A PEAK (0 0).
  THE NEXT GROUP IS (C H 2) WITH A PEAK (2 4).
  NO PEAK WITH APPROPRIATE AREA.
  THE NEXT GROUP IS (C H 2) WITH A PEAK (2 5).
  NO PEAK WITH APPROPRIATE AREA.
IS THIS WHAT YOU INTENDED?  :YES
PLEASE INPUT YOUR STMTS
:THE NEXT GROUP MUST BE CH2 (2 2) THIS COULD THEN BE FOLLOWED BY  CH2
WITH A SPLITTING OF 5 AND AN INTERACTION OF 2 BUT THIS WOULD BE FOLLOWED
BY A CH3 GROUP WHICH WOULD TAKE THE (3 2) PEAK WHICH WOULD TERMINATE THE
CHAIN LEAVING SOME ATOMS
// THE 'MEANING' EXTRACTED FROM THE STUDENT'S ARGUMENT
  THE NEXT GROUP IS (C H 2) WITH A PEAK (2 2).
  THE NEXT GROUP IS (C H 2) WITH A PEAK (2 5).
  THE NEXT GROUP IS (C H 3) WITH A PEAK (3 2).
  THIS TERMINATES THE CHAIN PREMATURELY.
IS THIS WHAT YOU INTENDED?  :YES
PLEASE INPUT YOUR STMTS
:SO THE CH2 GROUP MUST TAKE THE (2 4) PEAK AND THEN WE HAVE  CH2  (2 5)
AND  FINALLY A METHYL GROUP WHICH HAS THE (3 2) PEAK WHICH COMPLETES THE
ANSWER
// THE 'MEANING' EXTRACTED FROM THE STUDENT'S ARGUMENT
  THE NEXT GROUP IS (C H 2) WITH A PEAK (2 4).
  THE NEXT GROUP IS (C H 2) WITH A PEAK (2 5).
  THE NEXT GROUP IS (C H 3) WITH A PEAK (3 2).
  THIS IS THE SOLUTION.
```

FIG. 6. Shows the bactracking facility being used with a larger problem (again user replied are underlined).

```
IS THIS WHAT YOU INTENDED?  :YES
PLEASE INPUT YOUR STMTS
:ARGUMENT COMPLETED

WE ARE NOW CONSIDERING:
  THE NEXT GROUP IS (C O) WITH A PEAK (O O).
  THE NEXT GROUP IS (C H 2) WITH A PEAK (2 4).
  NO PEAK WITH APPROPRIATE AREA.
THIS ARGUMENT IS COMPLETELY CORRECT
WE ARE NOW CONSIDERING:
  THE NEXT GROUP IS (C O) WITH A PEAK (O O).
  THE NEXT GROUP IS (C H 2) WITH A PEAK (2 5).
  NO PEAK WITH APPROPRIATE AREA.
AN ARG WHICH WE HAVE RECONSTRUCTED FROM THE PARTIAL ONE YOU GAVE
IS THAT WHAT YOU INTENDED?:YES
THIS ARGUMENT IS COMPLETELY CORRECT
WE ARE NOW CONSIDERING:
  THE NEXT GROUP IS (C O) WITH A PEAK (O O).
  THE NEXT GROUP IS (C H 2) WITH A PEAK (2 2).
  THE NEXT GROUP IS (C H 2) WITH A PEAK (2 5).
  THE NEXT GROUP IS (C H 3) WITH A PEAK (3 2).
  THIS TERMINATES THE CHAIN PREMATURELY.
AN ARG WHICH WE HAVE RECONSTRUCTED FROM THE PARTIAL ONE YOU GAVE
IS THAT WHAT YOU INTENDED?:YES
THIS ARGUMENT IS COMPLETELY CORRECT
WE ARE NOW CONSIDERING:
  THE NEXT GROUP IS (C O) WITH A PEAK (O O).
  THE NEXT GROUP IS (C H 2) WITH A PEAK (2 2).
  THE NEXT GROUP IS (C H 2) WITH A PEAK (2 4).
  THE NEXT GROUP IS (C H 2) WITH A PEAK (2 5).
  THE NEXT GROUP IS (C H 3) WITH A PEAK (3 2).
  THIS IS THE SOLUTION.
AN ARG WHICH WE HAVE RECONSTRUCTED FROM THE PARTIAL ONE YOU GAVE
IS THAT WHAT YOU INTENDED?:YES
THIS ARGUMENT IS COMPLETELY CORRECT
DO YOU WISH TO SEE THE REASONING CHAINS WHICH YOU DID NOT EXPLORE:NO
DO YOU WISH TO CONTINUE:NO
$
STOP
PARSES TO:(STOP)
ANOTHER PROBLEM?:NO
**!
```

FIG. 6—cont.

EXPLANATION3, ASSERTION3 and ASSERTION4 are assumed. Figure 6 shows that these missing ASSERTIONs are hypothesised by this algorithm, which uses the last ARGUMENT found in FLalg as a basis for reconstructing further partial ARGUMENTs.

(iii) The ARGUMENT is subjected to a detailed analysis as clearly it contains an inconsistent ASSERTION. (All consistent solution paths are contained in the TRACE which is returned by the algorithm.)

2.3. THE NATURAL LANGUAGE INTERFACE

Burton (1976) has argued forceably *why* one requires a NL interface for teaching systems, namely so that the User is free to concentrate on the task in hand; this same author has argued too, that the interface should be "friendly" and should accept abbreviations, spelling errors and should accept semantically meaningful but syntactically invalid sentences. (The latter implies that the parser is able to skip over noise words and looks for *semantic* classes rather than syntactic entities and so shares many of the characteristics of the SOPHIE parser (Brown & Burton, 1975). Indeed, this approach to building NL interfaces derives from the work of Brown and Burton). The parser which we have implemented has the characteristics listed above: in addition as we are dealing with fairly complex ARGUMENTs we felt it was essential to have the facility to interactively build up, and amend EXPLANATIONs (Sleeman & Hendley, 1978).

The PARSER which we have implemented has 3 phases—the PRE-PARSER, the PARSER itself and the POST-PARSER. The essential tasks of the PRE-PARSER are to remove anticipated noise words from the input and to *segment* the EXPLANATION into ARGUMENTs and to further segment the several ARGUMENTs into ARGUMENT-COMPONENTS. The PARSER, which is implemented as a set of BCPL functions, scans the ARGUMENT-COMPONENTs looking for the anticipated semantic classes. If these are found then it returns the appropriate FL statements. If the PARSER is not successful then the scan is repeated, applying the spelling correction algorithm to each of the unrecognized words and finally by omitting the unrecognized words. If the parse still fails the PRE-PARSER is entered and a search is made for an alternative segmentation and the parse is repeated. When the input cannot be further segmented the PARSER provides the following feed-back:

(i) the next word in the best partial match;
(ii) the expected top-level semantic class.

The user then has the opportunity to retype the offending statement and also to retain or discard previous and subsequent statements in his input. After a statement has been amended the complete EXPLANATION is re-analysed.

The POST-PARSER in this system groups ARGUMENT-COMPONENTs into ARGUMENTs, presents the user with the NL equivalent of the FL statements and asks the user if they are what he intended. If this is rejected then he is asked to retype the EXPLANATION. The reasons for giving the user a chance to comment on the acceptability of the FL statements extracted from his input is threefold: firstly, this prevents detailed analysis of erroneous EXPLANATIONs, secondly it was felt that the "paraphrase" might help the user restate ARGUMENTs which are mis-handled by the system and thirdly it has been a *very* useful diagnostic tool during the debugging phase of the grammar. Figure 7 shows the user amending a component of his EXPLANA-TION and the use of the spelling correction algorithm, both on the original and amended EXPLANATION. We also note that the fourth component of his EXPLANATION would initially have been extracted as three components, (because "and" and "which" are treated as delimiter words) but the system combines these together when it discovers that this produces a more complete parse.

The facilities provided by this interface are very analogous to those provided by the more "portable" LIFER system (Hendrix, 1977) which has been designed to be a general NL interface. LIFER has the very useful ability to define both synonyms and paraphrases but it is not clear that this system would be able to cope with noise words which occur in this domain or that it would be able to cope with the situation where if concept A is encountered then B should follow, and the system must return a null value for B if it is not found after A. (This facility is essential in our case as it enables us to handle only partially specified ARGUMENTs; as we have seen, either the group or the peak can be omitted and the ASSERTION is still accepted.) The synonym and paraphrase facilities of LIFER are very interesting and it could be that incorporating these into our basic parser would have led to simplifications in the domain grammar. Only experience will tell whether naïve users will be able to handle such facilities.

2.4. POSSIBLE EXTENSIONS TO THE FSR MODES

The objective of this part of the project has been to analyse the EXPLANATIONs which users have given about a particular aspect of their earlier response, their

```
**!
CALL PSM
INPUT PROBLEM NUMBER:2
THE MOLECULAR FORMULA IS
(C 4 H 8 O)
IN OUR NOTATION THE SPECTRUM OF YOUR MOLECULE IS
((3 2) (3 0) (2 3))
$
REASON
PARSES TO:(REASON)
PLEASE INPUT YOUR STMTS
:THE FIRSTGROUP IS METHYL FOLLOWED BY CH2 WITH THE
(2 3) PEAK AND THEN WITH THE NULL PEAK WE HAVE THE KETONE
GROUP AND THE METHYLL GROUP WHICH HAS AN INTERACTION OF 3
AND ASPLITINGOF O WHICH IS THE SOLUTION
FIRSTGROUP = (FIRST GROUP)
METHYLL = METHYL
YOUR STMTS WERE SUCCESSFULLY PARSED UPTO
 (AND ASPLITINGOF O)
I DID NOT RECOGNISE ASPLITINGOF.
I WAS LOOKING FOR A GROUP OR A PEAK.
DO YOU WISH TO RETAIN THE FOLLOWING?
 THE FIRST GROUP IS METHYL.
 FOLLOWED BY CH2 WITH THE (2 3) PEAK.
 AND THEN WITH THE NULL PEAK WE HAVE THE KETONE GROUP.
 AND THE METHYL GROUP WHICH HAS AN INTERACTION OF 3.
:YES
DO YOU WISH TO RETYPE THIS STMT?
 AND ASPLITINGOF O.
:YES
:AND A SPLITING OF O
DO YOU WISH TO RETAIN THE FOLLOWING?
 WHICH IS THE SOLUTION.
:YES
YOU HAVE BUILT UP THE FOLLOWING
 THE FIRST GROUP IS METHYL.
 FOLLOWED BY CH2 WITH THE (2 3) PEAK.
 AND THEN WITH THE NULL PEAK WE HAVE THE KETONE GROUP.
 AND THE METHYL GROUP WHICH HAS AN INTERACTION OF 3.
 AND A SPLITING OF O.
 WHICH IS THE SOLUTION.
IS THIS WHAT YOU INTENDED?
:YES
SPLITING = SPLITTING
 THE FIRST GROUP IS (C H 3) WITH A PEAK (O O).
 THE NEXT GROUP IS (C H 2) WITH A PEAK (2 3).
 THE NEXT GROUP IS (C O) WITH A PEAK (O O).
 THE NEXT GROUP IS (C H 3) WITH A PEAK (3 0).
 THIS IS THE SOLUTION.
IS THIS WHAT YOU INTENDED?   :YES
PLEASE INPUT YOUR STMTS
:ARGUMENT COMPLETE
```

FIG. 7. Shows various features of the NL interface.

```
WE ARE NOW CONSIDERING:
 THE FIRST GROUP IS (C H 3) WITH A PEAK (U U).
 THE NEXT GROUP IS (C H 2) WITH A PEAK (2 3).
 THE NEXT GROUP IS (C 0) WITH A PEAK (0 0).
 THE NEXT GROUP IS (C H 3) WITH A PEAK (3 0).
 THIS IS THE SOLUTION.
UNSPECIFIED ITEM IN ARGUMENT
 THE FIRST GROUP IS (C H 3) WITH A PEAK (U U).
WHICH WE HAVE NOTED BUT WILL ACCEPT
THIS ARGUMENT IS COMPLETELY CORRECT
DO YOU WISH TO SEE THE REASONING CHAINS WHICH YOU DID NOT EXPLORE:NO
DO YOU WISH TO CONTINUE:NO
$
STOP
PARSES TO:(STOP)
ANOTHER PROBLEM?:NO
**!
```

FIG. 7—*cont.*

ASSERTION. But one might well ask questions about the robustness of the system and the likely problems which would be encountered if one were to allow a completely "raw" undergraduate chemist to converse with the system in the same way as he might discuss these same issues with a human tutor. Three types of extensions seem worth considering:

    (i) discussing further aspects of the algorithm;
    (ii) discussing the same aspects of the algorithm, but accommodating a greater range of expression;
    (iii) dealing with other *types* of omission.

Aspect (i) is considered a major draw-back of the current system and work is in hand to remedy this. Briefly we propose expressing the whole algorithm in a single data-structure which can be both executed and used as a basis for explanation (Sleeman & Hendley, 1978).†

    (ii) Here we would wish to point out that the grammar has already been extensively modified as a result of "field trials", and that these modifications have been straight forward to carry out because the grammar is written as a series of (relatively) independent functions.

    (iii) To consider this point, we shall need to understand how the various components in the system, namely the NL-FL interface and the Comparison Algorithm interact. It is worthwhile recalling that the NL-FL interface expects to find concept B having found concept A and if it in fact encounters concept C it will return a null value for concept B. The FL statements extracted from the Student's EXPLANATION thus contains a series of concepts and their values or an indication that no value was returned for an expected concept. The Comparison Algorithm copes with the following types of omissions:

    (a) unspecified and wrong failure messages;
    (b) partially specified ASSERTIONs;

† The MYCIN project (Shortliffe *et al.*, 1973) has shown one way to achieve this.

(c) partially specified ARGUMENTs (the system copes as we have seen with the situation where the user backtracks but does not repeat the "common" FACTs).

Essentially, we are saying that we have analysed a series of protocols and noted the various ways in which FACTs and DEDUCTIONs are expressed and have noted the (logical) omissions which were commonly made. The NL-FL interface which has been implemented is able to cope with many of these linguistic variants and with incomplete arguments; similarly the Comparison Algorithm is able to cope with the "imperfect" FL statements derived from these EXPLANATIONs.

The relationship between the various components is brought out nicely by considering two further extensions. Namely how to enhance the system to comment on ARGUMENTs which have ASSERTIONs missing from the "middle' of a series of ASSERTIONs (should this be thought desirable) and secondly by considering the use of the global ASSERTIONs which we noted in the observed protocols of Fig. 1.

The first enhancement merely involves modifying the Comparison Algorithm so that it will record a match between strings of FACTs such as F1F4 and F1F2F3F4. Trivial. The second case requires the *definition* of a new construction in the formal language to represent a Global ASSERTION, the interface must then be enhanced so that it includes a procedure which "spots" such global ASSERTIONs. Finally, the Comparison Algorithm would need to be enhanced to deal with the new FL statements and to process them appropriately. Namely, is the Global ASSERTION consistent with the resources remaining and does the conclusion itself, this time an ASSERTION (or the negation of an ASSERTION), follow from the global ASSERTION. Indeed one could argue that this particular case does not very easily fit into the framework which has been used to analyse the other FACT-DEDUCTION pairs and so this would be a major enhancement.

It seems more than likely that extensive field-trials would reveal still further forms of ARGUMENTs which have so far escaped our attention. We have however considered the following enhancements.

3. Enhancements

3.1. DISCERNING WHAT THE STUDENT IS ACTUALLY DISCUSSING

In the protocols discussed in this paper we have shown the user essentially replying with the information requested and at the level of detail anticipated by the algorithm. Namely, the user gave as his EXPLANATIONs a series of ASSERTIONs and a single failure message. Typically, however we might expect the user to reply with information which is totally irrelevant, to give reasons which lead the user to the ASSERTION or to give an irrelevant EXPLANATION. Analysing such protocols is obviously more difficult and we have suggested that this problem is essentially that of finding the appropriate "focus of attention".†‡ Work on this topic is progressing and will be reported later.

† It is likely that if the system has a very wrong expectation for an EXPLANATION then the parser will not produce an acceptable parse, and that there will be considerable interaction between the parser and the FSR module.

‡ A similar approach has been suggested by Miller & Goldstein (1976), their system will attempt to find an acceptable interpretation (parse in their terminology) for the student protocol given a series of ordered outline plans (which can be variants or "buggie" plans).

3.2. THE SEGMENTATION ALGORITHM

In section 2.3 we outlined the current segmentation algorithm. This is clearly a difficult problem and there are several situations which the algorithm cannot handle, namely:

$$F_{11} \quad F_{12} \quad \ldots \quad D_1 \quad D_2 \quad F_{21} \quad F_{22} \quad \ldots \quad F_{2m}$$
$$D_1 \quad F_{11} \quad \ldots \quad F_{1n} \quad F_{21} \quad F_{22} \quad \quad \ldots \quad F_{2m} \quad D_2$$

The first of these two cases is relatively straight forward to deal with as we would use the first DEDUCTION as the separator. The second is more difficult because one would need to know how many FACTs were required to "support" a particular DEDUC-TION. It is not possible to decide this issue in this case without analysing in detail the solutions returned by the algorithm. In the case of the chains of reasons we are helped by the fact that the FACTs are usually correctly ordered, but in a domain like the selection of a group where it is not possible to make this assumption it would be difficult if not impossible to do a satisfactory segmentation. Again the situation would be even more complex if we allowed certain FACTs to be omitted. However, given that we have access to various knowledge sources (including the number of FACTs required to "support" a particular DEDUCTION and the nature of these FACTs) we could *probably* suggest a possible segmentation to the user and ask for his comment (as we did in the case of hypothesized ARGUMENTs from incomplete ones).

3.3. PARSING WITH A MORE DEMANDING GRAMMAR

The parser which we are currently using has the ability to skip over a pre-defined number of noise words. Given this approach there is a fear that some highly significant detail could have been overlooked in the course of such a parse and so we suggest that the input should be reparsed with a more demanding grammar. (Having found that a parse exists one might argue that one is then prepared to invest further effort.) Ideally, one would be able to guide the "refined" parse by the output from the initial phase. Taken to its logical conclusion this suggestion could lead to a very different approach to parsing NL than has been previously tried.

4. Conclusions

The *raison d'être* for this piece of work was to see whether it would be possible to implement a system which would understand a User's EXPLANATION of his algorithm.† Our reason for wanting to do this was that we were convinced that this is a powerful teaching mode, and at the same time presented many interesting problems in producing a suitable natural language interface. From the point of view of pure NL work we could have been deemed to be undertaking a purely "engineering" task. On the other hand the analysis of the dialogues which we have given and the "heuristics" which we have built into the system to cope with incomplete arguments, may serve to reinforce several very important points which will have to be accommodated before systems which are in any sense "natural" can be built. We have seen many examples of people omitting what they considered to be *irrelevant* detail from their ARGUMENT,

---

† In a sense, the FSR module is producing automatically a model of a section of the student's algorithm, and thus this work is related to that of Brown & Burton (1977), Carr & Goldstein (1977) and Self (1974). This aspect of the PSM is discussed further in Sleeman (1979).

and we have designed our system so that it accepts these incomplete ARGUMENTs. The Comparison Algorithm accepts an incomplete ARGUMENT if and only if, it contains sufficient information to distinguish it from other ARGUMENTs in the domain (i.e. those returned in the TRACE). This seems to be an adequate discriminatory criterion for this domain, but we readily acknowledge that the problem of deciding what is and what is not relevant, is in general formidable.

Bobrow *et al.* (1977) have analysed dialogues which arise in another domain namely that of a Travel Agency and have also pointed out the incomplete and "unexpected" nature of many of these dialogues. Their frame-based system, GUS goes some considerable way to producing a system which can hold a "natural" dialogue in that domain and is highly suggestive about the solution of the more general problem. Similarly, Collins and Carbonell have analysed problem-orientated teaching dialogues and have noted that the dialogues contained a number of incomplete statements, and further they noted that the tutors were often able to produce explanations, even where they had incomplete information. These authors concluded their paper (Carbonell & Collins, 1973) with the wry comment that their ultimate objective was to implement a system which was as fuzzy thinking as a human tutor. We have similar aspirations for our own system.

This work was started when one of us, DHS, was associated with Professor R. F. Simmons' research group in Austin, Texas and was partly supported by grant number NSF 509X; similarly RJH has been supported by an SRC studentship. This system has been implemented on the Computer Based Learning Project's MODULAR ONE computer, and we are particularly grateful to A. J. Cole for programming assistance. We are also grateful for the comments which Ira Goldstein made on an earlier draft.

References

BOBROW, D. G. *et al.* (1977). GUS, A frame-driven dialogue system. *AI Journal*, **8**, 155–173.
BROWN, J. S. & BURTON, R. R. (1975). Multiple representation of knowledge for tutorial reasoning. In BOBROW, D. & COLLINS, A., Eds, *Representation and Understanding*. New York: Academic Press.
BROWN, J. S. & BURTON, R. R. (1978). Diagnostic models for procedural bugs in basic mathematical skills. *Cognitive Science*, **2**, 155–192.
BURTON, R. R. (1976). Semantic grammar: an engineering technique for constructing natural language understanding systems. *BBN Report No. 3453*.
CARR, B. & GOLDSTEIN, I. P. (1977). Overlays: a theory of modelling for CAI. *MIT AI memo 406*.
CARBONELL, J. R. & COLLINS, A. (1973). Natural semantics in AI. *Proceedings of IJCAI3*, pp. 344–351.
HENDRIX, G. (1977). LIFER: A natural language interface facility. *SIGART Newsletter*, February pp. 25–26.
MILLER, M. L. & GOLDSTEIN, I. P. (1976). PAZATN: a linguistic approach to automatic analysis of elementary programming protocols. *MIT AI Memo 388*.
PASK, G. (1975). TEACHBACK. In *Cybernetics of Human Learning and Performance*. Hutchinson.
SELF, J. A. (1974). Student models in CAI. *International Journal of Man–Machine Studies*, **6**, 261–276.

SHORTLIFFE, E. H. *et al.* (1973). An AI program to advise physicians regarding antimicrobial therapy. *Computers in Biomedical Research*, **6**, 544–560.

SLEEMAN, D. H. (1975). A problem-solving monitor for a deductive reasoning task. *International Journal of Man–Machine Studies*, **7**, 183–211.

SLEEMAN, D. H. (1979). Some current topics in intelligent teaching systems. *AISB Quarterly*, **33**, 22–27.

SLEEMAN, D. H. & HENDLEY, R. J. (1978). Following student reasoning. *University of Leeds Computer Studies Report*, **1**.

6. A structured planning and debugging environment for elementary programming†

MARK L. MILLER

Artificial Intelligence Laboratory, Massachusetts Institute of Technology, Cambridge, Mass. 02139, U.S.A.

How could an appropriately structured environment facilitate the acquisition of programming skills? Significant theoretical strides are needed before human-quality performance can be expected from a computer-based programming tutor. As an intermediate step, a system has been implemented which serves primarily as an editing language and diligent clerk. However, it differs from conventional programming environments in two crucial ways: (1) it interacts with the student using a vocabulary of concepts about planning and debugging, derived from an explicit model of the design process; and (2) it actively prompts the student with a menu of design alternatives, within the overall framework of a mixed-initiative dialogue. The current system is not a tutor; but the process of implementing and testing it has been instrumental in refining our model of the design process, thereby bringing us a step closer to realizing a computer-based programming tutor.

1. Introduction: a vehicle for studying programming knowledge

The astute employer would rather hire a skilled programmer with no background in FORTRAN, to write FORTRAN programs, than a new graduate trained specifically in FORTRAN. Why? That many languages have similar constructs, and that the veteran will know what to look for in converting to the new language, are only partial answers. What is it that the proficient programmer knows, that the beginner does not? The neophyte lacks knowledge of style, of strategy, of how to organize work on a large project, of how programs evolve, and of how to track down bugs.

This paper reports on an investigation of this knowledge, and describes a model which formalizes it as sets of rules. In accord with the above intuitions, only the lowest level rules in the model deal with the constructs of particular programming languages. The most important rules deal with plans (which are independent of the detailed form of the code), debugging techniques, solution-order (search) strategies for choosing what to work on next, and methods for exploring interactions among design alternatives.

As a vehicle for pursuing this investigation, we have implemented a computer environment called *Spade-0* which interacts with students who are learning to plan and debug elementary programs. Spade-0 prompts the student through an hierarchical planning process, encouraging the student to postpone premature commitment to the detailed form of the code. It explores the hypothesis that articulating one's problem-solving strategies facilitates learning, by providing a vocabulary of concepts for describing plans, bugs, and debugging techniques. It handles the routine bookkeeping tasks,

† This paper describes joint work carried out in collaboration with my doctoral thesis advisor, Ira P. Goldstein, whose significant contributions to its form and content are gratefully acknowledged. The research was performed at the Artificial Intelligence Laboratory of the Massachusetts Institute of Technology. It was supported by the National Science Foundation under Grant SED77-19279. The author would like to thank John Seely Brown and Derek Sleeman for editorial suggestions significantly improving this paper.

and understands commands which edit the plan–rather than the code–of the student's program.

Our long term research objective is to construct "artificially intelligent" learning environments capable of human-like tutoring. Our approach to this difficult goal is to construct less ambitious *limited didactic systems* as subgoals. These intermediate systems are tutorial in nature, but limited in scope. They do not display the insight or sensitivity which we ultimately desire, but they help us to explore various facets of cognitive and pedagogical theories. Spade-0 in particular has been specifically designed to support systematic variation of its configuration of features, an essential property both for validating the environment as a whole, and for assessing the relative contributions of each module.

2. Turtle Graphics serves as an example programming task

Although our investigation has touched on several problem domains, our most extensive efforts have fallen within the realm of Papert's (1971) "Logo Turtle" language for simple graphics programming. Turtle Graphics has been a helpful source of examples because: (1) the complexity of typical Logo programs is manageable, even though the potential difficulty ranges over a wide spectrum; and (2) we have ready access to considerable student performance data for introductory Logo sessions.

The minimal Logo turtle language consists of these commands:

FORWARD ⟨number⟩   ; Turtle moves ⟨number⟩ steps in current direction;
BACK ⟨number⟩   ; Turtle moves ⟨number⟩ steps in opposite direction;
RIGHT ⟨number⟩   ; Turtle turns ⟨number⟩ degrees clockwise;
LEFT ⟨number⟩   ; Turtle turns ⟨number⟩ degrees counter-clockwise;
PENDOWN   ; Subsequent FORWARDs, BACKs draw lines;
PENUP   ; Subsequent FORWARDs, BACKs do not draw lines.

The user extends the available set of commands by defining new procedures. Each new procedure may be defined to accept zero or more formal parameters; each line of the new procedure is either a call to one of the Logo primitives, or an invocation (with actual parameters) of some user-defined Logo procedure. Conditional statements (IF—THEN—ELSE) and looping constructs (WHILE—DO) are also available.

Figure 1 shows a Logo procedure and the "Wishingwell" picture which it draws; this serves as our example task. (WELL and ROOF are user procedures defined in the same fashion.)

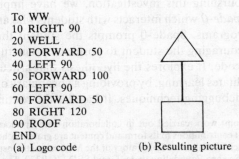

```
To WW
10 RIGHT 90
20 WELL
30 FORWARD 50
40 LEFT 90
50 FORWARD 100
60 LEFT 90
70 FORWARD 50
80 RIGHT 120
90 ROOF
END
```
(a) Logo code   (b) Resulting picture

FIG. 1. Wishingwell: a typical introductory Logo project.

A number of students (generally high school) have been asked to solve this task. Our usual procedure is to ask them to first describe the picture in English, then to draw it by hand. Next we ask them to think aloud as they design the program using the Logo system. We collect a verbal protocol as well as the typewritten transcript of the session. Except for the omission of typographical errors, the solution shown in Fig. 2 is typical.

```
E001    ? TO WW
E002    >  10 TREE
E003    >  20 WELL
E004    >  END

E005    ? TO WELL
E006    >  10 REPEAT 4 [20 30]
E007    >  20 FORWARD 100
E008    >  30 RIGHT 90
E009    >  END

E010    ? RUN WW
E011    ? CLEARSCREEN
E012    ? RUN TREE
E013    ? RUN WELL

E014    ? EDIT WW
E015    >  15 LEFT 90
E016    >  17 BACK 50
E017    >  END
```

FIG. 2. A typical student solution.

3. Modelling elementary programming

Spade-0 is based on an information processing model which accounts for this type of protocol.† While a complete description of this model is beyond the scope of the present paper, this section provides sufficient background information to explain the operation of Spade-0 and to argue that its implementation has been instrumental in suggesting refinements to the model.

The first thing which we notice about the protocol is that the problem-solving behavior can be partitioned into distinct phases or "episodes" (Polya, 1965). Even before the typescript begins, there is a phase of understanding the problem, that is, of converting the pictorial representation into some internal symbolic representation. The model does not address this: it requires as input a symbolic representation of the specifications for the desired picture (à la Goldstein, 1974) such as is shown in Fig. 3.

Parts of WW: Roof, Pole, Well.
Properties of Roof: Triangle, Horizontal.
Properties of Pole: Line, Vertical.
Properties of Well: Square, Horizontal
Relations Between Roof and Pole: Above, T-Connected.
Relations Between Pole and Well: Above, T-Connected.

FIG. 3. Specifications for Wishingwell.

† More precisely, we have devised a framework within which we model this and similar protocols. One model within that framework corresponds to the "ideal" student; other models are viewed as perturbations from the ideal student, and represent individual students. The current system does not use individual student models; however its design was derived using this overall framework, and a planned system will include provisions for automatically inducing individual student models.

(The specification language is based on common-sense predicates such as "is-a" and "is-part-of", and geometry-specific relations such as "is-above" and "is-connected-to".)

After understanding the problem, there is a phase of defining a procedure (E001–E009). The model claims that this definitional phase is the externally observable manifestation of an internal process of Plan Refinement. Other phases involve trying out the procedure (E010), localizing an error or "bug" (E011–E013), and repairing a bug (E014–E017). A separate "mode" is used to model each such phase: a mode is a packet of rules with its own interpreter. For example, Localization Mode is a set of rules which become active when Tryout Mode has discovered a bug, its job is to decide which part of the program is responsible for the error.

"Control Mode" is responsible for interrupting the normal flow of operations to switch modes, when appropriate. Control Mode includes rules such as:

(a) if in Tryout Mode and an error occurs, enter Localization Mode with a description of the error;

(b) if in Refinement Mode and the definition of a subprocedure is completed, enter Tryout Mode for that subprocedure, and

(c) if in Repair Mode and the underlying cause of the bug was found to be a missing step in the plan, enter Refinement Mode with the specification for that step as goal.

Since all of the rules within a given mode have the same overall purpose, each rule can be expressed more simply; the overall purpose can be procedurally encoded into the interpreter for that particular mode.

The next thing which we notice about the protocol is that there is no obvious relationship between the specifications (Fig. 3) and the code (Fig. 2).† In particular, the top level WW goal has *three* parts, but its code has first *two*, and later *four* steps. A human tutor might say that this student has undergone a *reformulation* process, whereby the problem description has been modified, replacing the original two subgoals of drawing a roof and a pole by the single subgoal of drawing a tree (Fig. 4). The *reason* for doing this is that the student has already written a tree program, which can now be used as a subprocedure. The model formalizes the human tutor's insight using a data structure called the *plan*.

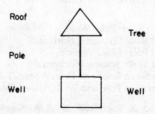

FIG. 4. Reformulating the Wishingwell in terms of a tree.

† Of course, there is no way to be certain that the student viewed the problem exactly as we have represented it in the specifications. However, the informal evidence in typical verbal transcripts tends to support this description.

The model classifies plans according to a particular taxonomy (Fig. 5). At the most general level, there are three categories of planning strategies: *Identification* with previously solved problems; *Decomposition* into simpler sub-problems; and *Reformulation* of the problem description in other terms. At more detailed levels the model provides elaborations of these techniques, specifying, for example, methods for recognizing interactions among sub-goals, and deriving a linear solution. Corresponding to each plan type is a rule specifying how to refine goals of that type.

This lends precision to the notion of the *plan* of a program. The plan is an hierarchical representation of the design choices among alternative plan types which led to the code (Fig. 6). A *chart* (Kaplan, 1973; Kay, 1973) is used to capture the notion of alternative partial plan versions. Its relevance here is that Spade-0 enables the student to access and modify this data structure, which can facilitate debugging or extending the program.†

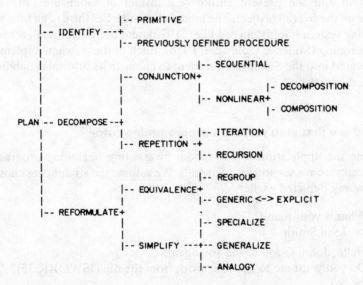

FIG. 5. A taxonomy of plans.

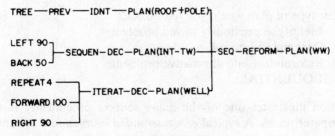

FIG. 6. Plan for WW.

† Assertions must be attached to various nodes of this structure in order to fully describe the plan. This "semantic and pragmatic annotation" is specified by the model but not implemented in Spade-0. (We will return to this point in a later section on the limitations of the current system.)

The model posits that certain types of bugs are an inevitable consequence of rational planning under limited resources and incomplete knowledge. Hence, a model of diagnostic and repair techniques complements the planning model. The diagnosis model traces the underlying causes of program malfunctions to specific erroneous choices during plan refinement mode.

The model is incomplete: a more thorough model would include additional modes, such as a phase of *criticizing* the program after its successful completion. Even if augmented in this way, it would be premature to claim any psychological support for the model. However, informal but detailed analysis of over a dozen student protocols has been encouraging. The resulting plan structures yield insights into the problem-solving behavior which: (a) would not otherwise be apparent; and (b) are consistent with introspective and retrospective accounts (Miller & Goldstein, 1977*b*).

Spade-0 was implemented to explore various aspects of this model. Other papers by Ira Goldstein and the present author (e.g. Miller & Goldstein, 1977*a*) provide perspective on the overall project. The model also underlies the design for an automatic programming system (Goldstein & Miller, 1976), and a protocol analyzer for elementary programming (Miller & Goldstein, 1976). Each of these, when implemented, will be incorporated into the Spade environment to enhance its tutorial capabilities (as will be explained later).

4. Spade-0 is a first step toward a programming tutor

To illustrate the application of the model to assisting beginning programmers, we present excepts from a session with Spade-0. We assume the student has chosen to draw the Wishingwell depicted earlier.

Q1. What is your name?
A1. > John Smith

Q2. Hello, John. Good to see you again.
    Do you want me to get your work from the file (JSWORK 35)?
A2. > No

Q3. OK. What name for the procedure you wish to plan today?
A3. > WW

Q4. What type of plan would you like to use?
    A.   Identify as previously solved problem.
    B.   Decompose into sub-problems.
    C.   Reformulate into alternative problem.
A4. > SEQUENTIAL

This interaction illustrates one of the many sources of difficulty in implementing practical computer tutors. A typical *computer aided instructional* system would reject the student's answer here, because it is not one of the choices which were offered. Yet, a human tutor would have no trouble understanding the student's response in this situation (despite an inherent ambiguity). Spade-0 addresses this by an abbreviation capability, which finds the shortest path between the current rule and the unexpected answer.

Q5. OK. I am assuming PLAN -> DECOMPOSE -> SEQUENTIAL.
    What are the main steps in this sequential plan?

A5. > Well Pole Roof

Q6. Do you want to include a SETUP step?

A6. > Later
    OK, John. I am postponing the [setup] of WW until later.

Q7. What now?

A7. > Go to the second [interface] of the sequential plan.

Q8. Do you want to include this optional interface?

A8. > Yes

One of the difficulties encountered in early versions of the system was that even trivial graphics programs have a considerable number of nodes in the chart structures which represent their plans. Because of this, there seemed to be no convenient way for the user or the system to unambiguously refer to nodes in the evolving structure. Requiring the student to label each node by its unique internal name (e.g. "G00037") was unacceptable. Yet, a design objective was that the student should be able to walk around freely in the structure, examine the choices at various nodes, edit nodes, attach assertions to nodes, and so on. This problem was resolved by two techniques: (1) a more elaborate parser was devised for disambiguating references to nodes; and (2) an advanced display capability was implemented, allowing the plan to appear on the screen, and the current node to be brightened.

Figure 7 shows the display screen at this point in the session. Several "windows" are employed. The teletype part of the interaction occurs on the lower half of the screen. The user's turtle picture is drawn in the upper right corner (currently only the cursor is visible in this region, since no drawing commands have yet been issued). Relegating the turtle display to one corner—rather than allowing it to usurp the entire top of the screen as in standard Logo—leaves several areas free for pedagogical purposes. The user's

```
┌─────────────────────────────────┬─────────────────────────────┐
│       PLANNING CONTEXT:          │       TURTLE DISPLAY:       │
│                                  │                             │
│    1    PLAN(WW)                 │                             │
│    2      DECOMPOSE              │                             │
│    3        SEQUENTIAL           │                             │
│    4 #        [SETUP]            │                             │
│    5 #      MAINSTEP(Well)       │                             │
│    6 #      [INTERFACE]          │                             │
│    7 #      MAINSTEP(Pole)       │                             │
│    8 #      [INTERFACE] ←        │                             │
│    9 #      MAINSTEP(Roof)       │                             │
│   10 #      [CLEANUP]            │                             │
│   11                             │                             │
│   12                             │                             │
│   13                             │                             │
│   14                             │                             │
│   15                             │                             │
│   16                             │                             │
├─────────────────────────────────┴─────────────────────────────┤
│  MODE: PLANNING  ||  EXPLORING: 0  ||  RULE: FRAG → [INTERFACE] │
└─────────────────────────────────────────────────────────────────┘
         Q8. Do you want to include this optional interface?
         A8. > Yes
```

FIG. 7. Spade-0 display screen during planning of WW.

skeletal plan is displayed in the upper left, and a line of "mode" information is available in the center. As the plan is displayed in the upper left, and a line of "mode" information is available in the center. As the plan is refined and modified (by the addition or deletion of nodes), its representation on the screen is updated accordingly. The current goal is brightened (indicated by an arrow), and each pending goal is flagged by the symbol "#". The mode line indicates the current rule mode, the exploration level (to be explained below), and a shorthand representation for rule governing the current interaction.

Note how the system exhorts the user to adhere to an hierarchical refinement process. The student is not distracted from understanding his problem and designing a high level plan, by a necessity to communicate with the machine in low level string-oriented editing commands. Nor do errors of programming language syntax obscure the student's task, since no code is ever typed by hand. Instead, the final program is computed from the student's answers to the multiple choice questions; hence typographical errors can be trivially noticed and immediately corrected.

At each step, Spade-0 chooses an appropriate next goal to pursue; but there is no requirement to accept its choice: interactions 6 and 7 illustrate the student ignoring the system's advice, and selecting a different goal to pursue instead. This illustrates how our desire to obtain feedback about the underlying model constrained the implementation. Although the system always encourages obeying the model, features are provided to allow violating it; and all such features are available at all times.

Enforcing these constraints requires some ingenuity. At the top level, the system contains a flexible driver loop, which invokes a scheduler to suggest which goal to pursue. Associated with each goal is a specific rule which it obeys; typically the rule will generate subgoals, each with a specified rule governing *its* expansion. The driver loop incorporates a powerful escape mechanism that allows the user to ignore the current goal at any time, activating a feature instead. This requires recording the status of each interaction in a global database, so that no information crucial to that interaction is lost if volatile storage (e.g., the push down stack of function invocations) is returned. As a result of this program organization, the dialogue may be interrupted at any point to perform any arbitrary computation; when resumed, Spade-0's knowledge of the user's goals is intact.

Spade-0's flexibility has enabled us to experiment with alternative configurations of features and rules. The system has already undergone several iterations of informal testing and revision, resulting in better formulations of the planning rules, and an improved understanding of the merits of various features. The LATER feature illustrated in the above scenario provides an example.

One of the modes in the underlying model is responsible for choosing which subgoal to work on next. The choice is determined by reconciling the competing indications of a weighted set of *preference rules*. Initially the preference rules favored a primarily top-down, left-to-right solution order. In informal experiments, graduate student subjects found this too restrictive, and used the LATER feature surprisingly often. For example, subjects invariably prefer to solve the POLE of WW *before* the preceding interface step.

To correct this, additional rules were added. At first, the new rules seemed *ad hoc*: other things being equal, solve main steps before interfaces; prefer direct neighbors to non-adjacent goals; prefer left-to-right order; prefer simple goals to more complex goals. In reviewing the new rules, however, a general principle emerged: *design decisions should be made in that order which minimizes the probable scope of future modifications.*

Of course, this *Least-Scope* principle cannot be implemented directly, since one cannot tell in advance what is likely to change. The new rules could not be *replaced* by the principle, but they could be *understood* as heuristics which tend to approximate it. Consider one of these new rules—main steps before interfaces—how does this approximate Least-Scope? One of the most common bugs in sequential plans, prerequisite clobbers brother goal (Sussman, 1973), involves an incorrect ordering of main steps. The repair technique is to re-order the main steps: the bodies of the main steps are unaffected; but interfaces must be re-designed. Likewise, "Top-Down Programming" is an excellent approximation to Least-Scope. But it is only one of several heuristics; in isolation, it is inadequate. The Least-Scope principle in turn suggests further refinements which might otherwise be overlooked: e.g. prefer simple goals to more complex goals *except* when the more complex goal constrains the simpler one.

Consider the following situation. The user is in the process of defining wishingwell. However, prior to completing either the initial SETUP or the first INTERFACE, the user requests execution of the program, obtaining an incorrect picture (Fig. 8). The scenario below illustrates the assistance Spade-0 can provide.

Q9. What now?
A9. > RUN WW

Q10. {Running WW . . . Done.} What now?
A10. > Debug

Debugging WW. The top level of WW contains 7 design decisions
which could be faulty. There are warnings attached to several
nodes in the plan for WW.

According to the model, the planner leaves warnings on nodes for which the design decision was arbitrary, to guide later debugging. This is reflected in Spade-0, in that the user may attach a warning to a node as a reminder of a possible bug. The system also adds warnings on its own when various conditions are satisfied. For example, use of the LATER feature results in a system-generated warning that a node may be incomplete. The presence of a warning increases Spade-0's suspicion that a given node is the locus of an error; and user-generated warnings are given greater weight.

Q11. Do you want to try to diagnose bugs in WW?
A11. > Yes

Q12. What now?
A12. >Warnings?
I am assuming DIAGNOSE –> PLAN? –> WARNINGS?.

The WW plan contains the following warnings:
    The [setup] goal of the sequential plan has not been completed.
    The first [interface] has not been completed.

Q13. What now?
A13. > Repair the [interface] between pole and well.

I see, John. You have concluded that the [interface] between pole and well has a semantic bug: specifically, the missing step, which is syntactically optional, is needed for this particular problem. Completing . . .

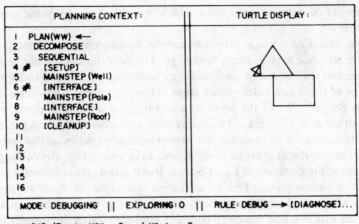

```
        PLANNING CONTEXT:                          TURTLE DISPLAY:
  I    PLAN(WW) ◄—
  2      DECOMPOSE
  3        SEQUENTIAL
  4  #       [SETUP]
  5          MAINSTEP (Well)
  6  #       [INTERFACE]
  7          MAINSTEP (Pole)
  8          [INTERFACE]
  9          MAINSTEP (Roof)
 10          [CLEANUP]
 11
 12
 13
 14
 15
 16

  MODE: DEBUGGING  ||  EXPLORING: O  ||  RULE: DEBUG ──► [DIAGNOSE]...
```

QIO (Running WW ... Done.) What now?
AIO. > Debug
Debugging WW. The top level of WW contains 7 design decisions
which could be faulty. There are warnings attached to several
nodes in the plan for WW.

FIG. 8. Spade-0 display screen during debugging of WW.

In order for a student to converse successfully with Spade-0, a certain amount of terminology must be mastered. Hence, the system contains a rudimentary tutoring module, which attempts to develop a shared vocabulary about plans, bugs and debugging techniques. The following scenario illustrates how new terms are introduced when appropriate situations arise.

Q11. The rule is: DEBUG –> [DIAGNOSE]+[REPAIR].
       Do you want to try to diagnose bugs in WW?

A11. > Yes

Q12. You have never used DIAGNOSE before.
       Would you like an explanation?

A12. > Yes

Diagnosis means figuring out which node in the plan represents an incorrect choice. There are four sources of evidence. (1) Aspects of the plan itself, such as warnings attached to nodes, may be examined. (2) The problem description can be checked, to ensure that a code segment has been written to achieve each goal. (3) A trace of the running process can be used to detect such mistakes as undoing previously accomplished steps. (4) The code can be scanned for unusual patterns such as consecutive calls to FORWARD with no rotations in between.

It should be emphasized that the tutoring module is extremely primitive. It consists of a small collection of *ad hoc* rules which: (1) decide when to interrupt the student, and (2) select one of the explanations from a database of pre-stored messages.

Suppose that the same student, still working on parts of wishingwell, wishes to try an entirely different plan. However, in order to encourage such exploration processes, many students need reassurance that the current state of the solution can be restored, should the alternative plan prove unsucccessful. Hence, although such human-engineering features may seem to be of only minor theoretical interest, their provision in Spade-0, as illustrated below, seems essential.

> Q14. What now?
>
> A14. > EXPLORE
>
> OK. The current solution has been recorded as exploration 3.
> To get it back, type "Restore 3".
>
> Q15. What now?
>
> A15. > Go to the decompose node of WW
>
> OK. The active plan for the decompose of WW is SEQUENTIAL.
>
> Q16. What now?
>
> A16. > Edit
>
> Editing the decompose of WW.
> Only one choice is left: Decompose -> Repetition.
>
> Q17. What now?
>
> A. Iteration
>
> B. Recursion
>
> A17. > A
>
> Q18. What now?
>
> A18. > RESTORE
>
> The last saved exploration was version 3. I am restoring version 3 of your plan for WW.
>
> John. The sequential version of the decompose for WW is now active.
>
> Q19. You were pursuing the first interface of the sequential plan.
> What now?

The effort involved in exploring unsuccessful alternate plans is rarely wasted. The efficient representational scheme allows all versions of all plans developed during previous explorations to remain available, and these "hung" subplans often turn out to be useful later on.

The importance of such system features is that they provide a flexibility which goes beyond our current theoretical framework. By monitoring the use of such features, we can discover ways in which the underlying model needs extension or revision.

5. Spade-0 is an experimental tool

We expect advanced versions of Spade to be of practical value in tutoring beginning programmers.† However, Version 0 is primarily intended as an experimental vehicle for exploring various facets of the underlying model of planning and debugging.

The following issues of design methodology are currently being investigated using Spade-0.

(a) Do users find the planning rules adequate; or are there planning concepts which cannot be expressed in this framework? Is there a single optimal set of rules, or should the system be tuned to each individual's "style"?

---

† We also believe that some of the ideas and techniques will prove helpful in the development of book-keeping assistants and "apprentices" for professional programmers.

(b) Do the plan structures generated by Spade-0 serve as useful documentation, aiding one programmer in understanding and modifying programs written by another?

(c) How many rules remain the same in moving from one task domain to another? We are in the process of designing problem solving models for the "blocks world," a set theory world, and an elementary calculator world.

(d) The "Later" feature (illustrated in interaction 6 of section 4) allows the user to deviate from the system's default solution order. Do novice programmers in fact make more frequent use of this feature than experts? Does Least-Scope predict the contexts in which experts find Top-Down programming inappropriate?

(e) How effective is the system in giving supportive practice in structured programming? Can its effectiveness be attributed to greater articulation of planning and debugging strategies?

The process of implementing and testing Spade-0 has already resulted in several refinements to our model. It led to the discovery of Least-Scope, a principle governing the order of design decisions which is more subtle than Top-Down. It changed our view of debugging, from an early grammar-based representation, to the current formulation as a separate mode, in which transformational procedures map plans into plans. Most recently it has focused our attention on the role of exploration. We are currently attempting to adapt the model to incorporate this phenomenon, and to formalize the ways in which other flexibilities in the system's features are employed.

6. Limitations and extensions

Spade-0, although useful as a tool, is not a practical tutor in its current form. Its limitations are instructive, however, providing insight as to the additional knowledge and expertise which would be required for a successful tutor. We will examine three such limitations.

1. Although a problem specification language for turtle graphics (Goldstein, 1974) plays a central role in the underlying model, Spade-0 does not use information in the problem description. This severely restricts its range of planning advice and debugging assistance, a limitation which cannot be surmounted merely by better human-engineering, by extending the collection of plan types, or by adding new features within the existing framework.

To address this difficulty, we have designed and are now implementing Spade-1, an improved environment, based on the use of Goldstein's predicate language to specify the problem description. The following proposed scenario illustrates how this extra information will enable a natural extension to the current system.

Q20. What is the name of this procedure?
A20. > WW

Q21. Please enter the problem description for WW.
A21. > WW is Roof, Pole, Well
     > Roof is-a Triangle
     > Pole is-a Line
     > Well is-a Square
     > Roof is-above Pole

> Pole is-above Well
> Roof is-connected-to Well
> Well is-connected-to Pole.

Q22. OK. The WW problem is well-defined. What now?

A22. > Roof Pole Well

These steps are Parts in the problem specification.

Q23. Are you pursuing a sequential decomposition plan?

A23. > Yes

Q24. OK. What now?

A24. > ADVICE

WELL is described as a square in the WW specification. The answer library contains a procedure, RECT, which draws rectangles. A square is a kind of rectangle. Hence, I suggest trying an identification involving RECT as the plan for WELL.

In the extreme case where the user requests advice about every decision, a module capable of performing "automatic programming," albeit within a limited domain, is required. For each plan type, the rules for propagating semantic and pragmatic annotation ("purpose" and "reason" assertions) downward through the plan must be specified. Goldstein & Miller (1976) present an early version of the design for such a module; a revised description will be presented in a forthcoming doctoral dissertation by Miller.

2. Even with the extension to Spade-1, the allocation of effort to detailed articulation of the plan would quickly begin to seem excessive as the student became more experienced: Spade-0's simple abbreviation capabilities will not suffice. Hence, we have designed Spade-2, a further improvement of the environment, based on the use of a chart-based parser (Kaplan, 1973; Kay, 1973) to infer the user's plan from fragmentary and implicit information at varying levels of detail. The following proposed scenario illustrates how Spade-2, with its plan parsing module, would represent a further extension of the system described here.

Q25. The current problem is Wishingwell.
     Its parts are Roof, Pole, and Well. What now?

A25. > Square.

Q26. I am assuming: Well has been solved by calling Square.
     What now?

A26. > Forward 100

Q27. OK. What now?

A27. > Triangle

Q28. I am assuming: Roof has been solved by calling Triangle.
     I am assuming: (Forward 100) was in-line code for Pole.
     I am assuming: the overall plan type is Sequential.
     The interfaces are still pending . . .

A preliminary design for the plan parser was presented in (Miller & Goldstein, 1976). Whether efficient implementation can surmount the inherently combinatoric nature of the plan recognition problem remains an open question; related work by Rich *et al.* (1978) and Waters (1976) is encouraging.

As the environment increases in sophistication, it becomes possible to contemplate reducing the highly structured style of interaction. For example, the user interface for Spade-2 could be engineered to closely resemble standard Logo. However, various advise-giving commands would be available, based on having inferred the student's plan. This presents a paradox: it is by no means obvious that a less structured environment is, in general, more conducive to learning. For example, the structured prompting of Spade-0 might be ideal for inculcating the virtues of outlining, in an essay-writing environment. Likewise, the optimal style of interaction may vary widely across individuals.

3. This dilemma draws attention to the most serious problem confronting Spade-0 and most similar systems: paucity of pedagogical theory. To approach human quality, computer tutors must become sensitive to such issues as: (i) "what constitutes a good hint?", (ii) "should the computer spontaneously interrupt the student to provide remedial advice?", (iii) "how often should the tutor intervene?", (iv) "how much should it say?", (v) "when should it say it?", and (vi) "how should it say it?". Considerable theoretical and experimental work will be necessary before such questions can be answered with any confidence.

7. Related work

Spade-0 is one of several recent efforts to apply artificial intelligence (A1) theory and techniques to the design of personal learning environments. The most closely related projects include: the SOPHIE electronics tutor (Brown *et al.*, 1974), the SCHOLAR geography tutor (Collins *et al.*, 1977), the WEST arithmetic tutor (Burton & Brown, 1976), Sleeman's (1977) tutor for interpreting nuclear magnetic resonance spectra, the WUMPUS Advisor of Carr & Goldstein (1977), the FLOW programming tutor of Gentner & Norman (1977), and Genesereth's (1977) MACSYMA Advisor.

A second area of related work concerns the construction of computer assistants for programmers. Most other projects have focussed on "apprentice" systems for expert programmers; this is primarily a difference in emphasis. A recent flurry of activity was initiated by Teitelman (1970). Winograd (1973) went on to further define the problem, which has since been explored by Hewitt & Smith (1975), and pursued by Rich & Shrobe (1976). Rich *et al.* (1978) are currently investigating assistant environments for developing Lisp programs such as hash coding schemes, and FORTRAN programs such as are found in the IBM Scientific Subroutine Library.

Many of the objectives and ideas leading to Spade-0 are descended from research scattered over a much broader arena. The need for a unified account of planning and debugging became apparent in recent dissertations by Sussman (1973), Goldstein (1974) and Sacerdoti (1975). The attempt to provide explicit normative rules of design methodology has analogues in the structured programming movement (e.g., Dahl *et al.*, 1972; Dijkstra, 1976). The search for psychologically viable information processing models of the design process is closely related to work by Newell & Simon (1972) and Brooks (1975). The goal of providing a programming curriculum which emphasizes problem solving concerns is inspired by the writings of Polya (1965) and Papert (1971).

8. Conclusion: the role of limited didactic systems

Even when the task is a simple arithmetic game such as WEST (Burton & Brown, 1976), designing an "artificially intelligent" computer tutor is an arduous task, beset by shortcomings of theory and technique. In order to progress to more challenging domains such as computer programming, intermediate subgoals must be established. Didactic systems with limited objectives can lay the foundations for later work on more sophisticated and complete tutors. They can drive theory evolution, and suggest alternative applications. They can direct attention to serious issues previously unnoticed, and away from bogus issues previously thought crucial. Moreover, the pedagogical mileage obtainable from a limited system can often be surprising.

The development of a structured planning and debugging environment illustrates how such an intermediate system can help. It has provided a useful research context for studying the knowledge which a programming tutor would need to convey, resulting in several contributions to date.

(a) The model underlying Spade-0, which codifies several categories of programming skill, has been elaborated and refined in several ways. The revised model unifies early theories of planning and debugging, and addresses additional questions such as the order of pursuing subgoals during planning. It appears to provide a cogent analysis of simple programming, and a coherent framework for extending the analysis to more complex programming.

(b) Spade-0, an environment for elementary programming, attempts to assist novice programmers by emphasizing the plan instead of the code. It introduces the student to a vocabulary for describing plans, bugs, and debugging strategies; it provides a learning-by-doing context for exercising an articulate problem-solving style; and it organizes the student's program development process by supportive prompting and mixed-initiative menu-selection editing.

(c) A set of experimental techniques have been devised for exploring models of design and learning processes in limited didactic systems. Those skills which are relevant to a given task are isolated, by systematically varying the configuration of features and rules, and by continuously monitoring the use of each capability in particular contexts.

We hope to make further contributions in the following directions: pursuing our experiments with Spade-0; extending the depth and breadth of the underlying model; and implementing Spade-1 and Spade-2. Whereas Spade-0 serves primarily as an experimental tool, Spade-1—which will be operational in the near future—should approach the threshold of practical utility. Spade-2 will take a bit longer; but we expect it to surpass that threshold.

The application of Artificial Intelligence techniques to the design of personal learning environments is an emerging enterprise with considerable theoretical interest and exciting practical potential. Limited didactic systems provide a medium for cultivating more refined cognitive and pedagogical theories; better theories in turn sustain less restricted and more effective systems. Such systems will increasingly supplement the guidance provided by human teachers; whereupon the manner in which knowledge is disseminated, in every field from computer programming to English composition, will be radically transformed.

References

BROOKS, R. (1975). A model of human cognitive behavior in writing code for computer programs. *Report AFOSR-TR-1084*. Carnegie–Mellon University.

BROWN, J. S., BURTON, R. R. & BELL, A. G. (1974). SOPHIE: A sophisticated instructional environment for teaching electronic troubleshooting (an example of AI in CAI). *Final Report, Report 2790 (A.I. Report 12)*. Bolt, Beranek and Newman.

BURTON, R. R., & BROWN, J. S. (1976). A tutoring and student modelling paradigm for gaming environments. In COLMAN, R. & LORTON, P. JR., Eds, *Computer Science and Education* (Advance Proceedings of the Association for Computing Machinery Special Interest Groups on Computer Science Education and Computer Uses in Education Joint Symposium, Anaheim, Cal.). *SIGCSE Bulletin*, **8**, (1); *SIGCUE Topics*, **2**, 236–246.

CARR, B. & GOLDSTEIN, I. P. (1977). Overlays: a theory of modelling for Computer Aided Instruction. *Artificial Intelligence Laboratory Memo 406 (Logo Memo 40)*. Massachusetts Institute of Technology.

COLLINS, A., WARNOCK, E. H., AIELLO, N. & MILLER, M. L. (1975). Reasoning From incomplete knowledge. In BOBROW, D. & COLLINS, A., Eds), *Representation and Understanding: Studies in Cognitive Science*. New York: Academic Press, pp. 383–415.

DAHL, O. J., DIJKSTRA, & HOARE, C. A. R. (1972). *Structured Programming*. Academic Press.

DIJKSTRA, E. (1976). *A Discipline of Programming*. Englewood Cliffs, N.J.: Prentice-Hall.

GENESERETH, M. R. (1977). An automated consultant for MACSYMA. In *Proceedings of the Fifth International Joint Conference on Artificial Intelligence*, Volume II, p. 789.

GENTNER, D. R. & NORMAN, D. A. (1977). The flow tutor: schemas for tutoring. *Technical Report 7702*. Center for Human Information Processing, San Diego.

GOLDSTEIN, I. (1974). Understanding simple picture programs. *TR 294*. Massachusetts Institute of Technology, Artificial Intelligence Laboratory.

GOLDSTEIN, I. & MILLER, M. (1976). Structured planning and debugging: a linguistic theory of design. *Artificial Intelligence Laboratory, Memo 387*. Massachusetts Institute of Technology.

HEWITT, C. & SMITH, B. (1975). Towards a programming apprentice. *IEEE Transactions on Software Engineering*, **1**(1).

KAPLAN, R. (1973). A general syntactic processor. In RUSTIN, R. Ed., *Natural Language Processing*. Courant Computer Science Symposium. New York: Algorithmics Press.

KAY, M. (1973). The MIND system. In RUSTIN, R. Ed., *Natural Language Processing*. Courant Computer Science Symposium. New York: Algorithmics Press.

MILLER, M. & GOLDSTEIN, I. (1976). PAZATN: a linguistic approach to automatic analysis of elementary programming protocols. *Artificial Intelligence Laboratory, Memo 388*. Massachusetts Institute of Technology.

MILLER, M. & GOLDSTEIN, I. (1977a). Structured planning and debugging. In *Proceedings of the Fifth International Joint Conference on Artificial Intelligence*. Cambridge, Mass.

MILLER, M. & GOLSTEIN, I. (1977b). Problem solving grammars as formal tools for Intelligent CAI. In *Proceedings of ACM77*.

NEWELL, A. & SIMON, H. (1972). *Human Problem Solving*. Englewood Cliffs, N.J.: Prentice Hall.

PAPERT, S. (1971). Teaching children to be mathematicians versus teaching about mathematics. *Artificial Intelligence Laboratory, Memo 249*. Massachusetts Institute of Technology.

POLYA, G. (1972, 1965). *Mathematical Discovery*, Volumes I and II. New York: John Wiley.

RICH, C., & SHROBE, H. (1976). Initial report on a LISP programmer's apprentice. *Artificial Intelligence Laboratory, TR 354*. Massachusetts Institute of Technology.

RICH, C., SHROBE, H., WATERS, R., SUSSMAN, G. & HEWITT, C. (1978). Programming viewed as an engineering activity. *Artificial Intelligence Laboratory, Memo 459*. Massachusetts Institute of Technology.

SACERDOTI, E. (1975). The non-linear nature of plans. In *Proceedings of the Fourth International Joint Conference on Artificial Intelligence*, Tbilisi, Georgia, U.S.S.R.

SLEEMAN, D. H. (1977). A system which allows students to explore algorithms. In *Proceedings of the Fifth International Joint Conference on Artificial Intelligence*, Volume II, pp. 780–786.

SUSSMAN, G. (1973). A computational model of skill acquisition. *Artificial Intelligence Laboratory TR 297*. Massachusetts Institute of Technology.

TEITELMAN, W. (1970). Toward a programming laboratory. In BUXTON & RANDELL, Eds, *Software Engineering Techniques*.

WATERS, R. C. (1976). A system for understanding mathematical FORTRAN programs. *Artificial Intelligence Laboratory, Memo 368*. Massachusetts Institute of Technology.

WINOGRAD, T. (1973). Breaking the complexity barrier (again). In *Proceedings of the ACM SIGIR-SIGPLAN Interface Meeting*.

7. The role of plans in intelligent teaching systems

MICHAEL R. GENESERETH

Department of Computer Science, School of Humanities and Sciences,
Stanford University, California, U.S.A.

Effective remedial instruction often requires information about the student's beliefs and misconceptions. One way of obtaining this information is by studying the student's efforts in solving problems that require knowledge of the subject matter. In some areas it is possible to design diagnostic tests that can pinpoint a student's misconception directly from his answers. However, in subject areas where there are several ways of solving a problem, it is helpful to consider not only the student's final answer but also his steps in producing it. This paper is concerned with automatically analyzing the steps of a solution to infer the student's problem solving "plan" and the use of that plan in generating remediation tailored to the student.

The notion of a problem solving plan is formally defined herein as a trace of the student's mental operations in deciding which steps to perform. With this view, plan recognition can be thought of as a complex parsing process, in which the student's mental operations comprise the grammar and the steps of his solution are the words. Once the plan is reconstructed, it can be analyzed to reveal the underlying beliefs and misconceptions, and it can be used to suggest remediation appropriate to the student's problem solving strategy. This paper describes several approaches to plan recognition and plan-based remediation and illustrates the particular approach taken in an automated consultant for MACSYMA called the Advisor.

1. Introduction

One of the keys to effective remedial instruction is information about the student's beliefs and misconceptions. This information can often be obtained by analyzing the student's efforts in solving problems that require knowledge of the subject matter. In some areas, it is possible to design diagnostic tests that can pinpoint a student's misconception directly from his answers. For example, in their work on the Buggy system, Burton and Brown developed a methodology for automatically generating diagnostic tests that discover the underlying problems responsible for a student's errors in subtraction. However, in subject areas where the student chooses his own problem or when there are several ways of solving a problem, it is helpful to consider not only the student's final answer but also his steps in producing it. This paper is concerned with the process of automatically analyzing a student's steps to infer his rationale for taking those steps and the use of this information in providing remediation tailored to the student.

1.1. THE STUDENT'S PLAN

The student's rationale is important because it is the link between his beliefs about the subject area and his solution. In the exercise of elementary arithmetic skills like addition and subtraction, this link is direct. The sequence of steps is fixed in advance, and the student simply executes the steps.† If there is an error, it can be localized by

† This assumes that the student already has command of some procedure, possibly an incorrect one. In actual practice, the student might revise his procedure while trying to apply it to a novel problem.

following the student's steps and comparing his actions with those of the correct algorithm. In more complex domains like algebra, geometry, and calculus, there is no fixed procedure that solves all problems. Consequently, the student must piece one together for each new problem, and generally there are multiple ways this can be done. Identifying a misconception in this type of situation is more difficult and requires an understanding of why the student chose the steps he did.

There is a crucial distinction here between the student's steps in solving a problem and his mental operations in selecting those steps. The steps of the solution manipulate the objects of the problem (e.g. mathematical expressions and equations in algebra, drawings and proofs in geometry); the mental operations take goals and beliefs as "inputs" and produce step sequences as "outputs". For example, given a polynomial to solve, a student must first recall an appropriate method (like using the quadratic formula) or invent one he hasn't seen before (say factoring); he must check the method's preconditions (like integer coefficients) and figure out how to satisfy them (e.g. multiplying through by a constant); and only then can he begin to carry out the steps.

Insofar as a trace of the student's mental operations explains why he chose the steps he did, it constitutes a rationale for the solution. If the operations are guaranteed to produce correct solutions (given correct facts about the actions and the problem area), then the trace constitutes a direct proof that the solution is correct. If the methods are merely plausible (e.g. the independence assumption in satisfying conjunctive subgoals), then the trace constitutes only a plausible argument but still captures the rationale. In what follows the word *plan* will be used to designate a student's solution, the relevant beliefs, and a trace of his mental operations in using these beliefs to produce the solution.

One advantage of recognizing the distinction between the steps of a solution and the mental operations that produce it is that it suggests what it means for a solution to "make sense". Even when a sequence of steps is incorrect, we sometimes deem the solution "reasonable" in light of revealed misconceptions on the part of the student. We snap our fingers and exclaim "Ah, I see what he's doing" and sometimes "But he's wrong about x". This often occurs in grading problem sets and quizzes where one tries to understand the student's problem solving "logic" in order to detect his misconceptions. One possible explanation for this is that we recognize the student's mental operations are correct and that the student's mistake is due to a misconception about the subject area.

As an illustration of this, consider the MACSYMA interactions in Fig. 1. MACSYMA (Mathlab) is a large, interactive computer system designed to assist mathematicians, scientists, and engineers in performing symbolic manipulation of mathematical expressions. For the purposes of this paper, the important thing to realize is that it has a large number of complex commands and options. The command lines (e.g. **C6**) are typed by the user; the display lines (e.g. **D6**) are MACSYMA's response. A command line may be terminated by a semicolon or a dollar sign; if the latter is used, the display is suppressed (e.g. line **C7** in Fig. 1c). Expressions are entered in linear form (e.g. $(3-2*z)/z$); colon is the assignment operator; and other commands are applied using functional notation (e.g. **Factor (D6, X)**). Parentheses delimit compound statements.†

---

† One of the advantages of using computers as a subject area is that all of the student's actions are explicit (as "C lines"), whereas in other domains only the intermediate results are shown (the "D lines"). One of the difficulties of applying the techniques described here to other domains is that these intermediate actions must first be identified.

(a)

(C6)   X ↑ 2 − Z*(X + X*Y − Y*Z);
(D6) $X^2 - Z(X + XY - YZ)$

(C7)   Factor (D6, X);
(D7) $(X - Z)(X - YZ)$

(C8)   Part (D7, 1, 2);
(D8)   Z

(b)

(C6)   X ↑ 2 − Z*(X + X*Y − Y*Z);
(D6) $X^2 - Z(X + XY - YZ)$

(C7)   Expand(D6);
(D7) $X^2 - XZ - XYZ + YZ^2$

(C8)   (A: Coeff(D7, X, 2), B: Coeff(D7, X, 1), C: Coeff(D7, X, 0))$

(C9)   (−B + Sqrt(B ↑ 2 − 4*A*C))/(2*A);
(D9)   Z

(c)

(C6)   X ↑ 2 − Z*(X + X*Y − Y*Z);
(D6) $X^2 - Z(X + XY - YZ)$

(C7)   (A: Coeff(D6, X, 2), B: Coeff(D6, X, 1), C: Coeff(D6, X, 0))$

(C8)   (−B + Sqrt(B ↑ 2 − 4*A*C))/(2*A);
(D8)   0

FIG. 1. (a) Arthur's solution by factoring; (b) Bertram's solution using the quadratic formula; (c) Carleton's incorrect solution.

In each of the cases in Fig. 1, the student was asked to solve the same problem, and each student used a different approach. Arthur's and Bertram's solutions are correct; and, even without knowledge of MACSYMA, one sees how they got their answers. Arthur obtained his solution by factoring the expression and extracting one of the factors. Bertram expanded the expression, picked out the coefficients, and plugged them into the quadratic formula. Carleton's solution is similar to Arthur's but is incorrect because it is missing the preliminary expansion. The **Coeff** command does not return the coefficient of its argument in all cases, as one might suspect. What it does do is to loop over the terms of the argument collecting coefficients of the variable raised to the desired degree. Since there are no terms in **D6** free of **X**, **Coeff (D6, X, 0)** returns **0**. The reason for the name is that the command *does* compute the coefficient when the argument is expanded. Although Carleton's solution is incorrect, to many people it seems reasonable in light of this misconception.

1.2. PLAN RECOGNITION

MACSYMA experts are quick to diagnose Carleton's misconception, even those who have not seen the problem before. The intermediate steps in solving the problem are important in making this determination, but an understanding of the student's plan is also essential in pinpointing the misconception. The reason is that, taken individually, the steps are correct; it's only their composition that's wrong. Note that it is not illegal to use the **Coeff** command on **D6**; in fact, it is often used on non-expanded polynomials in finding roots over polynomial domains. Its use in Fig. 1c is incorrect only because it was expected to produce the coefficient of **D6** to plug into the quadratic formula in line **C8**.

The work of the artificial intelligence community on planning suggests that it is possible to characterize the mental operations a person uses in devising a sequence of actions to solve a problem. Given this characterization, the plan recognition process can be automated. The task is a difficult one, especially where there is a possibility that the solution is incorrect, as in Carleton's case. However, a number of researchers have already presented plan recognition algorithms, including Genesereth (1978, 1981), Miller and Goldstein (1976), Schmidt *et al.* (1978) and Waters (1978).

In their work on computer-aided instruction, Brown and Burton pioneered the use of the expert comparison technique in diagnosing student errors. In SOPHIE-II (Brown *et al.*, 1976), WEST (Burton and Brown, 1976) and BUGGY (Brown and Burton, 1978), misconceptions were inferred by comparing the student's solutions with those of an automated expert or an expert with various bugs inserted. However, in none of these systems were the student's answers or actions used in ordering the search. Plan recognition is a way of using information about the student's actions in dealing with the combinatorics in domains where the number of reasonable solutions and bugs is too large for the expert difference technique to work effectively.

1.3. PLAN USE

In addition to helping pinpoint the student's misconception, studying his plan is advantageous in that it enables the tutor to offer remediation in the context of the student's problem and his approach to solving it. Consider, for example, the consultation session in Fig. 2. The "Advisor" in this case is a consultant for MACSYMA, and Carleton is the novice responsible for the session in Fig. 1c. After accepting a statement of Carleton's goal and complaint, the consultant looks at his work, suspects a misconception about **Coeff**, and confirms it with a question. He then corrects the misconception and offers an alternative in the form of the **Ratcoeff** command. This alternative fits nicely into the Carleton's plan, and its importance is emphasized by its use in context.

Consultant: Speak up!

Carleton: I was trying to solve D6 for X, and I got 0.

Consultant: Did you expect Coeff to return the coefficient of D6?

Carleton: Yes, doesn't it?

Consultant: Coeff(exp, var, pow) returns the correct coefficient of var^{pow} in exp only if exp is expanded with respect to var. Perhaps you should use Ratcoeff.

Carleton: Ok, thanks. Bye.

FIG. 2. An example of MACSYMA consultation.

This paper discusses some approaches to automating the process of plan recognition and using plans to detect misconceptions and provide remediation in context. Fundamental to this endeavor is a formal representation for plans. Section 2 offers a precise definition for the notion of a plan as a "dependency graph" relating a student's actions to his beliefs about the problem area and the actions involved via the planning methods he used in piecing together his solution. The recognition of plans in this representation is discussed in Section 3, and the confirmation of tentative plans is discussed in Section 4. Section 5 indicates how confirmed plans can be used in providing advice tailored to the student. The final section sums up the key points of the paper and indicates directions for future work.

At least one tutorial program has been written in which plan recognition is used to determine student misconceptions. The MACSYMA Advisor (Genesereth, 1978) is an automated consultant for MACSYMA. It is a program separate from MACSYMA, with its own data base and expertise. The Advisor accepts a description of a violated expectation from its user, tries to reconstruct his plan, and if successful generates advice tailored to his need. For example, the Advisor is capable of conducting the consultation shown in Fig. 2 (except for the natural language processing). Although the Advisor was developed as a MACSYMA consultant, this does not mean that the techniques are in any way restricted to MACSYMA, only that they have not yet been tested in other subject areas.

2. Plans

Intuitively, a plan is a program of action, or sequence of steps, designed to achieve a desired goal. In this paper, the notion of plans is extended to include an argument for how the steps achieve the goal in terms of the planner's beliefs about the problem area. In imputing a plan to a student's actions, there is an underlying assumption that each of those actions is in some way intended to contribute to the overall goal. For sure, student's often exhibit purposeful exploration not directed toward solving any particular problem, but for simplicity of explanation such possibilities are ignored here.

The part of a plan explaining how the sequence of actions achieves its goal can be thought of as a logical argument in which the goal is the conclusion and the actions and relevant facts about the problem area are the premises. The view taken here is that a trace of the goals and subgoals, methods and assumptions that a problem solver uses in generating a sequence of actions is an appropriate structure for such an argument. This idea of using a computational trace as an argument for the correctness of a solution is similar to the explanation facility of MYCIN (Shortliffe, 1974) and the dependency relations in EL (Stallman and Sussman, 1977).

If one of the user's beliefs about a problem area or the available actions are incorrect, then the resulting action sequence may not achieve its goal, even though all of the planning methods are correct. The MACSYMA session in Fig. 1c is an example. The user's strategy was flawless; it was his misconception about **Coeff** that led to the difficulty. Once that was corrected, he successfully solved the problem, using the same plan except with **Coeff** replaced by **Ratcoeff**.

In order to make this notion of plans precise, the following discussion will concentrate on a particular planner called MUSER (for MACSYMA user), designed to mimic the behavior of novice users of MACSYMA. MUSER takes as argument a goal specified in a formal, predicate calculus-like language and uses facts about MACSYMA and mathematics to produce a sequence of MACSYMA commands that computes the desired result. In doing so, it uses a variety of planning methods that either produce a complete plan or generate appropriate subgoals. The goal language and planning methods were chosen after analysis of several dozen scenarios of MACSYMA usage and include many domain-independent as well as domain-specific techniques. Only a few of these techniques are shown here.

2.1. GOALS

In MUSER goals take the form of abstract operations in which implementational details are left unspecified. There are several different types of goals, and each has a corresponding set of parameters. For example, the goal **(Obtain (Coefficient G6 X 2))** means to obtain an expression for the coefficient of X^2 in **G6**, either to print it out or pass as argument to some MACSYMA command. Note that this can be done either by finding an already computed expression (stored, say, as the value of some variable) or by computing it anew. Either implementation is satisfactory so long as it computes the desired expression. **(Achieve (Val (A 2) 6))** means to modify the environment so that the value of the array element **(A 2)** is **6**. As with **Obtain**, one can do this in a variety of ways, e.g. by creating a new array and assigning it to **A** or by using the array assignment command. Similarly, there are goals for testing facts, e.g. **(Test (Val (A 2) 6))**, and proving them without further testing, e.g. **Prove (Val (A 2) 6))**.

Many of MUSER'S goal types exist merely for expressiveness and efficiency and can be subsumed by others. For example, the goal **(Find (Coefficient G6 X 2))** means to obtain an expression for the coefficient of X^2 in **G6** that has already been computed, whereas **(Construct (Coefficient G6 X 2))** means to compute it anew. **(Transform a p)** means to convert the expression **a** into a mathematically equivalent expression that satisfies **p**. **(Achieve-by-round (all i (if (<i 10) (Val (A i) 0))))** means to set the first 10 elements of the array **A** to **0** by iteration.

2.2. PLANNING METHODS

The planning methods in MUSER are "mental operations" that add implementational detail to evolving plans. Each method has associated with it sets of input and output objects and a procedural definition. Each methods satisfies a particular type of goal and is annotated with prerequisites and postrequisites (conditions that must be true in order for the method to succeed and those which become true after it is executed). Some planning methods produce complete plans to achieve their goals; some merely generate subgoals; others are mixed in their effects.

The **Eval-a-variable** method satisfies a goal of the form **(Obtain goal)** and returns it as value. The procedural definition of **Eval-a-variable** is shown in Fig. 3. It uses the subroutine **Fetch** to search its data base for a variable **var** such that **Val(var) = goal**. (The "?" prefix here designates the symbol that follows it as a pattern variable. The "," prefix indicates that the value of the variable **g** is to be plugged into the pattern, i.e. it means "unquote".) If **Fetch** succeeds in finding an appropriate variable, **Eval-a-variable** adds a call to the MACSYMA evaluator to the evolving plan via the call to **Action**.

The **Fetch** subroutine used here is MUSER'S data base access method. It searches the data base for an assertion of the form specified in its argument and returns as a value a list of bindings for the existential variables in the pattern. The **Action** method is MUSER'S way of adding actions to its plan. It takes as arguments the name of a command and descriptions of its inputs and outputs. In the case of **Eval-a-variable**, the command

```
(defun Eval-a-variable (goal) ;Goal = (Obtain goal)
    (prog (var)
        (setq var (Fetch '(Val ?v ,goal)))
        (Action 'Meval var)))

(defun Valuate (fun arg) ;Goal = (Obtain (fun arg))
    (prog (prc com g)
        (setq (prc com)
                (Fetch '(all x (if (?p x) (= (, fun x) (?c x)))))
        (setq g (Obtain arg))
        (if (not (Fetch '(,prc ,arg))) (setq g (Transform g prc)))
            (Action com g)))

(defun Convert (arg form) ;Goal = (Transform arg form)
    (prog (com)
        (setq com (Fetch '(all x (and (= (?c x) x) (,form (?c x))))))
        (Action com arg)))

(defun Use-quadratic-formula (exp var) ;Goal =
    (prog (a b c)                          ;        (Obtain (Root exp var))
        (setq a (Obtain '(Coefficient ,exp ,var 2))
              b (Obtain '(Coefficient ,exp ,var 1))
              c (Obtain '(Coefficient ,exp ,var 0)))
        (Action 'Pquad a b c)))

(defun Solve-by-factoring (exp var) ;Goal = (Obtain (Root exp var))
    (Obtain '(First ,(Obtain '(Factors ,exp ,var)))))
```

FIG. 3. Some of MUSER's planning methods.

is **Meval**, the input is a variable, the output is the goal; and, when the plan is executed, the variable will be evaluated to obtain the desired expression.

The alternative to retrieving a pre-computed object is to construct a new one. The goal of the **Valuate** method is to produce an object defined as the value of some mathematical function **fun** applied to an argument **arg**. The strategy is to search the data base for a MACSYMA command that computes **fun**, given preconditions **prc** on the argument. The definition for **Valuate** is shown in Fig. 3. The outputs of the call to **Fetch** are the command **com** and the preconditions **prc**. **Valuate** then obtains the argument **arg**, transforms it into an expression that satisfies **prc**, and then adds **com** to the plan. The extension to multiple argument functions is straightforward.

The **Convert** method is intended to satisfy the goal **(Transform arg form)**, i.e. to produce an expression equivalent to **arg** that satisfies **form**. To do so, it searches the data base for a MACSYMA command **com** that preserves mathematical equivalence but achieves **form**. If it succeeds, it adds to the plan a call to **com** with argument **arg** and returns the answer. The definition is shown in Fig. 3.

In addition to the domain-semidependent methods shown here, MUSER also uses several domain-specific procedures. As examples, consider the procedures **Use-quadratic-formula** and **Solve-by-factoring** shown in Fig. 3. They have same goal but differ drastically in their strategies.

2.3. PLANS

Plans are dependency graphs that explain how a student's actions are supposed to achieve his goals in terms of his beliefs about the problem area and the actions involved.

Each goal is related to its subgoals and the actions used to achieve it by some planning method; and each method is annotated with its inputs and outputs. In particular, all calls to the **Fetch** subroutine are annotated with the data base assertions they retrieved.

Figure 4 shows a partial plan for transforming the expression **G6** to expanded form. The top box represents a planning method, with its goal written in the upper half and its name in the lower. The inputs and outputs are indicated to the left and right. In the **Convert** method, MUSER looks in its database for a subroutine that returns an expanded expression equivalent to its input and finds the assertion **(all x (and (= (Expand x) x) (Expanded (Expand x))))**. **Fetch** returns **Expand**, and it is added to the sequence of steps to be performed. In this plan the problem solver's **Expand** action is explained in terms of its goal **(Transform G6 Expanded)** and its underlying belief that **Expand** returns a mathematically equivalent but expanded version of its argument.

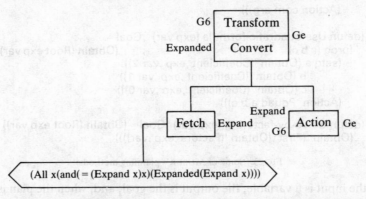

FIG. 4. Plan showing the **Expand** can be used to convert **G6** into its expanded form **Ge**. The goal is **(Transform G6 Expanded)**, and the planning method is **Convert**. **Convert**'s call to **Fetch** is annotated with the crucial fact about **Expand**, and the call to **Action** defines **Ge** as the result of executing **Expand** on **G6**.

Figure 5 shows a plan for computing the positive root of **G6** using the quadratic formula. As defined in Fig. 3, the **Use-quadratic-formula** method first computes the coefficients of the argument and then plugs them into the formula. These subgoals are indicated by the **Obtain** boxes connected to the **Use-quadratic-formula** box. For simplicity only the subplan for obtaining one of the coefficients is shown. The problem solver's choice in this case is to use the **Valuate** method. The assertion attached to the **Fetch** box indicates that **Coeff** does the job so long as the first argument is expanded. In order to obtain **G6** in expanded form, **Valuate** creates the subgoals **(Obtain G6)** and **(Transform G6 Expanded)**. In satisfying the **Obtain** subgoal, the **Eval-a-variable** method discovers that the variable **D6** has **G6** as value and starts off the plan with an evaluation of **D6**. In trying to transform **G6** to expanded form, **Convert** finds that the **Expand** command returns an expanded version mathematically equivalent to its argument. Hence, **Expand** is called on the value of **D6**, and the result **Ge** is passed as argument to **Coeff** along with the results of obtaining **X** and **1**. Finally, the coefficients are fed into the quadratic formula to obtain the root **G8**.

Figure 6 shows a plan for the user's effort in Fig. 1c. The problem in this case is that the user believes **Coeff**'s argument need only be a mathematical expression in order for **Coeff** to compute its coefficient. This erroneous belief is reflected in the predicate

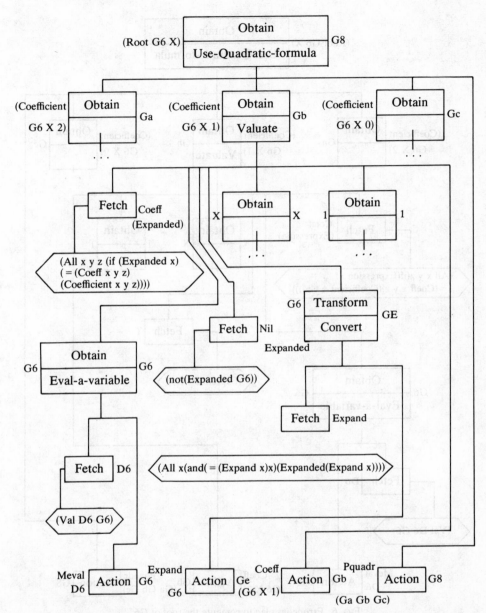

FIG. 5. Plan to compute the root of **G6** using the quadratic formula. The **Action** boxes at the bottom indicate the necessary steps in MACSYMA. The other boxes indicate the responsible planning methods.

Expression being returned by **Fetch**, which **G6** trivially satisfies; and, consequently, the **Transform** subgoal is not created (see the definition of **Valuate** in Fig. 3). Note that the structure of the plan here is correct, and so the action sequence "makes sense"; it's the premise that's wrong. If the premise were correct, the plan would constitute a flawless proof that **G8** is the root of **G6**.

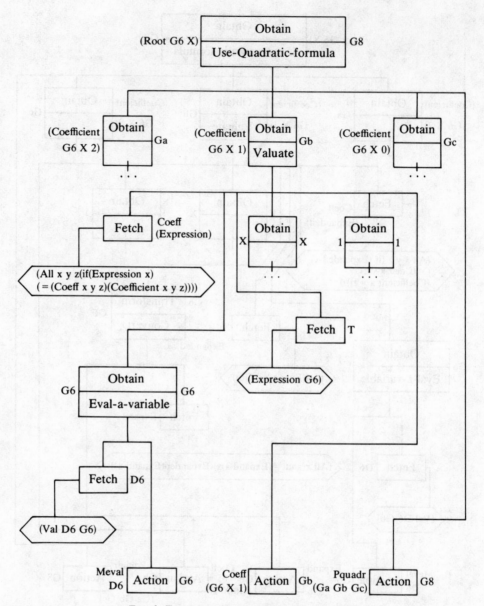

FIG. 6. Erroneous plan to compute the root of **G6**.

Figure 7 shows another plan to account for the session shown in Fig. 1c. In this case, the assertion about **Coeff** correctly lists **Expanded** as a precondition, and **G6** is obtained as before. However, the succeeding **Fetch** call indicates that the user believes **G6** to be expanded; and, therefore, the **Transform** subgoal is not created. Because **G6** is visible to the user, this mistake is less likely than the one in Fig. 6; but, when a user nests function calls, the intermediate expressions are not visible and such mistakes often arise.

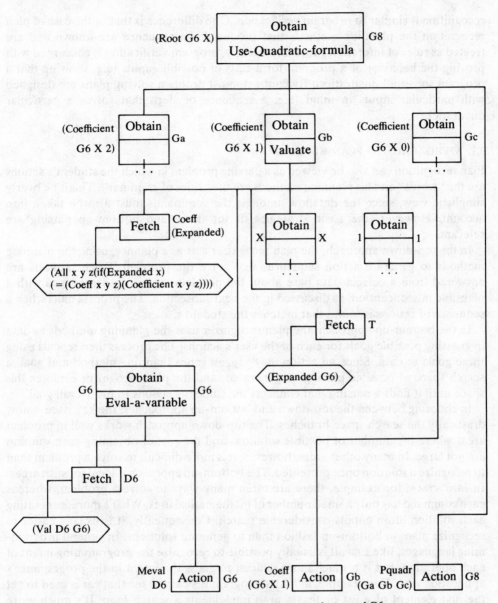

FIG. 7. Another erroneous plan to compute the root of **G6**.

3. Plan recognition

Plan recognition is the inverse of planning. A planner uses facts about its problem area to produce a plan that achieves its goal. A plan recognizer starts with a sequence of actions, reconstructs the problem solver's plan, and thereby infers the underlying beliefs.

As discussed in the last section, a plan is essentially a proof that a sequence of actions achieves its goal (in terms of the problem solver's beliefs). So, in a sense, plan recognition is similar to program verification. One difference is that in the case of plan recognition the planning methods that produced the sequence are known and are treated as rules of inference. More importantly, program verification is concerned with proving the behavior of a program for a class of possible inputs (e.g. showing that a program solves all quadratics). By contrast, most problem solving plans are designed with particular inputs in mind (e.g. a sequence of steps that solves a particular quadratic).

3.1. APPROACHES TO PLAN RECOGNITION

Plan recognition can also be viewed as a parsing problem in which the student's actions are the "words" and his planning methods are the "rules of grammar". This is an overly simplistic view, since the dataflow amongst the commands must also be taken into account. However, the basic strategies of top-down and bottom-up parsing are relevant.

In the top-down approach, the plan recognizer acts as a planner, using the planning methods to generate action sequences that solve the problem. **Fetch** requests are answered from a correct data base about the problem area or in accordance with a plausible misconception, as discussed in the next subsection. The process halts when a sequence of actions is found that matches the student's.

In the bottom-up approach, the plan recognizer uses the planning methods as data in guessing possible goals for each of the user's actions. The process then repeats using these goals as data. Since an action may suggest more than one method and goal, a search space of possible parsings is generated; and the plan recognizer explores this space until it finds a parsing that connects the student's actions to his overall goal.

In choosing between the top-down and bottom-up approaches, the key issue is how drastically the search space branches. The top-down approach works well in problem areas where the number of possible solutions and the cost of obtaining each solution are not large. In many other areas, however, it is more difficult to solve a problem than to recognize a solution once presented. The bottom-up approach is ideal for such areas. In MACSYMA, for example, there are often many ways to solve a problem, whereas each command has only a small number of mathematical uses. What's more, generating each solution often entails considerable search. Consequently, it is usually easier to recognize plans in bottom-up fashion than to generate solutions. In general programming languages, like LISP, it is usually possible to recognize the programming intent of each operation, but it is much more difficult to guess the intent in the programmer's application area. For example, in a LISP program it's easy to see that **car** is used to get the first element of a list or that a **prog** implements a search loop. It's much more difficult to guess that getting the first element of a list is equivalent to getting the real part of a complex number or the numerator of a rational number or that a search loop is a prime number program. The number of possible interpretations is simply too large.

3.2. HYPOTHESIZING MISCONCEPTIONS

Both the top-down and bottom-up approaches are complicated by the likelihood of misconceptions on the part of the student. Not only must the plan recognizer fill in the planning methods connecting the student's action to his goal, but it must also guess the student's beliefs and misconceptions.

One solution is for the recognizer to assume the student's beliefs are correct except for one or more hypothesized misconceptions. The program can then try to reconstruct the student's plan for each possible misconception or combination of misconceptions until it succeeds in finding a plan for the student's actions. The work of Brown and Burton on West tutor (Burton and Brown, 1976) and the Buggy system (Brown and Burton, 1978) exemplifies this approach. Although their programs do not use the student's intermediate work and do not reconstruct the student's plan, they do infer misconceptions from the student's final answers, largely by a "generate and test" approach. Given correct models of arithmetic expertise, both systems try to explain the student's error by proposing possible faults or omissions and checking for each whether it predicts the student's answers. Buggy's analysis is particularly sophisticated in that it can use a bank of test results, both correct and incorrect, to discriminate amongst possible faults.

A bottom-up version of this approach can be implemented by expanding the set of planning methods to include buggy methods as well as correct ones, with one buggy method per misconception. Such buggy methods could be constructed by copying the appropriate correct methods and modifying their **Fetch** calls so that they return values that reflect misconceptions. (In compiler terminology, this is called "constant folding".) In recognizing such buggy methods, the plan recognizer would also be inferring the corresponding misconception. The disadvantage of the approach is the large number of buggy methods that must be constructed in advance.

In point of fact, it is possible to build a program that recognizes plans with no hints whatsoever about the student's beliefs and misconceptions, so long as he uses a known set of planning methods. The MACSYMA Advisor, for example, is able to infer beliefs and misconceptions directly from the user's goal and actions and its corpus of planning methods. The Advisor also uses a set of buggy methods as described above but only for efficiency in recognizing common misconceptions.

The Advisor's plan recognition procedure is a hybrid top-down, bottom-up method. Planning methods are suggested in bottom-up fashion on the basis of the user's actions. The identity, inputs, and outputs of each action place constraints on the variables in the suggested method. To utilize these constraints, the method is symbolically evaluated in the forward and backward directions to propagate the information to the inputs and outputs of the method and to generate subgoal expectations. A variety of heuristics are used for associating expected goals with recognized methods. The inference of the student's beliefs (and misconceptions) comes when the propagated constraints on a method's variables reach any calls to **Fetch** and thereby constrain the contents of the student's data base.

As an example of its operation, consider how the Advisor would recognize the plans in Figs 6 and 7. When the plan recognition process begins, it has as data the relevant sequence of MACSYMA commands (the **Action** boxes) and a statement of the overall goal. The Advisor's first step is to determine which planning methods could have dictated the student's observed actions. At this point every method that contains a call to **Action** is a potential caller of every **Action** box. Information about the inputs and outputs of each action are propagated by symbolic execution to the inputs and outputs of the suggested methods. The Advisor then tries to pair up expected subgoals with the planning methods that have been suggested, on the basis of the methods' goal types, inputs, and outputs. For example, the overall goal **(Obtain (Root G6 X))** pairs up with the suggested method **(Use-quadratic-formula (Root G6 X))**. Similarly, the expected subgoal **(Obtain G6)** is paired with the suggested method **(Eval-a-variable G6)**, and the goal **(Obtain (Coefficient G6 X 0))** is paired with **(valuate (? G6 X 0))**, where the **?** signifies that the function being computed is unknown prior to the pairing. Since these pairings account for all of the student's actions and any implementation of a **Transform** subgoal entails additional actions, it can be concluded that no **Transform** subgoal was created, i.e. the student believed that **G6** satisfied the precondition **p** and so the **Fetch** condition in line 5 of **Valuate** succeeded. At this point the plan is complete except for the binding of the variable **p**. In order to guess the identity of **p**, the Advisor could just generate all possible predicates (like **Expanded, Univariate, Expression**, etc.) and any one would make a legal plan since there is not enough information in the user's actions to discriminate amongst the possibilities. However, since this is potentially a very large set, the program starts with 2 special cases: the correct precondition (i.e. **Expanded**) and the most general possibility (i.e. **Expression**). These two possibilities lead to the plans shown in Figs 6 and 7. Only if these fail to be confirmed (see next section) would the Advisor enumerate the other possibilities.

4. Plan confirmation and misconception detection

The goal of plan recognition, as described in the last section, is to generate plausible plans that explain how a given action sequence achieves its goal. In the event of ambiguities, remedial action cannot be undertaken until one or another of the possibilities is confirmed.

One obvious way of pruning the space of possibilities is to use knowledge about the individual student's beliefs and misconceptions. If it is known that the student understands particular facts, then there is little chance that his plan is based on contradictory facts, and any plan that mentions such misconceptions can be eliminated. Knowledge of this sort might be gleaned from his performance on other problems or from previous interactions with the tutor.

Where the available information on the student is insufficient to confirm a single plan, an alternative is to acquire the necessary information by interrogating the student about his plan. The Teiresias system (Davis, 1982) illustrates how a derivation tree can be presented to a person piecemeal, allowing him to confirm each step or, where a discrepancy is noted, to suggest an alternative. If the student agrees to all steps, then the plan must be a copy of his own. If not, then alternative plans that differ at the disputed step can be presented until he either agrees or no alternatives remain. One difficulty with this approach is that it requires that the student already be familiar with the system's formal vocabulary of planning methods. A second difficulty is that it can be very tedious when the size of the possible plans or the number of alternatives is very large. The possibility of having the student explain his own plan awaits further progress in natural language understanding.

An alternative that eliminates the need for the student to be acquainted with the system's problem solving vocabulary is to restrict the questioning to his beliefs about the problem area, i.e. to ask about the premises attached to each plan only. Of course, even if he agrees to all of the premises, this doesn't guarantee that he agrees to the plan. However, assuming there is some misconception amongst the assertions, it will be discovered by these methods, and appropriate remedial action can be taken.

The advantage of plans as defined here is that the underlying assumptions are explicit and, therefore, it is easy to detect misconceptions. One simply compares each of the assumptions with the correct facts and notes the discrepancies. For example, in Fig. 6, all of the premises are correct except for the one about **Coeff**. In Fig. 7, all are correct except for the one stating that **G6** is expanded. In larger plans than these, a misconception sometimes leads to false conclusions, which in turn are taken as premises later in the plan and lead to other false conclusion, etc. The result is that incorrect plans often contain more than one erroneous premise. However, in such cases, the underlying misconceptions are usually distinguishable because they have no dependency links connecting them to previous assertions.

Once the underlying misconception has been determined for each plan that explains the observed actions, there still remains the task of choosing a plan to ask about first. Two criteria are helpful in this regard.

The first criterion is parsimony, the assumption that the student has only one underlying misconception (or as few as possible). When choosing amongst possible plans, the MACSYMA Advisor, for example, asks about those plans with the fewest misconceptions and moves on to buggier plans only if it fails to get a confirmation. As an example, consider the MACSYMA session in Fig. 1c. One explanation of the student's behavior, in addition to the plans shown in Figs 6 and 7, is that the student believes that, in order for **Coeff** to work, the first argument must be, say, univariate (i.e. it must contain only one variable), and he believes that **G6** satisfies this condition. Both beliefs are incorrect, and neither has dependency links to other assertions in the plan, i.e. there are two independent misconceptions. Consequently, the Advisor would consider this possibility only after it had eliminated all of the plans with only single misconceptions.

A second criterion is that the misconception be plausible in light of the student's learning characteristics and experience. For example, in MACSYMA people often choose commands on the basis of their names; thus it is more likely that a novice would believe that **Coeff** computes an expression's coefficient than **Ratsimp**. Or, if a student had always observed that **Coeff** computes the coefficient (because it had only ever been called on expanded expressions), then the misconception of Fig. 6 is likely. The body of work on learning models has been steadily growing and may some day be of use in evaluating the relative likelihood of misconceptions (see Burton and Brown, 1976; Brown and van Lehn, 1980; Matz, 1981). However, at the moment, most of that work is inapplicable because it depends on knowledge of the student's experience, and this is generally unavailable to programs like the Advisor.

5. Advice generation

Once a plan has been confirmed and the misconception identified, remedial action can be undertaken. The misconception can be corrected, and the tutor can take the opportunity to offer the student an alternative. Since the information is provided in the context of a specific problem of interest to the student, the chances are good that it will be understood and remembered.

The best way to handle a detected misconception is pedagogical issue of some debate. One can simply tell the student what's wrong or lead him to discover it for himself through socratic dialogue. The Advisor uses the former approach. For example in Fig. 3, it tells the student how the **Coeff** command really works. In general, it supplies the correct information about a command whenever it discovers the student has a misconception about it.

Unfortunately, in the MACSYMA world, as in other problem areas, relaying the correct information about the wrong operation doesn't always lead the student to the right one. By providing this additional information, the tutor can help the student solve the problem and at the same time further its pedagogical aims. Of course, problems often have multiple solutions, and it isn't obvious which alternative to suggest.

One possibility is for the tutor to present the solution that is best or simplest according to an expert. For example, in the MACSYMA problem of Fig. 1c, the Advisor might have suggested that the student use the **Factor** command to compute the roots of the quadratic in a single step. Alternatively, it could have taken advantage of the situation to present material the student has not yet seen. Instead of telling him about **Ratcoeff** or **Factor**, it could have introduced MACSYMA's **Part** commands, which select parts of expressions, and could have shown him how to put them together in a program that solves quadratics.

Both of these criteria are independent of the student's approach to solving the problem. While both have advantages, a good tutor often prefers to tailor his advice to the student's problem solving strategy instead of presenting an entirely different approach. Another major advantage of plan recognition is that it provides the tutor with a record of the student's strategy to use in formulating remedial action. In response to a misconception, the MACSYMA Advisor, for example, searches its own (correct) data base with the same **Fetch** pattern that the student used in retrieving the erroneous belief; and, if the search succeeds, it conveys the answer to the student. In the consultation example of Fig. 3, this resulted in the offer of **Ratcoeff** as a substitute for **Coeff**. With this information, the student was still able to use the quadratic formula approach to solving the problem.

6. Conclusions

The MACSYMA Advisor was implemented as a test of the plan recognition approach to automated consultation. The methods to include in MUSER were determined after the analysis of several dozen sessions of novice MACSYMA use, and they account for all the non-exploratory behavior in the data in the sense that the humans' solutions can be generated from the MUSER methods. Working with MUSER as its student model, the plan recognition program was able to reconstruct the student's plan with very few questions. The results must be viewed with caution, however, since only three different problems were represented in the data.

6.1. REACTIVE ENVIRONMENTS

The Advisor's chief goal is to pinpoint and correct misconceptions on the part of the student. Misconceptions are often promoted by environments that do not provide immediate feedback after each action. This feedback could be of two types, viz. purely local feedback on the results of one's actions and more global feedback that takes into account the student's goals.

MACSYMA is a good example of an environment that provides local feedback. In the example of Fig. 1c, the user could have traced the problem to **Coeff** by displaying the value of each command rather than grouping several commands on a single line and suppressing the display. However, had the interaction been longer and the expressions larger, the feedback would probably have been less useful. If each step had to be checked by hand, what would have been the point of using MACSYMA? In this case only global feedback sensitive to the user's goal would have provided the necessary diagnosis. The same is true of Bertram's case, where each step produced reasonable looking results. In fact, his solutions (15 and 2) were simpler than the correct solutions. The point here is not to prove that local feedback is without value, but only to suggest that sensitivity to the student's plan is sometimes necessary.†

The Sophie-II system (Brown *et al.*, 1976) was an attempt to create a *reactive environment* of this sort, in which the system supplied feedback not only on the results of the student's measurements and replacements but also on their appropriateness to the diagnostic goal. Sophie made this evaluation by comparing the student's efforts to the actions of an expert diagnostician. The plan recognition approach is an attempt to generalize this activity to domains where the number of reasonable solutions is too large for the expert comparison technique to work effectively.

6.2. COMPLEXITY IN COMPUTER SYSTEMS

The complexity of theories in natural science very much reflects the complexity of the phenomena being modelled. For artifacts like computer systems, however, there is a prevalent belief that complexity can be eliminated by better design. If so, why not forget automated user aids and concentrate on making the systems easier to use? The problem is that there is a tension between ease of learning and ease of use once learned. Even if it were true that complexity were independent of "power", this conflict would remain.

MACSYMA is a good example. Many of its commands admit an ambiguity of interpretation on different problem areas. Some users think of **Coeff** as returning the full coefficient of its argument and are surprised to find that it doesn't. The suggestion is then made to rename **Ratcoeff**, which gets the full coefficient, to be **Coeff** and rename **Coeff** to be something innocuous like **Syncoeff**. Unfortunately there are users who are interested in obtaining roots of polynomials over polynomial domain, for which they need the syntactic version. Seeing **Coeff**, they would assume it is what they want and get the wrong answer. More importantly, the implementors of MACSYMA are loathe to perform the swap because more people would use the computationally expensive **Ratcoeff** even when the argument is already expanded. Another example is the existence in MACSYMA of several commands with hidden prerequisites and side-effects (that rob the system of its local feedback). Any suggestions to pass extra arguments or eliminate all non-explicit side-effects have met great resistance from the experienced users. As a result new users develop misconceptions, and plan-sensitive consultants become necessary.

In general, a consultant like the Advisor is necessary whenever one is faced with a problem solving situation in a domain one does not fully understand. The lack of knowledge may be incidental, as it is when the domain or device is fairly simple but time constraints make it impossible for the user to learn all that is necessary (e.g. using

† In point of fact, Macsyma users often don't take advantage of the available feedback and, when they do, frequently are still unable to identify the problem. Also, feedback tends to encourage lazy experimentation rather than careful thought. For example, in simplifying expressions novices blindly try all the automatic simplifiers instead of discriminating amongst them to determine the most suitable.

a calculator or oscilloscope). Or it may be essential, as when the domain is inherently complex (as in MACSYMA or algebra or natural science).

6.3. SUMMARY

The central idea in this paper is that plans can be viewed as dependency graphs that explain how a set of actions achieves its goal in terms of the problem solver's beliefs about the problem area. The planning methods used in creating the action sequence can be thought of as rules of inference in these graphs, and so the graphs very much resemble computation traces of the planning process. A number of plan recognition routines have been implemented that can reconstruct plans, even those based on misconceptions, directly from action sequences. The importance of plan recognition to research in intelligent teaching systems is that it provides a way to interpret a student's intermediate steps in problem solving. The resulting plans can be used to identify the student's misconceptions and to offer remediation in context. Much work needs to be done in building better planning models and making plan recognition procedures sensitive to the learning characteristics of the student; but, because of their demonstrated ability to recognize plans, various existing programs (like the MACSYMA Advisor) suggest the feasibility of the approach.

References

BROWN, J. S. & BURTON, R. R. (1978). Diagnostic Models for Procedural Bugs in Basic Mathematical Skills. *Cognitive Science*, **2**, 155–192.

BROWN, J. S. & VAN LEHN, K. (1980). Repair Theory: A Generative Theory of Bugs in Procedural Skills. *Cognitive Science*, **4**, 379–426.

BROWN, J. S., BURTON, R. R. & BELL, A. (1976). *Reactive Learning Environment for Computer Assisted Instruction*. Bolt, Beranek, and Newman, Inc., Report 3314.

BURTON, R. R. & BROWN, J. S. (1976). A tutoring and student modeling paradigm for gaming environments. *SIGCSE* **8**, 1, 236–246.

CARR, B. & GOLDSTEIN, I. P. *Overlays: a Theory of Modeling for Computer Aided Instruction*. MIT AI Memo 406.

CHEATHAM, T. E. & TOWNLEY, J. (1976). Symbolic execution of programs—a look at loop analysis. *Proceedings of the Symposium on Symbolic and Algebraic Manipulation*, pp. 90–96.

DAVIS, R. (1982). Teiresias: applications of Meta-level knowledge. In *Knowledge-based Systems in Artificial Intelligence* (R. Davis and D. B. Lenat, eds). McGraw-Hill, New York.

DEKLEER, J. (1979). *Causal and Teleological Reasoning in Circuit Recognition*. Ph.D. thesis, MIT AI.

GENESERETH, M. R. (1978). *Automated Consultation for Complex Computer Systems*. Ph.D. thesis, Harvard University.

GENESERETH, M. R. (1981). *Plan Recognition*. Memo HPP-81-10, Stanford University.

GOLDBERG, A. (1973). *Computer-assisted Instruction: the application of Theorem-proving to Adaptive Response Analysis*. Report No. 203, Institute for Mathematical Studies in the Social Sciences, Stanford University.

HEWITT, C. (1975). *Towards a Programming Apprentice*. Trans. on Software Engineering, SE-1, 1 IEEE, pp. 26–45.

MATHLAB GROUP (1977). *MACSYMA Reference Manual*. MIT Laboratory for Computer Science.

MATZ, M. (1981). A generative theory of high school algebra errors. Chapter 2 in this volume.

MILLER, M. & GOLDSTEIN, I. P. (1976). *Parsing Protocols Using Problem Solving Grammars*. MIT AI Memo 385.

SCHMIDT, C. F., SRIDHARAN, N. S. & GOODSON, J. L. (1978). The plan recognition problem. *Artificial Intelligence*, **11**, No. 1, 2, 45–83.

SHORTLIFFE, E. H. *MYCIN: a Rule-based Computer Program for Advising Physicians Regarding Antimicrobial Therapy Selection*. STAN-CS-74-465, Stanford University.

SLEEMAN, D. H. (1977). A system which allows students to explore algorithms. Proceedings of the 5th International Joint Conference on Artificial Intelligence.

STALLMAN, R. M. & SUSSMAN, G. J. (1977). Forward reasoning and dependency-directed backtracking in a system for computer-aided circuit analysis. *Artificial Intelligence*, **9**, 135–196.

STANSFIELD, J. L., CARR, B. & GOLDSTEIN, I. P. (1976). *WUMPUS Advisor I*. MIT AI Memo 381.

WATERS, R. C. (1978). *A Method for Automatically Analyzing the Logical Structure of Programs*. Ph.D. thesis, MIT AI.

8. Diagnosing bugs in a simple procedural skill

RICHARD R. BURTON

Xerox Palo Alto Research Center, Cognitive and Instructional Sciences Group, 3333 Coyote Hill Road, Palo Alto, CA 94304

To account for student errors in simple procedural skills, Brown and Burton (1978), proposed "the Buggy model." In the model, a student's errors are seen as symptoms of a "bug," a discrete modification to the correct skills which effectively duplicates the student's behavior. This paper describes an operational diagnostic system based on the Buggy model that has been used with several thousand students over the last two years to find systematic errors in the domain of place-value subtraction. Subtraction is used as a paradigmatic case for studying diagnosis; simple enough that it is possible to diagnose real students and complex enough to provide an interesting case study of the subtleties of diagnosing students in a natural setting.

A brief overview of the Buggy model and a framework for diagnostic systems using the model is presented. This provides both a framework for understanding the final diagnostic system and an appreciation of the subtleties of diagnosis. The complicating factors in diagnosis are presented and solutions to some of the complications are discussed.

Two diagnostic systems are described; one for dealing with standard tests and one for interactive diagnosis. The problems particular to each type of diagnosis are examined.

A definition of "subskill" (what a student must know to perform a skill) is derived from the set of observed bugs. Some uses of subskills are described and all of the subskills of subtraction are given.

1 Introduction

To account for student errors in simple procedural skills, Brown and Burton (1978), proposed "the Buggy model." In the model, a student's errors are seen as symptoms of a "bug," a discrete modification to the correct skills which effectively duplicate the student's behavior. As an example, consider the following two errors made by a student in the procedural task of subtraction:

$$\begin{array}{r} 500 \\ -65 \\ \hline 565 \end{array} \qquad \begin{array}{r} 312 \\ -243 \\ \hline 149 \end{array}$$

Both errors are accounted for by the bug named **0-n=n**.† The student is using a

---

†Bug names appear in bold type.

modification to the subtraction procedure which dictates that when the top digit in a column is 0, write the bottom digit as the answer for that column. Modifications may be the result of deleting part of the correct procedure, of adding incorrect subprocedures, or of replacing correct subprocedures by incorrect ones.

This chapter describes an operational system based on the Buggy model that has been used with several thousand students over the last two years to diagnose systematic errors in the domain of place-value subtraction. For the purposes of this chapter, subtraction is used as a paradigmatic case for studying diagnosis. Subtraction is simple enough that it is possible to diagnose real students in a natural setting and complex enough to provide an interesting case study of the subtleties involved. Initially the diagnostic system had a fixed, prespecified set of bugs, and it simply chose those bugs that maximally accounted for the student's behavior. As the range of erroneous behaviors to be diagnosed expanded, the space of possibilities became too large for these exhaustive search techniques. Also, many students have subtle variations of the 'taught" methods, make careless mistakes while following their correct or faulty procedures, and switch back and forth between old and recently-learned procedures. All of these factors complicate the diagnostic process and set the stage for the system to be described in this paper.

The first section presents a brief overview of the Buggy model and characterizes what we mean by diagnosis. Then the framework for diagnostic systems is presented using a simple system as an example. This provides both a framework for understanding the final diagnostic system and an appreciation of the subtleties of diagnosis.

The second section describes the complicating factors in diagnosis and indicates why the simple system must be extended. This discussion also mentions solutions to some of the complications.

The third section describes the diagnostic system that is used when students are given a prespecified test and the methods for dealing with the complications. The interactions between the heuristics of the system and the items on the test are examined. An interactive version of the diagnostic system is presented and the areas of problem generation and logical equivalence are considered.

The fourth section presents a definition of "subskill" (what a student must know to perform a skill) that is derived from the set of observed bugs. Some uses of subskills are described and an example of each of the subskills of subtraction is given.

1.1   PROCEDURAL NETWORK MODEL

When we set out to explain the causes of observed student errors, we knew a representation was required, but we did not know how complex the representation would need to be. We did not know what primitives or control structures would be appropriate so, in an attempt to avoid having our language shape the way we saw the data, we chose a representation language which allowed us freedom to capture each newly observed set of student errors in the way that seemed most appropriate to those errors. Thus our initial representation scheme was *ad hoc by design.*

The representation scheme distinguishes between goals and methods for satisfying those goals. For each goal there is a correct method of achieving that goal and, optionally, alternative correct methods and alternative incorrect or "buggy" methods. Methods are written in a stylized subset of the programming language, Lisp. The most frequent construct in the implementation of the methods is a call for other goals to be satisfied (i.e., breaking a goal down into subgoals). This led to the formation of "procedural networks" (Sacerdoti, 1977) which represent the goal-calling structure, the associated conditionals, the primitives and other information about the intention of the procedures along with diagnostic suggestions. All this information is represented in the form of a network. The network, however, is not meant to be a cognitive construct, but simply a framework for relevant pieces of information.

The observed data is represented in the network as procedures (methods and their variants) which mimic the behaviors of the students. To guarantee some generality (so that not every student could be hypothesized as having a different bug unrelated to any other bug or to the correct skill) the representation scheme was constrained in two ways. First, if a student was executing part of the procedural task correctly, the scheme's representation of that part of the student's behavior had to be the same as it was for a correct student. A bug, in other words, must be the least possible variant of the correct skill that mimics the behavior.

The second constraint was to distinguish between primitive and compound bugs. If we found a student who had behavior A and another who had behavior B and a third whose behavior was the combination of A and B, then this third behavior must be modelled in the representation as the composition of the bug A with the bug B. These two constraints led to numerous reworkings of the decomposition of the skill into subskills.†

1.2   DIAGNOSIS

There are many possible meanings of the term diagnosis, many different methods of testing or determining a diagnosis, and many different purposes to which

---

†From a psychological point of view, the procedural network representation is a *descriptive* tool. In particular, we are not proposing the procedural network as an alternative to, for example, the class of production rule models which try to model internal mental processes of the level of working memory. Our goal is to characterize the entire class of data we observe in a form that facilitates comparing descriptions of the data without worrying about underlying mechanisms. It seemed premature to focus on the possible mechanisms of a particularly well-formed subset of the data without first characterizing the entire range of phenomena.

diagnoses are applied. (Diagnosis is often referred to in some work as developing a model of the student.) We shall discuss the range of possible meanings and choose the one most pertinent to our work. The *dimension* of this range is a measure of the depth of understanding of what the student is doing.

The simplest level of diagnosis is determining whether or not a student has mastered a skill, and possibly the degree of mastery, represented by a numeric value. This level of diagnosis is not particularly useful for remediation, since one does not have any idea what parts of the skill need more work. It is interesting to note that without a model of the skill being tested, even determining that the student possesses the skill is hard. A student may have an almost arbitrarily complex perversion of the skill and produce the right answers for most typical problems. But without a good model, it is difficult to determine how much the boundary conditions of the skill have been stressed. If a test includes only examples that the student gets right, it will always be concluded that s/he has mastered the skill.†

A more complicated level of diagnosis is determining what subskills the student has not mastered (Friend, 1980). This technique has useful applications for both remediation and coaching/tutoring. The WEST coaching system (Burton and Brown) presents a system that determines which subskills a student does not know and uses that information to provide and control tutorial feedback. This level of diagnosis has its own set of problems that will not be touched upon until Section 4.3, in which a theoretical basis for formalizing the notion of subskills will be advanced.

The level of diagnosis appropriate for this paper is determining what internalized set of incorrect instructions or rules gives results equal to the student's results. *That is, we require of a diagnosis that it be able to predict, not only whether the answer will be incorrect, but the exact digits of the incorrect answer on a novel problem.* This means having a model of the student that replicates behavior on the problems observed so far and that *predicts behavior* on problems not yet done. It is clear that we require a model of the student's encoded skill to be sufficiently complete that it can be executed on new problems.

A usage of the term diagnosis that is still more specific than the above is to determine what has *caused* the student to develop his incorrect procedures. At present, diagnoses at this level are not very well understood and are beyond the scope of this paper. Brown and VanLehn (1980) have developed a principled theory that explains many of the observed bugs.

---

†Usually the determination of what problems to include (i.e., what possible mislearnings are detected by the test) is left to test-makers' intuitions of the kinds of mistakes they have seen other students make. A model of the procedural skill can provide insight into what the possible ways of mislearning a skill are and thus aid in the creation of diagnostic tests.

1.3   FRAMEWORK FOR THE DIAGNOSTIC PROCESS

In the next section we describe some of the complexities that a diagnostic system faces with real students. We begin by introducing, and exploring the shortcomings of, a simple prototypical system for diagnosing idealized student behavior using an executable model of the possible bugs. We shall direct our discussion by way of examples in subtraction. Many of these complications occur in other domains, but subtraction provides a particularly clear illustration of the problems.

1.3.1   A core but overly simple system: Naïve Diagnostic System

The leverage provided by the procedural network model is an efficient means for predicting the answer to any problem from any bug. The Naïve Diagnostic System compares the student's answers with the output of each bug run through the test and picks the *one* bug that gives the same answers as the student. (We will later discuss why there might not be exactly one.) Since there are only about a hundred and ten primitive bugs for subtraction (that we have identified so far), the computation is not overwhelming.

Figure 1 presents a sample "diagnostic table" that might arise from such a system for an idealized student. The diagnostic table provides a summary of how well a bug matches the student's responses on the given set of problems. The test problems with the correct answers appear at the top of the table. The student's answers appear on the next line, using the convention that "+" indicates a correct student answer. Each of the remaining pairs of lines provide the name of a bug and the answers produced by it under the assumption that the student had this and only this bug.

For each of these lines, a "***" means that the bug predicted the student's *incorrect* answer. A "*" means that the bug in that row would give the correct answer and also that the student got the correct answer. Thus "*" and "***" indicate agreement between the student's behavior and the predicted behavior of the bug, and positive evidence that the student has that bug. Negative evidence is portrayed in two ways: A "!" means that the bug in that row predicts the correct answer but the student gave a wrong answer. The number predicted by the bug is shown if it disagrees with both the student's and the correct answers.

Figure 1 shows a student who has the bug mentioned in the introduction, $0-n=n$. Also shown is the entry for the bug, "the smaller digit in each column is subtracted from the larger, regardless of which is on top" (called **smaller from larger**.) This bug generates the same answer as the student on the fourth problem but is not an acceptable diagnosis because it doesn't account for the entire set of student behavior.

This diagnostic system can go wrong in two ways: there may be more than one bug that exactly matches every answer given by the student; or there may be no bug at all that matches. If there is more than one bug and the system is

Problems and Correct Answers

45	40	139	500	312
-23	-30	- 43	- 65	- 243
22	10	96	435	69

Student Answers:

	+	+	+	565	149

$0 \cdot n = n$:

*	*	*	***	***

smaller from larger:

*	*	116	***	131

***	-	bug predicts student's incorrect answer
*	-	bug predicts student's correct answer
+	-	student's answer is correct

FIG 1. Student diagnostic table with bug $0 \cdot n = n$.

interactive, it can attempt to generate a new problem for the student so that it can distinguish between the bugs. (Finding such a problem can often be extremely difficult, as will be discussed in section 3.3.2.) If the student is not on-line (as is the case with standardized tests), the test given the student must be redesigned.†

The second way the simple diagnostic algorithm can go wrong is by having the student's behavior not emulated by any bug. In these cases, no bugs match all of the student's answers. With real students, there are many ways that this can happen. We will continue by examining some of them.

2 Complicating Factors in Diagnosis

2.1 PERFORMANCE LAPSES

The diagnostic situation is complicated by the fact that students sometimes really do make mistakes from fatigue, laziness, boredom, or inattention. This happens while they are following a buggy procedure as well as while they are following a correct one. A closely related problem is that students sometimes do things for reasons that are beyond the limits of the theory being used to determine consistency. For example, they may copy some answers from their neighbors or

†There are two properties that the test must have in order to prevent such ambiguous diagnoses from arising. One is to have, for each of the hundred bugs, at least one problem which causes a symptom for each bug. In the case that the student has only one bug, this bug can thus be distinguished from the correct procedure. The second property the test must have is to contain problems that distinguish between any two of the hundred bugs. For example if the test in Figure 1 included neither the third problem nor the fifth problem, it could not be determined whether the student had $0 \cdot n = n$ or smaller from larger. This does not mean that a diagnostic test need contain several hundred problems. Problems can be generated which test more than one bug at a time, producing distinct incorrect answers. For example, the tests we use in our data collection have these properties and contain only 20 problems. The problem of test construction will be addressed later.

get digits for their answers from nearby problems. This brings into question the notion of a consistent error: A student who always makes the rightmost digit in the answer be the same as the date is being completely consistent in a sense we have not included in our database. Consistency in the sense that we use it implies that the student will always give the same answer to the same problem and that the answer is completely determined by the problem alone.

To be of practical use, a system must find a student's systematic errors even in those cases where some non-systematic errors are present. This means that the diagnostic system cannot insist on exact matches between its proposed bugs and the student's behavior. The system must find the best match and then decide if it is really good enough to be a diagnosis. One major ramification of this fact is that hypotheses about a student's bug can not be rejected with the first piece of evidence to the contrary. This rules out a major class of diagnostic techniques which use problems that very few hypotheses explain to quickly reduce the space of possibilities.

2.2   ERRORS IN PRIMITIVE SUBSKILLS

Another source of inconsistency, or "noise" as we shall refer to it, is that specialized subskills that are assumed to be primitive in the model may, in fact, have errors. This can be seen in subtraction in the form of errors in the standard subtraction facts table such as $13-7=8$. One "solution" to this problem is to consider each fact to be a separate subskill and to consider all of the possible values of, for example, $13-7$ except 6 as being bugs.†

This approach has several problems. It is not applicable in the common case where facts-table errors are not consistent. It is unconfirmable in practice because a typical test of 20 items requires about 60 subtraction facts to be used. Since there are 100 subtraction facts, not every fact can be tried once, much less enough times to determine consistency. This solution also has the drawback that almost any answer can be "explained" as a compounding of facts-table errors which could swamp the diagnostic system with complex alternative theories.

2.3   SUBSKILL VARIANTS

Another source of noise is that repeated drilling on parts of the skill can lead to variants of the "standard" algorithm that cause the student to do correctly parts of problems that the bug predicts he would miss. For example, ten is learned as one of the subtraction facts by repeatedly solving exercises of the form, $10-y$. Based on this experience, students sometimes perceive the leftmost one and zero digits of a number (e.g., 1093) as being the single "digit" ten rather than as two digits, hence hiding cases where a bug such as $0-n=0$ might otherwise arise. Another

†Alternatively, one could postulate a model for doing "facts" and include this in the model of subtraction. One has then just pushed the problem down a level by assuming a different level of primitives which might themselves not be completely correct.

example arises because students are drilled on two-column problems requiring borrowing—they will often know how to borrow correctly in the units column of a problem but have a bug in the borrowing procedure in the remaining columns.

2.4   COMPOUND BUGS

Students often have mislearned more than part of the skill, and thus have a combination, or compound, of two or more primitive bugs.   In a recent experiment with approximately one thousand third-, fourth- and fifth-grade students, thirty-seven percent of the diagnoses were compound bugs (VanLehn, 1981). A straightforward way for the simple system to diagnose these students is for it to consider subsets of primitive bugs up to some cardinality. We have observed students with as many as four bugs in a single skill (see Figure 2). With 110 primitive bugs, this leads quickly to more hypotheses than can be feasibly examined (approximately 10^8) by exhaustive search. For the remainder of this section we explore heuristics to reduce the space of bugs, and describe the heuristics for searching the reduced space efficiently.

2.4.1   Reducing the space of compound bugs

Many of the arbitrary compound bugs, or compounds, will be logically equivalent in the sense of producing the same behavior. If only one member of each class of logically equivalent compounds is examined, the search space is reduced.

One grouping that suggests itself is to ignore the order of the bugs within the compound, so that the compound of bug A with bug B, denoted as {A B}, is the same as the compound of bug B with bug A, {B A}. This can easily be accomplished by canonicalizing the compounds by, for example, alphabetizing the component letters. There is, however, a useful interpretation that suggests itself for the difference between {A B} and {B A}, that being whether the correct model was perturbed by bug B then the result perturbed by bug A or vice-versa. Under this interpretation, the ordering indicates the order of perturbation in the model. (This is analogous to the decision in a production system of the order in which rules A and B are tried.) In many cases the bugs are independent so that the order of perturbation makes no difference. But independence is not always the case. In some cases, the preconditions of one of the bugs can subsume the preconditions of the other, preventing it from ever being tried. For these cases, the standardization must put bugs in order of decreasing specificity. For example, the bug 0-n=0 would be ordered before **smaller from larger**.

Another observation about grouping compound bugs into equivalence classes is that some bugs "hide" other bugs in the sense of preventing their preconditions from ever being met. In these cases, {A} is logically equivalent to {A B}. For example, the bug **smaller from larger** will hide any bug in the borrowing procedures so that their compound will be equivalent to **smaller from larger** alone. This is because **smaller from larger** redefines the column-subtracting procedure so that it never needs to borrow; any bug that has **trying to borrow** as one of its preconditions will never be tried.

31	53	23	2003	203	1043	520	10214	909	10300	70001
-11	-20	-8	- 24	-109	-505	-467	-8375	-458	- 546	- 391
20	33	15	1979	94	538	53	1839	451	9754	69610

Student Answers:

+	30	5	1	106	2	140	161	501	200	0

smaller from larger & $0 \cdot n = 0$ & $n \cdot 0 = 0$ & stop working when the bottom number runs out:

*	***	***	***	***	***	***	***	***	***	***

$n \cdot 0 = 0$:

*	***	!	!	4	508	!	!	!	!	!

stop working when the bottom digit becomes a blank:

*	!	***	79	!	!	!	!	!	754	610

smaller from larger:

*	!	25	2021	***	1542	147	18161	551	10246	70390

$0 \cdot n = 0$:

*	!	!	!		1038	60	1909	***	9800	70000

***	-	bug predicts student's incorrect answer
*	-	bug predicts student's correct answer
!	-	bug predicts the correct answer, but student's answer is incorrect
+	-	student's answer is correct

FIG. 2. Student diagnostic table with a compound bug. The diagnosis is a compound of the bugs smaller from larger, $0 \cdot n = 0$, $n \cdot 0 = 0$ and stop working on a problem when the bottom number runs out. The evidence for and against the individual primitive bugs is also included.

Canonicalization fails entirely in a few cases where bugs have overlapping preconditions which prevent there from being a single "right" order. Two orderings may be different from each other and different from any of their subsets. For example, the bug *when borrowing from a column in which the top and bottom digits are the same, borrow from the next column to the left instead* and the bug *when borrowing from a column with a zero as the top digit, change it to a 9 and return* have preconditions that overlap in problems requiring a borrow in a column which has zero over zero (e.g., 305-108). Thus {A B} is actually different from the bug {B A}; the first gets 107 for the answer while the second gets 297. Our representation makes the distinction between these two bugs so that both are representable.† (This problem presents itself in production system formalisms in the form of ordering of rules in the rule set. One consequence of this for diagnostic systems based on such production rules is that their diagnosis must, in

†The diagnostic compounding mechanisms use a canonical ordering routine so that this difference would not be "discovered" by the system itself.

some cases, include not only what the buggy rules are but also how they are ordered.)

There are also cases in which different combinations of bugs are the same (generate the same results on all problems) even though they are made from different primitives and can not be grouped for any principled reason. These cases are rare but do necessitate that the system be able to deal with multiple diagnoses. This also creates the additional annoyance that after determining that two bugs are the same, the system must then decide which is a more appropriate label for the diagnosis.

2.4.2   Heuristics to limit the search

While the number of hypotheses to be searched is greatly reduced by embedding knowledge about hiding and canonical ordering, the space is still too large to search exhaustively. One standard approach to limiting combinatorial search is to search only those compound theories for which there exists support in the data (a variant of "bottom-up" searching). The system limits its search to only combining primitive bugs for which evidence has been found. For this approach to succeed in finding a compound bug {A B}, there must be evidence for A and B separately. We will address the ramifcations of this limitation and methods for circumventing them in a later section.

Care must be taken when searching the space of compounds because primitive bugs do not always combine in simple ways. There are situations in which a bug will interfere with another bug in such a way as to cause the student to get the right answer on problems where one of the bugs would predict the occurrence of a wrong answer. For example, on the problem 313-208, a student who has both the **smaller from larger** bug and the **n-0=0** bug will get the right answer, 105. A student with the **smaller from larger** bug only will get 115. This has the important ramification for the diagnostic system that *it cannot eliminate a hypothesis just because it predicts that the student would miss a problem that he gets right.* Another complexity of bug combination is that two bugs that generate the same answers on all problems can each combine with the same third bug and generate different behavior. Two bugs generating the same behavior occur in the situation of needing to borrow from a column which has a zero on top. One bug **increments the zero to one instead of decrementing it** {A} and the other bug **decrements the bottom digit instead of the top** {B}. When each of these bugs is compounded with the bug 0-n=n {C}, however, we get different behavior. In the problem 304-159, the first bug compound {A C} will get 165 for an answer (because incrementing the zero has disabled the 0-n condition), while the second bug compound {B C} will get 245.†

---

†The situation here is actually slightly more complicated. The two bugs actually can be distinguished in the case where the digit below the zero is also zero or blank. In this case, the bottom zero can not be decremented. However, if each of the bugs is compounded with the bug **ignore columns in which there is a zero on top and a zero or a blank on the bottom** {D}, the compounds {A D} and {B D} are equivalent. When these compounds are compounded with 0-n=n, the resulting triples {A C D} and {B C D} are distinguishable again.

Allowing bugs in an executable model to be arbitrarily combined may result in the implementation problem of loops. For example, if the primitive bug of **moving from left to right instead of right to left** is not implemented very carefully, it can loop when combined with a bug in the recursive borrowing procedure that has built into it the notion of moving from right to left. These problems, once discovered, can be overcome by reimplementing the offending bugs.

3 The DEBUGGY Diagnostic System

3.1 METHOD OF DIAGNOSIS

In this section we will describe an extension of the Naive Diagnostic System. First we consider the off-line version, called DEBUGGY, then the interactive version, called IDEBUGGY. From each student the system has the answers for every problem on the test (and the test problems themselves). At a high level, DEBUGGY compares the student's answers with results of the primitive bugs, looks for combinations of the bugs that compare favorably, tries to explain the noise in the resulting set of compound bugs, and then chooses the best and decides if it is good enough to be a diagnosis. The details of these steps are discussed below.

3.1.1 Forming the initial hypothesis set

DEBUGGY begins by considering a fixed set of hypotheses that includes all of the primitive bugs and roughly 20 common compound bugs. (See Friend and Burton (1981) for a description of the 110 primitive bugs.) The results of all 130 bugs are compared with the student's answers. This comparison is used to determine the subset of the known bugs which will become the *initial hypothesis set*. The bugs in this subset form the basis for the compounding heuristics. The initial hypothesis set contains any bug that explains *at least one of the student's wrong answers*, and has what we refer to as full-problem evidence, meaning that it has correctly predicted the student's wrong answer on at least one problem.

An alternative to full-problem evidence for inclusion in the initial hypothesis set is single-column evidence which explains only a single incorrect column of the student's answer. For example, $0-n=0$ has single-column evidence in the problem $303-218=105$ because it explains the ten's column. A full-problem evidence scheme is used because it is efficient to obtain and is very constraining on the set of bugs. The latter is crucial since the search space grows rapidly with the number of primitive bugs considered for compounding.

There are two possible advantages to a single-column evidence scheme: theories can be ruled out quickly (by having to look at only the first column rather than the whole problem to find out that a hypothesis is not correct); and better candidates for compounding can be found (because the candidate only has to exhibit itself in a single column rather than in the whole problem). The first advantage is offset by the efficiency of the procedural network representation;

complete answers can be provided fast enough that time is not an issue. Even if a single-column evidence scheme were used, full-problem information would still be needed to check for interactions and determine the consistency of local-column theories across the whole problem. Thus, DEBUGGY uses full-problem evidence to constrain its initial hypothesis set. The second advantage is counteracted by the fact that, while single-column evidence does find more candidates for compounding, many of them are spurious. We will later discuss the use of single-column evidence to extend the initial set of hypotheses as needed.

3.1.2   Reducing the initial hypothesis set

The elements of the initial hypothesis set (bugs that completely explain at least one erroneous student answer) are combined to generate additional hypotheses particular to the student. Thus, the space of hypotheses considered for a student is limited to the powerset (set of all subsets) of the initial hypothesis set. Even this limited space is often too large to search exhaustively (not infrequently the full-problem evidence set contains around 20 bugs, leading to 20^4 hypotheses); so attempts are made to reduce the initial hypothesis set before looking for compounds.

Some bugs appear in the full-problem evidence set because they agree coincidentally with a student answer actually caused by a different bug. For example on the problem 700-5, the bug **adding instead of subtracting** will give the same answer as the bug **smaller from larger**. If this problem is the only piece of evidence for **adding instead of subtracting**, and if there is other evidence for **smaller from larger**, **adding** instead of subtracting will be removed at this stage, saving the system the necessity of exploring all compounds containing **adding** instead of subtracting as one of the constituents. Another reason primitive bugs in the initial hypothesis set may not be good candidates for compounding is that some are specializations of other bugs; if a student has a general bug, many of their answers will agree in places with its specializations. For example, **smaller from larger** is more general than **0-n=n**. If a student is following **smaller from larger**, some answers will be explainable by **0-n=n**. The subsumption heuristic will discard **0-n=n** in this situation.

The initial hypothesis set is reduced by finding and removing primitive bugs that are completely subsumed by other primitive bugs. A strict definition of subsumption is used because it is possible to remove a bug which should be one constituent of the final compound theory. The subsumption process considers all of the problems on the test before removing a bug. For this process, there are three classes of predictions by the bug. Ordered in terms of value, or "goodness," they are: (1) those that agree with the student's answer, (2) those that predict the correct answer when the student's answer is incorrect, and (3) those that predict a wrong answer different from the answer the student gave. For a bug A to be removed, there must exist another bug B such that A is the same or worse on every answer, and worse on at least one, than B. In particular, a bug will be kept if that bug predicts the right answer when the possible subsuming bug predicts a wrong answer. These retained bugs are more likely to compound well because the problems for which they predict the correct answer represent situations wherein they do not apply. Hence they would not interfere with other bugs that do explain the behavior.

3.1.3 Compounding the hypothesis set

Pairs of bugs in the reduced full-problem evidence set are formed and the resulting compound hypotheses are compared with the student's answers. If the compound explains more of the student's behavior than either of its constituent hypotheses, the compound is added to the set of hypotheses.

Any new compounds are paired with the existing hypotheses so that all subsets of bugs will be considered. There is a limit (currently 4) to how many primitives are allowed in a compound; compounds with more than this number of constituents are rejected. As an efficiency consideration, information stored in the network indicates which bugs hide which other bugs or subprocedures. For example, a link from the bug **smaller from larger** to the procedures for borrowing is used to store the fact that this bug will prevent borrowing from ever occurring. Such links are examined when a compound is first considered so that any attempt to compound **smaller from larger** with any bug of the borrowing procedures will be rejected immediately.

This "hill-climbing" algorithm, which needs independent reasons for belief in each of the pieces, is very efficient but occasionally misses a bug because it is not one of the considered hypotheses. In some cases, one of the bugs in the compound will completely cover the symptomatic cases for the other, making it impossible to get independent evidence for the covered bug. For example, consider the case of a student who has the bug **0-n=0** {A} compounded with the bug **when borrowing from a column with a 0 as the top digit, decrement the bottom digit of the column instead** {B}. There will never be any evidence for {B} (problems for which {B} alone predicts the students' wrong answer) because every problem causing {B} to generate a symptom will be further disturbed by {A}. Special cases like this are handled (once we discover them) by adding them to the starting list of bugs to be tried on every student. A related, more frequent problem occurs when bugs that are not logically covered appear to be so because the particular test being given did not happen to contain the right type of problems. This difficulty can be overcome in large part by the careful test-item selection that we will describe in Section 3.2. (Also we will discuss a general structure called a skill lattice that provides a means of identifying those bugs potentially covered by other bugs, both in general and for a specific set of test problems.)

3.1.4 Coercion - explaining the "noise"

During the compounding phase the system creates a structure that includes, for each of the primitive and compound bugs, the knowledge of where it agrees with the student and where it disagrees. After the structure is completed, the problem of noise is considered. The general approach is to try to find *rationalizations* for the discrepancies between the bugs' predictions and the student's actual answers. First, the set of hypotheses that have any chance of being selected as a diagnosis is chosen. The current selection criterion is whether the hypothesis explains a given percentage (currently 40 percent) of the student's symptoms. This cutoff saves time and prevents coercion from turning a theory for which there is very little evidence into a viable diagnosis. For any problem in which a selected hypothesis disagrees with the student's answer, an attempt is made to force the hypothesis into generating the student's answer by varying the hypothesis slightly with one or more coercions. In the example in Figure 3, the best hypothesis is coerced in two problems: in problem 5, by a variant that recognized one and zero as the "digit" ten; and in problem 11, by the fact-stable error, 15-8=8.

The coercions are designed to explain local variants of the bug and common performance lapses which would otherwise be counted against the bug. There are three types of coercions: facts-table errors, variants and predicted inconsistencies. Facts-table errors are limited to one facts-error per problem which is off by 1 or 2. (For example, the facts error 9-3=3 will not be considered because it is off by 3.) These limitations on the use of facts errors as coercions are imposed because any possible answer could be explained with enough facts errors. This procedure gets a large number of the cases that the human diagnosticians believed were facts errors from looking at the student's scratch marks. Variants are local modifications which allow bugs to be applied differently at boundary conditions. The set of looked-for variants includes considering the unit's column separately from the rest of the problem and treating the leftmost digits specially.

In certain cases, a bug will cause conditions that do not normally occur. In these cases, students may not have developed a consistent way of handling the unusual condition even though it is clear they are consistently following the original bug. For example, the bug **always borrowing whether or not the top digit is larger than the bottom** sometimes causes the result in a column to be larger than 9. Some students will truncate and use the units digit. Some students will write both digits in the answer. Some students will "carry" the extra ten back into the column it was borrowed from (thereby getting the correct answer). Some students will do a mixture of these. These three options are handled by predicted inconsistencies. Another example is that the bug **when borrowing from a column which has a zero on top, forget about the decrement operation** introduces the condition of having a zero on top that has been "touched" by a previous operation. Some students treat this condition as they would any other 0-n column. However other students will use 0-n=0 or 0-n=n in this column even though they will solve "untouched" 0-n columns correctly. (These are not considered to be bugs in their own right because they never appear in isolation; they apply only in conditions which don't arise unless there is another bug.) The set of inconsistencies that are predicted by a bug is stored in the network.

The coercions are applied to the buggy procedure. This means that a student can make a facts error while doing **smaller from larger** and the system will recognize it (see Figure 3). After coercions are done on each problem upon which the bug and the student disagree, an attempt is made to incorporate the coercions into the bug as pieces of the compound. This is done because in the evaluation phase a hypothesis is weighted down by the number of coercions it requires *unless the coercion is consistent throughout the test.*

The correct subtraction procedure is also coerced. This provides a reference plane as to how much of the student's incorrect behavior can be due to coercions. If a hypothesis with coercions does not explain the answers better than the coercions alone, it is not a very useful diagnosis. (As a side-effect, coercing the correct subtraction procedure also diagnoses those students with just facts-table errors.)

3.1.5　Choosing a diagnosis

After the coercion procedure, each bug is classified according to how well it explains the answers. The classification procedure is a refinement of the one described in Brown and Burton (1978). Briefly, it takes into account the number of predicted correct and incorrect answers as well as the number and type of mispredictions. Mispredictions which predicted a wrong answer when the student gave a correct answer are counted more negatively than mispredictions where the student got a wrong answer. (It is more likely that "noise" caused a student to miss an extraneous problem than that it caused him/her to get one right.) Coercions are counted negatively but not as negatively as mispredictions. Each type of coercion has its own weight so that different coercions can have differing effects on the final evaluation. For example, the variant of recognizing a one followed by a zero as 10 counts very little off. The goal of the classification procedure is to put each of the hypotheses into one of the classes: consistent bug (i.e., almost all of the student's errors are explained by the hypothesis); consistent bug but with other symptoms; some buggy behavior but not consistent; and unsystematic behavior.

The members of the highest non-empty class are then compared with each other and the best one is taken as the diagnosis. This final comparison allows simple theories that explain slightly less to be chosen over more complex theories. In actual use, the results of the entire diagnosis process are printed in order to improve the diagnostic process. Figure 3 provides excerpts of a diagnosis.

3.2　INTERACTION BETWEEN TEST AND DIAGNOSIS

An integral part of an off-line diagnostic program is the set of test problems that are given to the students. DEBUGGY includes automatic programs to measure various diagnostic properties of tests and symbiotic programs that aid test creation. One essential property for a test is that of distinguishing all of the bugs. One test

Problems and correct answers:

43	80	127	183	106	800	411	654	5391	2487	3005	854	700	608	3014
-7	-24	-83	195	-38	-168	-215	204	2697	5	-28	247	-5	209	-206
36	56	44	88	68	632	196	450	2694	2482	2977	607	695	399	2808

Student answers:

+	64	+	+	+	542	106	+	2604	+	1088	+	605	309	+

borrow across zero and borrow skip equal:

*	!	*	*	*&	***	***	*	***	*	***&	*	***	***	*

0·n=n:

*	***	*	*	*	768	216	*	!	*	*	705	!	3208

smaller from larger:

44	***	164	112	132	768	204	450	3306	*	3023	613	705	401	3212

***	-	bug predicts student's incorrect answer
*	-	bug predicts student's correct answer
!	-	bug predicts the correct answer, but student's is answer incorrect
+	-	student's answer is correct
&	-	coersion applied

FIG. 3. Diagnosis of compound bug with coercions and noise. The diagnosis is a compound of the bug when borrowing from a column with zero on top, leave that column alone and borrow from the next column to the left instead and the bug when borrowing from a column in which the top and bottom digits are the same, leave that column alone and borrow from the next column to the left. Problem 5 was coerced by the variant that recognizes one and zero as the "digit" ten thus blocking the first bug. Problem 11 was coerced by including the facts-table error 15-8=8 with the diagnosis for this problem. The best hypothesis did not predict problem 2 correctly, but it still had enough evidence to be chosen as the diagnosis. The bugs smaller from larger and 0·n=n are included because they explain the answer that is not explained by the first diagnosis. Note that even though there is positive evidence for them, there is substantial negative evidence against them as well.

analysis program determines the equivalence classses of bugs imposed by a test. That is, it determines which bugs give the exact same answers on every problem on the test. Using this program, we were able to design a test capable of distinguishing among 1200 compound bugs with only 12 problems! A second important property of a test is that it cause each bug to be invoked often enough to determine that it is consistent. The current tests that we are using are designed to cause each primitive bug to generate at least three errors. To accomplish this it was necessary to have 20 problems on the test.

Another important property of the test is that it generate answers that will serve as useful input for the diagnostic program. For DEBUGGY's compounding heuristics to be maximally effective, the test should be designed to test the subskills on different problems so as to maximize the chances of finding evidence for a bug in one subskill without the interference of a bug in another subskill. This can be difficult. For example, consider the test given the student whose diagnosis appears in Figure 2. Each of the four primitive bugs that are constituents in the final diagnosis have independent evidence in only one problem. If any of these problems had not been on the test, the diagnostic program would not have had the correct diagnosis in its search space of hypotheses. One possible alleviation is to use partial evidence (such as column evidence) to expand the number of primitive bugs considered for compounding. The interactive diagnosis system uses this solution. For off-line diagnosis, however, the test can be designed in advance to minimize this problem.

DEBUGGY includes a program based on the skill lattice (described in section 4) to find those subskills that are not being tested independently. The independence constraint opposes the goal of producing small tests because a small test must exercise as many skills as possible in each problem. The 12-problem test mentioned above requires several different skills in each problem. For isolating bugs in students who have primitive bugs, the test works very well. On the other hand, when a student with a compound bug misses a problem, it is sometimes difficult to recognize that fact from the primitive bugs separately. By adding more problems that use the subskills independently, the test increases the effectiveness of the diagnostic algorithm.

3.3 INTERACTIVE DIAGNOSIS

The DEBUGGY system described above is an off-line system. An interactive version of DEBUGGY (called IDEBUGGY) has also been developed. Interactive analysis has the potential for allowing a much faster, better-confirmed diagnosis because the problem sequence can be tailored to the student. IDEBUGGY uses many of the same internal routines as DEBUGGY with a quite different control structure. In addition, interactive use requires the techniques of problem generation and recognition of logical equivalence. Whereas DEBUGGY has been tested on thousands of students, IDEBUGGY has seen little use and hence the techniques are correspondingly less refined. The discussion of IDEBUGGY is included here in order to lay out the space of diagnostic techniques by pointing out differences between on-line and off-line diagnosis.

IDEBUGGY presents the student with problems and, using his answers, maintains (generates and evaluates) a set of hypothetical diagnoses from the set of primitive bugs and the space of compound bugs. After getting each student answer, a choice is made whether to give another problem or to stop and report the diagnosis. Thus, each new problem is determined by the state of possible hypotheses up to that point. When enough evidence for one hypothesis is collected, and there are no closely competing hypotheses, that hypothesis is returned as the diagnosis.

3.3.1 Organization of IDEBUGGY

IDEBUGGY is organized as a collection of tasks together with a heuristic strategy for deciding which task to do next. These tasks include such things as generating a good successive problem, reconsidering previously suspended hypotheses or deciding to produce a diagnosis. Before describing the operation of the tasks, we present a brief description of the context within which the tasks operate and of how the context originates. Each task is small in terms of the amount of computation it requires. A task changes the global context so that after it has run a different task will be choosen. This organization allows IDEBUGGY to either be directed by its own strategy heuristic or be guided in a symbiotic manner by a teacher or diagnostician. The global context consists of all hypotheses (primitive and compound bugs) that have been considered. With each hypothesis is noted how well it predicts a subset of the problems that have been given the student so far. An assumption made during design of IDEBUGGY (proved true in use) is that there are too many hypotheses to try all of them on every problem in interactive use. Thus, the set of hypotheses to compare with each student answer is carefully chosen to control the proliferation of hypothesis/problem pairs.

To start, the student's first problem is tried on a preselected list of common bugs. This provides an initial set of hypotheses. Before each task choice, the set of hypotheses that explain the observed behavior well enough to be considered reasonable diagnoses are selected as the "current set." The "current set" is an important factor for the decision of what task to do next. (The non-current hypotheses are saved for later consideration; no hypothesis is ever thrown away.)

The tasks available at each choice are:

(1) generate a simple problem;
(2) generate a problem that splits between the bugs in the current set of hypotheses;
(3) allow more-obscure bugs as hypotheses;
(4) create more hypotheses by extending (compounding) the current ones;
(5) reconsider previously suspended hypotheses;
(6) propose a diagnosis; or
(7) give up.

The choice of task is determined primarily by the size of the current set of hypotheses. If there is more than one bug in the current set, a problem is generated which splits between them. That is, a problem is found that will generate positive evidence for at most one subset. (The problems of doing this will be addressed in the next section.) If there is only one hypothesis in the current set, there are several alternatives: gain more support for this hypothesis by generating a problem that splits between it and the next-best hypothesis (even though the second best one is not good enough to be current); extend the current hypothesis by compounding it with other hypotheses and see if any of these do an equally good job of explaining the evidence; generate a problem which tests a subskill not yet tested so that other bugs are not overlooked; or propose the current hypothesis as the diagnosis.

If the current set is empty, IDEBUGGY can either consider more-obscure bugs for the hypotheses, combine existing hypotheses into compounds, generate simple problems which isolate single subskills, or give up if the student has already answered many problems. Generating problems which test subskills in isolation is done because the student's bug may be a compound. A problem which tests a single subskill may turn up one of the primitive constituents which can then be extended into a complete hypothesis.

When the decision is made to extend a hypothesis, it is combined with every hypothesis that has full-problem evidence, with every hypothesis that has single-column evidence and with a set of common primitive bugs. This allows many more possibilities than the heuristics used off-line, but since the number of problems given the student is less, the chances of getting extraneous evidence for inappropriate hypotheses is reduced. When a hypothesis has accumulated sufficient positive evidence, an attempt is made to coerce its negative evidence.

To reduce the amount of computation performed when a new student answer is received, a large number of the hypotheses are not tried on new data. Hypotheses that are in this state are referred to as "suspended" because they have been suspended from consideration by the program. Hypotheses are suspended when they have mispredicted more than a certain percentage of the student answers (currently 30 percent). Because a student may make performance errors in the first problems he does, the correct hypothesis can be suspended. To guarantee that the best hypothesis is found, suspended hypotheses are reconsidered whenever a current hypothesis has mispredicted more problems than the suspended hypotheses have. During reconsideration, each hypothesis is tried on problems it has not yet done, i.e., those the student answered while the hypothesis was suspended. If the hypothesis mispredicts one, it is suspended again. If it correctly predicts all of them, it is added to the set of current hypotheses.

3.3.2   Problem generation

The diagnostic system needs to be able to generate (or have prestored) problems with many different features. This need arises when the system has more than one hypothesis and requires a problem that differentiates between them. For any domain with a large number of hypotheses to consider, prestoring problems for all possible combinations of bugs is not practical. The system is therefore faced with the problem of generating problems to fill this need. A piece of leverage that the system does have is an executable model of the bugs that can determine whether or not any particular problem will differentiate between them (by running them and seeing if the answers are different), so the system only needs a generator that is likely to have the right features.

IDEBUGGY uses problem generators designed to produce problems specific to a small number of conditions (listed in Table 1). Each generator produces a problem sequence that is rich in problems containing their target condition, though not all the problems contain it. The resulting problems are filtered by actually running them through the models of the bugs to find the symptom-producing problems in the sequence. This freedom allows more randomness in the generation process which in turn avoids over-constraining the generated problems. For example, the generator for problems with the same digit in both the top and the bottom can be random about whether or not the columns on either side of that column require borrowing. This allows the single condition generator to be used effectively to generate symptoms for compound hypotheses. The generators are associated in the network with each primitive bug. For compound bugs, the generators for each of the primitives are cycled through the generators stored off the primitive bugs. In some cases two hypotheses will be very similar (two compounds, for example, that share common elements) and the above process will not find a problem that splits them. In these cases, an additional heuristic is used provided that the two hypotheses give different answers to one of the problems the student has already solved. Variants of the existing splitting problem are found by incrementing and decrementing some of its digits, adding extra columns on the left or right, or by deleting columns.

TABLE 1
Problem Generators

arbitrary problems
problems that do not require borrowing
problems that require borrowing
problems that have zero on the top
problems that have zero on the bottom
problems that require borrowing from zero
problems that borrow from two zeros in a row
problems that have the same digit on top and bottom in a column
problems that borrow from a column which has a blank on the bottom
problems that have a zero in the top and bottom of a column
problems that have one and zero as the leftmost digits
problems that have a one in the top number
problems that require a borrow from a column which has zero over blank
problems that require a particular subtraction fact

The "varying-an-existing-problem" heuristic is also used when attempting to gain confirming evidence for a hypothesis that explains most but not all of the student's answers. Problems similar to the ones that the hypothesis mispredicted are generated. If the mispredicted problems were careless errors, the new problems will increase the positive evidence for the hypothesis. If they were symptoms of a part of the student's bug that is not included in the current hypothesis, the new problems may provide some evidence as to what the missing piece is and will, at least, provide negative evidence against the current hypothesis so that it is not proposed (incorrectly) as a diagnosis.

3.3.3   Logical equivalence

In IDEBUGGY, logical equivalence is a significant problem because the program can waste a lot of time attempting to split logically equivalent hypotheses. The problem is differentiating when a bug {A B C} is logically equivalent to another bug {D E F} from when the problem that separates the two has not yet been found. Our heuristic solution is to use the problem generation techniques mentioned earlier to try to find a problem on which the two bugs differ (hence proving that they are not equivalent). If, after some suitably large number of attempts (500), they are not shown to be different, then the hypotheses are treated as if they were the same.† This is done by selecting the hypothesis with the simplest bug (or one of the simplest in case of ties) to remain in the current set and having the selected hypothesis point at the others. Whenever a new problem is tried on the selected member, however, it is also tried against all of the equivalent ones and any that are found to differ are split out.

4 Definition of Subskills

One interesting benefit of the database of bugs is that it is possible to define an intuitively appealing notion of subskill in a way that has many uses in the diagnostic process. The term "subskill" has been used in the diagnostic literature to informally refer to any part of the skill being talked about. Additionally, there have been attempts to characterize subskills in terms of groupings of test items or as pieces of a representation of the correct skill (Durnin and Scandura, 1973). These notions of subskill are too coarse to account for the range of behaviors captured by the database of bugs, in the sense that there is no direct correspondence between the bugs and any other notion of subskill. The primary limitation of existing characterizations of subskill is that they are driven from the correct skill and nothing else. *We have observed bugs, however, which have no vestiges in the correct skill.* For example, some students when borrowing will skip columns that have the same number on the top and the bottom. We would like to say that these students are lacking a subskill that a student who subtracts correctly has: knowing that the bottom number doesn't matter during a borrow operation. This subskill is the absence of a procedure in the correct skill. (There is an alternate view that the buggy student is making distinctions that are inappropriate for this skill.) Which things constitute subskills when left out of the correct skill can be determined empirically from the database of bugs.

A subskill is defined to be any isolatable part of the skill that it is possible to mislearn. This is determined from the database of primitive bugs by considering how they partition the set of all possible problems. Every bug separates the set of all possible problems into two partitions: those for which it generates the correct answer and those for which it generates an incorrect answer. Different bugs will often generate different partitions, though it is possible for two bugs to generate the same ones. For example, the bugs $0 \cdot n = 0$ and $0 \cdot n = n$ generate equal partitions because any problem that causes $0 \cdot n = 0$ to produce an incorrect answer also causes $0 \cdot n = n$ to produce an incorrect answer. The bugs are grouped into equivalence classes by the equality of their partitionings of the set of all possible problems. Each of the equivalence classes that arises from this analysis determines a *subskill*.

† This heuristic is useful because it uses "smart" problem generators and it gets better as the problem generators get better.

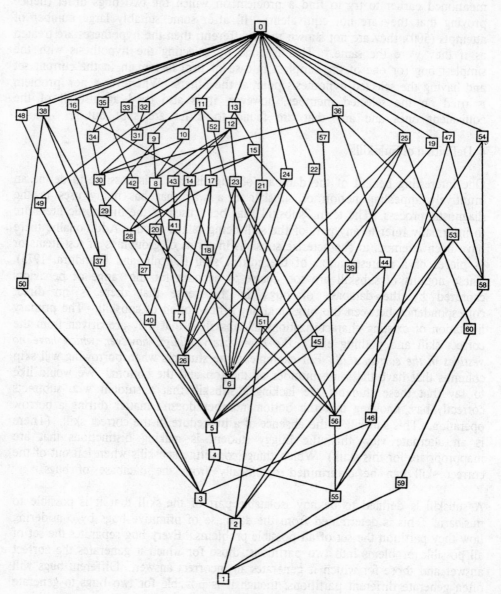

FIG. 4. Skill lattice for Subtraction

0	Correct skills
1	No subtraction skills
2	Subtract 0 from a number whose right-most digit is 0
3	Subtract 0 from a number
4	Subtract columns which are n-n or n-0

5	Subtract without borrowing
6	Borrow from some columns with a digit on the bottom
7	Borrow from columns whose answer is the same as their bottom digit
8	Borrow from a column with a 9 or a larger number on top
9	Borrow from a column with a larger top digit
10	Borrow from a column with zero on top when blank on bottom
11	Borrow from a column with zero on both top and bottom
12	Borrow from a column unless one is on top and a nonzero digit is on the bottom
13	Borrow from a column unless digit one is on both top and bottom
14	Borrow in two consecutive columns
15	Borrow from columns with the same digits on top and bottom
16	Borrow from columns that have nine as the bottom digit
17	Borrow from columns with the same nonzero digits on top and bottom
18	Borrow from columns which have an answer of zero
19	Borrow from the leftmost column when it has a non-blank in the bottom
20	Borrow more than once per problem
21	Can borrow then not borrow
22	Borrow from columns with two on the bottom
23	Borrow from leftmost columns or columns that have a non-one on top
24	Borrow from columns with top digits smaller than the bottom digits
25	Borrow from columns that have a top digit one less than the bottom digit
26	Borrow from the leftmost column
27	Borrow once in a problem
28	Borrow from columns that have the top digit larger than the bottom digit
29	Borrow from a column with the top digit greater than or equal to the bottom digit
30	Borrow from a column with a zero on top
31	Borrow from a middle (not leftmost) column with a zero to the left
32	Borrow from leftmost column of a problem whose form one followed by one or more zeroes
33	Borrow from a column with a zero on top and a zero to the left
34	Borrow from or into a column with a zero on top and a zero to the left
35	Borrow into a column with a zero on top and a zero to the left
36	Borrow from a column with a zero on top and a blank on bottom
37	Borrow into a column with a nonzero digit on top
38	Borrow into a column with a one on top
39	Borrow when difference is 5
40	Subtract columns with a one or a zero in top that require borrowing
41	Subtract columns with a zero in the top number that require borrowing
42	Subtract a column with a zero on top that was not the result of decrementing a one
43	Borrow into a column with a zero on top when next top digit is zero
44	Borrow from a column with a blank on the bottom
45	Borrow from a column with a one on top
46	Subtract numbers of the same lengths
47	Subtract a single digit from a large number
48	Subtract columns unless the same digit is on top and bottom
49	Borrow all the time
50	Subtract when one is in top
51	Subtract when neither number has a zero unless the 0 is over a 0
52	Subtract columns when the bottom is a zero and the top is not zero
53	Subtract when a column has a zero over a blank
54	Subtract numbers which have a one over a blank that is not borrowed from
55	Can subtract a number from itself
56	Subtract numbers with zeros in them
57	Subtract problems that do not have a zero in the answer
58	Subtract numbers when the answer is no longer than the bottom number
59	Subtract leftmost columns that have top and bottom digits the same
60	Subtract columns that have top and bottom digits the same*the same ones.

This gives rise to subskills that are of much finer grain than normally recognized. While in theory this leads to the consideration of an infinite number of problems, in practice one need only consider enough problems to completely distinguish between bugs.

The subskills can be placed naturally into a lattice by the relationship **gets correct answers on all the same problems and more.** The maximal element in the lattice is the skill of knowing how to subtract all possible problems (having all problems in the "correct" partition) and the minimal element is the lack of any subtraction skill at all (having no problems in the "correct" partition). Figure 4 presents the skill lattice for subtraction based on bugs we have observed. We obtained supporting evidence for this notion of subskill when, after determining the lattice, it was possible to identify and name all of the subskills produced. It is also worth noting that the subskills are independent of the representation chosen for the bugs; it stems only from their behavior.

The most surprising thing about the skill lattice for subtraction is its complexity. There are 58 subskills necessary for even this simple skill (approximately one for every two bugs). Another surprising thing is that many of the subskills are taken for granted, seemingly because the situations in which they occur are *not* recognized as decision points in the final skill. For example, students must learn to ignore the bottom number in a column they are borrowing from. This captures the intuition that part of expertise is knowing when to ignore what.

4.1   USES OF SKILL LATTICE IN TEST GENERATION

A subskill lattice can be created from any test by considering the way the bugs partition the problems on the test. The resulting lattice will be a homomorphic image of the maximal lattice resulting from considering all possible problems. Any nodes in the maximal lattice that are mapped onto the same node in the test lattice are not distinguishable by that problem set (assuming one is considering an answer as either right or wrong). This provides a measure of the extent to which one subskill may be hidden by another in the test. When designing a test for a diagnostic system that works by considering only the correctness of the answers, this mapping information is very useful. Testing two subskills together prevents students from demonstrating that they do know one of them if they don't know the other. For example it may be that every problem that involves subtracting a zero from a digit also involves borrowing. If a student cannot borrow, we will not know whether s/he can subtract a zero or not. Diagnostic systems such as DEBUGGY which try to predict the exact wrong anwers given have a better opportunity to separate the student's subskills. However, even these systems can benefit from subskill-independent tests when producing partial diagnoses for students who are not consistent.

4.2   USE OF SKILL LATTICE IN DIAGNOSIS

The skill lattice provides a useful heuristic for attacking the problem of having one bug **hide** the symptoms of another. In some situations, the diagnostic program is faced with the problem that its best current hypothesis {A B} explains some of the students' answers but not all of them. One explanation for this situation is that there is some other bug C which is also present, that is, the student actually has bug {A B C}. If {A B} is not covering C (i.e., there exists some problem for which C generates a wrong answer but both A and B generate the right answer), there will be some independent evidence that C is present (the problem that C predicts to be wrong) and the combination heuristic will try compounding {A B} and C. If, however, {A B} does cover C (because every problem for which C generates a wrong answer either A or B generates a wrong answer), there will never be any evidence for C separately, and {A B} would (potentially) have to be compounded with all other primitive bugs to discover {A B C}.

The skill lattice contains exactly the information to identify candidates for C. We first calculate the skill lattice using the problems the student has answered and find the union of A's and B's "incorrect partitions." This union defines a cut through the lattice such that all of the skills below this cut have "incorrect partitions" that are subsets of the union. The skills below the cut are covered by {A B} and any bugs of these skills are candidates for the hidden bug C. If this set is large, the problems predicted wrongly by the bug {A B} can be used to produce the candidates for C ordered by how well their "incorrect partition" matches the answers not explained by {A B}.

4.3   DIAGNOSIS TO THE SUBSKILL LEVEL

In the light of our characterization of subskills, we reconsider the possibility of diagnosing only on the basis of whether a student's answers are right or wrong. The method we used to define subskill depends only on which problems were missed, so it should be possible to determine which subskills are errant by only considering right versus wrong. Scoring test items as right or wrong is fast and there is the possibility that a very fast, simple diagnosis system could be built based on this technique by locating the student's template of right and wrong answers in the lattice. It is our belief that a fast system could be developed around this paradigm.

There is a limiting problem with this approach. From a practical standpoint, bugs of the same subskill may require different remediation. Consider two bugs of the borrow subskill: **leaving blanks in the answer in any column which requires a borrow, and decrementing the minuend digit in the first column that requires a borrow before adding ten to it.** These two bugs will be grouped together by any classification scheme that looks only at right versus wrong because they cause wrong answers on exactly the same set of problems (any problem that requires borrowing). However, it is clear that a student with the second of these bugs understands quite a lot about borrowing while the student with the first probably understands very little.

The use of the skill lattice also presents interesting possibilites in combination with methods used in DEBUGGY. In particular it provides a clue to the problem of "noise" by characterizing the problem-partitionings that are possible within the boundaries of the theory. If the student has a partitioning that is not in the lattice or constructable by combination of partitions that are in the lattice, the student's test must have "noise." Of course knowing that a student's solution contains noise is quite different from knowing where the noise is or what is producing it, but it is an interesting case of the program recognizing that something is beyond the limits of its theory.

Conclusions

We have described a system which has been used to diagnose consistent procedural bugs in more than a thousand students and which is still being used in classrooms. From this experience we have learned that diagnosis of real students using only the student's answers is difficult but possible if one has a strong model of the correct skill and its bugs. We have described techniques for implicitly reducing the size of the search considered during diagnosis and searching the reduced space in an efficient order. An important lesson from this discussion is that the diagnostic heuristics go hand in hand with test generation; one can be designed to overcome (to some extent) the limitations of the other. We also presented an empirically based definintion of subskill and explored some of its applications.

I would like to thank John Seely Brown and Kurt VanLehn for their support during the design and documentation of DEBUGGY, Jamesine Friend for poring over diagnoses and ferreting out troubles with the system and Bruce Buchanan for his many helpful comments on an early draft of this paper.

References

BROWN, J. S. & BURTON, R. R. (1978). Diagnostic models for procedural bugs in basic mathematical skills. *Cognitive Science*, **2**, 155–192.

BROWN, J. S. & VANLEHN, K. (1980). Repair theory: a generative theory of bugs in procedural skills. *Cognitive Science*, **2**.

DURNIN, J. H. & SCANDURA, J. M. (1973). An algorithmic approach to assessing behavioral potential: comparison with item forms and hierarchical technologies. *Journal of Educational Psychology*, **65**, No. 2, 262–272.

FRIEND, J. (1981). *Domain Referenced Adaptive Testing*. Xerox Cognitive and Instructional Sciences Report 10, Palo Alto, CA.

FRIEND, J. & BURTON, R. R. (1980). *Teacher's Manual of Subtraction Bugs*. CIS Working Paper, Xerox Palo Alto Science Center.

SACERDOTI, E. (1977). A structure for plans and behavior. In *The Artificial Intelligence Series*. Elsevier North-Holland, New York.

VANLEHN, K. (1981). *Bugs are not enough: Empirical Studies of Bugs, Impasses and Repairs in Procedural Skills*. Xerox Cognitive and Instructional Sciences Report 11, Palo Alto.

9. Assessing aspects of competence in basic algebra

D. SLEEMAN

The University, Leeds, U.K.

The paper reviews the potential uses of models in ICAI/CAI systems and outlines some of the earlier work in the area. The underlying design of the Leeds Modelling System, LMS, is outlined, and some details are presented of the current implementation, which given problem(s) and the student's answer(s) hypothesizes model(s) for the student.

The sets of rules and associated mal-rules used in the Algebra Modelling experiments are presented, together with the results of the recent experiment with pupils from a Leeds high school. A close correlation between the "bugs" diagnosed by LMS and those discovered during conventional diagnostic interviews was noted. This experiment clearly shows the diagnostic power of the system but does point to some shortcomings in the formulation of the Modeller. These shortcomings are analysed and the corresponding modifications are outlined.

1. Background to modelling work

A number of workers have argued that if a teaching system is to cope with the difficulties encountered by a student, it must have an accurate model of that student. One such framework (Hartley and Sleeman, 1973) suggested that an intelligent teaching system requires: knowledge of the problem domain; student model (history); list of (teaching) operations; means-ends guidance rules (which relate teaching decisions with conditions in the student model).

Some workers, among them Goldstein (1981), have advocated that the student should be represented in terms of the same skills as those used by the expert (he uses the term *overlay* model). Other workers have cautioned that naive user's problem solving should be studied in some detail and his difficulties and misunderstandings should be explicitly represented. (See Stevens and Collins' study on meteorology (Stevens *et al.*, 1981), Matz's (1981) study of high school algebra, Brown and Burton's (1978) use of ill-formed procedures with BUGGY and Sleeman's (1979) mal-rules for Algebra.) Further, several systems have been implemented which produce diagnostic models, principally GUIDON (Clancey, 1981), BUGGY (Brown and Burton, 1978) and LMS (Sleeman and Smith, 1981). It could be argued that the Self Improving Teaching systems implemented by O'Shea (1981) and Kimball (1981) also model student behaviour.

2. Outline of Leeds Modelling System. LMS

Two points arise from the earlier modelling work. First, whether it is possible to formulate the task of inferring a model to describe the student's performance, so that the number of combinations to be considered can be "contained". Note, LMS produces a (diagnostic) model but does not attempt to do any remedial teaching. The separation is quite deliberate and was necessary to evaluate the Modeller. That is the system, given

185

the problems to be worked and the student's answers, attempts to infer model(s) of the student's behaviour. LMS is considered to have succeeded when the inferred model(s) give the same answers as the student on the problem set. (Naturally, the model(s) can also be used predictively.) Secondly, to what extent it is possible to implement a domain-knowledge-driven Modeller (i.e. a Modeller which works in several domains). In an earlier paper (Sleeman and Smith, 1981) we describe a modelling system which addresses these issues; here we summarize the approach.

Suppose we are working in a domain where there are R applicable rules, and if at level L we only consider combinations which contain L rules, then there will be $L!$ combinations. Further, suppose that during the analyses of protocols, we noted M erroneous alternatives, or mal-rules (1), for each of the R rules then one can show that at level L there are

$$L! * (1+M)^L \tag{1}$$

combinations. (We have referred to this as the EXHAUSTIVE-GROUPED algorithm.)

In the SELECTIVE algorithm, we begin with a *single* rule, and verify that it is an acceptable model. That is, the person being modelled is able to cope with problems which are associated with this particular rule. In which case we move to the next level, level 2, and consider all the models which can be generated by adding an additional rule, rule 2. And so at level L, with no mal-rules, there are only L models to be considered. Again taking mal-rules into consideration gives

$$L * (1+M) \tag{2}$$

combinations. Table 1 shows the number of combinations generated by the different methods for several values of L and M.

TABLE 1

Shows the number of configurations produced for differing number of rules and mal-rules for the EXHAUSTIVE-GROUPED and SELECTIVE algorithms. (These values are produced using formulae 1 and 2 of Section 2, note that at each level only the configurations which contain L rules are considered)

		$M = 0$	$M = 1$	$M = 2$	$M = 3$
1	EXHAUSTIVE-GROUPED	1	2	3	4
	SELECTIVE	1	2	3	4
2	EXHAUSTIVE-GROUPED	2	8	18	32
	SELECTIVE	2	4	6	8
3	EXHAUSTIVE-GROUPED	6	48	162	384
	SELECTIVE	3	6	9	12
4	EXHAUSTIVE-GROUPED	24	384	1944	6144
	SELECTIVE	4	8	12	16
5	EXHAUSTIVE-GROUPED	120	3840	29 160	122 880
	SELECTIVE	5	10	15	20
6	EXHAUSTIVE-GROUPED	720	46 080	524 880	2 949 120
	SELECTIVE	6	12	18	24

We have evolved heuristics which eliminate functionally equivalent models and which thus further reduce the size of the search space. First, we assign each rule to a *priority* class. The first heuristic is that additional rules can be added both before and after a class but not between members of the class. The second heuristic is that more specialized rules must always precede general rules. Violation of this heuristic leads to models in which the more specialized rules are *never* activated; e.g. a terminating rule which has a null condition part *must* be the last rule. (A quantitative assessment of these heuristics is given in Sleeman and Smith, 1981.)

3. The Modeller

The analysis summarized in the last section assumes that the domain knowledge is modular, but makes no further assumptions about the actual representation. The Modeller, however, uses a Production Rule representation for the rules and mal-rules, and (hence) for the models. The models are Production Sets, PSs, which in turn are composed of a series of Production Rules, PRs. In general each PR has both a condition and the corresponding mal-rules are given in Fig. 4. Figure 5 gives a systems protocol for some "level 7" models solving a *particular* problem. (Note, the models are "executed" using a standard Production Rule interpreter; that is, the rule which "fires" corresponds to the first rule in the PS whose condition part is satisfied.) A schematic representation of the Modeller is given in Fig. 1.

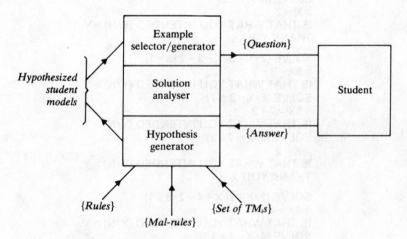

FIG. 1. A schematic representation of the Modeller.

For each problem domain, the Modeller must be provided with the following data:

(1) The R rules applicable in the domain.
(2) The associated mal-rules.
(3) The R Template- or Teaching-models which correspond to "ideal" models for each level (we shall use the notation TMi to represent the ith model).

(4) The priority of each rule.

(5) For each rule, information which indicates the rules it subsumes.

(6) A set of problems for each level which is adequate to discriminate between all potential variants.

(For a discussion of the assumptions made in LMS. 1 see Sleeman and Smith, 1981.)

```
THE LEVEL IS 7
SOLVE (2*X+4*X+4 = 16)
>X-3
FUNNY INPUT—OK AS FAR AS (1*X-3)
SOLVE (2*X+4*X+4 = 16)
>X = 3
IS THAT WHAT YOU INTENDED (Y/N) > N
SOLVE (2*X+4*X+4 = 16)
>6X+4 = 16
IS THAT WHAT YOU INTENDED (Y/N) > Y
SOLVE (6*X+4 = 16)
>6X+4-4 = 16-4
IS THAT WHAT YOU INTENDED (Y/N) > Y
SOLVE (6*X+4-4 = 16-4)
>6X = 16-4
IS THAT WHAT YOU INTENDED (Y/N) > Y
SOLVE (6*X = 16-4)
>6X = 12
IS THAT WHAT YOU INTENDED (Y/N) > Y
SOLVE (6*X = 12)
>X = 2
IS THAT WHAT YOU INTENDED (Y/N) > Y
THANK YOU . .

SOLVE (2*X+3*X-3 = 2*3+1)
>5X-3 = 7
IS THAT WHAT YOU INTENDED (Y/N) > Y
SOLVE (5*X-3 = 7)
>5X = 7+3
IS THAT WHAT YOU INTENDED (Y/N) > Y
SOLVE (5*X = 7+3)
>X = 2
IS THAT WHAT YOU INTENDED (Y/N) > Y
THANK YOU . .

SOLVE (2*X+2*X+4 = 2*8+1)
>4X+4 = 17
IS THAT WHAT YOU INTENDED (Y/N) > Y
SOLVE (4*X+4 = 17)
>4X = 21
IS THAT WHAT YOU INTENDED (Y/N) > Y
THANK YOU .
```

FIG. 2. Showing the facilities afforded by LMS's algebra interface. (The user's responses are underlined.)

Figure 2 shows the interaction between the Modeller and a student. There are several points worth noting about this dialogue:

(1) Expressions are only analysed if they are syntactically valid (the grammar is also given as data) and provided the student is satisfied with what he has typed. (It is clearly pointless to analyse something which the student realizes is a mis-typing.)
(2) The student is *not* required to solve a problem in a single step, but can successively simplify the equation.
(3) The refinement of a particular problem stops when the student gives:
(a) the correct answer;
(b) a form which is incorrect (i.e. reduces to an answer which differs from that of the original equation);
(c) when the number of refinement cycles exceeds the limit for the problem.

In all cases the system merely gives the neutral message "THANK YOU" and does not indicate whether or not the last form was correct. Because of point 3(c) above, it is hoped that the student will not infer that a premature termination implies an error.

N.B. Although we could have continued the modelling using the intermediary tasks "generated" by the student, we decided not to do this as these might involve higher level rules. (This extension, however, needs to be considered.)
(4) In this experiment, LMS does not stop at the end of a level even when it has discovered a consistent error, as we are essentially collecting data about the Modeller's performance.
(5) After a consistent error has been located, one can generate models for the next level based on either the (correct) Template Model or on the incorrect model discovered at the current level. This choice is made by the investigator. The system has been run in both modes. This experiment was run in "conservative" mode, namely the first; the other mode gives the Modeller the possibility of spotting multiple "bugs".

4. Rules for the Algebra Domain

In Fig. 3, we give a set of rules for this domain.

	LEVEL	PATTERN	"ACTION"
FIN	1	$(X = M)$	(M)
FIN2	2	$(X = M/N)$	(MN)
SOLVE	3	$(M*X = N)$	$(X = N/M)$ or (INFINITY)
ADDSUB	4	$(M + N)$	(evaluated)
MULT	5	$(M*N)$	(evaluated)
XADDSUB	6	$(M*X +/- N*X)$	$((M +/- N)*X)$
NTORHS	7	$(\text{lhs} +/- M = \text{rhs})$	$(\text{lhs} = \text{rhs} -/+ M)$
REARRANGE	8	$(+/- M +/- N*X)$	$(+/- N*X +/- M)$
XTOLHS	9	$(\text{lhs} = +/- M*X \text{ rhs})$	$(\text{lhs} -/+ M*X = \text{rhs}))$
BRA1	10	$(M*\langle N\rangle)$	$(M*N)$
BRA2	11	$(M*\langle N*X +/- P\rangle)$	$(M*N*X +/- M*P)$

FIG. 3. Rules for the algebra domain., where M, N and P are integers and where lhs, rhs etc. are general patterns (which may be null), and where $+/-$ means either $+$ or $-$ may occur and where $\langle$ and $\rangle$ are the "usual" algebraic brackets.

There are several points worth making:

(1) The rule REARRANGE, is a way of avoiding undue complication with many of the other rules.

(2) In view of these several artifacts the system merely checks that the student's equation reduces to the same *value*, and *not* that the rules needed to solve the student's current response is a subset of the rules needed to solve the original problem. This approach also avoids having for example, the rule NTORHS (see Fig. 3) and a rule which adds to both sides of the equation the negation of the number to be moved. (Fig. 2 shows the first problem being solved *without* using NTORHS and the second problem solved by using it).

	LEVEL	PATTERN	"ACTION"
MSOLVE	3	$(M*X = N)$	$(X = M/N)$
MNTORHS	7	$(\text{lhs} +/- M = \text{rhs})$	$(\text{lhs} = \text{rhs} +/- M)$
M2NTORHS	7	$(\text{lhs1} +/- M*X \text{lhs2} = \text{rhs})$	$(\text{lhs1} + *X \text{lhs2} = \text{rhs} -/+ M)$
M3NTORHS	7	$(\text{lhs1} +/- M*X \text{lhs2} = \text{rhs})$	$(\text{lhs1} *X \text{lhs2} = \text{rhs} +/- M)$
MXTOLHS	9	$(\text{lhs} = +/- M*X \text{rhs})$	$(\text{lhs} +/- M*X = \text{rhs})$
M1BRA2	11	$(M*\langle N*X +/- P\rangle)$	$(M*N*X +/- P)$
M2BRA2	11	$(M*\langle N*X +/- P\rangle)$	$(M*N*X +/- M +/- P)$

FIG. 4. Some mal-rules for the domain, using the same conventions as Fig. 3.

Figure 4 gives the mal-rules for this domain, and Fig. 5 shows all the models generated at level 7 which give unique answers with this problem-set. The application of some of these rules, e.g. M2NTORHS and M3NTORHS (models 3, 4 and 5 of Fig. 5), lead to some very strange intermediary states. There is value in considering the operation of such rules, as many children who do not have a "feel" for mathematics appear to operate at the level of crude symbol manipulation. Then having generated an "odd" expression such as those produced by M2NTORHS/M3NTORHS, they apply a "normalizing" operation to return the equation to a more familiar state and then continue processing, as if nothing had ever gone amiss! (The point will be discussed again when the students' interviews are considered.)

5. The experiment

An earlier pilot experiment verified that children were able to use the system. In this experiment, we were attempting to show primarily that the models inferred by LMS were the same as the difficulties diagnosed by an experimenter in a detailed interview. We were concerned to show that any problems reported by the Modeller were genuine and, moreover, to establish that the difficulties diagnosed by the experimenter were detected by the system. Secondly, we wished to see if the Modeller would detect the same difficulties in a number of sessions. (N.B. The Modeller merely tells the child how many of a set of problems s/he gets right—it does not give feedback after each problem; similarly, it was agreed that the interviewers would merely probe and not provide explanations.)

In the event six children, aged 14–15 years, and covering a range of abilities, had an hour-long session with LMS, and three days later they were given a "standard"

PS (MULT ADDSUB XADDSUB NTORHS SOLVE FIN2 FIN) EVALUATES
$(2*X+4*X+4=16)$ TO
RULE XADDSUB FIRES-RESULT IS $(6*X+4=16)$
RULE NTORHS FIRES-RESULT IS $(6*X=16-4)$
RULE ADDSUB FIRES-RESULT IS $(6*X=12)$
RULE SOLVE FIRES-RESULT IS $(1*X=12//6)$
RULE FIN2 FIRES-RESULT IS (2)
COMPLETE ANSWER IS 2

PS (MNTORHS MULT ADDSUB XADDSUB SOLVE FIN2 FIN) EVALUATES
$(2*X+4*X+4=16)$ TO
RULE MNTORHS FIRES-RESULT IS $(2*X+4*X=16+4)$
RULE ADDSUB FIRES-RESULT IS $(2*X+4*X=20)$
RULE XADDSUB FIRES-RESULT IS $(6*X=20)$
RULE SOLVE FIRES-RESULT IS $(1*X=20//6)$
RULE FIN2 FIRES-RESULT IS ((20 6))
COMPLETE ANSWER IS (20 6)

PS (M2NTORHS MULT ADDSUB XADDSUB SOLVE FIN2 FIN) EVALUATES
$(2*X+4*X+4=16)$ TO
RULE M2NTORHS FIRES-RESULT IS $(2*X+*X+4=16-4)$
RULE M2NTORHS FIRES-RESULT IS $(2*X+*X+=16-4-4)$
RULE ADDSUB FIRES-RESULT IS $(2*X+*X+=12-4)$
RULE ADDSUB FIRES-RESULT IS $(2*X+*X+=8)$
UNABLE TO FULLY EVALUATE THIS PROBLEM—FINAL STATE IS
$(2*X+*X+=8)$

PS (MULT ADDSUB XADDSUB M2NTORHS SOLVE FIN2 FIN) EVALUATES
$(2*X+4*X+4=16)$ TO
RULE XADDSUB FIRES-RESULT IS $(6*X+4=16)$
RULE M2NTORHS FIRES-RESULT IS $(6*X+=16-4)$
RULE ADDSUB FIRES-RESULT IS $(6*X+=12)$
UNABLE TO FULLY EVALUATE THIS PROBLEM—FINAL STATE IS
$(6*X+=12)$

PS (M3NTORHS MULT ADDSUB XADDSUB SOLVE FIN2 FIN) EVALUATES
$(2*X+4*X+4=16)$ TO
RULE M3NTORHS FIRES-RESULT IS $(2*X*X+4=16+4)$
RULE M3NTORHS FIRES-RESULT IS $(2*X*X=16+4+4)$
RULE ADDSUB FIRES-RESULT IS $(2*X*X=20+4)$
RULE ADDSUB FIRES-RESULT IS $(2*X*X=24)$
UNABLE TO FULLY EVALUATE THIS PROBLEM—FINAL STATE IS
$(2*X*X=24)$

PS (MULT ADDSUB XADDSUB SOLVE FIN2 FIN) EVALUATES
$(2*X+4*X+4=16)$ TO
RULE XADDSUB FIRES-RESULT IS $(6*X+4=16)$
UNABLE TO FULLY EVALUATE THIS PROBLEM—FINAL STATE IS
$(6*X+4=16)$

FIG. 5. All the unique models for level 7, solving a particular problem (with the systems TRACE facility
switched on).

interview with one of three experimenters. (The author did not take part in these
interviews, neither had the experimenters seen the students' protocols.) After these
diagnostic interviews it was planned to give each child a second session with the
Modeller, but in the event due to pressure on the system, this was only done with
pupil 3.

		MODELLING I	INTERVIEW	MODELLING II	SUMMARY
STUDENT 1 John	Level 5	2 EXEC-errors $8*x = 4*3+2*2-5 \Rightarrow$ $x = 9/8$			Indicates lack of attention when on system. Confusion between + and *
	Level 6	1 EXEC error $3*4+2*2 \Rightarrow 48$ (i.e. all *s)			
	Level 7	Change side, not sign $2x = 7*3 -1 -3*x \Rightarrow x = 17/5$ New MAL-RULE			
	Level 9		Perfect		
STUDENT 2 Sarah	Level 6	$5*x - 2*x = 2*3 - 4 \Rightarrow x = 3/2$			Slight problems—probably due to unfamiliarity with the system.
	Level 7	$3*x + 5 = 4*2 + 1 \Rightarrow x = 3/4$	Perfect		
	Level 7	CHANGE SIDE but not SIGN OF NUM			
STUDENT 3 Charlotte	Level 3	$4*x = 3 \Rightarrow x = 4/3$ (TWICE) $10*x = 3 \Rightarrow x = 18/3$ (READ-ERROR)	Level 8 (Pr11&12) $4+3*y = 5*3 +1 \Rightarrow 7y = 16$ $2 + 3*y + 2 = 16 \Rightarrow 5y + 2 = 16$ When asked to rework OK.	Level 8 OK here. So error seems to have been cleared up	Consistent error. Cleared up when attention was drawn to it.
	Level 4	$4*x + 3 - 2 \Rightarrow x = 5/3$,,			
	Level 5	$4*x = 4*3 - 4 \Rightarrow x - 2 = 2$,,			
	Level 8	ADDSUB before REARRANGE consistently so $4 + 3*x = 5*3 + 1 \Rightarrow 7x = 16$ (One value coincides with "proper" result)			

STUDENT 4 *Linda*	Level 3: MSOLVE 4*3 = 3 ⇒ x = 4/3 Level 4: EXEC 2x = 10 + 4 + 6 − 18 ⇒ x = 2 Level 8: New MAL 5 + 2*x = 3*2 + 1 ⇒ 10x = 7 4 + 3*x = 5*3 + 1 ⇒ 12x = 16 EXEC? 4 + 2 + 4*x = 5*5 + 2*2 ⇒ 4x = 8	Level 8: 2*y = 10 − 3*y ⇒ 2y − y = 7 (Pr13) *BUT* Level 9: 2*y = 14 + 6 − 3*y ⇒ 5*y = 20 OK (pr14) 2*y = 7*3 − 1 − 3*y ⇒ 2y + 3y ⇒ 21 − 1 (Pr15) —	Confusion over precedence in mixed cases both ON-LINE and with INTERVIEWER
STUDENT 5 *Andrea*	Level 5: 3*x = 4*4 + 7*2 ⇒ 3x = 46 i.e. (4*4 + 7)*2 Level 7: Change side without changing sign of NUMBER	Level 8: 4 + 3*y = 5*3 + 1 ⇒ 7y = 16(Pr11) 2 + 3*y + 2 = 16 ⇒ 5y + 2 = 16 (Pr12) 2*y = 10 − 3*y ⇒ 2y = 7y (Pr14) 2*y = 14 + 6 − 3*y ⇒ 2y = 17y ⇒ 4y = 17y/2y ⇒ y = 8½ 2*y = 7*3 − 1 − 3*y ⇒ 2*y = 21 − 1 − 3*y (OK) — [REWORKED Pr14 correctly when written down in stages.]	*Interview* shows confused over precedence in mixed cases. [Did not get to here in modelling session.]
STUDENT 6 *Rachel*	Level 5: 3*x = 4*4 + 7*2 ⇒ 3x = 12 + 14 EXEC	Perfect	One slight EXEC error.

Fig. 6. Summary of the "diagnoses" made by LMS and the interviewers.

5.1. SUMMARY OF RESULTS

The main points noted in the several stages of the experiment are given in Fig. 6. The following is a synopsis of the main observations:

(1) Careless copying errors:

$$\text{e.s.} \quad 4*X = 4+3-2 \Rightarrow X = 5/3$$
$$10*X = 3 \Rightarrow X = 18/3$$

(2) Some errors are clearly due to confusion of "+" and "*", for example:

$$3*4+2*2 \Rightarrow 48 \,[\text{i.e. } 3*4*2*2]$$

This could be merely due to the similarity of the two operators on the particular terminal. So we should experiment with a more legible character set, but perhaps we also need additional mal-rules.

(3) During the session with LMS, several students forgot to change the sign of an integer when moving sides, i.e. behaved as predicted by mal-rule, MNTORHS.

(4) MSOLVE was "activated" by two students in their sessions with LMS, once at the level expected and secondly at a higher level where it was therefore not detected.

(5) The major observation was the difficulties which several students had in deciding the precedence in "mixed" expressions. Figure 7 shows both student 3's interaction with LMS and examples worked in the interview. (For completeness, we also give the systems TRACE for the model which LMS inferred for this student on the second problem. N.B. We are *not* claiming that this is how the student arrived at *her* answer.) This certainly seems to have been a "hard" bug with this student. Interestingly enough, when asked by the experimenter if the solutions to these problems were correct, she did point out her errors and got this type of problem correct in her second session with LMS.

Students 4 and 5 had similar difficulties with problems presented by the interviewer but unfortunately they did not reach this level in their session with LMS. Figure 8 shows that student 5 got the first four problems wrong but got the apparently more difficult fifth problem correct. The explanation for this seems to be that the first 4 problems were worked largely in the student's head, whereas with the fifth problem more of the intermediary results were committed to paper. Our (tentative) conclusion is that the student knew the rule, but tended to overlook it when working problems "mentally". Note that in the third and fourth examples of Fig. 8 the student appears to be operating at the level of a "symbol manipulator" (cf. the mal-rules of Fig. 5; see Section 4 above) and then attempts to restore the intermediary problem to a more "familiar" form.

(6) In these sessions with LMS, we have observed a number of new mal-rules including:

$$M*N+P*Q \Rightarrow M*N*P*Q$$
$$M+N*X = \cdots \Rightarrow M*N*X = \cdots$$

In the earlier pilot we saw some other mal-rules which would complete this "set".

(a)

THE LEVEL IS 8

SOLVE $(5+2*X = 3*2+1)$
$>X = 1$
IS THAT WHAT YOU INTENDED (Y/N) $>$ Y
THANK YOU ..

SOLVE $(4+3*X = 5*3+1)$
$>X = 16/7$
IS THAT WHAT YOU INTENDED (Y/N) $>$ Y
THANK YOU ..

SOLVE $(2+3*X+2 = 16)$
$>X = 14/5$
IS THAT WHAT YOU INTENDED (Y/N) $>$ Y
THANK YOU ..

SOLVE $(5+3*X = 5*2-1)$
$>X = 9/8$
IS THAT WHAT YOU INTENDED (Y/N) $>$ Y
THANK YOU ..

SOLVE $(4+2+4*X = 5*5+2*2)$
$>X = 29/10$
IS THAT WHAT YOU INTENDED (Y/N) $>$ Y
THANK YOU ..

SOLVE $(5+3*X = 5+1*2)$
$>X = 7/8$
IS THAT WHAT YOU INTENDED (Y/N) $>$ Y
THANK YOU ..

YOU GOT 1 OUT OF 6 RIGHT
**MODEL FITTING VECTOR (1 6)
**THE STUDENT BEHAVES AS MODEL
((MULT ADDSUB XADDSUB REARRANGE NTORHS SOLVE FIN2 FIN))

(b)

$4+3*Y = 5*3+1$
$7Y = 16$
$Y = 16/7$

$2+3*Y+2 = 16$
$5Y+2 = 16$
$5Y = 16-2$
$5Y = 14$
$Y = 14/5$

(c)

PS (MULT ADDSUB XADDSUB REARRANGE NTORHS SOLVE FIN2 FIN) EVALUATES
$(4+3*X = 5*3+1)$ TO
RULE MULT FIRES-RESULT IS $(4+3*X = 15+1)$
RULE ADDSUB FIRES-RESULT IS $(7*X = 15+1)$
RULE ADDSUB FIRES-RESULT IS $(7*X = 16)$
RULE SOLVE FIRES-RESULT IS $(1*X = 16//7)$
RULE FIN2 FIRES-RESULT IS $((16 7))$
COMPLETE ANSWER IS (16 7)

FIG. 7. (a) Student 3's LMS protocol. (b) Student 3's interview performance with selected level 8 problems. (c) LMS system's protocol for the model inferred for this student on problem 2.

$$4+3*Y = 5*3+1$$
$$7Y = 16$$
$$Y = 16/7$$

$$2+3*Y+2 = 16$$
$$5Y+2 = 16$$
$$5Y = 16-2$$
$$5Y = 14$$
$$Y = 14/5$$

$$2*Y = 10-3*Y$$
$$2Y = 7Y$$
$$= 2Y-7Y$$
$$= -5Y$$

$$2*Y = 14+6-3*Y$$
$$2Y = 17Y$$
$$Y = 17Y/2Y$$
$$Y = 17/2$$

$$2*Y = 7*3-1-3*Y$$
$$2Y = 21-1-3*Y$$
$$2Y+3Y = 20$$
$$5Y = 20$$
$$Y = 4$$

FIG. 8. Interview with student 5—problems corresponding to levels 8 and 9.

5.2. A DETAILED ANALYSIS OF THE STUDENTS' PERFORMANCE

Table 2 gives a summary of this group's performance. From Table 2(a) we see that 221 out of the 248 problems were worked correctly; leaving 27 incorrect solutions.

With the current rules and mal-rules, 12 of the errors were diagnosed, leaving 15 undiagnosed. Table 2(b) shows that if we had made the mal-rules "global", i.e. detectable at all levels after they had been "introduced", then two further incorrect responses would have been spotted. Furthermore, if we had implemented the mal-rules

TABLE 2(a)

Problems worked	Correct solutions	Incorrect solutions	Diagnosed	Undiagnosed
248	221	27	12	15

TABLE 2(b)

		Undiagnosed		
Incorrect solutions	Diagnosed	Match mal-rule at another level	Proposed new mal-rules	Executive/ random
27	12	2	5	8[1]

[1] Of the 8 executive errors, 7 appeared in the first 3 levels.

encountered in these sessions, then a further five responses would have been diagnosed, leaving eight executive/random errors. It was further noted from the "raw" data, that seven out of the eight of these "executive" errors occurred in the first three levels. Thus we argue that students make far fewer "executive" errors once they have settled into the system.

Ignoring spurious "executive" errors and assuming the enhancements discussed above, 19 out of the remaining 20 incorrect responses would then be diagnosed. We do, of course, appreciate that this very high performance will not be achieved with a random cross-section of students, *until* we have built up a very large "library" of mal-rules.

6. Further Work

6.1. FURTHER DETAILS WITH THE SYSTEM

Clearly much more extensive trials are required and will be carried out shortly. (It is intended to incorporate the mal-rules discovered in this experiment and to modify LMS so that mal-rules are "global".)

6.2. IMPROVING THE SPEED OF LMS.1

Given a fixed set of rules and mal-rules, it is not necessary to generate the models when the student is on-line. Thus, it is desirable to split LMS into two parts: the first will create the models, and the second will present the problems to the student and will determine whether the student's behaviour falls within the space described by the models (that is by the current set of rules/mal-rules). Viewing the Modeller in this way helps one to appreciate that what is essentially an *inference* problem has been reduced to a *search* problem, cf. Meta-DENDRAL (Buchanan, 1974).

If one has a fixed set of problems, then a further increase in speed could be achieved, as once one has determined the models which give unique answers, these results could be saved and merely *accessed* during the on-line phase.

It was also noted that there were redundant rules in many of the models. That is the problems chosen were not sufficiently demanding to activate all the rules. There are two possible outcomes: first, that the problems should be made more demanding and, secondly, that the redundant rules should be removed. The latter implies that the domain is not strictly hierarchical and this can be exploited to affect a reduction in the size of the search space.

6.3. EXTENDING THE SET OF RULES/MAL-RULES TO COVER OTHER
ASPECTS OF ALGEBRA

It would be very instructive to see, for instance, whether the types of "mal-rules" observed by Matz (1981) could be captured in this representation.

6.4. GENERATING PROBLEMS TO DISCRIMINATE BETWEEN HYPOTHESIZED MODELS

As discussed in Sleeman and Smith (1981) it would be *possible* to generate a problem template which would distinguish between two hypothesized models, similarly to the way in which Meta-DENDRAL "grows" the condition part of its rules. However, this again would be too slow to be useable in the on-line phase, and so it is suggested that discriminatory templates should either be supplied as data or "grown" in the "off-line" phase of the Modeller. It is then merely necessary to "substantiate" the template in the on-line phase. (One needs to present the student with sufficient problems so that a reliable performance profile can be determined, this is clearly not always possible with a fixed example set.) The performance profiles anticipated include "ideal" behaviour, consistent use of mal-rule(s), inconsistent use of one or more mal-rules, consistent/inconsistent use of mal-rule(s) followed by "ideal" behaviour, behaviour not explained by the current set of rules and mal-rules (2).

6.5. COPING WITH "BUGS" AT A HIGHER LEVEL THAN WHERE THEY "SHOULD" OCCUR

The LMS protocols and the interviews give several examples of this occurring. And indeed with younger children one can expect to find much greater evidence of this. (Namely, when the problem is "hard", the student makes errors with rules with which he previously succeeded.) To accommodate this the system will have to be redesigned, in part.

6.6. COPING WITH THE SITUATIONS WHERE THE APPROPRIATE MAL-RULES ARE NOT PRESENT

In the above section we have assumed that the appropriate mal-rule was known to the system. When this assumption is not valid there appear to be several ways to proceed:

(1) Analysing protocols "manually" as at present and then subsequently enhancing the list of mal-rules.
(2) Generate mal-rules from rules given constraints for the syntax and semantics of mal-rules. (Again one could argue that this has some psychological validity.)
(3) Use the Version Space technique (Buchanan and Mitchell, 1978), to refine a "standard" rule given that using it the student got some problems right and others wrong.

Acknowledgements

M. McDermot and the pupils from Abbey Grange School, Leeds, and to Daniel, Toby and Thomas Satterthwaite for being guinea pigs with an early version of LMS.

J. R. Hartley, Professor K. Lovell and K. Tait for undertaking the diagnostic interviews with the children.

To Rutgers' Computer Science department for making their excellent LISP system available.

Dr N. S. Sridharan and Dr T. M. Mitchell of Rutgers for related discussions.

M. J. Smith for discussions in the early stages of the work.

S. A. France for allowing me to use his enhanced "Winston" matcher.

Notes

(1) Rules which "capture" an observed error, e.g. changing the *side* but not the *sign* of a number in an algebraic equation.
(2) The system will have to decide when the student's behaviour has "stabilized" and, hence, when additional examples will not illicit further information. Secondly, LMS must produce a (succinct) summary of the child's behaviour on each problem set.

References

BROWN, J. S. & BURTON, R. R. (1978). Diagnostic models for procedural bugs in basic mathematical skills. *Cognitive Science*, **2**, 155–192.

BUCHANAN, B. G. (1974). Scientific theory formation by computer. *Proceedings of NATO Advanced Study Institute on Computer Orientated Learning Processes*. Bonas, France.

BUCHANAN, B. G. & MITCHELL, T. M. (1978). Model-directed learning of production rules. In *Pattern-directed Inference Systems* (D. A. Waterman and F. R. Hayes-Roth, eds). Academic Press, New York.

CLANCEY, W. J. (1981). Tutoring rules for guiding a case method dialogue. Chapter 10 in this volume.

GOLDSTEIN, I. P. (1981). The genetic Graph: a representation for the evolution of Procedural Knowledge. Chapter 3 in this volume.

HARTLEY, J. R. & SLEEMAN, D. H. (1973). Towards intelligent teaching systems. *International Journal of Man–Machine Studies*, **5**, 215–236.

KIMBALL, R. (1981). A self-adapting, self-improving tutor for symbolic intesration. Chapter 12 in this volume.

MATZ, M. (1981). Towards a generative theory of high school algebra errors. Chapter 2 in this volume.

O'SHEA, T. (1981). A self-improving quadratic tutor. Chapter 13 in this volume.

SLEEMAN, D. H. (1979). Some current topics in intelligent teaching systems. *AISB Quarterly*, **33**, 22–27.

SLEEMAN, D. H. & SMITH, M. J. (1981). Modelling student's problem solving. *AI Journal*, 171–187.

STEVENS, A., COLLINS, A. & GOLDIN, S. E. (1981). Misconceptions in student's understanding. Chapter 1 in this volume.

10. Tutoring rules for guiding a case method dialogue

WILLIAM J. CLANCEY

Computer Science Department, Stanford University,
Stanford, California 94305, U.S.A.

The first version of an "intelligent computer-aided instruction" program built on MYCIN-like expert systems has been implemented. This program, named GUIDON, is a case method tutor in which the problem-solving and tutorial dialogue capabilities are distinct. The expertise to be taught is provided by a rule-based consultation program. The dialogue capabilities constitute teaching expertise for helping a student solve a case.

In this paper we describe the rule-based formalism used by MYCIN-like programs, and argue that these programs are not sufficient in themselves as teaching tools. We have chosen to develop a mixed-initiative tutor that plays an active role in choosing knowledge to present to a student, based on his competence and interests. Teaching expertise is represented explicitly, using a flexible framework that makes it possible to modify easily tutorial strategies and communicate them to other researchers. Furthermore, we argue that it is desirable to augment the domain expertise of MYCIN-like programs with other levels of domain knowledge that helps explain and organize the domain rules.

1. Introduction

How can we make the expertise of knowledge-based programs accessible to a student? Knowledge-based programs (Davis, Buchanan & Shortliffe, 1977; Lenat, 1976; Pople, 1977; Goldstein & Roberts, 1977) achieve high performance by interpreting a specialized set of facts and domain relations in the context of particular problems. These knowledge bases are generally built by interviewing human experts to extract the knowledge they use to solve problems in their area of expertise. However, it is not clear that the organization and level of abstraction of this performance knowledge is suitable for use in a tutorial program. We are exploring this problem in the GUIDON tutorial program, using the knowledge bases of MYCIN-like expert systems.

MYCIN is a knowledge-based program that provides consultations about infectious disease diagnosis and therapy (Shortliffe, 1974). In MYCIN, domain relations and facts take the form of rules about what to do in a given circumstance. A principle feature of this formalism is the separation of the knowledge base from the interpreter for applying it. This makes the knowledge accessible for multiple uses, including application to particular problems (i.e. for "performance") and explanation of reasoning (Davis, 1976).

We have most recently used the MYCIN knowledge base as the foundation of a tutorial system, called GUIDON. The goal of this project is to study the problem of transferring the expertise of MYCIN-like systems to a student. It is argued in this paper that MYCIN-like rule-based expert systems constitute a good basis for tutorial programs, but they are not sufficient in themselves for making knowledge accessible to a student.

In GUIDON we have augmented the performance knowledge of rules by adding two other levels: a "support level" to justify individual rules, and an "abstraction level" to organize rules into patterns. The components and tutorial uses of these levels are discussed in section 4.3. Secondly, the GUIDON system contains teaching expertise that is represented explicitly, and is independent of the domain knowledge base. This is expertise for carrying on a tutorial dialogue intended to present the domain knowledge to a student in an organized way, over a number of sessions. Section 3 describes design considerations for this tutorial dialogue, given the structure of the knowledge in MYCIN-like problem areas (described in section 2).

With the addition of other levels of domain knowledge and teaching expertise, GUIDON is designed to transfer the expertise of MYCIN-like programs in an efficient, comprehensible way. In doing this, we make contributions to several areas of research in Intelligent Computer-Aided Instruction (ICAI), including means for structuring and planning a dialogue, generating teaching material, constructing and verifying a model of what the student knows, and explaining expert reasoning.

However, we also argue that the nature of MYCIN-like expert systems makes it reasonable to experiment with various teaching strategies. The representation of teaching expertise in GUIDON is intended to provide a flexible framework for such experimentation (section 4). To illustrate the use of this framework in the first version of GUIDON, we present in this paper two sample interactions and describe the domain knowledge and teaching strategies used by the program (sections 5 and 6). The sample interactions and rule listings were generated by the implemented program.

2. Description of MYCIN-like expert systems

2.1. PROBLEM AREA AND FORMALISM

A major objective of the MYCIN system has been to provide a high performance, computer-based therapeutic tool designed to be useful in both clinical and research environments. MYCIN is a computer-based consultant that interacts with physicians in much the same way that human consultants do: it asks numerous questions about the state of the patient and provides advice about appropriate therapy. This requires development of a system that has a sound knowledge base, and that displays a high level of competence in its field.

The MYCIN knowledge base has been built over four years through interactions with physicians. This body of knowledge is represented as a collection of conditional sentences called "production rules." The production rule formalism provides a flexible and easily understood representation of facts and relations, and a simple interpreter of those facts (Davis & King, 1977). The MYCIN knowledge base currently contains approximately 450 such rules.† Each rule consists of a set of preconditions (called the

---

† In addition there are several hundred facts and relations stored in tables, which are referenced by the rules.

"premise") which, if true, justifies the conclusion made in the "action" part of the rule. An example is shown below.†

> IF (1) the gram stain of the organism is gram negative, and (2) the morphology of the organism is rod, and (3) the aerobicity of the organism is anaerobic, THEN there is suggestive evidence (0.6) that the genus of the organism is Bacteroides.

FIG. 1. Sample MYCIN rule.

2.2. VALIDITY OF THE KNOWLEDGE BASE

Two formal evaluations of MYCIN's performance have demonstrated that MYCIN's competence in selecting antimicrobial therapy for meningitis and for bacteremia is comparable to that of the infectious disease faculty at Stanford University School of Medicine (where MYCIN was developed) (Yu *et al.*, 1979a,b). From this we conclude that a rule-based consultant can be given the knowledge necessary for demonstrably high performance in a domain as complex and inexact as medicine. The fact that the formalism of production rules has been exploited in MYCIN to create a rich, high performance knowledge base for solving difficult, real world problems is an important starting point for demonstrating the advantages of using this representation of domain knowledge for tutoring.

2.3. DOMAIN OF APPLICATION

The production rule formalism used by MYCIN is widely applicable to tasks other than medicine, although it is by no means a "universal" language. Because the knowledge base is separate from the interpreter for applying it, it is possible to remove the medical knowledge and substitute a set of rules about a new domain.‡ The tutoring system we are developing will also work with problems and rules in another domain, assuming some parallels between the structure of the knowledge in the new domain and the structure of the existing medical knowledge. Thus, GUIDON is a multiple-domain tutorial program. The overall configuration of this system is shown in Fig. 2. (The representation of teaching expertise is discussed in section 4.) One advantage of this system is that a fixed set of teaching strategies can be tried in different domains, affording an important perspective on their generality.§

The EMYCIN system has already been used to demonstrate the applicability of the production rule formalism and interpreter to domains other than infectious disease diagnosis and therapy. For example, the SACON program‖ provides advice on structural analysis problems, such as the most appropriate materials for airplane wings under stresses of different sorts. In addition, the EMYCIN system has been used in two very

---

† In this paper, each precondition is called a "subgoal." If all of the subgoals in the premise can be achieved (shown to be true), then a conclusion can be made about the goal in the action.

‡ The domain-independent package, consisting of rule interpreter and explanation module is called "EMYCIN," which stands for "essential MYCIN." Development of this system is being continued by William van Melle and A. Carlisle Scott.

§ This method of integrating domain and teaching expertise can be contrasted with the design of early frame-oriented CAI systems. For example, in the tutor for infectious diseases by Feurzeig, Munter, Swets & Breen (1964), medical and teaching expertise were "compiled" together into the branching structure of the frames (dialogue/content situations). In GUIDON, domain and teaching expertise are decoupled and stated explicitly.

‖ Collaborative project with the MARC Corporation, Inc.

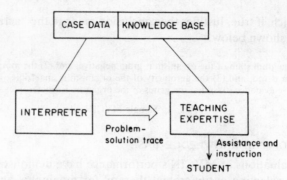

FIG. 2. Modules for a multiple-domain tutorial system.

different medical domains: interpretation of pulmonary function tests (Feigenbaum, 1977) and drug therapy recommendations for psychiatric patients (Heiser, Brooks & Ballard, 1978). It has also been used in a class exercise to diagnose and recommend fixes for problems in an automobile horn system (van Melle, 1974). In this paper, all examples and discussion will be based on the infectious disease knowledge base (the original MYCIN program).

2.4. OTHER REPRESENTATIONS FOR KNOWLEDGE BASES

Production rules have worked well in several domains (Feigenbaum, 1977).† However, other approaches for building knowledge-based systems are possible. For example, Pople successfully uses frame-like "disease hypotheses" (Pople, 1977) and Kulikowski uses a causal-associational network (Weiss, Kulikowski & Safir, 1977).

We do not argue here for or against the use of a production rule system as a foundation for tutorial programs; sounder representations of expertise may be found. But given the availability of a system with MYCIN's sophistication, there is good reason to experiment with it in a tutorial setting. It is quite possible that our use of the domain rules in a tutorial program will help us to design better formalisms for codifying expertise.

3. Development of a tutorial program based on MYCIN-like systems

In addition to the domain knowledge of the expert program, a tutorial program requires teaching expertise, such as the ability to tailor the presentation of domain knowledge to the student's competence and interests (Brown, 1977). The GUIDON program, with its teaching expertise and augmented domain knowledge, is designed to be an active, intelligent agent that helps make the knowledge of MYCIN-like programs accessible to a student.

It is possible to follow MYCIN's reasoning during a consultation by using the explanation system (one can ask WHY case data is being sought by the program and HOW goals will be (were) achieved). However, we believe that this is an inefficient process for learning the contents of the knowledge base. The MYCIN program is only a passive "teacher." It is necessary for the student to ask an exhaustive series of questions, if

† PROSPECTOR, the SRI program, was designed originally as a MYCIN-like system for consulting with geologists about mineral exploration sites.

he is to discover all of the reasoning paths considered by the program. GUIDON acts as an agent that keeps track of the knowledge that has been presented to the student in previous sessions and looks for opportunities to deepen and broaden the student's knowledge of MYCIN's expertise. Moreover, the MYCIN program contains no model of the user, so program-generated explanations are never tailored to his competence or interests. GUIDON's teaching expertise includes capabilities to measure the student's competence and to use this measure as a basis for selecting knowledge to present.

What kind of dialogue might be suitable for teaching the knowledge of MYCIN-like consultation systems? What strategies for teaching will be useful? Will these strategies be independent of the knowledge base content? How will they be represented? What additions to the performance knowledge of MYCIN-like systems might be useful in a tutorial program? These are some of the basic questions involved in converting a rule-based expert program into a tutorial program.

As the first step in approaching these questions, the following subsections discuss some of the basic ways in which MYCIN's domain and formalism have influenced design considerations for GUIDON. Section 3.1 describes the nature of the dialogue we have chosen for tutorial sessions. Section 3.2 discusses the nature of MYCIN performance knowledge and argues for including additional domain knowledge in the tutorial program. Sections 3.3 and 3.4 argue that the uncertainty of MYCIN's knowledge and the size of the knowledge base make it desirable to have a framework for experimenting with teaching strategies. This framework, which describes GUIDON as a discourse program and will provide the basis for future development of the system, is presented in section 4.

3.1. A GOAL-DIRECTED CASE DIALOGUE

In a GUIDON tutorial session, a student plays the role of a physician consultant. A sick patient (the "case") is described to him in general terms: his age, sex, race and lab reports about cultures taken at the site of the infection are provided. The student is expected to ask for other information that he thinks might be relevant to this case: e.g. did the patient become infected while hospitalized? Did he ever live in the San Joaquin Valley? GUIDON compares the student's questions to those asked by MYCIN and critiques him on this basis. When the student draws hypotheses from the evidence he has collected, GUIDON compares these conclusions to those that MYCIN reached, given the same information about the patient. We refer to this dialogue between the student and GUIDON as a "case dialogue." Because GUIDON attempts to transfer expertise to students exclusively through case dialogues, we call it a "case method tutor."

It is assumed that the student wishes to learn to solve the problems which MYCIN can solve. GUIDON's purpose is to broaden the student's knowledge of the evidence to consider in a particular problem by pointing out inappropriate lines of reasoning and suggesting approaches the student did not consider. An important assumption is that the student has a suitable background for solving the case; he knows the vocabulary and the general form of the task (using case data to reach a diagnosis). GUIDON can help him judge the relative importance of the evidence in specific cases. The criterion for having learned MYCIN's problem-solving methods is therefore straightforward: when presented with novel, difficult cases, does the student seek relevant data and draw appropriate conclusions?

Helping the student solve the case is greatly aided by placing constraints on the case dialogue. A "goal-directed" dialogue is a discussion of the rules applied to achieve specific goals. In general, the topics of this dialogue are precisely those "goals" that are concluded by MYCIN rules.† During the dialogue, only one goal at a time is considered; data that cannot be used in rules to achieve this goal are "irrelevant." This is a strong constraint on the student's process of asking questions and making hypotheses, A goal-directed dialogue helps the tutor to follow the student as he solves the problem, increasing the chance that timely assistance can be provided.‡

Our design of GUIDON has also been influenced by consideration of the sophistication of the students we expect to use it. We are designing the program for well-motivated students who are capable of a serious, mixed-initiative dialogue. Various features (not all described in this paper) make the program flexible, so that students can use their judgment to control the depth and detail of the discussion. These features include the capability to request:

(1) a list of descriptions of all data relevant to a particular goal;
(2) a subgoal tree for a goal;
(3) a quiz or hint relevant to the current goal;
(4) a concise summary of all evidence already discussed for a goal (data and rules that were mentioned in the dialogue);
(5) discussion of a goal (of the student's choice);
(6) conclusion of a discussion, with GUIDON finishing the collection of evidence for the goal, and indicating conclusions that the student might have drawn.

3.2. SINGLE FORM OF EXPERTISE

The problem of multiple forms of expertise has been important in ICAI research. For example, when mechanistic reasoning is involved, qualitative and quantitative forms of expertise may be useful to solve the problem (Brown, Rubenstein & Burton, 1978). de Kleer has found that strategies for debugging an electronic circuit are "radically different" depending on whether one does local mathematical analysis (using Kirchhoff's laws) or uses a higher level, functional analysis of components (Brown *et al.*, 1975). One might argue that a tutor for this domain should be ready to recognize and generate arguments on both of these levels.§

For all practical purposes, GUIDON does not need to be concerned about multiple forms of expertise. This is primarily because reasoning in infectious disease problem-solving is based on judgments about empirical information, rather than arguments based on causal mechanisms (Weiss *et al.*, 1977). MYCIN's judgments are "cookbook" responses that address the data directly, as opposed to attempting to explain it in terms of physiological mechanisms. Moreover, the expertise to solve a MYCIN case on this level of abstraction constitutes a "closed" world (Carbonell & Collins, 1977): all of the

† A typical sequence of (nested) goals is: to reach a diagnosis, to determine which organisms might be causing the infection, to determine the type of infection, to determine if the infection has been partially treated, etc.

‡ Sleeman (1977) uses a similar approach for allowing a student to explore algorithms.

§ See Carr & Goldstein (1977) for related discussion.

objects, attributes and values that are relevant to solution of a case are determined by a MYCIN consultation that is performed before a tutorial session begins†

It is possible that multiple forms of expertise might be applied to solve some of the problems in domains of other MYCIN-like expert systems, e.g. in solving structural analysis problems. Using GUIDON in these domains may suggest ways to use the production rule formalism to encode multiple forms of expertise.

Even though MYCIN's domain makes it possible for cases to be solved without recourse to the level of physiological mechanisms, a student may find it useful to know this "support" knowledge that lies behind the rules. Section 4.3 describes the domain knowledge we have found it useful to add to MYCIN's performance knowledge in GUIDON.

3.3. WEAK MODEL OF INQUIRY

Even though the MYCIN world can be considered to be closed, there is no strong model for ordering the collection of evidence.‡ Medical problem solving is still an art. While there are some conventions that ensure that all routine data is collected, physicians have not agreed upon a basis for numerically optimizing the decision of what to do next.§ For example, when offering assistance, should the tutor suggest the domain rule that most confirms the evidence that has already been collected, or a rule that contradicts this evidence?‖ It will be useful to experiment with various strategies for guiding the student's collection of case evidence.

3.4. LARGE NUMBER OF RULES

For every case GUIDON discusses with a student, MYCIN provides an "AND/OR" tree of goals (the "OR" nodes) and rules (the "AND" nodes) that were pursued during the corresponding consultation. This tree constitutes a trace of the application of the knowledge base to the given case.¶ Many of the 450 rules are not tried because they conclude about goals that don't need to be pursued to solve the case. Hundreds of others fail to apply because one or more preconditions are found to be false. Finally,

---

† There is always the possibility that a student may present an exotic case to the GUIDON that is beyond its expertise. While MYCIN has been designed to detect simple instances of this (i.e. evidence of an infection other than bacteremia or meningitis), we have decided to restrict GUIDON tutorials to the physician-approved cases in the library (currently over 100 cases).

‡ In Goldstein's WUMPUS program (Carr & Goldstein, 1977), for example, it is possible to rank each legal move (analogous to seeking case data in MYCIN) and so rate the student according to "rejected inferior moves" and "missed superior moves." The same analysis is possible in Burton and Brown's WEST program (Brown *et al.*, 1975).

§ See, for example, Sprosty (1963).

‖ MYCIN's rules are not based on Bayesian probabilities, so it is not possible to use optimization techniques like those developed by Hartley (Hartley, Sleeman & Woods, 1972). Arguments against using Bayes Law in expert systems can be found in Shortliffe (1974).

¶ Before a tutorial session, GUIDON scans each rule used by MYCIN and compiles a list of all subgoals that needed to be achieved before the premise of the rule could be evaluated. In the case of a rule that failed to apply, GUIDON determines all preconditions of the premise that are false. By doing this, GUIDON's knowledge of the case is independent of the order that questions were asked and rules were applied by MYCIN, so topics can be easily changed and the depth of discussion controlled flexibly by both GUIDON and the student. The procedure for constructing the trace is quite complicated and not all of the problems have been solved. Details will appear in later publications. This process of automatically generating a solution trace for any case can be contrasted with SOPHIE's single, fixed simulated circuit (Brown *et al.*, 1976).

typically 20% of the rules make conclusions that contribute varying degrees of belief about the goals pursued.

Thus, MYCIN interpreter provides the tutorial program with a lot of information about the case solution (see Fig. 2). It is not clear how to present this to a student. What should the tutor do when the student pursues a goal that MYCIN did not? (Interrupt him? Wait until he realizes that the goal contributes no useful information?) Which dead-end search paths pursued by MYCIN should the tutor expect the student to consider? For many goals there are too many rules to discuss with the student; how is the tutor to decide which to present and which to omit? What techniques can be used to produce coherent plans for guiding the discussion through lines of reasoning used by the program? It would be useful to have a framework that gave us the freedom to guide the dialogue in different ways. The rest of this paper shows how GUIDON has been given this flexibility by viewing it as a discourse program.

4. A framework for a case method tutorial program

One purpose of this tutorial project is to provide a framework for testing teaching methods. Therefore, we have chosen an implementation that makes it possible to vary the strategies that the tutor uses for guiding the dialogue. Using methods similar to those used in knowledge-based programs, we have formalized the tutorial program in rules and procedures that codify expertise for carrying on a case dialogue.

This section is relatively abstract. The reader may find it useful to consider the sample dialogues in Figs 7 and 8 before proceeding. The first subsection below lists forms of discourse knowledge that will be useful for a case method dialogue. Following subsections describe GUIDON's representation of this knowledge. Examples and details are provided in sections 5 and 6.

4.1. DISCOURSE KNOWLEDGE

Our implementation of GUIDON's dialogue capabilities makes use of knowledge obtained from studies of discourse in AI (Bobrow *et al.*, 1977; Bruce, 1975; Deutsch, 1974; Winograd, 1977). To quote Bruce (emphasis added):

> [It is] . . . useful to have a model of how social interactions typically fit together, and thus a model of discourse structure. Such a model can be viewed as a heuristic which suggests likely *action sequences* . . . There are places in a discourse where questions make sense, others where explanations are expected. [These paradigms] . . . facilitate generation and subsequent understanding (Bruce, 1975).

Based on Winograd's analysis of discourse (Winograd, 1977), it appears desirable for a case method tutor to have the following forms of knowledge for carrying on a dialogue.

(1) Knowledge about dialogue patterns. Faught (1977) mentions two types of patterns: interpretation patterns (to understand a speaker) and action patterns (to generate utterances). GUIDON uses action patterns represented as "discourse procedures" for directing and focussing the case dialogue. These are the "action sequences" mentioned by Bruce. They are invoked by tutoring rules, discussed in section 4.2.†

† Because of the constraints a goal-directed dialogue imposes upon the student, we have not found it necessary to use interpretation patterns at this time. They might be useful to follow the student's reasoning in a non-goal-directed dialogue.

(2) Forms of domain knowledge for carrying on a specific dialogue, Section 4.3 surveys the augmented domain knowledge available to GUIDON.

(3) Knowledge of the communication situation. This includes the tutorial program's understanding of the student's intentions and knowledge, as well as the tutor's intentions for carrying on the dialogue. These components are represented in GUIDON by an "overlay student model" (in which the student's knowledge is viewed as a subset of the expert program's) (section 4.4.1), a "case syllabus" (a lesson plan of topics to be sure are discussed, created by the tutor for each case) (section 4.4.2), and a "focus record" (to keep track of factors in which the student has shown interest recently) (section 4.4.3). Knowledge of the communication situation controls the use of dialogue patterns.

The following subsections give details about each of these forms of knowledge.

4.2. DISCOURSE PROCEDURES AND TUTORING RULES

The sequences of actions in discourse procedures serve as an ordered list of options—types of remarks for the program to consider making. For example, the procedure for discussing a domain rule (hereafter, d-rule) includes a step that indicates to "consider mentioning d-rules related to the one just discussed." Thus, a discourse procedure step specifies in a schematic form WHEN a type of remark might be appropriate. WHETHER to take the option (e.g. is there an "interesting" d-rule to mention?) and WHAT to say exactly (the discourse pattern for mentioning the d-rule) will be dynamically determined by tutoring rules (hereafter, t-rules) whose preconditions refer to the student model, case syllabus, and focus record (hereafter, referred to jointly as the communication model).

T-rules are generally invoked as a packet to achieve some tutorial goal.† T-rule packets are of two types:

(1) T-rules for accumulating belief—updating the communication model and determining how "interesting" a topic is are two examples.‡ Generally, a packet of t-rules of this type is applied exhaustively.

(2) T-rules for selecting a discourse procedure to follow. Generally, a packet of this type stops trying t-rules when the first one succeeds. The form of t-rules of this type is shown in Fig. 3. Knowledge referenced in the premise part of a t-rule of this type is described in subsequent sections. The action part of these t-rules consists of stylized code, just like the steps of a discourse procedure.§ A step may invoke:

   (a) a packet of t-rules, e.g., to select a question format for presenting a given d-rule;

   (b) a discourse procedure, e.g., to sequentially discuss each precondition of a d-rule;

---

† Packets are implemented as stylized INTERLISP procedures. This should be contrasted with the interpreter used by the expert program that invokes d-rules directly, indexing them according to the goal that needs to be determined.

‡ GUIDON uses "certainty factors" for representing the program's belief in something. Their value ranges between −1 and 1, with negative values signifying disbelief. See Shortliffe & Buchanan (1975) for discussion of their implementation and significance.

§ Discourse procedure steps also contain control information (e.g. for iteration) that is not important to this discussion.

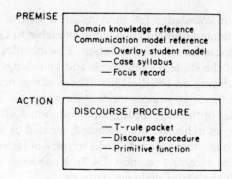

FIG. 3. Form of a tutorial rule.

  (c) a primitive function, e.g. to accept a question from the student, perform bookkeeping, etc.

Below is an outline of the t-rules currently being implemented in GUIDON. Except where noted, examples of these t-rules are presented in discussions of the sample tutorial dialogues in this paper.

  I. *T-rules for selecting discourse patterns*
    A. Guiding discussion of a d-rule.
    B. Responding to a student hypothesis.
    C. Choosing question formats.

  II. *T-rules for choosing domain knowledge*
    A. Providing orientation for pursuing new goals (not demonstrated in this paper).
    B. Measuring interestingness of d-rules.

  III. *T-rules for maintaining the communication model*
    A. Updating the overlay model when d-rules fire.
    B. Updating the overlay model during hypothesis evaluation.
    C. Creating a case syllabus (not implemented).

All of the t-rules in this paper are translated by a program directly from the INTER-LISP source code, using an extension of the technique used for translating MYCIN's rules. This accounts for some of the stilted prose in the examples that follow.

4.3. AUGMENTED REPRESENTATION OF DOMAIN KNOWLEDGE

The representation of domain knowledge available to GUIDON can be organized in three tiers, shown by Fig. 4.

  Subsequent sections briefly describe the components of each tier. Section 4.3.4 discusses how meta-level knowledge that describes the representation of MYCIN-like rules has been used in GUIDON for implementing a variety of tutorial strategies.

4.3.1. *Performance tier*

The performance knowledge consists of all the rules and tables used by the expert program to make goal-directed conclusions about the initial case data. The output of

```
┌─────────────────────────────────────────────────────────┐
│                                                           │
│          I. META-LEVEL ABSTRACTIONS: rule models         │
│                                        rule schemata      │
│                                                           │
│          II. PERFORMANCE: rules                           │
│                            lists and tables               │
│                                                           │
│       III. SUPPORT: definitions                           │
│                      mechanism descriptions               │
│                      justifications                       │
│                      literature references                │
│                                                           │
└─────────────────────────────────────────────────────────┘
```

FIG. 4. Domain knowledge organization into three tiers.

the consultation, an extensive AND/OR tree of traces showing which rules were applied, their conclusions, and the case data required to apply them, is passed to the tutor. GUIDON fills in this tree by determining which subgoals appear in the rules. In Fig. 5, "COVERFOR" signifies the goal to determine which organisms should be "covered" by a therapy recommendation; d-rule 578 concludes about this goal; "BURNED" is a subgoal of this rule.

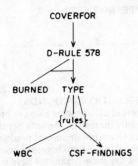

FIG. 5. The portion of the AND/OR tree of goals and rules created by the expert program which is relevant to the dialogue shown in Fig. 7.

Tutorial rules make frequent reference to this data structure in order to guide the dialogue. For example, the response to the request for help shown in Fig. 7 is based first of all on the rules that were used by the expert program for the current goal. Similarly, the t-rules for supplying case data requested by the student check to see if the expert program asked for the same information during the corresponding consultation (e.g. the "white blood count" in the sample dialogue of Fig. 7).†

D-Rule578 and its associated documentation is illustrated in Fig. 6.

4.3.2. Support tier

The support tier of the knowledge base consists of annotations to the rules and the factors used by them.‡ For example, there are canned-text descriptions of every

---

† Other possibilities include: the question is not relevant to the current goal; it can be deduced by definition from other known data; or a d-rule indicates that it is not relevant to this case.

‡ Rule justifications, author and edit date were first proposed by Davis (1976) as knowledge base maintenance records.

⟨abstraction level⟩

RULE-SCHEMA: MENINGITIS . COVERFOR . CLINICAL
RULE-MODEL: COVERFOR-IS-MODEL
KEY-FACTOR: BURNED
DUAL: D-RULE577

⟨performance level⟩

D-RULE578

If: (1) The infection which requires therapy is meningitis, and
     (2) Organisms were not seen on the stain of the culture, and
     (3) The type of the infection is bacterial, and
     (4) The patient has been seriously burned
Then: There is suggestive evidence (0·5) that pseudomonas-aeruginosa is one
        of the organisms (other than those seen on cultures or smears)
          which might be causing the infection
UPDATES: COVERFOR
USES: (TREATINF ORGSEEN TYPE BURNED)

⟨support level⟩

MECHANISM-FRAME: BODY-INFRACTION . WOUNDS
JUSTIFICATION: "For a very brief period of time after a severe burn the
      surface of the wound is sterile. Shortly thereafter, the area becomes
      colonized by a mixed flora in which Gram pos organisms predominate.
      By the 3rd post burn day this bacterial population becomes dominated
      by Gram neg organisms. By the 5th day these organisms have invaded
      tissue well beneath the surface of the burn. The organisms most
      commonly isolated from burn patients are *Pseudomonas*,
      Klebsiella-Enterobacter, *Staph*. etc. Infection with *Pseudomonas*.
      is frequently fatal."
LITERATURE: Macmillan BG: Ecology of Bacteria Colonizing the Burned Patient
      Given Topical and System Gentamicin Therapy: a five-year study, J
      Infect Dis 124:278–286, 1971.
AUTHOR: Dr. Victor Yu
LAST-CHANGE: 8 September, 1976

FIG. 6. Domain Rule 578 and its associated documentation. All information is provided by a domain expert, except for the "key-factor" which is computed by the tutor from the rule schema and contents of the particular rule. See section 4.3.3.

laboratory test in the MYCIN domain, including, for instance, remarks about how the test should be performed. Mechanism descriptions provided by the domain expert are used to provide some explanation of a rule beyond the canned text of the justification. For the infectious disease domain of MYCIN, they indicate how a given factor leads to a particular infection with particular organisms by stating the origin of the organism and the favourable conditions for its growth at the site of the infection. Thus, the frame associated with the factor "a seriously burned patient" shows that the organisms originate in the air and grow in the exposed tissue of a burn, resulting in a frequently fatal infection.

4.3.3. Abstraction tier

The abstraction tier of the knowledge base represents patterns in the performance knowledge. For example, a rule schema is a description of a kind of rule: a pattern of preconditions that appears in the premise, the goal concluded about, and the context of its application. The schema and a canned-text annotation of its significance are formalized in the MYCIN knowledge base by a physician expert. This schema is used by the tutor to "subtract off" the rule preconditions common to all rules of the type, leaving behind the factors that are specific to this particular rule, i.e. the "key factors" of this rule. Thus, the key factor of d-rule 578 (see Fig. 6), the fact that the patient has been seriously burned, was determined by removing the "contextual" information of the name of the infection, whether organisms were seen, and the type of the infection. Examples of the use of key factors occur throughout the hypothesis evaluation example (Fig. 8), particularly in lines 4–9.

Rule models (Davis, 1976) are program-generated patterns that represent the typical clusters of factors in the expert's rules. Unlike rule schemas, rule models do not necessarily correspond to domain concepts, though they do represent factors that tend to appear together in domain arguments (rules). An example from the MYCIN data base shows that the gram stain of an organism and its morphology tend to appear together in rules for determining the identity of an organism. Because rule models capture the factors that most commonly appear in rules for pursuing a goal, we are experimenting with their use as a form of "orientation" for naïve students. Details will be provided in later publications.

4.3.4. Use of meta-knowledge in tutorial rules

Meta-knowledge of the representation and application of d-rules plays an important role in t-rules. For example, in the first dialogue excerpt (Fig. 7) GUIDON uses function templates† to "read" d-rule 578 and discovers that the type of the infection is a subgoal that needs to be completed before the d-rule can be applied. This capability to examine the domain knowledge and reason about its use enables GUIDON to make multiple use of any given production rule during the tutorial session. Here are some uses we have implemented.

(1) Examine the rule (if it was tried in the consultation) and determine the subgoals that needed to be achieved before it could be applied; if the rule failed to apply, determine all possible ways this could be determined (perhaps more than one precondition is false).
(2) Examine the state of application of the rule during a tutorial interaction (what more needs to be done before it can be applied?) and choose an appropriate method of presentation.

---

† A function's template "indicates the order and generic type of the arguments in a typical call of that function" (Davis & Buchanan, 1977).

(3) Generate different questions for the student.
(4) Use the rule (and variations of it) to understand a student's hypothesis.
(5) Summarize arguments using the rule by extracting the "key point" it addresses.

The ability to use domain knowledge in multiple ways is an important feature of a "generative" tutor like GUIDON.† Flexible use of knowledge permits us to write a variety of tutoring rules that select and present teaching material in multiple ways. This is important because we want to use the MYCIN/GUIDON system for experimenting with teaching strategies.

4.4. COMPONENTS OF THE COMMUNICATION MODEL

The components of the communication model are (1) an overlay student model, (2) a case syllabus and (3) a focus record.

4.4.1. The overlay student model

The d-rules that were fired during the consultation associated with this case are run in a forward direction as the student is given case data.‡ In this way, GUIDON knows at every moment what the expert program would conclude based on the evidence available to the student. We make use of knowledge about the history and competence of the student to form hypotheses about which of the expert's conclusions are probably known to the student. This has been termed an "overlay" model of the student by Goldstein, because the student's knowledge is modelled in terms of a subset and simple variations of the expert rule base (Goldstein, 1977). Our work was originally motivated by the structural model used in Burton and Brown's WEST system (Brown et al., 1975).

Special t-rules for updating the overlay models are invoked whenever the expert program successfully applies a d-rule. These t-rules must decide whether the student has reached the same conclusion. This decision is based upon:

(1) the inherent complexity of the d-rule (e.g., some rules are trivial definitions, others have involved iterations);
(2) whether the tutor believes that the student knows how to achieve the subgoals that appear in the d-rule (factors that require the application of rules);
(3) the background of the student (e.g. year of medical school, intern, etc.);
(4) evidence gathered in previous interactions with the student.

These considerations are analogous to those used by Carr & Goldstein (1977) for the WUMPUS tutor.

4.4.2. The case syllabus

Before a human tutor discusses a case with a student, he has an idea of what he wants to discuss, given the constraints of time and the student's interests and capabilities. Similarly, in later versions of GUIDON a case syllabus will be generated before each

† Generative CAI programs select and transform domain knowledge in order to generate individualized teaching material. See Koffman & Blount (1973) for discussion.

‡ This is one application of the problem solution trace. The structure of this trace permits the program to repetitively reconsider d-rules (indexing them by the case data referenced in the premise part), without the high cost of reinterpreting premises from scratch.

case session.† We would like the syllabus to give GUIDON a global sense of the value of discussing particular topics, especially as depth of emphasis will impact on the student's understanding of the problem's solution. The syllabus of the type we are proposing provides consistency and goal-directedness to the tutor's presentations.

The syllabus will be derived from the following:

(1) The student model—where does the student need instruction?
(2) Professed student interests (perhaps the case was chosen because of features the student wants to know more about).
(3) Intrinsic importance of topics: what part does this information play in understanding the solution of the problem?
(4) Extrinsic importance of topics: given the universe of cases, how interesting is this topic? (A datum that is rarely available is probably worth mentioning when it is known, no matter how insignificant the evidence it contributes.)

We believe that these considerations will also be useful for implementing automatic selection of cases from the consultation library.

4.4.3. The focus record

The purpose of the focus record is to maintain continuity during the dialogue. It consists of a set of global variables that are set when the student asks about particular goals and values for goals. T-rules reference these variables when selecting d-rules to mention or when motivating a change in the goal being discussed. An example is provided in section 5.1.

5. T-rules for guiding discussion of a goal

In this section we consider an excerpt from a dialogue and some of the discourse procedures and tutoring rules involved. Suppose that a first-year medical student has just read about treatment for burned patients suspected to have a meningitis infection. His microbiology text mentioned several organisms, but it wasn't clear to him how other factors such as the age and degree of sickness of the patient might affect diagnosis of an actual case. GUIDON is available to him, so he decides to ask the program to select a relevant case from the MYCIN library for a tutorial session.

The program begins by invoking the discourse procedure CASE-DISCUSSION. One of the first steps is to choose a case. At this point the student described the case he wanted using keywords ("burned meningitis patient").‡ GUIDON selected the case and set the scene for the student. There is one pending culture from the CSF (cerebral spinal fluid, where meningitis infections occur). In the excerpt below (Fig. 7), the dialogue has reached the subtask of determining the organisms which might be causing

---

† Goldstein's "syllabus" and BIP's "Curriculum Information Network" are fixed networks that relate skills in terms of their complexities and dependencies. The syllabus discussed here is a program-generated plan for guiding discussion of a particular problem with a particular student.

‡ Student input to the GUIDON program is in the form of menu options and simple English phrases that are parsed using keyword analysis and pattern matching routines developed for MYCIN's question-answering module (Scott et al., 1977; Shortliffe, 1974).

the infection. (Annotations appear in curly brackets { }; student input follows double asterisks; line numbers are referred to in subsequent discussion of this example.

1   You should now proceed to ask questions that will enable you to make a
       hypothesis about the organisms (other than those seen on cultures or
       smears) which might be causing the infection.

5   {Initiative is given to the student; he may ask for more
            data; make a hypothesis; or use a special option.}

    ** HOW IS THE FACT THAT THE PATIENT IS BURNED RELEVANT?

10   {One option is to ask how a piece of data is relevant to the
           current goal.}

       The fact that patient-326 is seriously burned will be used to
       conclude that *Pseudomonas aeruginosa* is one of the organisms which might
15   be present (in addition to those seen on cultures or smears) [Rule 578].

    ** HELP

        {The "help" option is a request for assistance: the student
20   asks "where do I go from here?"}

       Try to determine the type of the infection: bacterial, fungal, viral,
    or TB.

25   {To provide help, GUIDON chose: (1) a rule to discuss
           (D-rule 578 was chosen because the dialogue just focused
           on it); and (2) a method of presentation—"tell the
           student to finish incomplete subgoals mentioned in the
           rule." Thus, a new topic is set up, "the type of the
30   infection." Initiative is returned to the student . . .}

    ** WHAT IS THE PATIENT'S WBC?

       The white count from the patient's peripheral CBC is 1·9 thousand.
35

        {The tutor observes that this question is relevant to the
           new topic and provides the requested data. The dialogue
           continues in this goal-directed manner . . .}

FIG. 7. Sample interaction: gathering data.

When the student requested help (line 17), the program had been following the pattern for discussing a goal. The request for help led to the invocation of tutoring rules. The teaching strategy represented by these t-rules is to provide help for a goal by suggesting a d-rule to the student. The discourse procedure that provides help in this context first invokes a packet of t-rules that will choose a d-rule to mention to the student. The second step is to invoke a packet of t-rules that will choose a presentation method.

5.1. CHOOSING A D-RULE TO MENTION IN ORDER TO PROVIDE HELP FOR A GOAL

D-rule 578 (see Fig. 6) was chosen because it became the focus of the discussion when the student asked about the relevance of the "burned" factor. That is, when the student asked the question in line 8, a variable was set to indicate that the most recent factor referred to for this goal was "burned" (the "focus topic"). Then when the packet of t-rules for choosing a d-rule to present was invoked, the following t-rule succeeded:†

T-RULE26.03

If: The recent context of the dialogue mentioned either a
     "deeper subgoal" or a factor relevant to the current goal
Then: Define the focus rule to be the d-rule that mentions this
       focus topic

This example illustrates how the communication model guides the session by controlling t-rules.

Often there is no obvious d-rule to suggest to the student. It is then useful for the tutor to have some measure of the "interestingness" of a d-rule at this time in the discussion. The t-rules presented below are applied to a set of d-rule candidates, ranking them by how strongly the tutor believes that they are interesting.

5.1.1. Change in belief is interesting

One measure of interest is the contribution the d-rule would make to what is currently known about the goal being discussed. If the d-rule contributes evidence that raises the certainty of the determined value of the goal to more than 0·2, we say that the value of the goal is now significant.‡ This contribution of evidence is especially interesting because it depends on what evidence has already been considered.

Like all t-rules, this determination is a heuristic which will benefit from experimentation. In t-rule 25.01 we have attempted to capture the intuitive notion that, in general, change in belief is interesting: the more drastic the change, the more interesting the effect. The numbers in the conclusion of t-rule 25.01 are certainly factors that indicate our relief in this interestingness.

T-RULE25.01

If: The effect of applying the d-rule on the current value
     of the goal has been determined
Then: The "value interest" of this d-rule depends on the effect of
       applying the d-rule as follows:
       a. if the value contributed is still insignificant then 0·05
       b. if a new insignificant value is contributed then 0·05
       c. if a new significant value is contributed then 0·50
       d. if a significant value is confirmed then 0·70
       e. if a new strongly significant value is contributed then 0·75
       f. if an insignificant value becomes significant then 0·80
       g. if an old value is now insignificant then 0·85
       h. if belief in an old value is strongly contradicted then 0·90

† T-rule numbers are of the form: ⟨procedure number that invokes the rule⟩ . ⟨index of the rule⟩. Thus, t-rule 26.03 is the third rule in discourse procedure number 26.

‡ For example, if the goal is the "organism causing the infection" and the certainty associated with the value "Pseudomonas" is 0·3, then this value is significant.

0

5.1.2. *Use of special facts or relations is interesting*

In contrast to t-rule 25.01, the measure of interest in t-rule 25.06 below is static. We would like to make sure that the student knows the information in tables used by the expert program, so we give a d-rule that references a table special consideration.

T-RULE25.06

If: The d-rule mentions a static table in its premise
Then: Define the "content interest" to be 0·50

5.2. GUIDING DISCUSSION OF A D-RULE

Returning to our example, after selecting d-rule 578, the tutor needed to select a method for presenting it. The following t-rule was successfully applied:†

T-RULE2.04

If: (1) The number of factors appearing in the d-rule which need to be
            asked by the student is zero, and
     (2) The number of subgoals remaining to be determined before the
            d-rule can be applied is equal to 1
Then: Substep i.   Say: subgoal-suggestion
       Substep ii.   Discuss the goal with the student in a goal-directed
                     mode [Proc001]
       Substep iii. Wrap up the discussion of the rule being considered
                     [Proc017]

The premise of this t-rule indicates that all preconditions of the d-rules can be evaluated, save one, and this d-rule precondition requires that other d-rules be considered. The action part of this t-rule is a sequence of actions to be followed, i.e. a discourse pattern. In particular, substep "i." resulted in the program printing "try to determine the type of the infection . . ." (line 22). The discourse procedure invoked by substep "ii." will govern discussion of the type of the infection (in simple terms, a new context is set up for interpreting student questions and use of options). After the type of the infection is discussed (relevant data is collected and hypotheses drawn), the tutor will direct the dialogue to a discussion of the conclusion to be drawn from d-rule 578.

Other methods for "suggesting a d-rule" are possible and are selected by other t-rules in the packet that contained t-rule 2.04. For example, the program could simply tell the student the conclusion of the d-rule (if the d-rule can be evaluated based on data currently available to the student), or quiz the student about the d-rule, or sequentially discuss each precondition of the d-rule, and so on.

6. T-rules for responding to a student's hypothesis

A student's hypothesis provides the tutor with considerable evidence about his knowledge of the d-rules. It is an excellent opportunity for the tutor to update the model of the student's understanding and use that model to make instructive remarks. The chief strategy behind the tutorial remarks illustrated below is to state evidence directly or to use simple true-false questions when the overlay model shows that student is probably ignorant of the rules to apply (lines 11–17), otherwise use fill-in and multiple choice questions that are intended to "entrap" the student (lines 19–45).‡

† "Say: ⟨label⟩" designates something the program will "say" to the student. The label is useful for debugging, because every "print statement" is uniquely labelled.
‡ Please note that lines 4–6 and 41–43 have been paraphrased to illustrate work in progress.

{After presentation of relevant case data . . .}

1   ** I THINK THAT THE ORGANISMS PRESENT ARE DIPLOCOCCUS-PNEUMONIAE,
         PSEUDOMONAS-AERUGINOSA, AND NEISSERIA-MENINGITIDIS.

         Good. The age of the patient gives evidence for concluding that
5   *Diplococcus-Pneumoniae* might be present (Rule 507). The fact that the
         patient has been seriously burned is good reason to suspect *Pseudomonas
         aeruginosa* (Rule 578). Both conclusions apply because the infection
         which requires therapy is meningitis, no organisms were seem on a gram
         stain of the culture, and the type of the infection is bacterial.
10
         The age of the patient also leads one to suspect *Neisseria
         meningitidis* (Rule 507). Do the fact that the infection was acquired
         while the patient was hospitalized and information about the diseases to
         which the patient has been exposed support this conclusion?   **   NO
15
         Right, this would be good reason to rule out *Neisseria meningitidis*
         (Rule 561).

         What facts about this case tell you that the organisms which might be
20   present are: *E. coli* and *Klebsiella pneumoniae*?
         ** HELP
             {The student was expected to describe each factor
             with a phrase, one per line. Help is provided by
             listing all relevant factors for the current goal.}
25   Choose from:
         1. The patient does not have a TB risk factor and the patient's
                 x-ray is not abnormal
         2. Otitis-media and Epigolottitis are not among the diagnoses
                 which are consistent with the patient's clinical history
30   3. The white count from the patient's peripheral CBC is less than
                 2·5 thousand
         4. The infection was acquired while the patient was hospitalized
         5. The patient has been seriously burned
         6. None of these
35
         ** 1   3   4   {This question was a form of "entrapment." Notice
                             that the choices all appear in Fig. 9.}

         You're right about the WBC (Rule 557) and the evidence gained from
40   the fact that the infection was acquired while the patient was
         hospitalized (Rule 545). However, the lack of a TB risk factor and a
         normal x-ray is weak evidence that *Mycobacterium-TB* is not one of the
         organisms which might be present (Rule 160).

45

FIG. 8. Sample interaction: hypothesis evaluation.

"Entrapment," as used here, involves forcing the student to make a choice that will
reveal some aspect of his understanding.† In this example, all choices listed (lines

† Many of GUIDON's question-asking strategies resemble the "Socratic" strategies formalized by Collins
(1976), probably because our production rule representation of domain knowledge makes it convenient to
think in terms of "relevant factors" for a determining the "value of a goal" (terms we share with Collins).
However, the relation between factor and goal in MYCIN is not necessarily causal as it is in the network
representation used by Collins.

26–33) actually appear in rules applied by MYCIN (see Fig. 9). When the student wrongly chose number 1 ("TB risk factor and abnormal x-ray"), GUIDON indicated how that evidence actually was used by MYCIN.

6.1. UPDATING THE OVERLAY STUDENT MODEL AFTER A STUDENT HYPOTHESIS

Figure 9 illustrates how the overlay model is updated for the hypothesis in Fig. 8. T-rules are invoked to determine how strongly the tutor believes that the student has taken each of the relevant d-rules into account. That is, a packet of t-rules (packet number 6 here) is tried in the context of each d-rule. Those t-rules that succeed will modify the cumulative belief that the given d-rule was considered by the student. T-rule 6.05 succeeded when applied to d-rules 545 and 557. While the student mentioned a value that they conclude (pseudomonas) (clause 1 of the t-rule), he missed others (clause 3). Moreover, he did not mention values that can ONLY be concluded by these d-rules (clause 2), so the overall evidence that these d-rules were considered is weak (-0.70).†

T-RULE6.05

If: (1) The hypothesis does include values that can be concluded by
        this d-rule, as well as others, and
    (2) The hypothesis does not include values that can only be
        concluded by this d-rule, and
    (3) Values concluded by the d-rule are missing in the hypothesis
Then: Define the belief that the d-rule was considered to be -0.70.

After each of the d-rules applied by MYCIN is considered independently, a second pass is made to look for patterns. Two judgmental tutorial rules from this second rule packet are shown below. T-rule 7.01 applied to d-rule 578: of the d-rules that conclude pseudomonas, this is the only one that is believed to have been considered, thus increasing our belief that d-rule 578 was used by the student. T-rule 7.05 applies to d-rules 545 and 561: the factor NOSOCOMIAL appears only in their premises, and they are not believed to have been considered. This is evidence that NOSOCOMIAL was not considered by the student, increasing our belief that each of the d-rules that mention it were not considered.

T-RULE7.01

If: You believe that this domain rule was considered, it concludes a
    value present in the student's hypothesis, and no other rule that
    mentions this value is believed to have been considered
Then: Modify the cumulative belief that this rule was considered by 0·40

T-RULE7.05

If: This domain rule contains a factor that appears in several rules,
    none of which are believed to have been considered to make the
    hypothesis
Then: Modify the cumulative belief that this rule was considered by
    -0.30

Future improvements to this overlay model might make it possible to recognize student behavior that can be explained by simple variations of the expert's d-rules.

† The certainty factor of -0.70 was chosen by the author. Experience with MYCIN shows that the precise value is not important, but the scale from -1 to 1 should be used consistently.

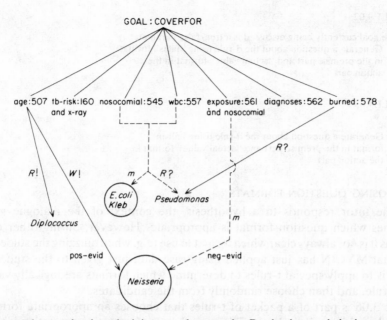

FIG. 9. Interpreting a student hypothesis in terms of expert rules. D-rules that conclude about organisms to "cover for" are shown with their key factors (see Fig. 6). Circled values are missing from the student's hypothesis (e.g. *E. coli*) or wrongly stated (e.g. *Neisseria*). Dotted lines lead from rules the student probably did not use. *m*, Evidence link that the tutor deduced is unknown to the student; *R* and *W*, links to right and wrong values that the tutor believes are known by the student; !, unique link; expert knows of no other evidence at this time; ?, questionable; tutor is not certain which evidence was considered by the student. *R*? means that the student stated this value; it is correct; and more than one d-rule supplies evidence for it.

(1) Variation in the premise of a d-rule: The student is using a d-rule that fails to apply or applies a successful d-rule prematurely (he is misinformed about case data or is confused about the d-rule's premise).

(2) Variation in the action of a d-rule: The student draws the wrong conclusion (wrong value and/or degree of certainty).

6.2. PRESENTATION METHODS FOR D-RULES THE STUDENT DID NOT CONSIDER

Returning to our example, after updating the overlay model, the tutor needs to deal with discrepancies between the student's hypothesis and what the expert program knows. The following t-rules are from a packet that determines how to present a d-rule that the student evidently did not consider. In our example, t-rule 9.02 generated the question shown in lines 11–17 (of Fig. 8). T-rule 9.03 (a default rule) generated the question shown in lines 19–43.

Apply the first tutorial rule that is appropriate:

T-RULE9.01

If: (1) The d-rule is not on the syllabus for this case, and
    (2) Based on the overlay model, the student is ignorant
        about the d-rule
Then: Affirm the conclusions made by the d-rule by simply
       stating the key factors and values to be concluded

T-RULE9.02

If: The goal currently being discussed is a true/false parameter
Then: Generate a question about the d-rule using "facts" format
        in the premise part and "actual value" format in the
        action part

T-RULE9.03

If: True
Then: Generate a question about the d-rule using "fill-in"
        format in the premise part and "actual value" format in
        the action part

6.3. CHOOSING QUESTION FORMATS

When the tutor responds to a hypothesis, the context of the dialogue generally
determines which question format is appropriate. However, during other dialogue
situations it is not always clear which format to use (e.g. when quizzing the student about
a rule that MYCIN has just applied using case data just given to the student). Our
strategy is to apply special t-rules to determine which formats are logically valid for a
given d-rule, and then choose randomly from the candidates.

T-rule 3.06 is part of a packet of t-rules that chooses an appropriate format for a
question based on a given d-rule. The procedure for formatting a question is to choose
templates for the action part and premise part that are compatible with each other and
the d-rule itself.

T-RULE3.06

If: (1) The action part of the question is not "wrong value," and
     (2) The action part of the question is not "multiple choice,"
         and
     (3) Not all of the factors in the premise of the d-rule are
         true/false parameters,
Then: Include "multiple choice" as a possible format for
        the premise part of the question

T-rule 3.06 says that if the program is going to give a conclusion that differs from that
in the d-rule it is quizzing about, it shouldn't state the premise as a multiple choice. Also,
it would be nonsensical to state both the premise and action in multiple choice form.
(This would be a "matching" question—it is treated as another question type.) Clause 3
of this t-rule is necessary because it is nonsensical to make a multiple-choice question
when the only choices are "true" and "false."

As can be seen here, the choice of a question type is based on purely logical properties
of the rule and interactions among question formats. About 20 question types
(combined premise/conclusion formats) are possible in the current implementation.

7. Final remarks

We have argued in this paper that it is desirable to add teaching expertise and other
levels of domain knowledge to MYCIN-like expert programs if they are to be used as
educational programs. Furthermore, it is advantageous to provide a flexible framework
for experimenting with teaching strategies, for we do not know the best methods for
presenting MYCIN-like rule bases to a student.

The framework of the GUIDON program includes knowledge of discourse patterns and the means for determining their applicability. The discourse patterns we have codified into procedures permit GUIDON to carry on a mixed-initiative, goal-directed case method dialogue in multiple domains. These patterns are invoked by tutoring rules, which are in turn controlled by a communication model. The components of this model are a case syllabus (topics the tutor plans to discuss), an overlay model (domain knowledge the tutor believes is being considered by the student), and a focus record (topics recently mentioned in the dialogue). Finally, we observed that meta-knowledge about the representation and use of domain rules made it possible to use these rules in a variety of ways during the dialogue. This is important because GUIDON's capability to flexibly reason about domain knowledge appears to be directly related to its capability to guide the dialogue in multiple, interesting ways.

Furthermore, we have augmented the performance knowledge of MYCIN-like systems by making use of support knowledge and meta-level abstractions in the dialogue. The problem-solving trace provided by the interpreter is augmented by GUIDON to enable it to plan dialogues (by looking ahead to see what knowledge is needed to solve the problem) and to carry on flexible dialogues (by being able to switch the discussion at any time to any portion of the AND/OR solution tree).

Development of GUIDON is still in its early stages. The procedures and rules described in this paper constitute the basic foundation of the program, but much experimentation remains to be done. We are just at the stage of trying the program with medical students; no formal experiments have been run at this time. The program has not been applied to all of the various EMYCIN domains, though we foresee no difficulties in this implementation. It remains to be seen just how domain independent the tutorial strategies are, or whether a mixed-initiative dialogue is even suitable for computational problems like that in the MARC domain of structural analysis.

Early experience with this program has shown that the tutor must be selective about its choice of topics if the dialogues are not to be overly tedious and complicated. That is, it is desirable for tutorial rules to exert a great deal of control over which discourse options are taken. Future development of GUIDON will focus on the use of the case syllabus for controlling the tutorial rules; we believe that it is chiefly in selection of topics and emphasis of discussion that the "intelligence" of this tutor resides.

The following people read earlier drafts of this paper and provided thoughtful remarks: Jan Aikins, Avron Barr, Jim Bennett, John Brown, Bruce Buchanan, and Adele Goldberg and Derek Sleeman. I would especially like to thank Bruce and Avron for allowing me to use portions of a working paper that we wrote together.

Many people have contributed their ideas to the MYCIN program over the past 5 years. The GUIDON project would not have been possible without their effort.

This research was sponsored in part by grants from ARPA (Contract Title MDA 903-77-C-0322) and NSF (MCS 77-02712).

References

BARR, A., BEARD, M. & ATKINSON, R. C. (1976). The computer as a tutorial laboratory: the Stanford BIP Project. *International Journal of Man-Machine Studies*, **8**, 567–596.

BOBROW, D. G., KAPLAN, R. M., KAY, M. *et al.* (1977). GUS, a frame-driven dialog system. *Artificial Intelligence*, **8** (2), 155–173.

BROWN, J. S. (1977). Uses of AI and advanced computer technology in education. In *Computers and Communications: Implications for Education*. New York: Academic Press.

BROWN, J. S., RUBENSTEIN, R. & BURTON, R. (1976). Reactive learning environment for computer-aided electronics instruction. *BBN 3314*.

BROWN, J. S., BURTON, R., MILLER, M., DE KLEER, J., PURCELL, S., HAUSMANN, C. & BOBROW, R. (1975). Steps toward a theoretic foundation for complex, knowledge-based CAI. *BBN 3135*.

BRUCE, B. C. (1975). Generation as a social action. In SCHANK, R. & NASH-WEBBER, B. L., Eds. *Theoretical Issues in Natural Language Processing*. pp. 74–77.

CARBONELL, J. R. & COLLINS, A. (1973). Natural semantics in Artificial Intelligence. *Proceedings of the 3rd IJCAI*, pp. 344–351.

CARR, B. & GOLDSTEIN, I. (1977). Overlays: a theory of modelling for CAI. *MIT AI Lab. Memo 406*.

COLLINS, A. (1976). Processes in acquiring knowledge. In ANDERSON, SPIRO & MONTAGUE, Eds, *Schooling and Acquisition of Knowledge*. Hillsdale, N.J.: Erlbaum Associates.

DAVIS, R. (1976). Applications of meta level knowledge to the construction, maintenance and use of large knowledge bases. *AIM-283*. Stanford University.

DAVIS, R., BUCHANAN, B. & SHORTLIFFE, E. H. (1977). Production rules as a representation for a knowledge-based consultation program. *Artificial Intelligence Journal*, **8** (1).

DAVIS, R. & BUCHANAN, B. G. (1977). Meta level knowledge: overview and applications. *Proceedings of the 5th IJCAI*, pp. 920–927.

DAVIS, R. & KING, J. J. (1977). An overview of production systems. In ELCOCK, W. E., *Machine Intelligence* **8**: *Machine Representations of Knowledge*. John Wiley.

DEUTSCH, B. G. (1974). The structure of task-oriented dialogs. *IEEE Symposium for Speech Recognition*, pp. 250–253.

FAUGHT, W. S. (1977). Motivation and intensionality in a computer simulation model. *AIM-305*. Stanford University.

FEIGENBAUM, E. A. (1977). The art of Artificial Intelligence: I. Themes and case studies of knowledge engineering. *Proceedings of the 5th IJCAI*, pp. 1014–1029.

FEIGENBAUM, E. A., BUCHANAN, B. G. & LEDERBERG, J. (1971). On generality and problem solving: a case study using the DENDRAL program. *Machine Intelligence*, **6**. Edinburgh University Press.

FEURZEIG, W., MUNTER, P., SWETS, J. & BREEN, M. (1964). Computer-aided teaching in medical diagnosis. *Journal of Medical Education*, **39**, 746–755.

GOLDSTEIN, I. (1977). The computer as coach: an athletic paradigm for intellectual education. *MIT AI Lab. Memo 389*.

GOLDSTEIN, I. & ROBERTS, B. R. (1977). Nudge, a knowledge-based scheduling program. *Proceedings of the 5th IJCAI*, pp. 257–263.

HARTLEY, J. R., SLEEMAN, D. H. & WOODS, P. (1972). Controlling the learning of diagnostic tasks. *International Journal of Man–Machine Studies*, **4**, 319–340.

HEISER, J. F., BROOKS, R. E. & BALLARD, J. P. (1978). Progress report: a computerized psychopharmacology advisor. *Proceedings of the 11th Collegium Internationale Neuro-Psychopharmacologicum*, Vienna, Austria.

KOFFMAN, E. B. & BLOUNT, S. E. (1973). Artificial Intelligence and automatic programming in CAI. *Proceedings of the 3rd IJCAI*, pp. 86–94.

LENAT, D. B. (1976). AM: an Artificial Intelligence approach to discovery in mathematics as heuristic search. *AIM-286*. Stanford University.

POPLE, H. E. (1977). The formation of composite hypotheses in diagnostic problem solving—an exercise in synthetic reasoning. *Proceedings of the 5th IJCAI*, pp. 1030–1037.

SCOTT, A. C., CLANCEY, W. J., DAVIS, R. & SHORTLIFFE, E. H. (1977). Explanation capabilities of production-based consultation systems. *American Journal of Computational Linguistics*, Microfiche 62.

SHORTLIFFE, E. H. (1974). MYCIN: A rule-based computer program for advising physicians regarding antimicrobial therapy selection. *Ph.D. dissertation* in Medical Information Sciences, Stanford University. Also, *Computer-Based Medical Consultations: MYCIN*. New York: American Elsevier, 1976.

SHORTLIFFE, E. H. & BUCHANAN, B. G. (1975). A model of inexact reasoning in medicine. *Mathematical Biosciences*, **23**, 351–379.

SLEEMAN, D. (1977). A system which allows students to explore algorithms. *Proceedings of the 5th IJCAI*, pp. 780–786.

SPROSTY, P. J. (1963). The use of questions in the diagnostic problem solving process. In JACQUEZ, J. A., Ed., *The Diagnostic Process, Proceedings of a Conference Held at the University of Michigan*, pp. 281–308.

VAN MELLE, W. (1974). Would you like advice on another horn? Unpublished paper, Stanford University.

WEISS, S. M., KULIKOWSKI, C. A. & SAFIR, A. (1977). A model-based consultation program for the long term management of glaucoma. *Procceedings of the 5th IJCAI*, pp. 826–832.

WINOGRAD, T. (1977). A framework for understanding discourse. *AIM-297*. Stanford University.

YU, V. L., BUCHANAN, B. G., SHORTLIFFE, E. H., WRAITH, S. M., DAVIS, R., SCOTT, A. C. & COHEN, S. N. (1979a). Evaluating the performance of a computer-based consultant. *Computer Programs in Biomedicine*, **9**, 95–102.

YU, V. L., FAGAN, L. M., WRAITH, S. M., CLANCEY, W. J., SCOTT, A. C., HANNIGAN, J. F., BLUM, R. L., BUCHANAN, B. G. & COHEN, S. N. (1979b). Antimicrobial selection by a computer—a blinded evaluation by infectious disease experts. *Journal of the American Medical Association*, **242**, 1279–1282.

11. Pedagogical, natural language and knowledge engineering techniques in SOPHIE I, II and III

JOHN SEELY BROWN, RICHARD R. BURTON AND JOHAN DE KLEER

Xerox Palo Alto Research Center, Coyote Hill Rd, Palo Alto, California, CA 94304, U.S.A.

This paper provides an overview of the pedagogical and knowledge-engineering techniques in SOPHIE I, II and III. From the pedagogical perspective, we focus on the kinds of interactive instructional scenarios that have been made possible by integrating explicit models of domain expertise into the instructional medium itself. We provide both concrete examples and discussions of their significance. From the knowledge engineering perspective, we focus on a set of abstractions and techniques that have enabled us to build intelligent systems that are efficient, habitable and exceptionally robust.

1. Introduction

1.1 HISTORY AND OVERVIEW

The research described in this paper took place over a five-year period and centered around three different SOPHIE systems. Work began on what was to become SOPHIE I in early 1973 when two of us, Brown and Burton, were at the University of California at Irvine. The Air Force had expressed interest in using computers in their advanced electronic-troubleshooting course, particularly in the laboratory section; and we were interested in exploring interactive learning environments that encouraged explicit development of hypotheses during problem-solving by facilitating the communication of the student's ideas to the machine and by enabling the machine to critique them. We recognized electronic troubleshooting as a particularly good application domain. While at Irvine, the general-purpose electronic simulator, SPICE, (Nagel and Pederson 1973) was obtained, an appropriate electronic device was chosen for study (the IP-28 regulated power supply), and protocols were collected of experts troubleshooting the IP-28.

In the summer of 1973, the project moved to Bolt, Beranek and Newman, Inc. in Cambridge, Massachusetts. The next year saw the development of a SPICE model of the IP-28 which was capable of being faulted, a fledgling natural language interface, a semantic network database of information about the IP-28, and implementation of the basic pedagogical and inferential ideas. By the end of 1974, a version of SOPHIE I was being used in exploratory experiments [Brown, Burton and Bell 1974, 1975]. During the following year, the habitability and robustness of the system were improved through continuous usage. Our major addition during this time was a dialogue mechanism that allowed the natural-language interface to handle a large number of elliptic and anaphoric expressions that arise in a troubleshooting context. By early 1975, SOPHIE I was essentially completed [Brown and Burton 1975].

Most of SOPHIE I's intelligence resided in a collection of procedural specialists that judiciously selected, set up and ran "critical" experiments on a general-purpose circuit simulator.   This allowed SOPHIE I to evaluate a student's hypotheses, critique his measurements and handle almost any question presented in the context of electronic toubleshooting.

SOPHIE II, built the following year, was an extension of SOPHIE I designed to be self sufficient for field testing [described in Brown, Rubinstein and Burton, 1976]. This required additional pedagogical components as well as supporting course material.   Of special pedagogical interest is its expert troubleshooter, which enabled students to insert arbitrary faults into the circuit and watch the expert locate them.   The key pedagogical benefit comes from the expert explaining both its tactics for choosing measurements and, more importantly, its higher level strategies for attacking the problem.   In this manner, the student is not only exposed to the general strategic principles of problem-solving, but also sees them applied to a problem of his own making. The expert uses decision trees to guide its measurements and contributes little to the technology of building intelligent systems.   It did, however, enable us to investigate the structure of explanations for flexible, intelligent systems such as SOPHIE III.

SOPHIE III was developed over a two year period starting in 1976. There were a variety of motivations for it.   First, the experiments run with SOPHIE II pointed out additional capabilities needed by a coach or automated lab instructor.   Our ability to implement these capabilities required (a) a more powerful and human-like reasoning engine, (b) techniques for modelling the student and (c) coaching strategies that limited the coach's interruptions of the student and governed its suggestions when it did break in.   This latter problem also required understanding how explanations could be synthesized from the collection of non-uniform inference strategies we expected to use.   Exploring all these issues simultaneously on a task domain that stretched our ability just to build the expert, seemed unwise.   Thus, in the SOPHIE III we concentrated on building an expert electronics reasoner [de Kleer 1976, Brown 1977] that had some of the characteristics necessary to facilitate the student modelling and coaching subsystems. Concurrently, we chose to explore the more complex aspects of the coaching and student modelling components on the considerably simpler task domains of games [Burton and Brown 1981] and elementary mathematics [Brown and Burton 1978, Burton 1981], domains for which the building of a reasoning engine could easily be done.

In addition to our desire to study issues of explanation, the SOPHIE III project was started for the second reason of exploring the tradeoffs between generality and efficiency in building intelligent systems.   SOPHIE III sought to mix very general knowledge of electronics with very specific device-dependent information hopefully resulting in a system both general and efficient.

The third reason for building SOPHIE III was to explore expanding the role of the coach to be more like that of an on-the-job consultant.   In particular, we wanted a system that could track and advise the student as he was working on a real piece of equipment, not just on one being simulated in the computer. To this end, we wanted to understand more about how to merge intelligent job performance aids with on-site job training.

1.2 PEDAGOGICAL OVERVIEW

Perhaps a comment is in order concerning the kind of troubleshooting expertise that we seek to develop in users of the SOPHIE environment.   Many troubleshooters typically have great difficulty fixing familiar devices with unusual faults or unfamiliar devices for which they have had no specific training. This is *not* the kind of troubleshooter we wish to develop.   Instead, we focus on producing a skilled troubleshooter with a sufficiently good conceptual — albeit qualitative — understanding of electronics to be able to develop appropriate diagnostic steps on his own, to digest new information from technical manuals and to troubleshoot unfamiliar equipment.

However, much more than the art of troubleshooting can be learned by studying the troubleshooting process. People who are skilled at operating complex equipment often exhibit proficiency at handling the unusual situations or casualities that inevitably arise. Their ability to "patch" their routine procedures or to back out of a weird state they accidently produce, often requires the kind of common-sense, causal understanding that we seek to instill in our expert troubleshooters.

1.2.1 Reactive Learning Environments: A Philosophy

The educational paradigm developed in the SOPHIE systems focuses on experiential learning which capitalizes on episodic memory for encoding instantiations and ramifications of generic knowledge.   When engaged in laboratory activities, students are forced to apply their factual knowledge to solve problems.   The problem-solving process gives rise to experiences that structure the factual knowledge. To facilitate this style of learning, the student must be encouraged to formulate, test and witness the consequences of his own ideas and must be freed from worry about possible catastrophic consequences. Because the student's ideas have arisen while attempting to solve a problem, they are anchored to a personally meaningful context; it is within this context that the idea is best explored with the student. The system should be able to critique the student's ideas. In addition, the system should watch for situations in which, while working on one problem, the student produces an effect that illustrates a principle he has just learned. If he fails to perceive this connection, the system should call his attention to it, providing him with the choice of pursuing it.

Supporting metaphors for this style of learning environment stem from coaching, apprenticeship and laboratory instruction, in which technology can be used in three ways.   First, it can make experimentation *easier* for the student. Second, technology can make experimentation *safer*.   Third, technology can be used to help students *learn from their mistakes*. All three benefits of technology have been realized in our project, but the emphasis has been on helping students learn from their mistakes, especially as it applies to automating the role of a coach or lab instructor.

1.2.2 Kinds of Knowledge and Activities to Impart It

There are many different kinds of knowledge that need to be interwoven in order to establish a sound framework for expert troubleshooting.   Troubleshooting *strategies* are responsible for controlling the sequence of measurements to be made. A good example is the "half split" strategy which directs the troubleshooter to choose his next measurement so that its result will halve the current set of hypotheses about what is at fault (assuming all are equally likely). Closely allied to strategies are the troubleshooting *tactics* which concern the ease of making one class of measurements over another. For example, voltage measurements are usually easier to make than current measurements and, unless the device is already disassembled, external measurements are easier to make than internal ones.

In addition, the good troubleshooter must have sufficent *understanding of electronic laws, of circuit components and of the overall functional organization of the device* to enable him to draw conclusions from his measurements.   For example, he must be able to deduce whether a transistor is faulty from observations of its input/output behavior. He must know simple electronic laws (i.e. Ohm's and Kirchoff's) in order to propagate known measurements into new areas of the circuit.   And to understand the more global consequences of his current set of measurements, he must have an understanding of the causality of underlying *circuit mechanisms* — of how negative feedback works, for example, or of how one component faulting might cause another to fail.

2. Pedagogical Techniques

In this section we discuss the various kinds of pedagogical environments that have been developed and explored with SOPHIE I and II. By so doing we hope to provide a sense of the educational challenges that must be faced in moving from an AI-oriented kind of research to one more concerned with cognitive and user-related issues. This section shows how SOPHIE's components form an integrated system and describes some of the pedagogical techniques being investigated. We focus on the SOPHIE II system because it is an extension of, and includes all of the features of, SOPHIE I.

2.1 SOPHIE II

The SOPHIE II system is a collection of components, each designed to foster activities that present to the student (or facilitate his discovery of) the kinds of knowledge needed for expert troubleshooting in electronics. These components consist of: 1) a "canned" articulate expert troubleshooter; a simulated laboratory (SOPHIE I); 2) a limited automated laboratory instructor or coach (SOPHIE I); 3) a variety of computer-based games; and 4) a collection of written material describing how to understand the function of a particular piece of equipment.

2.1.1 Articulate Expert Troubleshooter

The beginning student's first activity with the SOPHIE system is watching the articulate expert troubleshooter locate a fault. The articulate expert troubleshooter was designed to provide students with a nonthreatening, graceful introduction to the capabilities of the overall SOPHIE system and to expose them to expert strategic and tactical reasoning. To enhance the student's interest the student is allowed to choose which function block of the device is to be faulted and the symptoms it is to manifest. Once the expert succeeds in locating the faulty function block, the student is given the chance to locate the particular faulty component within that block.

Unlike many AI systems the articulate expert foregoes the goal of general applicability to attain cogent explanations, especially pertaining to strategic issues. The underlying mechanisms of the expert are based on decision trees annotated with schema for producing explanations about troubleshooting a particular circuit. Since the annotations are prestored and constructed by hand, they can be made as insightful and structured as desired. Futhermore, since the annotations are associated with nodes in a decision tree and since any node can be reached by only one path, their exact context is known ahead of time. Each node has several schema with the choice depending, primarily, on how often the student has activated this node.

2.1.1.1 Brief Description of the Interaction

The interaction proceeds as follows: The "expert" first explains the procedure of the lesson — that it is going to try to isolate a faulted functional block selected by the student. Since the student will know what is wrong with the instrument (at a block level), he will be asked to predict qualitatively the results of measurements at the time they are made by the expert.

Next, the "referee," a program responsible for inserting student-specified faults and verifying student predictions, asks which block is to be faulted. The student may select any of the seven functional blocks in the IP-28, the device being debugged. Depending on the selection, the referee may ask for more specific information about how the external behavior of the block should be affected by the fault. The student knows only the selected external behavior, not the actual component fault, and will have to make predictions based only on this external behavior. The referee only installs faults which produce clear qualitative symptoms; the student should be able to propagate the symptoms through the device.

Next, the expert attempts to locate the fault, explaining its strategy as it goes. Before the expert makes each measurement, the student is asked to predict the qualitative behavior of the instrument (will the measured value be too high, too low or about right?). Depending on the particular approach taken by the expert, it may ask the student a question or two about what can be determined from the measurements made up to that point and comment on his response.

If the student makes a wrong prediction, the referee takes over to demonstrate the actual behavior of the faulted instrument. It does this by posing the laboratory module of SOPHIE a question, chosen to demonstrate the real behavior. The SOPHIE lab responds with an actual measurement, and the referee restates the measurement qualitatively, in terms of the expert's question. If the student doesn't know the answer to one of the expert's questions, he may ask for help. The referee will ask SOPHIE, as above, and summarize the answer.

When the expert has decided what block contains the fault, it announces this to the student, along with the final bit of reasoning which led to the conclusion. The student is asked whether the conclusion is correct and whether he would like to isolate the actual component fault. If he would, a summary of the expert's measurements (expressed as answers to SOPHIE lab inquiries) is printed, and the student is put into a SOPHIE lab with the faulted device. A history list of the measurements made by the expert during this session is provided so that the student may review them and their associated values. He thereafter may make any measurements he wishes, propose hypotheses, replace components and so on, as in a normal lab session.

2.1.1.2 Educational Rationale

There are several pedagogical reasons for conducting a dialogue between the student and the expert. The first is to convey a useful debugging strategy to the student. The expert views the device in terms of discrete boxes which interact in known ways. It has, in other words, a high-level causal and teleological model of how the circuit works.† Without having to make measurements inside functional blocks themselves, the expert is able to determine which block contains the fault.

A second reason for providing the expert debugging interaction is that it allows students practice envisioning the consequences of symptoms and faults, a skill that taxes their causal understanding of electronics in general and the circuit in particular. It also helps students become better at checking their own hypotheses. A final motivation for using the expert is to present a gentle introduction to the SOPHIE lab. When the student makes an erroneous prediction, he witnesses the referee using the SOPHIE lab to determine the right answer. A beginning student is thereby exposed to a variety of acceptable questions and wordings for later use during his own SOPHIE lab interaction. As a result, when he is given the opportunity to isolate the actual component fault within the faulted block, he has a good idea of how to use the lab without needing explicit instruction.

2.1.1.3 Evolving Models

One way of viewing the process of learning how to debug a device is to think of the student as moving from static to dynamic models. For example, in the case at hand, his initial understanding of the power supply might be summarized by the simple statement of intent: "The supply puts out a fixed voltage." This model contains no variables or internal constructs and is thus essentially static. A more refined model contains provision for one contingency: "The supply puts out a fixed voltage, unless its current limit is exceeded, in which case it puts out less." The model develops to encompass internal parts and more interactions: "The power supply puts out a voltage equal to the reference voltage, unless. . . ." and so on. More and more variables are added as the understanding of the power supply improves.

Mechanisms are required for pointing out to students the mismatches between their developing models and the real-world situation. Conflicts of model with fact

---

†When we speak of a teleological model, we refer to a model in which intended purposes are described.

are the raw material from which better models are made. The expert debugging interaction provides many small opportunities of this sort for students to improve their understanding. Every time a student makes a wrong prediction, he has an opportunity to go through a "What? That can't be! Aha!" cycle which improves the accuracy of his world view.

In order for such conflicts of model and fact to be used, they must be perceived by the student. To extend this notion, we chose to alternate lab and expert activities. Either alone is less effective than the combination. This is because troubleshooting provides not just motivation but periodically a set of seemingly contradictory observations. When the same contradictory observations are subsequently made by the expert, the student pays heightened attention to its method of successful resolution. Often the escapes from seeming-dilemmas focus the student's attention on details or complexities previously overlooked. Conversely, things which concern the expert — reasons for inference, caveats, and the like — may not be assimilated by the student on first sight but may make sense later in a debugging problem which he can solve by appealing to them.

2.1.1.4 Expert Debugging Strategies

The debugging tree used to implement the expert, as we said, incorporates only one of the many overall approaches which might have been employed. Its important characteristics are that it causes the expert to operate at a function-block level, to rely on qualitative measurements, to utilize multiple substrategies and to make measurements which are teleologically significant.

There are several reasons for operating at a function-block level. Most inexperienced troubleshooters tend to begin their testing at a very local level. In a circuit of even moderate complexity, such an approach will usually lead to wasted time and components. A function-block model of the instrument is a convenient mental shorthand for grouping collections of components, thereby enabling a higher-level approach and simplifying behavioral predictions about sections of the circuit.

The expert's debugging strategies rely only upon qualitative measurements. The sort of causal reasoning promoted by this qualitative approach develops the student's tendency to think logically. Chains of the sort, "Well, this is too high, so this must be too high, and *this* therefore, too low..." or "If this goes down, then that must go up..." are important insights. Additionally, qualitative measures fit in well with the level and kind of explanation experts make. We did not want to present many arguments which depended on the actual values of measurements in the circuit, because we felt that to do so would be unrealistic in situations where the device was unfamilar to the student. Extensive experience with a particular device may in fact yield student rules like "If the output voltage is between 33 and 35 volts, replace D5." Such rules, while perhaps valid for repair of familiar equipment by average troubleshooters, do not teach concepts and do not generalize to other situations.

We emphasize that our expert is not committed to any single strategy, but to several. For example, if the output voltage of the power supply is high under light load, the expert has the choice of either a conservative, or a more radical, top-level strategy:

A. *Milk-the-front-panel*: Extract as much information as possible from observations of the device under different settings and loads, before proceeding to internal measurements, if necessary. As an important caveat:

A'. *Don't-kill-the-goose*: To keep from blowing the circuit, when milking the front panel, be sure not to set up the panel and put loads on the system that would ordinarily invoke the protective mechanisms of the circuit but that may now be malfunctioning.

B. *Formulate some, though not necessarily all, possible hypotheses:* In particular, don't spend exorbitant cognitive resources on convincing yourself that you have considered all possible hypotheses before checking out the more likely of the ones you have generated.

By offering both approaches, we expose a student to alternative ways of attacking the problem letting him witnessing an expert that is flexible enough to use different strategies for specific reasons.

Finally, the strategies support measurements which, in part, require reasoning about the purposes of each of the function blocks, i.e., teleologically reasoning. This means that each measurement is based on some function-related differentiation of blocks within the device.

A more general top-level strategy is also employed by the expert: split the space of hypotheses. The significant point is that, in order to use this idea, the expert must carry along several competing hypotheses simultaneously. Instead of proposing a single fault and making it the sole consideration of a test, the expert consistently mentions several possibilities among which a given test will differentiate. This kind of strong inference is much more powerful than testing a single hypothesis at a time.

2.1.2 SOPHIE Lab

The SOPHIE lab (part of the original SOPHIE I system) consists of two major components: 1) the automated lab instructor or coach and 2) the simulated laboratory workbench containing various instruments for making measurements and models of both the broken and the working device.

2.1.2.1 The Workbench

The workbench was designed with several pedagogical goals in mind. First it has to encourage students to run their own mini-experiments to explore the workings of the circuit. The mini-experiments consist of first modifying any component in the circuit and then determining the circuit's behavior by performing any set of measurements. To enable this experimentation, the lab provides the capability of saving the current experiment (context) and setting up a new one. Each such experiment forms a layer in a context tree.† Since measurements were easy to make, students could quickly assess the internal workings of the given device with respect to various modifications or faults.

---

†At any point, the student can push to a new layer and set up a minor variant of his immediate exploration or return back into the middle of a prior experiment. Our goal was to create an environment in which the student could develop a train of thought, with freedom to return and pick up any thread he wished.

An important aspect of the workbench was that it freed the student, and laboratory instructor as well, from having to worry about unforeseen consequences of a proposed modification or fault insertion. Many propagations are sufficiently subtle that even an expert's modifications may unexpectedly blow other components in the device.† This freedom enables students to engage in such useful exercises as finding a fault that does *maximal* damage; an exercise they find intriguing and from which they learn a lot about causality in the circuit.

Understanding causality, at least at the qualitative level of how a faulty component can affect a healthy one, is important. A special mechanism was added to SOPHIE's general-purpose circuit simulator, enabling the overall simulator to capture and portray this qualitative unfolding of causal fault propagation. The mechanism for performing propagation will be discussed further in the knowledge engineering section of the chapter.

2.1.2.2 The Simple Coach

The SOPHIE I system implements a limited coach that performs various checks on the student as he troubleshoots a given fault. The most sophisticated monitoring checks the logical redundancy of his measurements. In particular, the coach has sufficient logical prowess to detect if a proposed measurement *could possibly* contribute any new information about the fault. If not, the measurement is redundant.

The coach is also responsible for checking the logical consistency of all student hypotheses. In the extreme case, if the student offers no fault hypotheses prior to requesting that a component be replaced, SOPHIE does not replace it until he states precisely what he thinks is wrong with it. After the student offers a hypothesis, the coach determines whether it is consistent with the information deducible from his prior measurements. If it is not consistent, the coach identifies which past measurements contradict his current hypothesis. At times we have set up the SOPHIE environment so that if the student, by chance, guesses the actual inserted fault, but his current set of measurements have not yet ruled out other possible ones, the actual fault will be shifted to one of the logically possible remaining ones.

As with any coach, ours tries not to overburden the student with criticism. It uses both a notion of recency and of conspicuousness to choose among the measurements that contradict his hypothesis, leaving it to the student to request older and more subtle ones. In addition, the coach also delineates the measurements that support his hypothesis as well as a third class, those that are consistent with it.

The coach's final activity is to answer student questions. For example, students often want to know if a particular component *could* blow if some other given component were shorted. As we will discuss in section 4, the coach handles its various tasks by, metaphorically speaking, dropping into the background, setting

---

†One of the initial motivations for building this system stemmed from the need of having an environment into which instructors could insert faults without unexpectedly damaging the rest of the device. This need is enhanced when one considers inserting faults into real equipment such as complex reactors or boilers that can become unstable in surprisingly subtle ways.

up and running its own set of experiments on its copy of the workbench, abstracting the results and formulating a response to the student's query or hypothesis. But to answer the above kind of question, the coach must use its teleological and causal understanding of the device to figure out what boundary conditions (e.g., front panel settings of the device, loads on the device, etc.) would most likely blow the component in question. Thus, in answering this kind of question, the coach exposes the student both to the search for ways of setting up the device and to the consequences of running the device in those situations.

2.1.2.3 SOPHIE Gaming Environment

A game was developed in which one player inserts a fault which another player must then find. The game begins with one person (the "inserter") introducing an arbitrarily chosen fault into the circuit and setting the front panel controls so as to exhibit some external symptom in the device. The other person (the "debugger") must then find the fault by performing a sequence of measurements. Each measurement has an associated cost that roughly reflects the degree of difficulty of making that measurement on a real instrument. For each measurement the debugger makes, the inserter must predict whether the result of the measurement will be higher, lower or approximately the same as that in a working instrument. After the debugger successfully locates the fault, the inserter is given a score of the total cost of the debugger's measurements multiplied by the percentage of times the inserter correctly predicted the outcome. *Thus, it is to the advantage of the inserter to choose a difficult fault but not one so difficult that he can't predict its consequences.* The debugger, of course, attempts to isolate the fault using the least expensive sequence of measurements. The debugger announces a guess by replacing the component believed to be faulted. If the wrong component is replaced, the cost is increased a substantial amount. After each successful fault discovery, the roles are reversed and another game initiated.

The game was designed with two instructional goals in mind. First, we wanted a self-motivating activity that promoted cost-effective troubleshooting. Second, we wanted an activity that required the student to exercise his causal and teleological understanding of the device. To do well at this game requires both kinds of skill. Causal and teleological understanding is forced into application by requiring the inserter to predict the qualitative behavior of the circuit. To begin with, since the inserter must specify how to set the front panel controls to manifest a symptom, he dares not choose a fault whose impacts and implications he cannot project. In addition, he must successfully predict the qualitative response of the circuit at any location measured by his opponent, the debugger. This can deepen his understanding in two major ways. First, if he can guess the troubleshooting strategy that his opponent will choose, he can reflect on his ability to envision the qualititative consequences of a proposed fault at the measurement points favored by his opponent's strategy. Second, when his opponent's measurements diverge from his expectations and are off the direct causal path from the fault to the symptom, he will be forced to think about parts of the circuit he otherwise might not have bothered to master.

An extension of this two-person game to a team game, each team comprised of two people, leads to extraordinarily productive interactions. Teams are more adventuresome, more willing to probe the limits of their understanding. The discussion of possible ramifications that arise just choosing a fault, for instance, often requires substantial pooling of the team members' information as well as correction of each other's misconceptions. Similarly, when deciding on which next measurement to make, the members will often discuss the possible ramifications of each suggested measurement.

2.1.2.3.1 Using Teams to Generate Protocols on Strategic Thought:

An interesting by-product of using teams is that it provides a beautifully simple "window" into the strategic reasoning patterns and knowledge of the individuals [Brown, Rubinstein and Burton 1976]. The kinds of discussions or arguments that unfold between the team members provide us with detailed information about their strategic reasoning. This includes not only the reasons why a given measurement is being selected but also why some other is *not* being selected. It also helps solve another problem plaguing the general use of protocols in studying reasoning: getting subjects to articulate what they are thinking without becoming self-conscious and thereby altering their natural problem-solving behavior. However, in this situation we find that team players are far less self-conscious than the single informant and that they make and defend hypotheses, plan and revise strategies, and explain things to each other in what appears to be a natural way. Likewise, in collecting a protocol of a subject who is working alone, it is extremely difficult to get insights into why he rejects certain moves; subjects usually feel no need to justify why they don't do something. Instead, the single subject invariably focuses on the more tactical issues of how to accomplish his objective. In the two-person team environment, the arguments that naturally arise involve attempts to justify or defeat a proposed move. The record of these justifications provides a rare opportunity to see strategic reasoning unfold and defended.

2.2 TYPICAL SEQUENCE OF ACTIVITIES WITH SOPHIE

There are many ways in which all the above learning activities might be woven into a coherent training course on electronic troubleshooting. In order to provide a feeling for one such sequence we will briefly describe a twelve hour mini-course that we used to conduct a variety of experiments. The first two hours of this course consisted of a brief introduction to the SOPHIE followed by an intensive study of an instructional booklet reviewing material on basic electronics as related to regulated power supplies, as well as a more detailed explanation of the particular power supply device to be used. This material was rounded out by a question-answering period and an informal discussion on troubleshooting strategies.

In the second period, students alternated between using the expert debugger of SOPHIE II and doing troubleshooting in the SOPHIE lab using preselected faults. Unassisted troubleshooting provided good impetus for paying close attention to what the expert was saying; the students quickly realized that troubleshooting this instrument was harder than it appeared.

The third session consisted of two activities. The first exploited SOPHIE's simulator fully — students were given the task of finding the faults which propagated to blow out a specified component, thus gaining practice in predicting possible causes of secondary faults. In the second activity, students were joined into two-person teams to engage in more troubleshooting practice.

In the last three-hour period the teams were pitted against each other in the troubleshooting game. After several go-rounds, we broke up the groups and gave each individual some final troubleshooting exercises. For this concluding activity we stressed cost-effective troubleshooting as well as the use of SOPHIE's coach.

2.3 NON-STANDARD USES OF SOPHIE

2.3.1 A Resource Manager

The metaphor of coaching implicitly combines two activities: that of detecting the lack of understanding or faulty reasoning on the part of the student; and that of explaining to the student the critical remedial pieces of knowledge. In numerous cases, detection is considerably easier than remediation. In these situations, it might be advantageous to use SOPHIE in conjunction with a human instructor, with SOPHIE detecting the student's misconceptions and the instructor remediating them.

More generally, consider a laboratory setting with many students and one human laboratory instructor. It is relatively easy to create mock-up workbenches so that any measurement taken by a student while he troubleshoots is monitored and fed into a central SOPHIE coach. When the automated coach detects that a student is stuck in a loop, or is about to make a senseless replacement, then it can notify the instructor to explain the needed remediation to the student. In this way, the instructor need not waste time peering over his students' shoulders; he can count on the system to pinpoint potential opportunities for explanation. He then can employ his own tutoring strategies to decide whether to interrupt the student and, if so, what to say. In this scenario, the automated coach is saving both the instructor's time and effort in that detecting educationally useful moments in a troubleshooting session is very taxing even in a one-on-one situation.

Although the coach in SOPHIE I could perform the important task of detecting instances of inconsistent hypotheses and redundant measurements, a good laboratory instructor should be sensitive not only to mind bugs but also to opportunities to illustrate general principles in particular situations that arise while troubleshooting. As we will see in section 4, SOPHIE III is designed to capitalize on these latter occurrences, and is capable of detecting a wide range of situations that instantiate generic electronic laws. In the same spirit, it can also detect, without a simulation of the piece of equipment, interesting situations directly from measurements made on the broken piece of equipment, itself.

2.3.2 Distributed Instructional Systems and Generative CAI

Considering the cost of the computational resources needed to implement the fully general simulated laboratory and coach, and also wanting to set the stage for exploring versions of the above "resource management" scheme, we implemented a distributed instructional scheme. We used Apple II's, low-cost micro-computers, as work stations coupled to (in principle) a fast mainframe computer containing SOPHIE's general-purpose circuit simulator. The computational capabilities of the mainframe could be used to automatically generate voltage tables characterizing the behavior of the circuit for a *prespecified* set of faults as well as for its normal working behavior which could then be stored locally on the micro-computers. The micro-computer was inexpensively made to "look" like a simulated workbench by attaching to it a bitpad tablet on which actual color photographs of the desired printed circuit board or schematic were laid.   In the micro, a model of the photograph is constructed, making it possible to use the tablet's pen as a simulated voltage probe. With this setup, the student can make any measurement he wishes simply by using the tablet's pen to touch the appropriate terminal on the photograph.

The micro not only simulates the broken (or working) device, but keeps track of all of the student's measurements and attempted component replacements.   It can also accurately record the time at which each measurement was made. The student can review the measurements he has taken and ask for prestored help. After he finishes his troubleshooting exercises, the history of his interactions can be transferred to the mainframe and critiqued, off-line, by the SOPHIE coach. The coach can then determine what set of faults the student should try the next day and automatically create the database for the micro's table-driven simulator.

3. Natural Language Engineering

This section provides an overview of the abstractions underlying the natural language interface of the SOPHIE systems and describes lessons we learned using it with students.   Readers are referred to [Burton 1976] and [Burton and Brown 1979] for more details.

The goal of SOPHIE's natural language interface is to successfully understand whatever sentences users type into the system.   It presupposes that users have a fair amount of knowledge of electronics and are seriously engaged in troubleshooting a circuit. These assumptions are an integral part of the "world view" that has been designed into SOPHIE, limiting the scope of interactions. The natural language interface was built by using an engineering approach that took advantage of these constraints.   We developed two techniques: the first was a technique for incorporating the domain semantics into the parsing process that we called "semantic grammars" (because it uses a grammar that is based on semantically meaningful categories). Semantic grammars provide an approach to the construction of efficient, friendly, natural-language-like interfaces. The second technique was a dialogue mechanism that robustly handled the constructs that arise in conversation. We refer to these techniques as natural language *engineering* techniques because their goal is the production of useful widgits, not necessarily the furthering of our understanding of the language-understanding process.   In particular, there are many important problems in linguistics and the psychology of language for which semantic grammars are inadequate, and there are classes of dialogue phenomena not addressed by our dialogue mechanism.

The requirements for the natural language interface to an intelligent tutoring system are efficiency and friendliness over the class of sentences that arise in a dialogue situation.   The major leverage points that allow us to satisfy these requirements are (a) limited domain and (b) limited activities within that domain. In other words, we know the problem area, the type of problems the students are trying to solve, and the way they should be thinking about the problem in order to solve it. In SOPHIE's case, the domain is electronic troubleshooting, and the limited activities are taking measurements and developing hypotheses. This is manifested in SOPHIE's view of the world as consisting of an electronics lab with a broken circuit and a virtual lab instructor that can be called upon for criticism or advice.

One representation of the interface to this world is a set of objects and functions or operations upon them. The functional form (a Lisp form) by which one causes things to happen contains a function name (indicating the operation to be performed) and arguments (indicating the objects of the operation). The functional form for measuring the current thru R9, for example, is: (MEASURE CURRENT R9). One view of the task of the natural language interface is to translate the users queries from English into this functional representation. In this view, the functional representation language provides a target output language for the natural language interface. The functional forms which result from parsing the student's statements play a dual role in SOPHIE's operation. In their more obvious role, they are evaluated to carry out the desired operation. In their less obvious role, they serve as data objects that get manipulated by the dialogue mechanism.

As we experimented with early versions of SOPHIE, it quickly became clear that the system needed a model of the dialogue as well as of the lab itself. When the system exhibits intelligence by answering a student's questions or criticizing his ideas, the student invariably assumes the system has intelligent conversational abilities as well. For example, following his question "*what is the base emitter voltage of Q6?*", the student quite naturally asks "*what about Q3?*" This second query, like any containing ellipsed or anaphoric phrases, presupposes a dialogue context. The functional representation for the query contains uninstantiated items which serve as place holders for the meaning that will be gotten from the conversational context. The history list, as will be detailed later, provides the necessary model for the conversational context.

3.1 SEMANTIC GRAMMAR

In semantic grammars, the possible statements to the system are characterized in terms of the underlying concepts (functions and objects) of the domain. The input language is described by a set of grammar rules that give, for each function or object, all possible ways of expressing it in terms of other constituent concepts. Each rule has associated with it a method for building the meaning of its concept from the meanings of the constituent concepts. This allows the semantic interpretation to proceed in parallel with the recognition. Because the method also has the ability to stop the rule if the semantic interpretation fails, the semantics can be used to guide the parser. For example, the rule for <MEASUREMENT> expresses all of the ways in which a student can refer to a measurable quantity and also supply its required arguments. This rule can be used to find out about measurements ("*Is the voltage at the collector of Q5 correct?*") as well as to make them.

3.2 THE DIALOGUE MECHANISM

While involved in a problem-solving session, users assume dialogue context in many of their statements. The following statements occur naturally and require context to understand:

{In a context where the student has mentioned Q6}

What is the voltage at the base?

At the collector?

What about the current through the emitter?

Is that right?

What about Q5?

SOPHIE's dialogue mechanism accepts these. Viewed from the functional representation standpoint, the mechanism basically permits argument replacement, function-name re-use and argument re-use. These operations correspond to powerful, frequently occurring dialogue constructs including forms of pronominal reference, anaphorae and ellipsis. *"What is the voltage at the base?"* and *"set it to 50 ohms"* are examples of functions missing arguments. *"What about Q5?"* and *"thru R9?"* are examples of arguments missing surrounding forms. *"At the collector"* is an example of both a missing argument (to the function COLLECTOR) and a missing surrounding form (a function to apply to the collector of a transistor).

The functional representations returned by the parser for these sentences contain place holders for the missing pieces of information. For example, the functional form representation for *"What about Q3?"* is (REFERENCE Q3 ?). REFERENCE occurs when there is an argument in need of a surrounding form. The "?" position provides a place holder for the "meaning" of this ellipsis and is filled in with the functional form of that meaning when it is determined from the dialogue context. The functional representation for *"What is the voltage at the base?"* is (MEASURE VOLTAGE (BASE (PROREFERENCE (TRANSISTOR) ?))). In this form, PROREFERENCE marks that something has been deleted or pronominalized and "?" provides a place holder for the deleted construct. The second argument contains type information about the deleted construct that is determined from the sentence context. (In this case the list of acceptable types has only one element, TRANSISTOR, because transistors are the only parts which have BASES.)

The candidates for the missing parts of a statement are supplied by the dialogue context model, a list of the previous functional forms. The search for the missing items is guided by the type information either taken from the given object or supplied in the functional form. Although the view of dialogue constructs as supplying functional forms and arguments handles a large, useful class of queries robustly, there are many classes of dialogue phenomena it does not seek to deal. See [Webber 1979] and [Grosz 1978] for more general approaches.

3.3 IMPORTANCE OF PARAPHRASE; A SIMPLE EXPERIMENT

Having a system recognize alternative wordings of the same thought is important because our experience indicates that individuals; 1) phrase questions in a variety of ways and 2) they are poor at paraphrasing. In an informal experiment to test the habitability of a system, we asked a group of students to write down as many forms as possible of asking a particular question. The students each came up with one phrasing very quickly but had difficulty thinking of any others. Surprisingly, nearly all of their first phrasings were different, indicating the difficulty of accepting the first phrasing in all cases.

3.4 EXPERIENCES

The natural language interface to SOPHIE took approximately two man-years of effort, and evolved over the course of four years. Although extensions were made as the capabilites of SOPHIE increased, the primary impetus for change was the difficulties encountered by users. The dialogue mechanism is one feature that was added as a result of users' experiences. All during the use of the natural language interface, any query not understood was automatically sent as a message to one of the designers. This facility allowed the monitoring of SOPHIE's use, even at remote sites on the ARPA network. The non-comprehended sentences were saved and used as a "test" set for new modifications to the grammar. In the end, the natural language front end reached the state of being easily usable by electronics students. The entire system was fast, taking less than 150 milliseconds for almost all inputs, and robust, correctly handling more than 90 percent of queries.

Abbreviations and spelling correction are important to reduce the required amount of typing. This is not to say that users would be happier with an abbreviated command language; naive users tend to use full English queries. But as the naive user becomes involved in the troubleshooting process, he occasionally tries a new (often shorter) phrasing, an ellipsis or an abbreviation. If the system accepts it, the user incorporates the phrasing into the known accepted language base and continues to use it. (Although it is interesting to note that when, due to heavy system load, response time slowed down to more than about 5 seconds, the dialogue constructs disappeared and the student's format reverted to that of complete sentences.) The critical concept is that the system allow users to move from complete sentences to their own particular short command languages without rejecting very many intermediate statements along the way. The continuum from full sentences to cryptic, ellipsed abbreviations allows users to find their own comfortable method of expression.

When a user's query is not completely specified, or ambiguously misspelled, the system should provide unambiguous indication of what it has changed or overlooked to understand his request. The user may have meant something else and be very much misled by the response. For example in the following excerpt:

What is the current through R11?

Across R9?

the system interprets the second query as asking for the current through R9. The student, however, may be asking for the voltage across R9 rather than the current thru it; believing that the semantics of "across" would override the recent mention of the quanitity "current." To forestall misunderstanding, SOPHIE always responds to every query with a complete sentence describing the query as well as the answer. In this case, SOPHIE would respond with *"The current through R9 is 10 milliamps."* This solution does not work all the time; apparently the users' predispositions toward their own hypotheses sometimes override their ability to read/perceive what is being said, leading them to overlook all except the part of the response that is consistent with what they believed their query to be.

The system should have and present to the user a consistent model of its capabilities. Serious problems arise when the user does not have an acccurate model of the limits of the system. If the user thinks the system has more capability than it does, he will continually be asking things that the system can't understand. If the user does not know about a system capability, he will never use it. A natural language interface does not help because the interface does not provide any scope to the system. With a menu interface, the user has at least some idea of the capabilities of the system. In SOPHIE we attacked this problem by having the natural language component recognize common misconceptions about its world view well enough to provide remediation. An example is given in the following student query and system response:

>> COULD Q1 OR Q2 BE SHORTED?

I can only handle one question, hypothesis, etc. at a time. The fact that you say "OR" indicates that you may be trying to express two concepts in the same sentence. Maybe you can break your statement into two or more simple ones.

Another more complex example is:

>> WHAT IS THE CURRENT THROUGH NODE 4?

The current through a node is not meaningful since by Kirchoff's law the sum of currents through any node is zero. Currents can be measured through parts (e.g., CURRENT THROUGH C6) or terminals (e.g., CURRENT THROUGH THE COLLECTOR OF Q2).

The system response to the question addresses the student's misconception of where current is measured and, more importantly, gives the user some indication of how to ask for the information he wants; because C6 and the collector of Q2 are two of the terminals connected to node 4.

There are several limitations about the domain that made it appropriate to the semantic grammar technique. Since the user interacts with the system in the same way he would interact with a laboratory, few questions involve quantifiers. Also, relative clauses are not an appropriate way of asking direct measurement questions. These limitations are not inherent in the semantic grammar framework. More complex constructs, in particular quantification, have been implemented in applications of LIFER (Hendrix 1977) which uses a similar framework. In addition, the framework has been applied to other domains, such as in ACE (Sleeman and Hendley 1981) which analyzes student explanations about NMR spectra interpretation. RUS [Bobrow 1978] which began as an attempt to look into domain-independent semantic grammars, has developed a redefinition of the role of syntax in natural language and resulted in an efficient method for mixing syntax and semantics.

3.5 GRAMMAR REPRESENTATIONS

Two representations for semantic grammars were explored in SOPHIE. The first was the direct encoding of the grammar in Lisp code. In this encoding, each grammar rule was hand-coded as a Lisp function that typically checked for certain words or classes of words in the input, advanced the input, called other Lisp functions to look for other non-terminals, and built the interpretation of the rule. This has the advantage of not requiring a separate grammar formalism or parser, thus both reducing the overhead of getting started and allowing use of the powerful INTERLISP debugging environment in developing the grammar.

In this formalism, *fuzzy parsing*, the ability to skip words in the input sentence, was explored. When few and unsophisticated concepts were accepted, almost anything with the right words could be taken to mean the same thing, allowing recognition of some sentences that would not have been otherwise recognizable. As the complexity of the phrasings increased though, particularly with the inclusion of ellipsis recognition, the fuzziness led to troublesome misunderstandings. With two important exceptions, our experience showed that fuzziness caused more problems than it solved. The first exception is the fuzziness technique of ignoring words that are not in the system's dictionary. By informing the user of unknown words and trying to make sense of the remainder, the system can bypass many adjectives, adverbs and expletives. The second exception is the technique of ignoring words that are left over after a successful parse. The user should, of course, be told which words are being ignored.

The second representation for semantic grammars arose out of necessity. As the grammar became more complex, the Lisp implementation became hard to understand, so the grammar was translated into the *augmented transistion network* (ATN) formalism. The ATN has the advantages of being more concise, having factored expressive power and having a better development environment. In our ATNs, the structure built on the arcs and returns from the final state, is the "semantic interpretation" of the sentence, not its syntactic structure.

An initial efficiency advantage which the direct Lisp encoding had over the ATN, being executable directly as machine code, was overcome by the construction of an ATN compiler [Burton 1976, and Burton and Woods 1976]. The ATN formalism can be used to develop a range of interfaces, from simple keyword interfaces to highly complex, general schemes, with very little loss of efficiency. In addition, since the code produced by the compiler does not require the large Lisp environment, the compiler can be straightforwardly changed to produce code for microcomputers. This would allow the ATN formalism to be used for interfaces that are developed in a large machine environment but run as part of systems on small machines.

4. Knowledge-Engineering Techniques

Our intent in this section is to focus on the techniques that we have used to construct efficient and robust intelligent tutoring systems.† Achieving both efficiency and robustness is of paramount importance. Efficiency is needed because the attention span of students, even highly motivated ones, is often considerably shorter than that of the typical user of other knowledge-based expert systems; and robustness is needed because the questions asked, hypotheses proposed and experiments tried by students just learning a subject often are (or appear) bizarre.

We will discuss here two systems, SOPHIE I and SOPHIE III. Since most of the knowledge-engineering techniques in SOPHIE I were published some time ago

†By robustness, we mean able to work under many circumstances; particularly, providing an appropriate response to an unanticipated student action.

[Brown and Burton 1975, Brown, Burton and Bell 1974], we will limit the discussion of SOPHIE I to (1) the central abstractions of that work and (2) some of the misconceptions that surround the use of simulations as an inference tool. Understanding the strengths and inherent weaknesses of SOPHIE I will also set the stage for describing SOPHIE III. The later system reflects a major departure from SOPHIE I in its underlying knowledge-engineering techniques.

The "expert troubleshooter" in SOPHIE II focused on the problem of good explanations of problem-solving knowledge. Its "intelligence" resulted from straightforward applications of well-known knowledge-engineering techniques, primarily decision trees, and thus will not be discussed further.

4.1 SIMULATION-BASED INFERENCE SCHEMES: SOPHIE I

SOPHIE I utilized a simple but powerful idea that had already proved effective in one of the first major expert systems, Dendral [Lindsay, et al., 1980]. Both SOPHIE I and Dendral achieve their logical prowess by obtaining leverage from some powerful and robust non-AI tools, augmented by collections of rules (or procedural specialists) that "intelligently" use the tools and their results. In Dendral's case, the primary tool is an elegant mathematical algorithm for enumerating all the subgraphs of a graph without generating isomorphs. In our case the primary tool is the general-purpose circuit simulator, SPICE, which is in continued general use by circuit designers. Various knowledge-based specialists in SOPHIE I transform a given problem into a set of subproblems, each of which can be solved by executing an appropriate model on the simulator, critiquing the intermediate results, and infering an answer to the original problem from the resulting data. In other words, SOPHIE I, when presented with a question to answer, a hypothesis to evaluate, or a measurement to check for redundancy, sets up its own set of "experiments" and from the results, infers an answer to the question. There are, however, numerous problems merely in determining the precise experiment(s) necessary to gather sufficient information for infering an answer.

The following few sections will explore both the strengths and weaknesses of using simulations as the core of an inference engine. We will also discuss some unusual ways that simulation can be used in inference tasks.

4.1.1 Strength and Weaknesses of Simulations

There are two primary reasons for exploring ways to use simulation as part of an inference scheme in the domain of electronics: 1) there is a vast amount of electronic expertise already neatly encoded in simulation models, particularly for the generic components (diode, transistor, etc.); and 2) behind the simulation algorithms, there is a vast amount of mathematical expertise that efficiently implements a calculus for "reasoning" with these models. We are given a strong domain model; we need only find clever ways of using it.

Robustness Requirements When Using Simulations for Inference

4.1.1.1 Implicit Assumptions in the Models

The most characteristic shortcomings of nearly all simulations is that they have a large number of presuppositions built into them, many of which are implicit even to their designers.   Applying a simulation in a new context can be problematic since its implicit assumptions may be violated. This is especially true when using simulations to reason about potential consequences of faults (hypothetical or real), because faults can so drastically alter the internal workings of a system that the faulted system violates even the most basic, common-sense rules of any intentionally designed artifact (e.g. man-made device). In such cases, not only are the implicit assumptions of the original simulated system apt to be violated but even the mathematical techniques being used to "solve" or run the simulation can have their assumptions violated.

These observations are not limited to just electronic simulations. In fact, they are more likely to occur in other domains (reactors, hydraulic systems, and weather models, for example) where the simulation models are more likely to be tied to an already existing physical system. In such cases, the designers of these simulations are apt to let their understanding of the overall system suggest what aspects of the system's individual components need be captured. This leads to ad hoc models which subtlely depend on the system working as intended [see deKleer and Brown 1981 for an extensive discussion of this point, especially as it applies to robust mental models].

It is difficult to predict whether a proposed context on which to execute the simulation or a modification to its structure will transgress the assumptions of the model.   Worse, it is not always possible to detect, even after running the simulation, that a transgression has occurred; the model may still produce plausible behavior which is, in fact, wrong. Only if a trangression manifests itself by having the simulation "diverge" (so that no solution is found) is the state easy to detect.

The need to make explicit all the caveats underlying the overall simulation model — or, at least, to characterize its domain of applicability — is more crucial for the use of simulations as an AI tool than for their normal use. In normal use, it is often the designer who invokes the models on a new, perhaps hypothetical, situation and who will often intuitively know if an implicit assumption is being violated. But an AI system, such as SOPHIE I, generates deep within its inference chain hypothetical modifictions to a model that may make little sense to the expert and hence violate all kinds of implicit assumptions. In addition, an obvious use of an "intelligent" shell around a simulator is to have it rapidly generate a vast collection of hypothetical situations which is apt to stress the boundaries of the models in novel ways. In both of these cases, reliable use of the simulation models mandates that the assumptions/caveats be explict and checkable.

Fortunately, the general-purpose simulator that was used in SOPHIE I had relatively few bothersome, implicit assumptions (although our own extensions to it and the various circuit specific, functional simulations built especially for SOPHIE were plagued with such problems).   One proposed counter-assumptional experiment had an external voltage source (a fully functional storage battery) being hooked up to the *output* terminals of the regulated power supply. Such a modification had never occurred to us because it violates the core meaning or use of a power supply: to deliver voltage, not absorb it.† It turned out that we had built into the functional simulator a teleological assumption that the system was in either a current-limiting or a voltage-limiting mode — a reasonable asumption for a regulated power supply. But, with the battery hooked to its output terminals, it was no longer functioning even as a power supply, let alone a regulated one. Although the general-purpose simulator could handle this experiment, the functional simulator, hand-tailored to allow extremely fast simulations of the given power supply, completely failed to model, even qualitatively, what actually happens.

4.1.1.2 Models of Fault Modes

Another complicating factor in using simulations, especially to handle hypothetically faulty components, is the difficulty of characterizing all the possible behaviors of a malfunctioning component. This difficulty becomes accentuated in dealing with the models for primitive components since the program or mathematical transfer function for a primitive is often structurally opaque. The opacity results from the fact that the transfer function is derived empirically and hence its internal structure doesn't necessarily stand in any meaningful relationship to the internal structure of the component; perturbations to the internal structure of the component (faults) in this case have no obvious correspondence to perturbations of its model. This makes using the working model of the component as a guide for constructing the faulty model a problematic venture.

4.1.2 Simulation Used as Part of the Inference Machinery

For many of the capabilities needed by SOPHIE I, simulation is only part of the solution. In the next section we shall describe simulation capabilities, how simulations fit into the solution and what auxilliary mechanisms were added.

4.1.2.1 The Need to Capture Causality

The kinds of simulators most often used in electronics rely on "relaxation" methods for solving the system of equations characterizing circuit behavior. Although these techniques are extraordinarily powerful, the intermediate solution states they pass through bear little resemblance to any kind of causality underlying the circuit. Indeed, the circuit itself is represented as a set of constraints and the sought-after behavior is that which *simultaneously* satisfies all the given constraints. Nevertheless, students and experts alike can best understand a circuit, and remember their understanding, if an "explanation" reveals some of the underlying causality. Thus, to be able to get maximal pedagogical leverage from the simulation, we need to find ways of getting causal information. Two possible strategies come to mind: (1) deduce some of the circuit's underlying causality from the solution space of the constraint equations; or (2) factor the system of constraints and simulation methods so that the relevant parts of the system's

---

†Of course from another perspective this experiment is not quite so absurd since one might use a regulated power supply to charge a battery and one might also make the mistake of trying to charge a completely charged battery.

underlying causality are not hidden by relaxation. In SOPHIE I, we chose the second alternative.

4.1.2.1.1 Capturing Causality

As a first step, the appropriate level of causal abstraction must be identified. In SOPHIE's case the most important aspect of causality pertains to fault propagations: if a component faults, what other components will blow as a result? We factor the simulator's constraints into two classes, one comprising the normal constraints of electronic laws, the circuit's topology and its component values, and the other comprising *meta-constraints* characterizing the conditions at which components will blow, e.g. power dissipation factors etc.†

This factoring into constraints and meta-constraints allows the relaxation-based simulator to be augmented with two local procedural experts or specialists. The first specialist isolates all violations of the meta-constraints in the database produced by the simulator and if it locates more than one component that is overstressed it determines which one of these will blow first. Then, a second domain specialist determines how that component will fault; whether it will open, short or beta shift. The simulation model of the circuit is then modified to reflect this additional fault and the simulator is again called to construct a new layer in the database. The whole process is recursively repeated until the simulator produces a database that satisfies all of the meta-contraints. This final database is then returned along with the sequence of fault propagations that led to it. This combined structure contains the desired causality of fault propagation and the fixed point of the constraint equations, each being generated by a technique optimized for the task. This composite structure can then be used to answer questions about the consequences of the proposed hypothetical modification, to generate causal explanations concerning fault propagation or, perhaps, to drive a graphics system to animate the propagation.

4.1.2.2 Determining "Interesting" Experiments to Run

Answering certain classes of questions requires not only the ability to *run* the simulation model but also the ability to reason *about* the model itself. The need for both is most easily seen by considering questions that contain an implicit existential quantifier. Take, for example, the seemingly simple question "If X is shorted will Y blow?" The implied quantifier becomes clear in the following rephrasing: "Does there exist a boundary condition for the simulation such that, if X is shorted, it will lead to Y being blown?" The problem here is analogous to the classical problem of program testing: choosing a set of test data such that if the program has a bug, it will be manifested on that data. This analogy also illustrates

---

†This provides another subtle example of an implicit assumption built into the simulation. The mere fact that we choose excess power dissipation as being the significant feature underlying a component's failure through fault propagation signifies a belief that in the circuits we are handling, very fast but short lived potential spikes won't exist. In normal power supplies, that is a fair assumption. But, if such spikes are present, transistors will fail when the potential of the spike is great enough, even though its power is arbitrarily small. If a component were to fail so that it generated such a pulse or pulse stream, this assumption would be violated, leading to a potential divergence between the model and the physical system.

that just running more successful experiments or data sets does not necessarily improve the chances that the program is bug-free. Running even an infinite number of test cases, all of which exercise the same aspects of the program, will not guarantee more than does just a single experiment. The test cases must be independent with respect to the operation of the program. This means that what makes one experiment or data set "logically" different from another depends on the logic of the program.

Although the above observation is well known in programming methodology, its analogy in the use of simulations is not so well appreciated. Much of the power in using simulations as an inference engine stems from heuristics for determining "interesting" boundary conditions for the simulation.

Given the question "If X shorts will Y blow?", the heuristic calculus used to construct a set of boundary conditions first determines the function blocks containing the components X and Y. The calculus then determines how to set up the loads and control settings on the device so as to activate those functional blocks.

4.1.2.3 Hypothesis Evaluation

In SOPHIE I, evaluation of a hypothesis is the process of determining its logical consistency with respect to the information derivable from the current set of measurements.† Note that a hypothesis can be logically consistent with the known information and still not be what is actually wrong with the circuit. For example, if no measurements have been performed then any syntactically correct hypothesis is acceptable.

For a given hypothesis, the hypothesis evaluation specialist partitions the current set of measurements into three classes: one containing the measurements contradicted by the given hypothesis, another containing the measurements logically entailed by the hypothesis and the last class containing those measurements independent of the logical consequences of the given hypothesis.

These partitions are determined by taking into consideration all the logical implications derivable from the given hypothesis. If, for example, the hypothesis concerns Q3's base being open, there need be no direct or obvious measurement on Q3 that indicates whether it is working or not. By taking into consideration both the local and global interactions of components in the circuit, measurements arbitrarily far away from Q3 may be used to support or refute the hypothesis.

Simulation can be used to determine the consequences of a hypothesis much as it was used to infer the consequences of the assertional part of a hypothetical question. In particular, it is used to construct a "hypothetical world" specified by the hypothesis (e.g., "Q3 must have its base open"), and in that hypothetical world, all the student's measurements are "replayed." If the values of any of these measurements are not *qualitatively* equivalent to the ones observed by the student in the faulted circuit, then a counterexample or inconsistency has been established.

---

†A hypothesis concerns the state of a given component: a capacitor being shorted, a resistor being open, a transistor being shorted, etc.

4.1.2.4 Hypothesis Generation (Theory Formation)

The method of constructing the set of those hypotheses or faults consistent with the currently observed behavior of the faulted device uses the venerable "generate and test" paradigm. First, a backward-working specialist, the PROPOSER, examines the value observed for an external measurement and, from that observation, determines a list of all possible significant hypotheses which explain it. Because the PROPOSER is not endowed with enough knowledge to capture all the complex interactions and subtleties of the circuit, it can err by including hypotheses inconsistent with the observed behavior.

A second specialist, the REFINER, "simulates" each fault on the current hypothesis list to check whether it explains all the measurements that the student has taken. The REFINER must take into consideration all of the complex interactions overlooked by a simple theory of the circuit. Depending on the REFINER's simulator to check out all the subtle consequences of a proposed hypothesis, however, leads to a major problem; in order for a hypothesis to be simulated, it must be a fully instantiated fault. The hypothesis "the beta of the Darlington amplifer is low," for example, does not make clear *what* the proposed beta is, just that it is lower than it should be.

It is the job of a third specialist, called the INSTANTIATOR, to take an underspecified fault and instantiate it. The INSTANTIATOR uses several techniques to determine a potentially consistent specification of an underspecified fault. The most general of these techniques is a simple hill-climbing strategy in which a specific value for the fault "schema" is guessed and then partially simulated (enough to determine the external behavior). From the result of that simulation another guess is made, until finally a value is found that causes the desired behavior. Because this strategy executes the simulation many times, a special-purpose, functional simulation model is used that runs several orders of magnitude faster than the general-purpose simulator.

4.1.2.5 Determining Redundant Measurements

Perhaps the most complex logical task performed by SOPHIE I is the task of verifying whether or not a given measurement *could* possibly add any new information about what might be at fault.

Our approach to handling this task stems from an analogy for how one might prove the independence of an axiom set. If one is trying to establish that a new axiom is independent from a given collection of axioms, one might try to construct a "possible world" for the original axiom set which is not a possible world for the augmented axiom set.

In our case, we view each measurement-value pair as an axiom or assertion and proceed according to the above analogy. The set of hypotheses constructed by the hypothesis generator serves as the set of all possible world models which are consistent with the known measurements.

Although this technique has proved to be very powerful, for many pedagogical uses it is too powerful.† Some of the redundant measurements it detects can be

---

†This is the one area in which SOPHIE repeatedly surpasses its designers.

explained by a single step argument. However, others it detects equally easily take a large number of "logical" steps to explain. The disadvantage of the technique is that it can't distinguish between these two cases. What is needed is a human-like reasoning scheme capable of detecting redundancies on its own. This leads to our discussion of SOPHIE III.

4.2 SOPHIE III

The basic theme of the overall SOPHIE project has been to avoid restricting the actions of the student while allowing the computer to act as a coach, to assess the student's understanding and to guide him to a better understanding of electronics and troubleshooting. Building such laboratory requires a system which (1) allows the student to take the initiative, (2) is able to make significant inferences about the circuit from the student's measurements, and (3) is able to explain those inferences.

Meeting these requirements individually is difficult; in SOPHIE III we wanted to achieve them simultaneously. SOPHIE I allowed the student complete freedom of measurement and employed an extremely powerful inference strategy, but it could not explain the reasoning behind many of its inferences. SOPHIE II, on the other hand allowed the student very little initiative, used only a simple inference strategy, but was capable of very subtle explanations of its electronics and troubleshooting deductions.

	STUDENT INITIATIVE	INFERENCES	EXPLANATION
I	Yes	Powerful	Poor
II	Very Little	Weak	Good
III	Yes	Powerful •	Good

Our approach in constructing SOPHIE III was to base its inference techniques on those that we observed experts and students using. By making SOPHIE's inferencing strategies more akin to those used by the student, we could begin to determine which deductions the student was using, construct a model of his abilities, then use this model to generate explanations in familiar terms.

We also needed a fundamentally different and more human-oriented inference scheme because we wanted to investigate using SOPHIE as a computer-based consultant for on-job-site training as an intelligent job-performance aid. We thus wanted SOPHIE III to be able to work from measurements being performed on *real, physical equipment*, completely independently of any kind of circuit simulator.

4.2.1 Knowledge Engineering Perspective

The knowledge-engineering task of building SOPHIE III has several interesting features. First, the pedagogical emphasis demands an unusual amount of attention be paid to explanation of deductions. Because one goal is to help the student learn, explanation must be considered equally as important as deduction. Consequently, more of SOPHIE III's computational resources are spent in recording deductions and manipulating justifications with their underlying *assumptions* than in actually making the deductions in the first place.

Another capability not usually required by knowledge-engineering systems is that SOPHIE III must be able to hypothesize and reason about a student's partial understanding of electronics and troubleshooting. To do so, it must possess many logically redundant strategies since it can't assume the student will know the best ones. Thus many conclusions it produces have numerous independent proofs, each with its own set of justifications and assumptions.

A third complication facing SOPHIE III stems from the fact that electronics (and electronic troubleshooting) is a complex problem domain, part of which has been formalized, part of which has not, especially in terms of the causal calculii tacitly used by human experts. Because of the complexity, we were faced with either restricting ourselves to formalized aspects of the domain or working out a framework to systematically include the collection of ad hoc rules and inference mechanisms needed for the poorly understood part of the domain. We chose the latter course, and our strategy for building the electronics expert was to encode as much of the knowledge in the most general form possible. To complement the general knowledge, circuit-specific knowledge provided by electrical engineering needs to be included in the expert. The explanations of the circuit-specific knowledge, are supplied by the electrical engineer and are attached to each knowledge rule. In contrast, explanations for deductions made from the generic electronic laws do not presume any particular circuit and thus can be constructed from the steps taken by the inference mechanism used to make the deduction.

It would have been easier to encode much of the general knowledge as circuit-specific knowledge. We chose not to for three reasons. First, general knowledge has a very parsimonious structure making it relatively easy to analyze its limitations. Second, the more powerful the general knowledge, the less circuit-specific knowledge is necessary. Third, circuit-specific knowledge, since it is encoded from the engineer's particular analysis, is liable to undermine robustness since it reflects his underlying assumptions.

In SOPHIE III the circuit-specific knowledge is only employed after the general knowledge has made as many deductions as possible. Thus, the circuit-specific knowledge is aimed directly at those situations in which the general knowledge fails. Because of its known limited context, circuit-specific knowledge can be put in a canonical form, the number of ad hoc rules can be minimized and the determination of whether enough circuit-specific knowledge has been included to succeed is made much easier.

The generic electronic knowledge is solely concerned with the states and the behaviors (voltages and currents) of primitive components (e.g., diodes, transistors). This general knowledge is used by an inference scheme based on propagation of constraints which deals with simple inequalities rather than of single numeric quantities. Although, this feature complicates the constraint propagation, it both makes it possible to handle many kinds of inferences humans actualy perform and provides a rudimentary notation for expressing *qualitative* constructs.

The circuit-specific knowledge is organized around a structural decomposition of the circuit. A circuit is a designed artifact, consisting of a collection of weakly interacting modules. Each module is, itself, a circuit in its own right and can be likewise decomposed. The modules behave cooperatively to produce the behavior of the overall circuit. The key to the circuit-specific knowledge is having terms to express the behavior of these modules. The circuit specific knowledge consists of rules about how the behaviors of modules affect the behaviors of other modules: Neighboring modules affect each other as well a being influenced by the behavior of their lower-level, constituent modules. Constructing the right kind of knowledge structure which, in part, reflects a structural decompostion of the given circuit enables these rules to be systematically encoded where one kind of rule forms the inheritance in the knowlege structure and the other kind of rule forms transformation between "neighbors" of the structure.

Perhaps surprisingly, neither the general nor circuit specific reasoning engine has any direct knowledge of troubleshooting. The troubleshooter is a separate and general system, whose knowledge base is extremely small and is totally dependent on the electronics expert module. The troubleshooting module examines the deductions which the electronics expert does or could potentially make. This requires that it has intimate familiarity with both the electronics expert databases and inference mechanisms. The troubleshooter's simplicity results from the fact that the electronics expert module explicitly records each assumption it makes, and these are scrutinized by the troubleshooter in order to determine why the circuit is not functioning as it should.

The existence of the parasitic troubleshooter does not affect the deductions the electronics expert can make, but it does require that every deduction be augmented by a precise justification recording the inference mechanism and circuit data used. The success of the troubleshooter stems from the fact that in the troubleshooting task some component, necessarily, is not behaving as it should. If a component is not behaving as it should the electronics expert will eventually encounter a irreconcilable contradiction since its model of the circuit will differ from the actual faulty instance that is being debugged. Every inference the electronics expert makes, implicitly involves some assumption (the component is behaving as specified by its manufacturer) about a component or piece of circuit wiring. When the circuit contain a fault, these assumptions must be made explicit. In troubleshooting, a contradiction is an extremely informative event since it indicates which assumptions are violated, narrowing the field of possible faulty components. The entire troubleshooter is based on this one idea, an idea that will be substantally expanded later in this chapter.

The cost incurred by this elegant scheme is that the inference mechanism of the electronics expert must always supply accurate and exhaustive justifications and assumptions for all of its deductions. A single exception could render the troubleshooter impotent. To some extent this same organizational cleanliness is also demanded for generating coherent explanations, but the added constraint of this troubleshooting scheme now necessitates that the electronics expert's deductions be void of any hidden presuppositions.

4.2.2 The Architecture of SOPHIE III

SOPHIE III consists of three major expert modules: the electronic expert (which consists of two submodules), the troubleshooter and the coach. The electronics expert which received, by far, the most work utilizes mostly general electronic knowledge with some circuit-specific knowledge (in this case, regarding the IP-28 regulated power supply). One of its submodules, LOCAL utilizes the general knowledge and contains, among other things, a local constraint propagator, hence its name. The other submodule, CIRCUIT, is responsible for handling all the circuit-specific knowledge. The other two experts, the coach and the troubleshooter, are both self-contained and circuit-independent. The coaching expert examines those deductions to determine whether or not to interrupt or advise the student. The coaching expert is only partially implemented; the biggest unimplemented portion is the user model and interruption capabilities. The troubleshooting expert is relatively small, using the electronics expert to evaluate hypothetical measurements, and then choosing the most informative one. All three experts operate using only the information known to the student (measurements and schematic), from which they make as many (often redundant) deductions as possible.

The architecture of the electronics expert is a composite of several very different inference techniques. The circuit-specific reasoning can be roughly broken into two types. The first is a rule-based system which uses voltages and currents, propagated by LOCAL from the current set of measurements to determine the behaviors of circuit modules. The second mechanism determines what the component fault modes can cause the symptomatic module behaviors. The fundamental problem of intercommunication between different reasoning types is elegantly solved in SOPHIE III with a common language of justifications and assumptions: Each deduction made by any of the reasoning types simply records the reasons for and assumptions under which the deduction was made. This justification/assumption database, just as in a general-purpose truth-maintanence system, can be oblivious to the different kinds of reasoning that underlie each deduction step. This is also the database from which the troubleshooting expert works.

Three types of reasoning are involved in the electronics expert each with its own knowledge structure, complete with inference mechanism and database (see Fig. 4.1). The propagation database contains quantitative deductions about voltage and currents (e.g., output voltage is 30 volts) made by using the models of the components. The qualitative database contains assertions about the operating regions of the components, voltages, and currents (e.g., output current is low, transistor Q5 is off). The database for the third knowledge structure, the behavior-tree, consists of the possible behavioral modes of components and circuit modules (e.g., R5 is open, the current source is anemic).

4.2.3 The Local Propagator

The local propagator (LOCAL)† forms the basis for the electronics expert. It uses general knowledge of circuit laws to determine what further voltage and current consequences can be determined from the measurements that have been made. The deductions of the local propagator are used not only for their simple explanatory

†The propagator used in SOPHIE III is similar to Stallman and Sussman's EL which is also based on propagation of constraints [Stallman & Sussman 77]. LOCAL differs from EL in that it uses assumptions more widely and is capable of manipulating simple forms of inequalities.

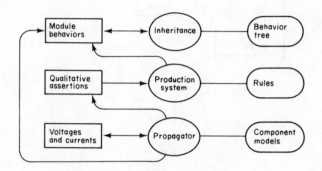

FIG. 4.1. Electronics Expert

capability, but for reference by the other two experts. In this section we will focus on the troubleshooting consequences of a measurement. In order for a measurement to provide useful information we must have some expectation about its value.

This local propagator may appear simple, but the variety of subtle problems with which it must grapple make it quite complex. The biggest obstacle is the necessity for generality — it must deal with arbitrary measurements in arbitrary circuits. But the profit we gain is great; because it is the only part of SOPHIE III that has to reason upon the measurements and circuit topology directly, it greatly simplifies the other experts which need only refer to LOCAL's deductions.

The propagations of even a single measurement can be quite deep. Suppose the resistor we have been using as an example occurred in the circuit Fig. 4.2. Suppose we measured the current in R13 to be 1 milliampere. Since the resistance of R13 is 100 ohms, the voltage across it must be .1 volts. But the voltage across R13 is the same as the voltage across the base-emitter junction of Q6. We know that a silicon transistor conducts no current when the base-emitter voltage is less than .6 volts so the current flowing in each of the resistor terminals must be zero. Now consider the node N9 which connects to R13, Q6 and R16. The current flowing out of R13 and Q6 must be flowing into resistor R16 so the current flowing through R16 is 1 ma. As just shown, a single measurement can lead to the calculation of a lot of information about other circuit values. The local propagator of SOPHIE III is an attempt to formalize this "If $A = x$, then $B = y$" kind of reasoning. It keeps records of each deduction so that explanations can be generated and examined when troubleshooting.

Although the concept of propagation applies to both AC and DC circuits, at present SOPHIE III only models DC behavior. This is sufficient to model the quiescent behavior of circuits, and adequate for modelling power supplies since they (except

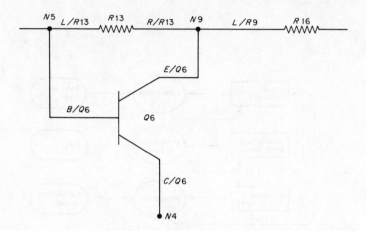

FIG. 4.2. A Current Limiter

for switching regulators) can be understood almost entirely from the quiescent point of view. The circuits consist of resistors, diodes, zener diodes, capacitors, transistors, switches, potentiometers and DC voltage sources. Each component has a expert associated with it which constantly checks to see whether the currents or voltages on its terminals are measured or calculated; as soon as a value is discovered for one, it is used to deduce voltages and currents on the others. Since the terminals and nodes are shared with other devices, these new currents and voltages in turn trigger other component experts. The process continues until no new information can be determined.

In order to explain propagations, a record is kept of which device's expert made the deduction. Propagations are represented as:

    (⟨type⟩ ⟨location⟩ (⟨reason⟩ ⟨component⟩ ⟨arg⟩) ⟨assumptions⟩).

The ⟨type⟩ is either "VOLTAGE" or "CURRENT." The ⟨location⟩ is a pair of nodes for a voltage, a terminal for a current. The ⟨reason⟩ is a token describing how the device expert made the propagation.

The circuit consists of components whose terminals are joined (two or more) at nodes. Since terminals, unlike nodes, are always attached to components we adopt the convention of labelling them by ⟨terminal-type⟩/⟨component⟩. Currents are normally associated with terminals, voltages with nodes. In Fig. 4.2, L/R13, R/R13, B/Q6, E/Q6, and C/Q6 are terminals, and N5 and N9 are nodes.

The simplest propagations are those involving the Kirchoff voltage and current laws. Kirchoff's current law states that if all but one of the terminal currents of a component or node are known, the remaining one can be deduced:

```
(CURRENT T/1 (MEASUREMENT)) = 1
```

The current in terminal T/1 is measured to be 1 ampere.

```
(CURRENT T/2 (MEASUREMENT)) = 2
```

The current in terminal T/2 is measured to be 2 amperes.
(CURRENT T/3 (KIRCHOFFI N1) ()) = -3

The current in terminal T/3 is determined to be -3 amperes by using Kirchoff's current law (abbreviated KIRCHOFFI) to node N1 (which has only three terminals).

Kirchoff's voltage law states that if two voltages are known relative to a common point, the voltage between the other nodes can be computed:

(VOLTAGE (N1 N2)) = .5
(VOLTAGE (N2 N3)) = 6
(VOLTAGE (N1 N3) (KIRCHOFFV N1 N2 N3) ()) = 6.5

The voltage from node N1 to node N3 is calculated by Kirchoff's voltage law (abbreviated KIRCHOFFV) by summing the voltage from N1 to N2 with the voltage from N2 to N3.

Ohm's Law is equally easily illustrated:
(CURRENT R1) = 1
(VOLTAGE (N1 N2) (RESISTORI R1) (R1)) = 100

The voltage across the resistor is determined from the current through it by an instance of Ohm's Law (abbreviated RESISTORI). This propagation assumes the resistance of the resistor (100 ohms) has not changed and thus the assumption R1 is added to the ⟨assumptions⟩.

or,

(VOLTAGE (N1 N2)) = 100
(CURRENT R1 (RESISTORV R1) (R1)) = 1

These three kinds of calculations, or propagations, can be combined into a very simple propagation theory. First, Kirchoff's voltage law can be applied to every new voltage discovered in the circuit. Then for every node and component in the circuit, Kirchoff's current law can be applied. Finally, for every resistor having a newly discovered current in or voltage across its terminal, the Ohm's law can be applied to determine further propagations. If the study of the characteristics produces any new voltages or currents (via RESISTORV or RESISTORI propagations) the procedure is repeated.

This procedure is easily implemented, but strategies are needed to avoid making duplicate propagations. The simplest strategy is to only consider newly discovered values for making deductions and to not reapply the propagation of a component model to itself.

4.2.3.1 Component Experts

LOCAL has an expert for each type of device it models. These experts are based on the mathematical electrical engineering models, but are implemented with the propagation scheme outlined in the previous section. Each component of a given type must be modelled in the same way. If, for example, one transistor in the circuit were modelled differently from the others without there being some significant physical difference in the transistors, the modelling would have presumed the functionality of the overall circuit.

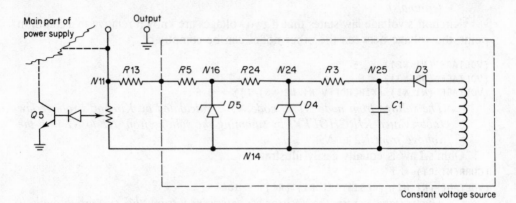

FIG. 4.3. Constant Voltage Source

Transistors, diodes, and zener diodes have discontinuous regions of operation. Each region is characterized by a fundamentally different behavior and the region usually needs to be identified before any values can be propagated. The diode is the simplest kind of semiconductor device; its only characteristic is that when it is reverse-biased (current can flow in only one direction through a diode), the current through it must be zero. From the zener diode we know that if the current through it is greater than some threshold, then the voltage across it must be at its breakdown voltage. Conversely if the voltage across the zener diode is at less than its breakdown voltage, then the current through the diode must be zero.

Suppose voltage measurements at the output and across D5 have just been made:

```
(VOLTAGE (N15 N14)   (MEASUREMENT)) =                            30
(VOLTAGE (N16 N14)   (MEASUREMENT)) =                            34
(VOLTAGE (N16 N15))  (KIRCHOFFV N16 N14 N15) ()) =                4
(CURRENT R5          (RESISTORV R5) (R5)) =                     .003
(CURRENT D5          (ZENERV D5) (D5)) =                          0.
```

The voltage across the zener D5 is less than its breakdown, therefore the current through it must be zero.

```
(CURRENT R4          (KIRCHOFFI N16) (R5 D5)) =                 .003
(VOLTAGE (N24 N16)   (RESISTORI R4) (R4 R5 D5)) =               7.18
(VOLTAGE (N24 N14)   (KIRCHOFFV N24 N16 N14) (R4 R5 D5)) =     41.18
(VOLTAGE (N24 N15)   (KIRCHOFFV N24 N16 N15) (R4 R5 D5)) =     11.18
(CURRENT D4          (ZENERV D4) (D4 R4 R5 D5)) =                 0.
```

The voltage across zener D4 is less than its breakdown.

```
(CURRENT R3          (KIRCHOFFI N24) (D4 R4 R5 D5)) =           .003
(VOLTAGE (N24 N25)   (RESISTORI R3) (R3 D4 R4 R5 D5)) =         4.90
```

```
(VOLTAGE (N25 N14)  (KIRCHOFFV N25 N24 N14) (R3 D4 R4 R5 D5)) =   46.1
(VOLTAGE (N25 N16)  (KIRCHOFFV N25 N24 N16) (R3 D4 R4 R5 D5)) =   12.01
(VOLTAGE (N25 N15)  (KIRCHOFFV N25 N24 N15) (R3 D4 R4 D5 D5)) =   16.01.
```

We will have much more to say concerning the device experts later. First, though, the numeric values of the propagations must be examined in much greater detail since they are the source of a major complexity in the local propagator, LOCAL.

The device rules utilized in LOCAL are general. This propagator fulfils three roles in the articulate electronics expert. First, it determines the electrical consequences of measurements. Second, it predicts other measurements, assuming non-faulted components. And third, the predictions made by the propagator are used to interface to higher-order knowledge.

4.2.3.2 Range Arithmetic

All measurements in the circuit and all circuit parameters have some degree of error. The errors in circuit parameters originate from the fact that manufacturers cannot make perfect components and instead guarantee their specifications to within certain tolerances. (Typically the resistance of a resistor is only within 10 % of its specified value.) Similarly, the meter used to measure circuit quantities can only measure voltages and currents to certain accuracies (typically 2 % error). A further limitation is that the meter has a minimum range; SOPHIE's meter cannot accurately measure below .1 volt or below 1 microamp. These effects, though artificially introduced into SOPHIE, are representative of what the student would encounter with real circuits. Because the numerical computations performed by the device experts introduce truncation and roundoff errors, it makes more sense to propagate either values *and* their tolerances, or ranges of values. Consequently, the basic arithmetic operations performed by the device experts are modified to accommodate the tolerances associated with each measurement and circuit parameter. Inducing these problems reflects our concern for being able to coach the student as he works on real, physical circuits.

There are a variety of ways to introduce tolerances into the propagated quantities. SOPHIE III utilizes a very simple scheme, representing each quantity by a range indicating its extreme values. A range Q is described by $[Q_L, Q_H]$ which indicates $Q_L \leq Q \leq Q_H$. No probability distributions are maintained. Consider the example of a resistor expert. If we know the current through a resistor is between 2.9 amperes and 3.1 amperes ($I = [2.9, 3.1]$), and its resistance is 100 ohms with a 10% tolerance ($R = [90, 110]$), Ohm's Law tells us that the voltage across the resistor must be between 261 and 310 volts ($V = IR = [2.9, 3.1] \times [90, 110] = [261, 341]$).

By using range notation, a great deal of additional knowledge can be included in the device models. For example, knowledge that the current through a diode is always positive can be expressed by the range $[0, \infty]$. To prevent problems incurred by using ranges, two modifications must be introduced to the simple propagation scheme: first, propagations with very wide ranges must be stopped; and second, new values which are only marginally better (only marginally narrower ranges) than old ones must be ignored since they probably are the result of iteration.

4.2.4 Passive Troubleshooting

In addition to simple propagation, two other kinds of knowledge are required to troubleshoot. The first, which might be called "passive troubleshooting" is concerned with gathering information about the correctness of components from measurements. The second, "active troubleshooting" knowledge is needed to choose new measurements to make. In SOPHIE III the passive troubleshooting knowledge is incorporated into LOCAL as an extension of the propagator. The active troubleshooting is implemented with an independent articulate expert, and is parasitic on the entire electronics expert; it will be discussed later.

4.2.4.1 Coincidences, conflicts and corroborations

In this section we develop a simple but general strategy for deducing the correctness of circuit components based on information obtained by the propagation. We assume that the error in the circuit is that some component is not functioning according to its specifications, that the overall circuit was correctly designed, that the circuit contains no wiring errors, and that the circuit contains only one fault.

The discovery of a known value for a point for which we already know a predicted, propagated value is called a *coincidence*. When the two values are equal, we call the coincidence a *corroboration* — when they differ we call it a *conflict*. Coincidences provide information about the assumptions made in the propagation: Corroborations verify them and conflicts indicate at least one of them is in error. This simplistic notion must be substantially adapted before it can be useful in actual troubleshooting.

Its difficulty is that corroborations do not always imply that the components involved in the derivation are unfaulted. A component should only be considered unfaulted as a consequence of a corroboration if a fault in it would significantly modify its propagated values. This is not, in general, the case. The two most common exceptions occur when the circuit isn't manifesting a symptom or when a particular propagation does not depend significantly on one of its underlying assumptions.

Although a component is faulted, the overall system may still be functioning correctly. (The fault may only manifest itself under certain load conditions, for example.) Therefore a corroboration provides no information if the system is not manifesting a symptom under the specified external conditions (e.g., load and control settings).

The system may be exhibiting a symptom, but the way the faulted component causing the symptom is used in a particular propagation may not be significant. This occurs most commonly when a large quantity is added to a small quantity since the range of the large quantity completely swamps the contribution of the smaller quantity. A similar situation arises when the propagation multiplies an input value by zero. A propagation which uses the same component twice is also suspect since the two uses may cancel each other out. We call those assumptions which corroborations remove from suspicion primary assumptions, and those that do not, the secondary assumptions.

If all propagations consisted of simple arithmetic operations these rules would suffice to distinguish between primary and secondary assumptions. There is, however,

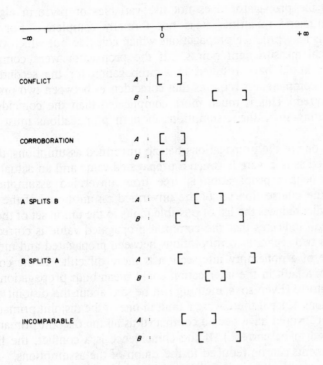

FIG. 4.4. Range Comparisons

one other kind of propagation which is based on a comparison of quantities. For instance, a transistor model may test the base-emitter voltage to check whether it is below a certain threshold and if so, conclude that the transistor must be off and therefore have zero collector current. If the base-emitter voltage is propagated to be some value below this threshold, the collector current being independently determined to be zero is not sufficient to corroborate the assumptions since the base voltage could be quite different (but below the threshold) without affecting the collector current.   The assumptions underlying comparison to thresholds must, of necessity, always be secondary.

It is fairly easy to record and summarize the results of coincidences.   A corroboration removes from suspicion all the primary assumptions. Similarly, a conflict removes from suspicion all assumptions not mentioned in the instigating propagation.   The summary of all the coincidences is the union set of all the components removed from suspicion.

4.2.4.2 Consequences of ranges on coincidences

A comparison between two ranges can have one of five results (see Fig. 4.4): (1) values contradict, (2) values corroborate, (3) first value splits second, (4) second value splits first, and (5) no comparison possible†.

Because the propagator does not use variables or perform algebra but only propagates numeric quantities it is not formally complete. For example, two measurements may produce propagations which coincide but which do not coincide at the original measurement points. If the propagator were complete, the first measurement would have resulted in a propagation for the second measurement point. This incompleteness requires that coincidences between two propagations also need to analyzed. This is much more complicated than the coincidences we have been considering since the assumptions of both propagations must be taken into account.

If either one of the propagations has no unverified assumptions, the coincidence can be handled as if it were between a propagated value and an actual measurement. However, if neither propagation is free from unverified assumptions the result depends on the intersection set of the unverified assumptions. If the intersection is empty, a conflict reduces the list of possible faults to the union set of the assumptions; a corroboration indicates that the common propagated value is correct, and can be considered as two separate corroborations between propagated and measured values.

The case of a nonempty intersection is more difficult. If the coincidence is a corroboration, a fault in the intersection could mean both propagations are incorrect yet corroboratory. (Even so, something can be said about the disjoint assumptions in the propagations, since if there were a fault in one of the disjoint primary assumptions the coincidence would have been a conflict; thus all the disjoint primary assumptions can be verified to be correct.) If the coincidence is a conflict, the list of possibly faulty components can be reduced to the union of the assumptions.

It is very tempting to remove from suspicion all components mentioned in the intersection, just as in the case of a conflict, and claim that correct propagations from a single (albeit incorrect) value must always corroborate each other; or, equivalently, that each point in the circuit has only two values associated with it — a correct value and a faulted value predicted by the propagator. Unfortunately, the claim is not valid.

4.2.4.3 Component Fault Modes

The theory of coincidences makes no presuppositions about the kinds of fault modes in which a component can be. But physical structure dictates that each component can only be faulted in a small number of characteristic ways. Since fault modes are not arbitrary and each fault mode has a distinct affect on propagations through the faulty component, a great deal more information about a component's faultedness can be obtained from propagations and coincidences. One very powerful strategy, called *conflict-trace*, examines the conflicting propagations to identify what

†The last alternative indicates that it is sometimes useful to propagate two independent values for the same quantity. The splitting possibilities can be intelligently dealt with. If the value for A splits the value for B, then if A is valid, B must be valid (though not vice-versa). For example, since A:[3 , 4] splits B:[0 , 10], the validity of A implies the validity of B. But if B were valid, A might be [7 , 8], still spliting B but contradicting with the original [3 , 4]. If A is not known to be valid, we must wait till it is proven before using this information. However, in a single-fault theory a very interesting deduction can still be made for this case: Every assumption of B which does not occur in A is corroborated. A split is just a kind of corroboration in which one of the propagations is much stronger than the other.

fault modes could have caused the particular conflict. Often, although a component may participate in the conflict, there is no fault mode in which it could cause the symptom, thus it must be blameless. Common fault modes for components are:

RESISTOR	open, shorted, high or low.
CAPACITOR	shorted or leaky.
DIODE	open or shorted.
ZENER DIODE	breakdownhigh or breakdownlow.
TRANSISTOR	beta-low, beta-high, all-junctions-open, ...

(The transistor has so many possible fault modes that it is impossible to choose succinct labels for each.)

Each component fault mode is characterized by a particular behavior. LOCAL does not utilize propagation models for the behavior of fault modes; instead, it has a collection of deduction strategies to detect what fault mode a component is in. Each of these deduction strategies is based on the common behavioral model of each device. There are four basic fault-detection strategies, each of which either is an integral part of the propagator, or examines the justifications for the propagations generated. *Excess* deductions result from LOCAL propagating into a component a voltage or current which drastically exceeds its rating, thereby indicating that it could be in a particular fault mode. *Inconsistent* deductions serve to rule out component fault modes whose behavior is inconsistent with the propagations. *Behavior* deductions are more subtle, and are based on the assumption that if a component is faulted and the overall circuit is manifesting a symptom, the faulty component must be manifesting a symptom. The *conflict-trace* strategy, unlike the previous three, does not participate in the propagations.

The conflict-trace inference strategy is the most complex of the four fault-mode detection strategies. It is a separate deduction mechanism independent of the propagator which is only invoked when a conflict or excess deduction determines some propagation to be high or low. Suppose that through a long propagation chain, we determine the current through a resistor and use Ohm's Law to predict the voltage across it. A subsequent measurement indicates this predicted voltage is too low. If the resistor is truly faulted, its resistance must be too high or be open. On the other hand, if it is not faulted the current supplied to it must have been too low; the process then recurses examining the component that was used to deduce that high current. (In either case, the resistor cannot be in the fault modes shorted or low.) For a single conflict, this technique will rarely verify more components, but it will always rule out faulted modes for each component involved.

One of the advantages of employing the fault modes is that more information can be gained from multiple conflicts: One conflict may indicate that if the resistor is faulted it must be high or open while another indicates that if the resistor is faulted it must be low or shorted. The combination of these two conflicts indicate the resistor is unfaulted.

In any justification each component expert has recorded how each component contributes to the propagation. This information can be used to determine the fault mode of the component, or which erroneous input propagations (if any) could cause the observed symptoms. Consider the example of a high voltage deduced by applying Ohm's Law. The resistor expert will have recorded the justification of the voltage with an annotation that it used a current to deduce a voltage by Ohm's Law. The necessary conflict-trace rule is: "All current-to-voltage propagations, produced by a resistor, that are too high indicate either that the resistor is shorted or low, or that the resistor's input current is too high."

The conflict-trace deductions are performed by a separate propagator which, instead of propagating ranges, through the circuit topology, propagates the tokens "high" and "low" through the justification of the problematic propagation. The tokens refer to whether the propagation is higher or lower (the ranges do not overlap) than was actually measured. The potential difficulty is that, if a component occurs more than once, it is not easy to tell which contribution dominates. To avoid this problem, LOCAL performs the entire conflict-trace deduction as one unit, identifying which fault modes on which components could have caused the observed symptoms and localizing the fault to the union of these. Thus, if the same resistor occurs twice in the same conflict, one explained by high or open and the other explained by low or shorted, no deduction about that resistor will be made other than it is under suspicion.

4.2.4.4 The Model for a Diode

Although every component of a given type behaves in the same basic way, the fine details of its behavior are controlled by its parameters. These parameters are determined by the manufacturer, not by the component's use in the circuit. For example, every resistor obeys Ohm's Law, but with varying resistance. The model for the diode is specified by eight parameters, each parameter is listed with its value for D6:

I_{MIN} : the maximum allowable reverse current flow, -1 microampere.
I_{MAX} : the maximum allowable forward current flow, 1 ampere.
V_{MIN} : the minimum voltage across the diode, -50 volts.
V_{MAX} : the maximum voltage across the diode, .8 volts.
I_{OFF} : defines the diode OFF state, 1 microampere.
I_{ON} : defines the diode ON state, 2 microamperes.
V_{OFF} : defines the diode OFF state, .3 volts.
V_{ON} : defines the diode ON state, .45 volts.

These parameters are used by the diode expert to propagate new currents and voltages. If a newly discovered voltage is less than the threshold required to turn on the diode, the diode cannot be conducting very much current; on the other hand, if the new voltage indicates the diode is on, the diode must be conducting a significant amount of current:

A new voltage $V = [V_L, V_H]$ causes the propagation: If $V_H \leq V_{OFF}$, propagate the range $I = [-\infty, I_{ON}]$, otherwise if $V_L \geq V_{OFF}$ propagate the range $I = [I_{ON}, +\infty]$.

FIG. 4.5. Diode Voltage Parameters

(Note that we could not even express this rule without ranges.)

The propagations which result from a new current are analogous:

A new current $I = [I_L, I_H]$ causes the propagation: If $I_H \leq I_{OFF}$, propagate the range $V = [-\infty, V_{OFF}]$, otherwise if $I_L \geq I_{ON}$ propagate the range $V = [V_{ON}, +\infty]$.

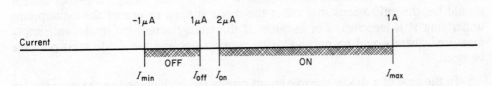

FIG. 4.6. Diode Current Parameters

Components have certain maximum limits which cannot be exceeded without destruction. These limits have three effects: They modify the above propagations, allow the model to explicitly detect faulty behavior, and allow some ranges to be propagated before any measurement is made. Wherever $+\infty$ or $-\infty$ appears in the above rules, they should therefore be replaced with the appropriate maximum or minimum parameter. Potentially faulty behavior can be detected by comparing the new propagation with the diode's maximum specifications:

If $I_H \leq I_{MIN}$ the diode must be shorted or I must be too low (I has a lower value than it should have). If $I_L \geq I_{MAX}$ the diode must be shorted or I is too high. If $V_L \geq V_{MAX}$ the diode must be open or $V = $ high.

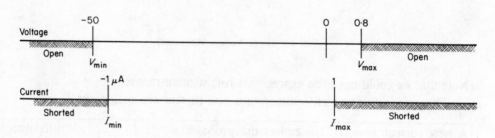

F$_{IG}$. 4.7. Diode Ratings

The expressions "I = high" and "V = high" indicate that a conflict-trace model must be applied to whichever component deduced the voltage or current that triggered the diode expert. The disjunction in the rule "If $V_L \geq V_{MAX}$ the diode must be open or V = high" states that one of "diode is open" or "V = high" must be true. Since "V = high" indicates the propagated value for the voltage is higher than it should be, this rule asserts that either the diode is open or one of the assumptions underlying V is incorrect. For instance, if the voltage across the diode was simply measured, there would be no underlying assumptions and the diode must perforce be open.

In the case of a diode, the maximum ranges can be included in the propagation database before any measurements are made.

Certain propagations are inconsistent with the diode being in a particular fault mode. If the voltage across a diode is greater than zero, it cannot be shorted since the definition of shorted is that the voltage across the diode is zero. Similarly if the current through a diode is greater than zero it cannot be open.

If $V_L \geq .1$ the diode cannot be shorted. If $I_L \geq I_{OFF}$, the diode cannot be open.

The behavioral deductions from a propagation are based on the assumption that the circuit contains only one fault and that it is currently manifesting a symptom. If the voltage across the diode is less than some maximum, the diode cannot be open since it cannot be causing a symptom. If the current through the diode is less than enough to warrant it being considered on, it cannot be shorted since if it were shorted and causing a symptom it would be conducting a significant amount of current.

If $V_H \leq V_{MAX}$ then the diode cannot be open. If $I_H \leq I_{ON}$ then the diode cannot be shorted.

When the value propagated by the diode leads to a later conflict, the fact that the propagation was high or low can be used to determine the fault modes in which the diode could be. The diode model can make six different propagations: (1) from a new voltage deduce that the diode is on and propagate the corresponding current, (2) from a new voltage, deduce that the diode is off and propagate the corresponding current, (3) from a new current, deduce that the diode is off and propagate the corresponding voltage, (4) from a new current, deduce that the diode is on and propagate the corresponding voltage, (5) add extreme maximum and minimum voltages to the propagation database before any measurements are performed, (6) add extreme initial maximum and minimum currents.

The conflict-trace rules associated with each of these six propagations are very complex, and therefore we have included only the one; for the first case (1). This conflict-trace rule will presume all the preceding diode rules. If the current propagated by the diode model is high (i.e., the predicted is higher than the measured), the diode must be shorted since the current flowing through it must be less than I_{MIN}. No erroneous value of the voltage propagated into the diode can cause this symptom since there is no valid region of operation in which the diode current is less than I_{MIN} (I_{MIN} is negative, and represents the maximum reverse current flow).

On the other hand, if the propagated current flowing through the diode is low (i.e., the predicted is lower than the measured), the diode must be shorted, or the voltage across the diode is high (indicating that the diode is off rather than it being on).

For the propagation $V \rightarrow I$ diode off: If $I = $ high, diode must be shorted, and symptom cannot be caused by V. If $I = $ low, diode must be shorted, or $V = $ high.

The diode being open never arises since a voltage low enough to indicate the diode is off will also trigger the behavioral deduction that the diode cannot be open.

4.2.5 Coaching and Active Troubleshooting

The articulate electronics expert makes predictions (propagations) from student measurements deduces their effect on the faultedness of circuit components. These deductions form the basis from which the coach monitors the student's troubleshooting progress. LOCAL might discover that the student consistently made redundant measurements indicating his lack of understanding about how a transistor operates. The coach might ask the student, following some measurement, whether some component was faulted and so discover whether the student understood corroborations. Coaching interactions such as this are supported by the deductions of the electronics expert. However, the skill of troubleshooting is not as much concerned with the consequences of measurements as it is with the choice of which measurement to make. SOPHIE III's coach must be able to comment on the quality of the student's measurements, as well as to suggest new ones. To this end, SOPHIE III employs a second expert, the articulate troubleshooting expert. Although the troubleshooting expert and the electronics expert construct a database of the deductions necessary to support coaching interactions, the coaching expert was never fully implemented. Instead SOPHIE III employed a skeletal coach which served mainly to suggest the kinds of coaching interactions that might be possible.

The skeletal coach of SOPHIE III always answers the student's questions, but can only initiate interactions just after the student states his choice of measurement, and again just after he obtains its results. Some measurements automatically can be determined to be uninteresting since they involve a coincidence with a narrow numeric range, based on verified assumptions. In such cases the coach will point out to the student that the measurement would be uninteresting, and the student can then inquire about the details. On the other hand, if the measurement is interesting, it is guaranteed to propagate new voltages and currents which may or may not remove more components from suspicion.

In order to determine the quality of a measurement, SOPHIE III requires a theory of troubleshooting. The goal of troubleshooting is to remove as many components from suspicion as efficiently as possible. Thus, the basic dimension by which to judge the quality of a student's measurement is the number of new components it removes from suspicion (easily determined by the articulate electronics expert). The coach should not critique a student measurement though, solely on this basis; it should only critique if it knows of some more informative measurement.

Measurements are evaluated by hypothesizing their coincidences with propagations. The quality (score) of the potential measurement is the *expected* number of components that it would remove from suspicion. The expected value is the sum of two products: — the number of components that would be verified by a corroboration times the probability of a corroboration, plus the number of components that would be verified by a conflict times the probability of a conflict. The student is therefore critiqued only if he makes a measurement with a score significantly lower than optimum, and is complimented if he makes a near-optimal measurement.

A surprising feature of this coaching strategy is that the student may be critiqued even if he makes a measurement that verifies more components than the optimal measurement would. For example, he might make one measurement which localizes the fault to forty components, then make a second measurement (which causes a conflict) which localizes the fault to one component. If a corroboration would have verified only one component, the choice of measurement is a very poor one (there was only a slim probability that the component was at fault). The student could be critiqued for his successful measurement — it was pure luck that he found the fault, since the expected value of that measurement was low.

The troubleshooting expert can also be used to make measurement suggestions when the student asks for them. It is a simple matter to identify the measurement with the best score. The explanation for the proposed measurement is simply a description of what components the coincidence could potentially verify and why. This measurement-suggestion mechanism can be used as a troubleshooter in its own right, with the student merely making the measurements, watching the expert explain the reason for the measurement, and explaining its consequences.

The coaching strategy presented thus far is not very good. This simple coach presumes to know all there is to know about electronics and presumes to have a totally accurate model of the student at all times. Unfortunately, because the electronics expert is far from exhaustive, a student who appears "lucky" may just, in fact, be smarter than the computer-based expert. A more conservative critiquing strategy would be to only critique the measurement if the hypothesized outcome matched. A less devastating, but nonetheless serious, problem is that during the early phases of troubleshooting the propagator may not know of hypothetical measurements that are close to the theoretical optimum. Before the first conflict the list of suspect components contains approximately all the components in the circuit. A near-optimal measurement, which should coincide with a propagation that uses half the components, is unlikely that such propagations would occur. On the other hand, once a single conflict is found, optimal measurements can be found which coincide with subpropagations (e.g., intermediate propagations halfway between the original measurements and the site of a conflict) of the conflicting propagations.

Aside from the fact that the expert does not make all possible inferences nor construct an adequate model of the student's capabilities, there are a variety of better coaching strategies available. For example, the coach might question the student when the expert discovers some important result in order to check whether the student has made the same deduction. Whenever the student makes a measurement which appears suboptimal, the coach could begin questioning the student about which components were faulted, and so diagnose which troubleshooting strategies the student does not understand.

4.2.6 The Need for Higher-Level Knowledge

There are still serious difficulties in tracking the troubleshooting of the student; this is particularly evident early in a debugging scenario. The first measurement, one even a neophyte debugger would perform, is to measure the output. This is probably the single most informative measurement he can make, LOCAL can do nothing with it. Only after the student has made a number of measurements can enough values be propagated· to derive some useful coincidences. In this opening sequence, the troubleshooter, no matter what is skill level, is basing his measurements on a different theory than the one LOCAL is using.

The expert is missing all the the attributes of "understanding how the circuit works." It does not understand the causality or the teleology of the circuit; in fact it does not even have a hierarchical description of the functional components. It employs a myopic local view of the circuit and thus fails to encompass the global mechanism through which the circuit functions. Its myopic view is only appropriate when the fault has been isolated to some module or group of components; it is entirely inappropriate for making initial measurements.

Our current state of knowledge about causal and teleological reasoning is of insufficient depth to permit their inclusion in the expert in a general way. Instead, we summarize the results of such reasoning and use these to make deductions. This new knowledge, unlike the propagator, is circuit-specific and must be changed for every new circuit SOPHIE III encounters. There are two principles we employ to encode this circuit-specific knowledge. First, we impose a strict discipline upon its form, making addition, modification and explanation of higher-level knowledge easier. Second, the propagator and its underlying mechanisms for handling assumptions and fault modes are used as a way of simplifying the deductions that the higher-level knowledge needs to make. Consider a simple example, suppose we had the rule "if output voltage is low, the regulator is shorted." The output voltage can be determined in a number of ways, one of which is by measuring the current in the load and using Ohm's Law to determine the voltage across it. The rule tells us that if the voltage is directly measured to be low, the regulator must be shorted. If the current is measured to be low, then either the regulator is shorted or the load is open or high. By utilizing the propagator and using the assumptions of the propagation (in this example, that the resistance of the load hasn't changed) to modify the consequences of the higher-order rules we need only one rule to handle both of these circumstances.

In addition to losing generality, we also lose some capacity to make intelligent explanations since the higher-level rules are made by the person who constructs the rules and not by LOCAL. Fortunately, there are four effects that mitigate this loss. First, the rules are relatively primitive, and thus any particular troubleshooting deduction will use a sequence of them, thus admitting a kind of deductive argument but with prestored explanation for each step in the sequence. Second, the rigid discipline on the form of the higher-order rules makes it much easier to impose a coherent structure on the rules. Third, the use of the propagator limits the necessary rules to a small essential core. Fourth, whatever contributions LOCAL makes to each deduction can be completely explained in terms of general electronic laws.

Although a circuit is constructed from components, it is more easily understood as consisting of a small number of interacting modules which in turn, consist of other modules. All of the circuit-specific knowldge is organized around these modules and their behaviors. The hierarchy of modules of a circuit are represented by a tree, the root of which is the circuit itself, the nodes of which are its modules and submodules, and the leaves of which are its components. Reasoning about module behaviors is of three types. First, a module's behavior is determined by the voltages and currents on module ports noted by LOCAL. Second, its behavior has implications for its submodules and parent modules. Third, the behavior of one module can causally affect the behavior of a neighboring one. The first kind of reasoning is implemented with a quantitative-qualitative map and a collection of rules for maping qualitative circuit values to module behaviors. The second is implemented by an inheritance mechanism called the behavior-tree. And the third is handled by a modification of the same rule-based system which detects module behaviors.

4.2.6.1 Module modes

Just like components, modules can be considered to have behavioral modes. One of the advantages of employing module behaviors is that they refer to "natural" internal states. These states must always be deducible by considering the module as a black box and looking at its input-output behavior. The identification of the "natural" module modes is a difficult process. One major difficulty is that modules usually have four or more terminals, while components usually have only two. To circumvent this difficulty, the mode of a module is directly identified with its behavior on one chosen port. For example, the mode of the constant current source is determined by its output voltage and current.† The modes used in SOPHIE III were chosen on the basis of simplicity, and the majority of them have only one or two (high and low) faulted modes. The exact choice of modes does not matter much, but it is critical that the different reasoning strategies which utilize modes agree upon the behavioral meaning of a module's modes, otherwise SOPHIE III will encounter irreconcilable contradictions.

A module is operating in a faulted mode if it is exhibiting the symptom specified by the semantics of the mode description and contains a fault causing that symptom. A module which contains no faults is by definition operating in a valid mode. A module can be exhibiting the symptoms of a faulted mode, yet be in a valid mode because some component external to the module faults‡. The possible fault modes need not be disjoint. Also the same component fault can cause two different behaviors depending on the precise shift in parameter value and the control settings.

Knowing a module's behavior provides information about its parent and constituent modules behaviors. These necessary deductions are not easy; a given constituent behavior can produce different behaviors in the parent, and even the same component fault mode may cause different module behaviors. The reasons for this difficulty are that component fault modes are not totally specified (e.g., R8 being high can mean R8 has a resistance between 3 and ∞ ohms) and that different control settings can cause the same component fault to manifest slightly different circuit symptoms. The knowledge engineer must construct a circuit-specific knowledge structure which indicates how each module's behavior contributes to the behaviors of its parent. We call this structure the behavior-tree (although it is really a lattice). Every node in the behavior-tree corresponds to a behavior mode of a module. The downward edges (see Fig. 4.8) from a node correspond to the behaviors of its submodules that could cause the node's own behavior; the upward edges from a node correspond to the parent behaviors that the node can cause.

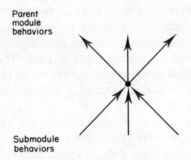

Parent module behaviors

Submodule behaviors

FIG. 4.8. A Node in the Behavior Tree

The terminals of the behavior tree are the fault modes of the components.

†Because we have no principled way of choosing the behaviors, some care must be taken since the extreme case is a one-to-one mapping of faulty module behaviors to constituent component faults.

‡This could be more general. We should include the possibility that a module may be faulted but not manifesting any symptom.

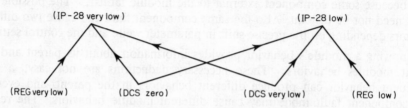

FIG. 4.9. Part of the IP-28 Behavior-Tree

A node in the behavior tree is completely specified by the module name and the mode it is in which can be abbreviated (<module> <mode>). Fig. 4.9 describes a small part of the IP-28 behavior-tree.

The behavior (IP-28 very-low) can be caused by (REG very-low), (DCS zero), or (DCS very-low). The behavior (IP-28 low) can be caused by (DCS zero), (DCS very-low), or (REG low). Note that (DCS zero) and (DCS very-low) can cause both (IP-28 very-low) or (IP-28 low).

The following sections will describe an inference strategy which uses the behavior-tree to deduce new module behaviors. The knowledge engineer need not be aware of this mechanism, but he must obey certain constraints when constructing the behavior-tree if this mechanism is going to be effective. The basic constraint is that the behavior-tree must be complete, so that anything not mentioned in the behavior-tree can be assumed to be impossible or false. The behavior tree must:

(1) Include every possible mode a module can be in (faulty and valid).

(2) Show every faulty behavior as causing at least one other faulty behavior (except for the overall module).

(3) Include all possible ways in which a module can affect a parent.

(4) Include every fault of every component†.

These constraints are important since they, in effect, imply that the behavior-tree and its module behaviors have a distinct unique meaning.

4.2.6.2 Detecting a module's behavioral mode

All of LOCAL's deductions are constantly monitored to see if some module's behavior is yet known. This monitoring process consists of two stages. The first

†Some faults immediately cause others, so these are left out of the tree by the single fault presuppostion.

detects interesting values discovered by LOCAL and adds these to a qualitative database, and the second uses this database to make assertions about module behaviors.

The propagator watches module ports and when voltages and currents are discovered it adds the qualitative values, corresponding to their ranges, to the database. This correspondence is specified by a translation table indicating what numeric values correspond to which qualitative value. Since the propagator uses ranges, some values may overlap more than one qualitative value. To handle this case, the electronics expert computes the intersection of the results that the each of the overlapping values individually.

As an example, consider the watch-point at the output of the IP-28 voltage reference (the voltage between nodes N11 and N14). The translation table is (high $\geq$ 31.0 $\geq$ eq $\geq$ 27.0 $\geq$ low). The numbers in the table delineate the different qualitative ranges. If the voltage is above 31.0 volts (VOLTAGE (N11 N14) high) will be added to the qualitative data base. If the voltage lies between 31 and 27, (VOLTAGE (N11 N14) eq) is asserted. The voltage [30 , 32] overlaps high and eq, so this voltage results in the assertion (VOLTAGE (N11 N14) (OR high eq)). This disjunction is handled by first deducing all of the consequences of (VOLTAGE (N11 N14) high) and then all of the consequences of (VOLTAGE (N11 N14) eq), and only permanently recording those consequences which are common to both. SOPHIE III employs 12 other watch-points to model the IP-28.

The detection rules which trigger on the qualitative database assertions need not pinpoint the exact behavioral mode of the module. They can determine that the module is in one of a set of possible modes (a localization), or determine that the module cannot be in some mode (an elimination). The mechanism for localizing and eliminating module behaviors is analogous to those used to deal with the fault modes of components: A deduction cannot eliminate a faulty behavior if the module contains a component about which the deduction makes an assumption.

The detection rules can also trigger on the states of components. Semiconductor components can have many states, each modelled by a distinctly different characteristic behavior. The component experts add their state into the qualitative database.

Module behaviors are not disjoint. Thus, it is not only necessary to know all the possible behaviors of a module, but also which behaviors are inconsistent with each other. For example, the regulator behavior low is inconsistent with behavior high, but not with behavior very-low. As with component fault modes, all localizations are transformed to the equivalent eliminations and recorded as such. Components are treated as degenerate modules whose behaviors correspond to the modes of its single constituents.

The rules for the variable voltage reference of the IP-28 are:

```
(VOLTAGE (N11 N14) HIGH) -> (LOCALIZE VARIABLE/REF high ok)
(VOLTAGE (N11 N14) EQ) ->  (LOCALIZE VARIABLE/REF ok)
(VOLTAGE (N11 N14) LOW) -> (LOCALIZE VARIABLE/REF low)
```

Ok is added in the first case because the IP-28 voltage-reference is designed to actively correct a low voltage on its output terminal, but not a high voltage. Thus if a low voltage appears, the voltage reference must be faulted, but if a high voltage appears some external module could also be supplying a voltage to its port. This latter

274 J. S. BROWN, R. R. BURTON AND J. DE KLEER

possibility never arises in normal operation, but can in faulty operation.

4.2.6.3 Reasoning with the Behavior-Tree

The behavior-tree is used by SOPHIE III to make inferences about module behaviors. The inference mechanism operates solely on a database which records the eliminated behavioral modes of modules. All localizations are converted to their equivalent eliminations so we need only consider inferences resulting from an elimination. The underlying idea is that when a faulty behavior is eliminated it can no longer cause, or be caused by any other behaviors. Eliminating a node involves searching up and down the behavior-tree for other behaviors to eliminate. If a faulty node is eliminated, the nodes below it can no longer be the cause; each of these lower nodes is examined to see whether it can still cause any other behavior, and if not, it too is eliminated. Analogously, if a mode is eliminated it can no longer cause any of its parents, so each parent behavior it can cause is examined to see whether it still can be caused by another behavior, and if not it too can be eliminated. One elimination can thus recursively generate many more. If all possible faulty behaviors of a module are eliminated, the module cannot be faulted.

Elimination and localization of valid behaviors are handled similarly, although more simply. While a faulty behavior can be caused by a faulty behavior in any one of the submodules, a valid behavior only results if all of the submodules are behaving validly. Thus the elimination of a valid node has no direct consequences on the nodes below it since the elimination of any one of these subnodes alone would be sufficient to eliminate the node itself. On the other hand, when a valid mode is eliminated its parent node cannot happen unless it could also be caused by an alternative valid mode of the module. If all possible valid behaviors are eliminated, the module must be faulted.

The remaining kinds of inferences are concerned with handling deductions about faultedness in general. If a module is determined to contain a fault, all of its parent modules are, by definition, also faulted. Since a particular faulty mode need not be known, this is achieved by eliminating all of the valid modes of the parent modules. Under the single-fault assumption and the fact that modules do not overlap, any sibling modules are automatically unfaulted. These mechanisms are sufficient to handle all the necessary deductions about behaviors. Consider the rule that if a module is unfaulted, all of its submodules are unfaulted. This is a simple consequence of the fact that all of its faulty behaviors have been eliminated and therefore its submodules have no possible faulty behaviors either. Similarly, if a parent module is known to contain a fault, and only one of its siblings can still contain a fault, that sibling contains the fault.

The propagations which cause the original elimination may have underlying assumptions which modify the consequent eliminations and localizations. These assumptions must be carried along during the recursive eliminations and localizations, continuously enforcing the restriction that an elimination of a faulty mode cannot depend on an assumption about the module in question. Eliminations of valid modes can, of course, depend on the module itself. When an illegal elimination of a faulty behavior occurs, the recursive eliminations are still attempted. The underlying assumptions may refer to only some of the components of the module, in which case the elimination will still lead to deductions about that part of the module which does not overlap with the underlying assumptions of the original elimination.

4.2.6.4 Non-hierarchical interactions

By far the majority of SOPHIE III's circuit-specific rules detect module modes. The behavior-tree, unfortunately, only captures hierarchical module interactions, and thus fails to capture many of the causal interactions between same-level modules. The state-to-state rules used by SOPHIE III, which are used to handle this latter case, can be divided into three categories. The first kind of rule, and also the most common, deduces that a module's neighbours are unfaulted when the module itself is unfaulted. The second identifies the causes for why a module behaves sympomatically, even though unfaulted. The third is a particularly inelegant type of rule that eliminates faulted modes of modules which are topologically distant from the watchpoint. We have tried to avoid rules of this last sort, but SOPHIE III employs three of them to capture the global interactions of non-neighbouring modules†.

The first kind of state-to-state rule concerning correct behavior, concentrates on determining neighbors to be correct. Often, when a module is discovered to be unfaulted and behaving normally (as distinguished from being unfaulted but behaving symptomatically) its "suppliers" and "consumers" can also be determined to be behaving normally, and hence to be unfaulted. Consider an example from the IP-28. The constant-voltage reference of this power-supply (see Fig. 4.3) consists of a raw DC voltage which is first regulated to 56 volts and then regulated down to 36 volts. The only supplier of power to the 36-volt regulator is the 56-volt regulator, and the only consumer of the 56 volt output is the 36-volt regulator. If voltage of the second reference is 36 volts, it is operating normally and unfaulted, and the 56-volt regulator must be unfaulted and operating normally. So the module-detection rule,

(VOLTAGE (N11 N16) EQ) -> (LOCALIZE 36V/REG operating-ok)

triggers the state-to-state rule,

(36V/REG operating-ok) -> (LOCALIZE 56V/REG operating-ok),

which, in turn, triggers the state-to-state rule,

(56V/REG operating-ok) -> (LOCALIZE LQ/DCS operating-ok).

(The LQ/DCS is the source of raw unregulated DC for the reference.)

The second type of state-to-state rule is somewhat analogous except that it is concerned with the faulty behavior that can be caused by neighbouring *faulty* behaviors. Consider the voltage-reference example again. If the output of the 36-volt regulator is low it is either faulted, being supplied with a bad signal (the 56-volt regulator is low), or being presented a bad load (the output filter of the voltage reference is shorted). Earlier we presented the mode-detection rule as:

---

† To some extent, all of the rules are inelegant. If we were going to allow circuit-specific knowledge it would have been more parsimonious to construct a qualitative causal model of the circuit which could be used to derive the state-to-state rules. Unfortunately we were unable to do so. It should be noted, however, that the reason so many rules are required (39, including the detection rules) is that we needed to track a student's potentially pathological measurements. If we were solely concerned with optimal troubleshooting, a dozen of the detection rules would have been sufficient.

(VOLTAGE (N11 N16) low) -> (LOCALIZE 36V/REG low ok),
but to facilitate the propagation rules we write it as,

(VOLTAGE (N11 N16) low) -> (BEHAVIOR 36V/REG low)

The effect is the same, except that the module-mode propagation rule can now trigger on the BEHAVIOR assertions:

(BEHAVIOR 36V/REG low) -> (BEHAVIOR 56V/REG low)
...

The effects of these rules can propagate through neighbouring modules, .e.g.,

(BEHAVIOR 56V/REG low) -> (BEHAVIOR LQ/DCS low).

These type of rules are powerful because they allow us to conclude, after all the possible BEHAVIOR rules have applied, that any module not mentioned in a behavior assertion must be unfaulted. This follows from our requirement that every possible cause for a module's faulty behavior must be included in the rule set. In effect, we have a disjunctive localize, e.g., the above example becomes a (OR (LOCALIZE 56V/REG low) (LOCALIZE 36V/REG low) (LOCALIZE LQ/DCS zero) (LOCALIZE VC/POT low) ...).

The third and last type of state-to-state rule is an exception rule to handle the cases which do not fit either of the previous two patterns. They are all of the form:

<measurement> -> (ELIMINATE <module> <mode>).

This pattern is the same as that for the module mode detection rules, but unlike those rules, the measurement takes place away from an input-output port of the module. For example, one of the three such rules for the IP-28 is:

(VOLTAGE (N11 N14) EQ) -> (ELIMINATE Q5 sh/op/op).

(The transistor mode sh/op/op is the collector open, and the base shorted to the emitter.) There are two components between Q5 (see Fig. 4.10) and either of nodes N11 and N14. Unfortunately, this rather inelegant rule is needed. This particular fault mode for Q5 makes the voltage regulator inoperative, and also shorts the output of the· voltage reference to the output of the overall power-supply. The voltage reference is very weak, so the main power-supply will dominate. Thus, if the output of the voltage-reference is normal, Q5 must not be shorted in this way. (If it were, it would not be voltage regulating, causing the voltage across the reference to be high.) This is a very subtle inference which would not be generally possible without a rather sophisticated causal and teological model of the IP-28.

4.2.6.5 Troubleshooting with circuit-specific knowledge

Although the inferences made by the circuit-specific knowledge are more powerful than LOCAL's, their structure is simpler. All circuit-specific knowledge can be reduced to a collection of if-then rules making it easy to calculate the consequences of hypothetical measurements. The same techniques for using the general knowledge to score measurements apply to the circuit-specific knowledge. Recall that the best strategy is to identify a measurement with the maximum expected information value. The scores of each of the measurements considered by the general troubleshooter are augmented by the information gained from ensuing circuit-specific deductions. In addition, measurements at each of the watch-points in the circuit's translation table are considered and their expected value computed. Thus SOPHIE III can troubleshoot the instrument by itself. Early in the troubleshooting the measurements at module ports will have higher scores (at the watch-points); later in the troubleshooting the scores for hypothetical coincidences with propagations will be higher.

The troubleshooting coaching strategy remains unchanged. However, the computation of expected values by the troubleshooting expert must be extended further than just the addition of circuit-specific knowledge seems to suggest. Consider the case where the student makes a measurement which is neither at a watch-point, nor at an earlier propagation. Such measurements can be useful when they propagate into a watch-point (which happens fairly often because the student's opinion of the module boundaries differs from the expert's). Because only the expected value is of any use, SOPHIE III computes an approximation to the expected value of the student's measurement by hypothesizing different outcomes. Since SOPHIE III does not use this expensive strategy to evaluate the other hypothetical measurements, its expected for hypothetical measurements will always be lower than they actually are. It does not consider the influence of propagations into multiple watchpoints, or into a watchpoint but with underlying assumptions unless computing the expected value of a student's actual measurement (in which case the computational cost is justified). Therefore, the possibility exists that SOPHIE III may make slightly suboptimal measurements. Fortunately, the result is that the coach criticizes the student less, rather than more, than it actually should.

4.2.7 Problems With SOPHIE III's Electronics Expert

The electronics expert, although extremely powerful, suffers from several limitations. These limitations take two forms: those resulting from SOPHIE III's incompleteness and those resulting from SOPHIE II's inconsistency.

Contradictory deductions (inconsistency) are the consequence of making presuppositions about the circuit behavior which don't necessarily hold for the system or fault in question. There are three primary sources responsible for contradictions: the presupposition of a single fault, the presupposition that all fault modes are known, and the presupposition that a symptom must be caused by a component being in a fault mode. Fortunately, there are techniques which could be employed in SOPHIE to handle the situations that violate these presuppositions.

The single-fault presupposition is the most pervasive. Almost every deduction employed by SOPHIE III relies on it. Without it a corroboration cannot logically be used to verify the underlying components nor can a conflict be used to verify the components that aren't mentioned in the underlying assumptions that lead to the conflict. Much of the reasoning mechanism of the behavior-tree is no longer valid.

The case of the single-fault presupposition is indicative of the other two. Without making these presuppositions, powerful troubleshooting cannot occur; adhering to them too stringently can lead to irreconcilable contradictions. These presuppostions are thus very good heuristics for troubleshooting and should be assumed to hold only until evidence is discovered to the contrary. In this light, they should be treated as *defeasible assumptions* subject to explicit reasoning, much like the component assumptions of LOCAL. They are, in essence, a deeper level of assumptions, examined only when all the component assumptions have been eliminated. Every deduction made by LOCAL which depends on the single-fault presupposition should explicitly include this fact as an underlying assumption of that deduction. Unlike the component assumptions, these *presuppositional assumptions* influence the inference mechanism making the deductions. Although when we built SOPHIE III we had some ideas of how to handle this situation as a special case, it is the pioneering work of John Doyle [79] that suggests a general framework for defeating such assumptions, to elegantly alter the inference mechanism, and to efficiently reinstate only those previous deductions that are still valid. Within this extended framework, the troubleshoooting module, which mainly works on assumptions and justifications produced by the expert reasoning engine, would become just a special case of a more powerful reasoner that was capable of "deliberating" over its own actions and theories.

We have been discussing one alternative to the single-fault case, that of multiple independent faults. A more common case is that of multiple consequential faults. The single-fault heuristic often works well for such multiple faults. Frequently, the component that originally faulted will no longer be manifesting a symptom since the consequential fault has effectively made the originally faulted component appear unfaulted by isolating it.

The second presupposition, that SOPHIE III presumes all possible faults are known, is again good heuristic, but again does not always hold. Topological faults such as a short between two nodes which do not share a common component (e.g., two geometrically adjacent, but topologically distant, components which have been physically bent so that their leads touch) or an open node which disconnects two or more components from two or more others are such violations. A more subtle violation occurs with component fault modes, since it is hard to hypothesize all the ways in which a component can fault. Obviously a diode cannot turn into a battery, but under extremely rare conditions it can turn into a resistor that is neither open or shorted. This can cause problems for the behavior-tree mechanism, since the module may end up in a mode which was not hypothesized by the knowledge engineer. Fortunately, this is not usually a problem for SOPHIE III, since if no component is manifesting a symptom, the overall system cannot be manifesting a symptom. Nevertheless, just as with the single-fault assumption, this one should also be included as an assumption underlying every deduction involving an individual component or module.

The third important presupposition, that a circuit symptom is a direct consequence of some component behaving symptomatically, is only true for circuits which do not have some kind of "memory." Suppose a device had a circuit breaker on its input which blew every time the power supply was plugged in. The power supply is manifesting a symptom, but every component is functioning correctly: LOCAL would encounter an irreconcilable contradiction. The problem is, of course, that the circuit breaker "remembers" that some component was behaving symptomatically, even though the component might not be doing so at present. This type of fault is notoriously hard to find since the troubleshooter does not get the opportunity to see the faulted component manifest its symptom. Note the strong similarity between this situation and that of consequential faults: In both cases the source fault must be discovered without the propagations of LOCAL.

5 Conclusions and Theoretical Observations

There are many promising directions along which the work described in this chapter could have continued. However, two very different problems, one pragmatic and one intellectual, stood in our way. The pragmatic issue was the need for large address space and personal lisp machines; the intellectual issue was our increased awareness that we did not really know what it it meant to "understand" how a complex piece of equipment works. In particular we did not know what mental models the experts had of a given system's functioning, nor did we know how these models were learned, for they certainly weren't explicitly taught.

The computational issue that we faced with SOPHIE III was that it barely fits into the address space of a PDP-10 (256K). SPICE, SOPHIE I and SOPHIE III each already occupied its own separate address space so nothing could be gained by running SOPHIE III .stand-alone. This made it extremely difficult to extend SOPHIE III, especially to expand its coaching capabilites along the lines developing out of our coaching research on mathematical games. Address space limitations were not our only concern: To do "formative" evaluations, discovering the *reasons* for the pedagogical success and failures of our system, we needed the speed of efficient, dedicated Lisp machines. Without this speed, student reactions to the long and unpredictable delays often swamped our experimental probes.

5.1 MENTAL MODELS AND EXPLANATIONS

The issue concerning the need for a theory of human understanding of complex systems, in particular circuits, was clearly the more challenging one. Indeed, much of our recent research has been directed at attacking this problem. It quickly became clear to us that the work that went into SOPHIE II and III on explanation put the cart before the horse. We had no adequate theory of what it meant to understand a circuit and hence no well defined "target" model of what we wanted the student to learn. As a consequence no real theory of explanation was forthcoming.

In our experiments with SOPHIE I and II we substantiated that the beginner and expert alike prefer to reason about the circuit in qualitative and causal terms. The students preferred qualitative explanations and were only comfortable about their understanding if it was in terms of a qualitative causal mechanism. SOPHIE III's only reference to causality is in the precompiled explanations for its circuit-specific rules. It could not generate new ones nor could it expand old ones. A significant step toward the necessary robust theory of causality was achieved the following year by de Kleer, in his doctoral dissertation presenting a theory of qualitative causal reasoning about electronics [de Kleer 1979]. Although his target system is primarily concerned with building robust systems, his theory has turned out to provide a basis for constructing human-oriented explanations.

Our fledgling theory of mental models [de Kleer & Brown 80] is based on mapping the system's physical structure into a network of causal relationships among its parts. The links of this network represent the set of ways in which one part can affect another, and define a limited causal epistemology in the spirit of Reiger [1977]. The causal network is a mental model that is, metaphorically speaking, "runnable in the mind's eye." It is more than just a qualitative simulation or envisionment for it makes explicit causal attributions to the events unfolding in the simulation. But it is derivable from the above mentioned envisionments.

It is important to realize that these mental models are not equivalent to various animations of how a system's behavior unfolds. At best, such animations *implicitly* manifest the underlying causality of a system and the observer must attribute the right kind of causal link to each observable internal event. A theory of mental models makes explicit this attribution process.

Since these mental models are at least in principle executable they are subject to the same problems as are the implicit assumptions buried in simulations of a given system. This casts a new light on all of the robustness considerations that we discussed in the SOPHIE I section since the ideal mental model that we wish to eventually impart to the user should be as free as possible from hidden assumptions. Attempting to characterize ideal mental models, or at least ones with maximal probability of being useful for answering unanticipated questions or predicting the consequences of novel casualties, has led us to explore a set of esthetic principles for critiquing the models — even those which are consistent with the known facts. These principles also provide a gradient or direction for the progress of learning. The goal of this learning is to maximize the robustness of the models

Our central esthetic is the "no function in structure" principle. This principle states that the rules for specifying the behavior of any constituent part of the overall system should in no way refer, even implicitly, to how the overall system functions. Fully satisfying this principle ensures that the behaviors of each of the system's parts can be represented and understood in a context-free manner, independent of the overall system. Failing to adhere to this principle leads to the understanding of how the system functions being predicated on some aspect of how it functions (i.e., a circularity).

Since this principle suggests, a direction along which the learner can progress, it not only establishes a target mental model, but suggests possible *sequences* of explanations. Explanations themselves, however, should not necessarily obey these principles. Often it is best to initially violate the "no function in structure" principle, thereby providing an easily understand explanation from which to develop a more robust mental models. A good overall explanation would be a sequence of models in which the amount of function in structure decreases.

Perhaps the most unexpected aspect of this project has been how our ideas for building efficient and robust reasoning engines have provided useful distinctions and techniques for attacking the purely cognitive issues of mental models. This fact is even more remarkable in the case of SOPHIE I since no attempt was made to make its reasoning schemes psychologically relevant. An underlying theme for mental models has turned out to be the manipulation of underlying assumptions, just as it did in our reasoning and troubleshooting schemes in SOPHIE III. We see this as the unifying mechanism for any future SOPHIE-like system: The utility of assumptions is that they are a central vehicle for qualitative reasoning.

Acknowledgments

The SOPHIE project has been influenced and helped by numerous people. We are especially indebted to Alan Bell for the substantial amount of work he did on SOPHIE I. Richard Rubenstein and Ned Benhaim helped a great deal on SOPHIE II. We are also grateful to Ed Gardner for making possible the original SOPHIE project and to Harry O'Neil and Dexter Fletcher for their constant encouragement and willingness to shelter the project from various bureaucratic constraints. The project was initially funded by the Air Force Human Resource Laboratory at Lowry Air Force Base and later by DARPA/CTO and the Tri-Service training laboratories. Numerous people have read preliminary drafts and have made invaluable suggestions. Bruce Buchanan, Bill Clancey, Jaime Carbonell, Dan Bobrow and Rachel Rutherford deserve special thanks for their patience and insights.

References

BOBROW, R. J. (1978). *The RUS System*. Bolt Beranek and Newman, Inc., Report 3878.

BROWN, A. L. (1976). *Qualitative Knowledge, Causal Reasoning, and the Localization of Failures*. MIT AI TR-362.

BROWN, J. S. (1977). Remarks on building expert systems. In *Proceedings of the Fifth International Joint Conference on Artificial Intelligence*, pp. 1003–1005.

BROWN, J. S. & BURTON, R. (1975). Multiple representations of knowledge for tutorial reasoning. In *Representation and Understanding* (D. Bobrow and A. Collins, eds). Academic Press, New York.

BROWN, J. S. & BURTON, R. R. (1978). Diagnostic models for procedural bugs in basic mathematical skills. *Cognitive Science*, **2**, 155–198.

BROWN, J. S., BURTON, R. R. & BELL, A. G. (1974). *SOPHIE. A Sophisticated Instructional Environment for Teaching Electronic Troubleshooting (An example of AI in CAI)*. Bolt Beranek and Newman, Inc., Report 2790.

BROWN, J. S., BURTON, R. R. & BELL, A. G. (1975). SOPHIE. A step towards a reactive learning environment. *International Journal of Man Machine Studies*, **7**, 675–696.

BROWN, J. S., RUBINSTEIN, R. & BURTON, R. R. (1976). *Reactive Learning Environment for Computer Assisted Electronics Instruction*. Bolt Beranek and Newman, Inc., Report 3314.

BURTON, R. R. (1976). *Semantic Grammar: An Engineering Technique for Constructing Natural Language Understanding Systems*. Bolt Beranek and Newman, Inc., Report 3453, ICAI Report 3.

BURTON, R. R. (1982). Diagnosing a simple procedural skill. Chapter 8 in this volume.

BURTON, R. R. & BROWN, J. S. (1979). Toward a natural-language capability for computer-assisted instruction. In *Procedures For Instructional Systems Development* (H. O'Neil ed.). Academic Press, New York.

BURTON, R. R. & BROWN, J. S. (1982). An investigation of computer coaching for informal learning activities. Chapter 4 in this volume.

BURTON, R. R. & WOODS, W. A. (1976). A compiling system for augmented transition networks. *Proc. Coling*, **76**.

DE KLEER, J. (1976). *Local Methods for Localizing Faults in Electronic Circuits*. MIT AI AIM-394.

DE KLEER, J. (1979). The origin and resolution of ambiguities in causal arguments. In *Proceedings of the Sixth International Joint Conference on Artificial Intelligence*, pp. 197–203.

DE KLEER, J. & BROWN, J. S. (1980). Mental models of physical mechanisms and their acquisition. In *Cognitive Skills and their Acquisition*. Erlbaum, New York.

DOYLE, J. (1979). A truth maintenance system. *Artificial Intelligence*, **12**, 231–272.

GROSZ, B. (1978). Discourse knowledge. In *Understanding Spoken Language* (Donald E. Walker, ed.), pp. 229–344. North-Holland, New York.

HENDRIX, G. G. (1977). *The LIFER Manual: A Guide to Building Practical Natural Language Interfaces.* SRI International, Technical Note 138, Menlo Park, California.

LINDSAY, R. K., BUCHANAN, B. G., FEIGENBAUM, E. A. & LEDERBERG, J. (1980). *Applications of Artificial Intelligence for Organic Chemistry: The Dendral Project.* McGraw-Hill, New York.

NAGEL, L. W. & PEDERSON, D. O. (1973). Simulation program with integrated circuit emphasis. *Proceedings of the Sixteenth Midwest Symposium Circuit Theory.* Waterloo, Canada.

RIEGER, C. & GRINBERG, M. (1977). The declarative representation and procedural simulation of causality in physical mechanisms. *Proceedings of the Fifth International Joint Conference on Artificial Intelligence,* pp. 250–255.

SLEEMAN, D. H. & HENDLEY, R. J. (1982). ACE: a system which analyses complex explanations. Chapter 5 in this volume.

STALLMAN, R. M. & SUSSMAN, G. J. (1977). Forward reasoning and dependency-directed backtracking in a system for computer-aided circuit analysis. *Artificial Intelligence,* **9**, 135–196.

WEBBER, B. L. (1979). *A Formal Approach to Discourse Anaphora.* Garland Press, New York. (Also published in 1978 by Bolt Beranek and Newman, Inc., TR-3761.)

WOODS, W. A., KAPLAN, R. M. & WEBBER, B. L. (1972). *The Lunar Sciences Natural Language Information System: Final Report.* Bolt Beranek and Newman, Inc., Report 2378.

12. A self-improving tutor for symbolic integration†

RALPH KIMBALL

Xerox Corporation, OPD Systems Development, Palo Alto, California, U.S.A.

A *tutor for a problem solving domain* is defined to be a computer program that (1) transmits problem solving heuristics, (2) generates appropriate expository examples, (3) deals with arbitrary student-initiated examples, (4) handles a wide range of student backgrounds, and (5) is capable of acquiring superior problem solving approaches from the students themselves. In this paper it is shown that, for suitably structured problem solving domains, a computer-assisted tutor can be constructed that meets the above criteria, and in addition does not need to be initialized by a "grand master" problem solver. The results of tutoring freshmen calculus students with such a tutor built for the subject area of symbolic integration are reported.

1. The evolution of computer-based learning systems

During the 1960s computer-assisted instruction (CAI) emerged as the great panacea that would simultaneously educate our school children and college students, provide a stimulating new medium that would never be boring, and utilize computers in a particularly socially-responsive way. Of course, given the benefit of looking back from 1981, we know that our expectations for CAI were naive and far too high. We underestimated the costs of providing CAI, we overestimated the attractiveness of the medium (thousands of school children banged away on Model 33 Teletypes far longer than now seems possible), and most seriously, we just did not appreciate the inherent complexity of providing even the most minimally responsive teaching via a deterministic program.

By the end of the 1960s it was becoming apparent to those who were trying to provide a serious level of CAI service that CAI was not going to live up to its inflated expectations. The limitations of these primitive interactive CAI programs were finally appreciated and more realistic goals were adopted. A more sober, low-profile form of CAI has been preserved from that time through the present date.

Nevertheless, the promise of providing "intelligent" computer-assisted learning systems remained as a significant goal for education and computer researchers. A number of quite different approaches emerged during the 1970s, especially from the artificial intelligence research community. In most cases considerable emphasis was placed on allowing the student to pose unexpected or unanticipated responses, thereby giving the student partial or complete control over the learning episode.

A number of successful systems simply provided an *environment for exploration*. These systems contained no explicit notion of student goals, performance, or state, and had no built-in capacities to direct the student toward some purposeful behavior. The

† This paper describes research performed between 1969 and 1972 in collaboration with my thesis advisor Richard Smallwood. His contributions are gratefully acknowledged. The computer resources were provided by the Institute for Mathematical Studies in the Social Sciences at Stanford University under NSF contract GJ443X.

pedagogical assumption was that the student's inate curiosity would lead him to explore and learn in a self-motivated way.

In my view, although these systems were useful and provocative, they tended either to present such a limited universe that good students would exhaust the interesting dimensions of the system fairly quickly, or they were sufficiently deep that enculturation, rather than training, was required which could only be achieved through continuous and expensive user support. My most serious criticism of the environmental approach is that the systems provided no facilities for detecting, rescuing, or motivating the student who was in trouble. Seymour Papert's Turtle system is an example of the "limited universe environment", and Alan Kay's Smalltalk system is an example of the "enculturated environment".

Other systems tried to provide a much more structured approach to giving the student freedom. Sleeman and Brown refer to these systems as *intelligent tutoring systems*. In contrast to the environments for exploration, most of these systems contained explicit notions of student goals, performance and state, and always were prepared to direct the student toward purposeful behavior. This and other chapters in this book describe the principal examples of intelligent tutoring systems developed in the 1970s.

2. An intelligent tutor for symbolic integration

In order to motivate the reader's curiosity about how an intelligent tutor might be built, we present now a sample dialogue from a real computer calculus tutor implemented in LISP at Stanford University in 1972. Note that the tutor is an expert at symbolic integration heuristics, algebraic manipulation, *and* teaching students! The following protocol was actually observed, and is presented verbatim. The large characters are those typed by the student, small italicised text is expository material inserted in the present article only, and everything else (normal face) is typed by the tutor:

(INTEGRATE) *Student's command to LISP to start the tutoring program.*

Hello! What is your name?

Ruth

Hello again, Ruth

Have you ever studied partial fraction expansion?

The tutor recognizes the student Ruth and asks if she has learned partial fraction expansion yet. She had previously answered "yes" to all the other techniques.

no

Ok, do you have a problem?

no

All right, I will select one for you!

Thinking for a moment . . .

At this point the tutor retrieves Ruth's approach probability matrix from an external file, constructs an appropriate prior estimate, calculates the expected example distance for each problem in the example archive, and chooses the problem with the highest resulting value. All of these terms and others encountered below are explained in the accompanying article.

Ok, Ruth

Our integral is $\int X \log (X)\, dX$

What shall we do to solve it? **sub** *Ruth has chosen substitution*

Can you think of a substitution? (YES, HELP or EXIT)

> *We are now in the substitution program and Ruth has 3 choices: 1) specify her own choice of substitution; 2) receive a hint from the tutor; 3) abort substitution altogether and return to the original integral.*

yes

Let U = $\log (X)$

> *The tutor prompts the student with "Let U = " and she responds with her choice. Successive substitutions would involve the variables V, W, ...*

Ok, Ruth

we will let U

equal log (X)

> *At this point the tutor calculates $dU = 1/X\, dX$ and tries to find dU in the integrand. Since the search was unsuccessful, the tutor then solves $U = \log (x)$ for X so that the substitution can be carried out.*

Thus X

equals e^U

and dX

equals $e^U\, dU$

which we substituted into the integrand

Our new integral is now $\int U\, e^{2U}\, dU$

Please type Good, Bad or Giveup

> *Now that the student has applied substitution, the tutor lets her choose whether to go on with this new integral. "Good" will cause this new integral to become the "official" new transformation, "Bad" will return us to the start of the substitution routine for another try, and "Giveup" will abort substitution to return to the original integral.*

bad

Can you think of a substitution? (Yes, Help or Exit)

> *We are now back to the original integral.*

help

I can't find a suitable substitution! Will exit . . .

> *The tutor couldn't find a substitution that it felt led to a simpler integral. The point, of course, is that substitution was not a very good choice for this problem. Notice however that the tutor intervention threshold was not tripped when the student specified substitution. The intervention parameter is deliberately set high enough so that the student has some latitude to try poor guesses and see the results.*

Ok, Ruth

Our integral is $\int X \log (X)\, dX$

What shall we do to solve it?   : **help**

> *Now the student wants a hint from the tutor.*

I suggest you try integration by parts.

> *Integration by parts was the tutor's highest priority approach for this problem description state.*

What shall we do to solve it?   : **parts**

> *The student has taken the hint and asks for integration by parts.*

Integration by parts!

We will use the notation

$$\int U\, dV = UV - \int V\, dU$$

Can you think of a choice for U? (Yes, Help or Exit)

> *The student has essentially the same choice as she did upon entering the substitution program.*

help

How about letting U = log (X)

> *Here the tutor uses its "wired-in heuristics" to choose.*

Can you think of a choice for U? (Yes, Help or Exit)

yes

Let U = **log (X)**

> *Apparently the student is somewhat unfamiliar with integration by parts, since she did not even attempt to guess a choice for U.*

Ok, Ruth

we will let U = log (X)

thus dV = X dX

hmmmm . . .

> *A slight pause as the computer utilizes a simple set of "wired in" heuristics to find the integral of dV. If the tutor cannot solve the integral of dV by the known integral routine, simple substitution, or simple trigonometric substitution, the student is so informed and the tutor returns to asking for a choice of U.*

An intriguing choice!

thus $V = \dfrac{X^2}{2}$

and $dU = \dfrac{1}{X}$

We now have $\int X \log(X) \, dX$

$$= \frac{X^2 \log(X)}{2}$$

$$- \int \frac{X}{2} \, dX$$

Please type Good, Bad, Again, Solve or Giveup

Good allows the student to exit with the new integral; Bad recycles back to the beginning of integration by parts for a new choice of U; Again lets the student integrate the new integral by parts again; Solve lets the student solve for the original integral if at least two consecutive integrations by parts have been done; Giveup aborts integration by parts and returns with the original integral.

Good

Ok, Ruth

Our integral is now $\int X \, dX$

times $\dfrac{-1}{2}$

Extraneous coefficients are always factored out of the integrand

What shall we do to solve it? :**known**

The students often used "guess" at this point to guess the answer to simple integrals. "Known" however simply provides the answer once the known integral is successfully identified. Notice that the student has now completed the problem. If this problem had dragged on one more step, the tutor's problem length threshold would have exceeded and the tutor would have taken the student back to the beginning of the problem to suggest help in finding a better solution.

Very Good!

The answer to this integral

is $\dfrac{-X}{4}$

Adding the term from integration by parts

we have $\dfrac{2X^2 \log(X) - X^2}{4}$

plus an arbitrary constant . . .

You did that problem in 3 steps compared to 2 for me!

My Solution

1. Integration by parts
2. The known integral routine

Your Solution

1. Substitution
2. Integration by parts
3. The known integral routine

One of the most effective features of the tutor is this problem comparison. Even though the student does not see the exact step-by-step solution of the tutor, the comparison of the solution outline is usually revealing.

Thinking for a moment . . .

The tutor now adds the pattern of responses generated by this problem to the statistical summary for Ruth, checks the alarm threshold, and returns to the starting point of the whole process.

Ok, do you have a problem?

We have now come back to the starting point shown above.

3. Defining a tutor for a problem solving domain

In this article a tutor especially suited for solving *posed problems* in some arbitrary domain of discourse is described. A number of fairly strong assumptions are made about the nature of the problem domain, and the desirable student goals. In particular, it is assumed that

expertise in problem solving is a matter of *judgement* gained from experience, not a matter of efficiently applying a deterministic rule (e.g. symbolic integration seems to be interesting but we all know that symbolic differentiation is not);

this problem solving judgement depends mostly upon the human's perception of the problem's surface or initial appearance, rather than upon explicitly performing a look-ahead computation and evaluating a succession of transformed results;

the tutor's best advice does not always lead to a solution (this is actually a consequence of the first assumption);

if the best advice fails to be productive, then there exists "second-best advice", and so on;

one or more metrics can be devised that provide a "goodness" ordering on completed solutions to a given problem;

the point of the tutor is to stimulate the students to produce "better" solutions, i.e. to exhibit better judgement.

In the context of such a problem solving domain, it is assumed that desirable behavior for the tutor includes

demonstrably transmitting its own problem solving judgement to the student;

choosing appropriate expository examples for the student to work, both to strengthen weak student skills, and to provide a "grab-bag" challenge for the student;

dealing with unexpected and arbitrary examples brought to the tutor by the student;

altering the tutorial strategy depending not only upon the student's overt performance, but upon known omissions in the student's prior background; and finally

learning superior problem solving approaches from the student, if in fact the student demonstrates them.

The remainder of this article describes a particular implementation of such a tutor for symbolic integration. All of the above objectives are not only achievable in terms of the design of the tutor, but have been demonstrated in practice on real students.

4. An analytic model for how people solve integration problems

The solution of symbolic integration problems seems to meet nicely the above mentioned criteria for a problem solving domain. While it is true that powerful "non-traditional" computer algorithms have been developed to solve symbolic integrals (Risch, 1969), it is still the case that the vast majority of mathematicians use "judgement" as the primary tool for solving this class of problem. A number of other practical problem solving domains suggest themselves that offer hope of fitting into the same framework, particularly medical diagnosis and machine trouble-shooting. Note that activities such as chess playing seem to fit poorly to these domain requirements.

The goal of symbolic integration is to apply a series of transformations to a symbolic expression until it becomes a "known" expression that has an automatic answer. The "known" symbolic integrands are a small list, including x^n, the trigonometric functions $\sin(x)$ and $\cos(x)$, the hyperbolic functions $\sinh(x)$ and $\cosh(x)$, and the exponential function e^x.

We have already decided that human problem solvers approach symbolic integrals by examining the surrace characteristics, or form, of the expression and then choosing a particular solution approach. In order to compare the heuristics of two different problem solvers (or of the tutor and the student), we make the following additional assumptions:

any given problem solver categorizes all possible problems into disjoint classifications, depending on the problem's form. Actually this is not as strong an assumption as it sounds, since if there are a finite number of possible approaches, then all possible problems must necessarily be divided up into equivalence classes, depending on how they are approached. The equivalence classes (or some combination of equivalence classes) are exactly the disjoint problem states desired. Also,

although we do not claim that the tutor's and student's classification schemes for problems are identical, we assume that it is desirable to gravitate the student toward the tutor's classification scheme. And, at certain times in the computation of global tutorial responses (such as selecting the best next problem, or deciding if the student is in "dire" trouble), we make the strong simplifying assumption that the tutor's and student's problem classifications *are* the same. The general tutorial theory developed here allows for the alteration and evolution of both the student's and tutor's classification schemes, although this aspect was not implemented in the actual integration tutor.

Given a symbolic integration problem, the standard technique is to try one of a set of basic approaches to see if the integrand can be transformed into something more tractable. When the new integrand does seem simpler, then it replaces the original problem, and the procedure begins anew. If the integrand does *not* seem simpler (or equivalently if the user discovers after further transformations that the new integrand is a dead end), then a different approach is applied to the original problem. Thus the act of solving an integration problem involves guiding the expression through a series of transformations until it lands in the "known" classification.

It is useful to regard the problem solving episode as progressing from one *state* to another. In general, the state is characterized by the current expression to be solved, all of the history that led from the original expression to the current expression, and the user's state of mind. Needless to say, such a general state definition is difficult to deal with, since a complete representation of the problem history and the user's state of mind seems unachievable. However, by making certain judicious assumptions, and by defining the notion of state carefully, we can arrive at a model of the student solving symbolic integrals that is very useful. This model will allow

systematic updating in response to user actions;

the development of metrics to compare the abilities of one student with another or with the tutor;

a framework to be constructed that represents the *tutor's* expertise;

an absolute (as opposed to relative) estimate of how long it takes the student to solve problems of any given type;

a framework for choosing remedial problems of the greatest benefit to the individual student; and

a framework for describing the effects of learning.

Note that the student himself never deals with his own model. The student model serves only to guide the computer tutor when it needs to make a decision.

Let us proceed to develop some of the model's basic attributes, explicitly noting our assumptions as we proceed. The probability that the problem solver, when presented with a random expression of classification i, will transform it into one of classification k can be written as p_{ik}. Now if the probability of the problem solver choosing approach j for this particular transformation is a_{ij}, then we can directly write

$$p_{ik} = \sum_j a_{ij} b_{ijk} \tag{1}$$

where b_{ijk} is the probability that if an integral of classification i is transformed by the student with approach j, that the resulting integral will be of classification k. We call the a_{ij}'s the *approach probabilities*, and the b_{ijk}'s the *result probabilities*.

Both the approach probabilities and the result probabilities have direct physical significance to the student. The approach probabilities are especially important because they embody the heuristic judgement of the student. Most of the detailed manipulations of the student model will involve the approach probabilities. The result probabilities are a measure of how effective the student is in completing a transformation of an expression from one classification to another, and tend to measure his manipulative skills rather than his judgement.

In the absence of any simplifying assumptions, the approach probabilities are very complicated indeed. In general they are time varying, they depend on the path taken from state to state, and there is no way to measure them objectively. In order to proceed we must seek a method of defining the problem solving states, and a restricted regime in which all three of these difficulties can be avoided. Our first task will be to remove the dependency of the transition probabilities p_{ik} from the path taken from state to state. In examining equation (1), we will assume that the path dependencies must all reside in the approach probabilities a_{ij}, since the result probabilities b_{ijk} are only a measure of manipulative skill, which seems fairly unrelated to path history. Or to put it another way, we will ignore in this tutor the issue of manipulative skill and assume that we will just correct without penalty or comment any manipulative "goofs". In the actual integration tutor, this point was even more strongly emphasized, since the tutor actually carried out the manipulations after the student named the desired approach.

In order to claim that the approach probabilities are independent of the previous path taken, we must deal with two sources of path dependence:

The approach probabilities will certainly change immediately if the student chooses some approach that fails. We can hardly claim that he has returned to the same state to try again!

The approach probabilities will evolve gradually over time, as the accumulated weight of success and failure of approaches taken in given states changes the student's judgement.

There is a subtle difference between these two sources of changing approach probabilities. It is quite possible that the student will, with good motivation, try an approach that fails, then subsequently try a "second choice" that succeeds, and in the end not change his long term approach probabilities at all. In this case the student may rationalize that the problem was one of those "special cases" where the primary indicated approach does not work, but where the second indicated approach does. Here we would expect the long term approach probabilities not to change. Of course, this is most likely to happen when the student is fairly experienced.

If we define our problem solving states to include specific *failure states*, then we can remove the contribution of the first source of path dependence. If S is an arbitrary problem solving state associated with expressions of a certain form, then the mth failure state associated with S, namely $S(m)$, is defined to be the state arrived at immediately after being in state S and trying approach m unsuccessfully. Now we see that the approach probabilities associated with S cannot be dependent on failures encountered in S, since by definition this shunts the student not back into S but into a failure state.

The second source of path dependence cannot be maneuvered around in the same way, since this source represents true long term changes in the student's problem solving judgement. However, if we assume that these changes happen *not at the moment of application of a successful approach, but at the successful completion of the entire problem*, then during the actual course of a given problem, all of the probabilities must remain constant. This allows us to make the full claim that the approach probabilities a_{ij}, and hence the transition probabilities p_{ik}, remain fixed, keeping in mind the augmented failure state definition and this new assumption of learning "discontinuities". To pay for this assumption, however, we must posit the existence of a learning process, which under the appropriate circumstances, causes readjustments in specific approach probabilities to account for the effects of discovering a new efficacious approach or of suffering repeated failures. The sudden, or discontinuous nature of these probability changes, is actually supported by the data collected from students using the integration tutor. These results are discussed in detail later in this article. The specific form of the learning process will be discussed below.

We are now in a position to make the final assumptions needed for the problem solving model.

We assume that all variations in time of the true transition probabilities are due to learning, and that these changes are entirely subsumed by the discontinuous learning process model. (Thus we are ignoring the changes in approach probabilities that, for instance, a hangover might create).·

We assume that our state of information about the student prior to any exposure to the tutor can be adequately summarized by an ad hoc set of approach probabilities, known as the *zeroth prior estimate*.

We assume that in the absence of learning, we can update the probabilities that represent the student by using Bayes' theorem, namely

$$\{a|E\} = \{E|a\}\{a\}/\{E\} \tag{2}$$

where $\{a\}$ represents the student's unconditional approach probabilities, $\{a|E\}$ represents the student's approach probabilities given that event E has occurred, $\{E|a\}$ represents the probability of the event E taking place given the student's approach probabilities, and $\{E\}$ represents $\{E|a\}$ summed over all possible approach probabilities, i.e. the unconditional probability of event E taking place. $\{a\}$ is called the *prior estimate* of a, and $\{a|E\}$ is called the *posterior estimate* of a. This formula is to be used as a "pump", where the prior estimate $\{a\}$ is presented, and the resultant posterior estimate $\{a|E\}$ is computed. When the next event takes place, the old posterior estimate becomes the new prior estimate, and so on.

It should be recognized that these last two assumptions are not trivial, and have deep philosophical ramifications. The significant step in these two assumptions is allowing the existence of a zeroth prior estimate. Most *decision theorists* are comfortable with this step because they are willing to use even intuitive guesses as a way to get off the ground with the zeroth prior estimate before the data, namely event E, has been recorded. After all, decision theorists *must* make decisions! In many real world cases, the exact choice of the zeroth prior estimate makes little difference after real data from measured events begins to be processed by the information updating model. Finally, the notion that one can assign an "uncertain" probability to an event, even when little is known about the event, has strong intuitive appeal. Most classical probability theorists cannot bring themselves to allow the existence of a well-defined prior estimate, and they offer philosophical absurdities, such as proofs of the existence of Atlantis, as arguments that Bayes' theorem can be misused. The argument cannot be settled on technical grounds, because the issue of the legitimate existence of a prior estimate is not mathematical, but rather philosophical. The philosophical issue is whether the zeroth prior estimate "belongs" to the observer and is available for use (the Bayesian approach), or whether the zeroth prior estimate "belongs" to the universe and is thus inherently unobservable. In any case, we will take the view of the Bayesian decision theorist because we believe that a zeroth prior estimate of a student's approach probabilities is a legitimate thing to possess. Note that the *accuracy* of the zeroth prior estimate is not the main issue, only our right to possess it.

With these assumptions under our belt, we can now summarize our model of the problem solving process in traditional technical terms. The model of solving symbolic integration problems has been shown to be a discreet-time Markov process, to which we apply a Bayesian information updating process to account for observed student responses, and to which we apply an ad hoc probability updating process to account for hypothesized discontinuous learning events.

In Appendix 1, we present without proof or further motivation the mathematical details of the model, sufficient to perform all necessary record keeping and calculations. The interested reader can find a complete derivation of the equations in (Kimball, 1973).

5. The tutorial strategy

Now that we have posited an analytic model for how the student solves problems, the tutor is in a position to maintain elaborate and responsive bookkeeping as a result of the student's actions. What is missing then, is a strategy for what to do with all this knowledge about the student when it becomes time to make a decision.

We begin by designing an overall flow chart for the tutor's performance, given the following goals:

At sign-on, the student must be identified, and the tutor must determine if the student wishes to be exposed to any previously untried areas. The assumption is made that the tutor often will be used in conjunction with a course where the various approaches to solving integrals will be taught sequentially. Thus the tutor needs to know what approaches to avoid recommending if they have not yet been introduced.

The tutor must give the student the opportunity to pose his own problem, and the tutor must perform just as well as if the tutor had selected a problem of its own.

If the student has no problem, the tutor must select one that the student has not seen before and is particularly suited to the needs of the student.

The tutor must tell the student what approach it thinks is best when it is asked.

The tutor must be able to recognize wild, or very unlikely approaches, suggested by the student, and make immediate comment. However, the student must be able to proceed with his choice if he wishes.

Upon completion of each problem, the tutor must perform a global evaluation of the student's strong and weak areas. If the student seems to be grossly diverging from the tutor's beliefs about problem solving, then the tutor must select a special example suited to the trouble areas of the student, and must walk the student through it step by step.

After each problem is completed, the tutor must present a comparison of the approach it would have used to solve the problem against the approach taken by the student.

If the student solves the problem in a way recognized as superior by the tutor, then the tutor must incorporate the student's solution into its own repertoire in such a way that subsequent tutoring help immediately reflects this change.

The flow chart that implements the above goals is given in Fig. 1. The remainder of this section is devoted to describing how these goals are achieved.

The first step of a student session requires the tutor to ask the student if there are any new, previously unexplored approaches that have been learned since the last session. The tutor should avoid selecting problems or giving hints involving approaches that the student has never seen before. The tutor is not assumed to be able to present a *curriculum* or a *lecture* that would educate the student about an unknown approach. Of course, the tutor could in theory drop into a "CAI-mode" to present new material, but in the research described here, this step was not taken. Whenever the student lets the tutor expand the list of allowable problem solving approaches, the tutor in effect grows the $M \times N$ matrix of approach probabilities to accommodate columns for the new approaches, and initializes the new entries with an ad hoc set of "zeroth prior" estimates to seed the information updating model.

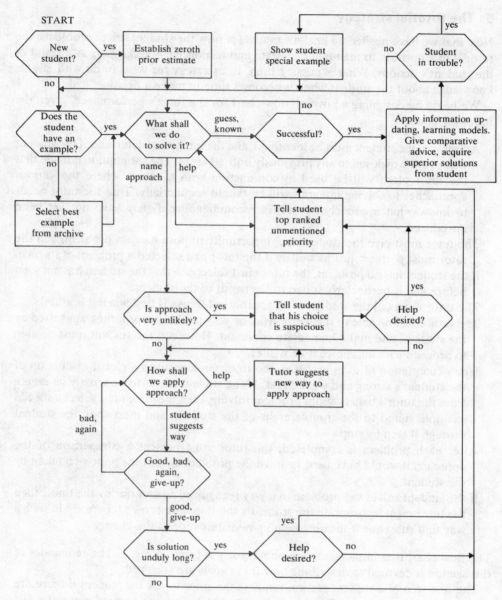

FIG. 1. The flow diagram of the tutor.

In the next step of a student session, the tutor asks the students if they have a problem of their own they would like help on from the tutor. If so, then they type it in, and the main-line dialogue begins. While this facility was used occasionally, it was found that the students greatly preferred to let the tutor choose a problem of its own from its "grab-bag" archive of problems. In order to choose a problem that was particularly well-suited to the student's current needs, the tutor scanned through its entire list of 130 problems, applying a metric to choose the best one. In order to develop the metric described below (and later to be able to give hints), the tutor had to possess its own approach probabilities, which we will label A_{ij}.

The tutor's approach probabilities were not assigned arbitrarily, but were accumulated by having an expert work all 130 problems in the grab-bag archive, and recording the approaches chosen in every problem state. Thus, with every problem in its archive, the tutor had a set of ordered pairs of the form

$$\text{(state } ID, \text{ approach } ID) \tag{3}$$

that described the path taken to solution. As we shall see, this representation of the expert's solutions, together with the model of the student's probabilities, provided the basis for all the tutor's decisions.

Now that we have a set of approach probabilities for both the student and the tutor, we can make some interesting comparisons. For instance, for each problem description state, we can calculate a tutor-student distance D_i, where

$$D_i = \sum_j |A_{ij} - a_{ij}|. \tag{4}$$

Now if we knew in advance what responses the student would make, we could select the problem from the archive that would minimize the total tutor-student distance

$$D_{\text{TOTAL}} = \sum_i D_i \tag{5}$$

posterior to working the problem. Lacking this perfect information, we could nevertheless calculate the probability that the student, somewhere in his solution would choose approach j in state S_i, given his approach probabilities a_{ij} and his transition probabilities p_{ik}:

$$P\{j|S(i)\} = \delta_{ik}a_{ij} + p_{ki}a_{ij} + \sum_l p_{kl}p_{li}a_{ij} + \sum_{l,m} p_{kl}p_{lm}p_{mi}a_{ij} + \cdots \tag{6}$$

where $\delta_{ij} = 1$ if $i = k$, else $\delta_{ik} = 0$. The change in D_{TOTAL} could then be estimated by carrying out this calculation on each candidate problem for all possible states and approaches.

Apart from the computational complexity of this scheme, there are two significant objections to its use. First, we would find that all problems of the same initial description state would give identical predicted contributions to the change in D_{TOTAL}. This would leave us with a choice to make among a possibly large number of problems. The second objection is that such a computation ignores the solution used by the tutor for the particular problem except insofar as it contributes to the tutor's approach probabilities. What is needed is a model to predict what relation a student's particular solution will have to the tutor's particular solution.

To pose such a model, we assume that if the tutor-student distance for a given state is large, the student is more likely to enter failure states and more likely to get into situations where the tutor gives him a hint that may change his problem solving approaches. Note that we refrain from simply using the tutor's record of the problem solution for giving hints, since the point of the tutor is to develop judgement, not to teach someone else's specific solutions. The hint giving strategy is explained in more detail below.

Thus a reasonable measure of a candidate problem from the archive is the set

$$\{D_i, D_j, D_k, \ldots, D_m\} \tag{7}$$

of tutor-student distances for states encountered in the tutor's solution. The *expected example distance* D_E of the candidate problem is the weighted sum

$$D_E = D_i + p_{ij}D_j + p_{ij}p_{jk}D_k + \cdots + p_{ij}\cdots p_{nm}D_m \tag{8}$$

where the transition probabilities are those of the student. This expected example distance has the following desirable features: (1) it is computationally tractable; (2) its value is proportional to the expected occurrence of tutor hints and comparisons that would change the student's approach probabilities; (3) it depends on the entire tutor solution and will yield very few ties among candidate problems; and (4) since it is weighted by the student's transition probabilities, it takes into account the possibility that the student may diverge from the tutor's solution.

To select an example from the archive, the tutor calculates the expected example distance for all the unworked problems in the archive, eliminating those using approaches unknown to the student, and chooses that problem that *maximizes* D_E.

In the next step of the student session, whether the problem has been presented by the student, chosen from the archive, or is a transformed partial solution, the tutor asks the student the generic question "What shall we do to solve it?". The student then can name an approach (from a standard list of all possible approaches), ask for help, or quit entirely. Usually the student will name an approach. At this point the tutor makes a decision whether the approach chosen is so inappropriate that a special comment should be made. As a pedagogical principle, the calculus tutor was designed so that interruptions at this stage were quite infrequent and were reserved only for the most wildly unlikely choices of approach. Thus, for instance, the choice of "substitution" never triggered an intervention by the tutor, because substitution was used so often over all problem types that it could never be considered wildly unlikely. In order to decide systematically when to intervene, an *unusual approach threshold* was defined as

$$H_i = \varepsilon_i [\max_j a_{ij,\text{tutor}}] \tag{9}$$

where ε_i is an adjustable quantity settable anywhere between 0 and 1. (In practice, a value of $\varepsilon = 0 \cdot 25$ was used.) Thus the threshold is a certain fraction of the tutor's response frequency for the most likely approach in that state. For states with a single preferred approach, the threshold will be tripped more easily by a wrong approach. But for states with no clear-cut choice, it will be very hard to trip the threshold. The unusual approach threshold is exceeded whenever approach j chosen by the student in state S_i satisfies

$$a_{ij,\text{tutor}} < H_i \tag{10}$$

In other words, the tutor looks at its own priorities to decide if the student chose an approach below the tutor's relative frequency threshold. When the threshold is tripped, all that happens is that the student is asked if he wants help. If he doesn't, then he can proceed onward with his choice. Note that if the student has a problem that requires an unusual approach, and he has already tried several approaches unsuccessfully, the tutor assigns both itself and the student to the proper failure state. The expected approach probabilities in these failure states are altered as described later in equation

(13), and the threshold is not triggered unnecessarily just because an unusual approach is needed.

A critical part of the student-tutor interaction comes when the student asks for help. At this point the tutor must respond from its own knowledge of how to solve the problem. Of course, the crucial point is that the tutor does not know how to solve the problem! If a tutor is to respond to arbitrary student problems and solution paths, it cannot store certain prescribed solutions in its memory. In fact, many subjects, including methods of integration, allow multiple solution paths for their problems. The tutor cannot use the particular solution stored in its archive since the student either suggests his own problem or else often deviates from the solution path recorded with the tutor's problem. Thus when the student asks for help, the proper response must be derived from the tutor's approach probabilities. When the student asks for help, the tutor suggests the highest probability approach. Successive requests for help yield successively lower priority approach choices. We thus state the principle:

> The tutor provides approach choice advice by presenting the student with its own approach choice priorities.

It is possible that the most highly recommended approach will not solve the problem. The student should be prepared to fail occasionally, even with "good" advice, and start the problem over again using the next most highly recommended approach. Since the student is learning a process of problem solving, rather than the solutions to isolated problems, even such negative experiences will broaden his judgement by causing him to search for less likely solution schemes.

After a student names an approach, he enters a subprogram specifically designed for the approach. He is now exposed to the second level version of "What shall we do to solve it?". In this case the student can suggest a solution scheme (such as "let $u = x$" in a substitution, or "let $u = e^x$, $dv = \sin(x)\,dx$" in integration by parts, or "apply the half angle identity" in trigonometric identities. Alternatively the student can ask for help. Following the application of the approach, the student has a chance to view the result and accept it; reject the result and try again; accept the result and apply the approach again; or give up on the approach altogether. When the student asks for help within the application of an approach, we take the pragmatic view of applying a set of "wired-in" heuristics to choose the right sub-approach. The choice of problem description states should always be made so as to reduce the role that wired-in heuristics play. In the calculus tutor, once an approach was chosen, the decision about how to apply that approach could be done deterministically in nearly every case.

Following the application of an approach, the tutor checks the problem solution as of that point to see if the solution is getting unusually long. It is often possible to perform a very large number of steps on a simple problem without triggering the unusual approach threshold. In order to establish a *problem length threshold*, we calculate the mean and variance of the expected number of steps to solution, given that the problem originally started in state S_i. Defining κ as a positive number (taken as $\kappa = 2 \cdot 0$ in practice) known as the problem length threshold parameter, we can write the problem length threshold for state S_i as

$$J_i = \nu_i + \kappa \sigma_i, \tag{11}$$

where ν_i is defined in equation (A7), and σ_i is the standard deviation of the expected number of steps to solution and is given by

$$\sigma_i^2 = (2\tau - I)v - v \,\square\, v, \tag{12}$$

where the box notation $\square$ refers to the term by term multiplication of two matrices of similar dimension, i.e. if $C = A \,\square\, B$, then $c_{ij} = a_{ij}b_{ij}$ (see Howard, 1971).

In a similar fashion to the unusual approach threshold, the tutor will not force the student to do anything if the problem length threshold is exceeded, but will simply ask him if he wants help.

The student can continue to apply approaches to a problem indefinitely. Each such application involves one loop of the lower central portion of the flowchart in Fig. 1. Eventually the student will reduce the problem to a simple recognizable form. If this form is a "known" integral, then the student may simply type "known" to finish the problem. The student may at any time try to guess the final answer, or he may abort a solution by typing "quit".

Following the completion of a problem, the tutor updates its prior estimates of the student's approach probabilities by using the information updating and student learning models described earlier. The tutor then prints a summary of those approaches used by the student together with a list of those approaches that were used by the original expert if the problem is from the tutor's archive. This is a very effective way for the student to compare his problem solving schemes with those of the tutor, particularly if he has solved the problem without tripping either of the thresholds or asking for a hint.

In the last step in the process the tutor scans the tutor-student distances for each problem description state. A third threshold, known as the "alarm threshold", governs whether the tutor stops to show the student a completely worked problem or not. If so, then the tutor scans a special list of remedial problems that are stored with their complete and detailed solutions, calculating expected example distances for these, in much the same way as for the general problem archive, except that the tutor knows there will be no deviance by the student from the selected solution path. Since this action is relatively heavy-handed, the threshold is set rather high, and the check against the threshold is only made every four problems.

Much of the value of the tutoring process we have developed in this section depends on the tutor being a good problem solver itself. In particular, the approach probability convergence schemes we have proposed for problem selection and hint generation would be counterproductive if the student was a better problem solver than the tutor. In this case the tutor would be attempting to bring the student down to its own level. The use of this tutorial scheme would also be severely restricted if the tutor required initialization by some kind of grand master of the subject. Therefore a most important development in our tutorial theory is a self-improvement strategy for the tutor.

The tutorial system as we have described it thus far is well suited for modification of the tutor's strategies. Except for the wired-in heuristics, all tutorial responses are determined by the state of the student's model, the tutor's approach probabilities, and the problem archive.

The real problem is to identify a criterion for superior student solutions. In particular the tutor cannot recognize brilliance in the solution of a problem that does not exist in its own archive. For the calculus tutor we shall make the simple assumption that length of problem solution is a measure of superiority. Thus whenever the student produces a solution of an archive problem that is shorter than the tutor's solution, the tutor will remember the student's solution by replacing its archive entry of state-approach pairs and updating its approach probability matrix. The tutor must of course reject solutions that end by quitting, or involve the guessing approach. In this way the tutor's basis for heuristic decisions can eventually be altered by the students.

6. The symbolic integration experiment

Methods of integration was a good choice of subject for this tutorial system for a number of reasons. As a subject in a calculus course, it is almost never taught as an algorithmic procedure (like differentiation). Rather the emphasis is on the acquisition of a number of techniques like substitution, integration by parts, and partial fraction expansion. Although the student is often given problems solvable by the same approaches, the real challenge is the recognition of the correct approach, rather than the details of the approach application. In addition, most problems can be solved by any one of several approaches involving different technique choices and different lengths of solution, thus providing the tutor a complete range of possible student results to judge. This unusually rich problem solving structure is ideal for testing the generality of the tutorial methods proposed in the previous sections.

In the initial phases of development of the integration tutor, it was hoped that the state definitions could be kept completely independent of problem solving considerations. The goal was to have each state unambiguously defined so that the tutor could know which state the student was in. Although this remains as an ideal, it was found that in certain situations a state definition dependent upon the way the problem is solved is preferable to the pure problem structure approach.

For instance, in the case of problems involving simple variable substitution leading directly to "known" integrals, integral solvers overwhelmingly recognize these problems as a distinct class based on the substitution approach. Although one could define this class exclusively using structural properties (the presence of a term and its derivative), the motivation for doing so is still based on the way the student solves this class. The key point is that virtually every integral solver solves these problems with a simple variable substitution, and it is unrealistic for the tutor to lump these problems into other classes that could yield a variety of possible hints. Thus in the choice of states for the integration tutor, we create two special states: "recognized substitutions"; and "recognized trigonometric substitutions". All other states are defined solely by their structural properties. The list of problem description states and the list of possible approaches are as follows:

1. Known integrals	1. Identification of known integrals
2. Recognized substitutions	2. Ordinary substitution
3. Recognized trigonometric substitutions	3. Integration by parts
4. Trigonometric and hyperbolic functions	4. Trigonometric substitution
5. Exponential functions	5. Trigonometric identities
6. Arc-trig and arc-hyperbolic functions	6. Separation of the sum
7. Fractional powers of functions	7. Polynomial division
8. Combinations of types 4 and 5	8. Completion of the square

9. Combination of types 4 and 7   9. Partial fraction expansion
10. Combination of types 5 and 6   10. Conjugation of the denominator
11. Combination of types 5 and 7   11. Expansion of a power
12. Combination of types 6 and 7   12. Returning to the previous integral
13. Polynomial functions   13. Guessing the answer
14. Other   14. Giving up

It is merely a coincidence that there are the same number of states and approaches in these lists. In addition to these problem description states, there are a number of special states, including "trapping states" corresponding to the solved problem, and to the aborted problem, as well as all of the possible failure states. The failure states were not actually considered explicitly (in the sense of creating entries for them in the data structures of our various models) because a simple "failure parameter" was built into the tutor that assumed that in the failure state the probability of the failing approach would be penalized by a constant factor λ, i.e.

$$a_{ij,\text{posterior}} = \lambda a_{ij,\text{prior}} \tag{13}$$

for the failing approach, and the remaining approaches' probabilities would be increased by a compensating factor that preserved normalization. Thus the actual data structures in the tutor remained fairly simple. In practice the value of λ was measured from real students, and was determined to be about $\lambda = 0.7$ (λ was measured by looking at how often the "failing approach" was re-chosen in the failure state).

The calculus tutor was written in LISP 1.6, a dialect of LISP developed at the Stanford Artificial Intelligence Laboratory. Since a typical tutorial session involved substantial algebraic manipulation, the tutor depended on REDUCE, a comprehensive algebraic manipulation system, written by Hearn at the University of Utah (1970). Although some minor formatting clean-up was done by the tutor, all algebraic manipulations including differentiation were then sent to REDUCE. Note that REDUCE had no routines for performing integration. The integrations performed by the calculus students were accomplished by the successive application of the called-for approaches. All of the approach machinery, including processing of the student responses, manipulation of the student models, variable substitution, trigonometric substitution, integrating by parts, polynomial division, trigonometric identities, and partial fraction expansion were done by the tutor. The resulting human driven integrating system was quite powerful and could solve in general closed form such difficult integrands as $1/(1+x^4)$.

7. Experimental results

Although the tutor was in continuous use by the author and others over a period of about a year (June 1971 to June 1972), the main experimental results were obtained from an intensive study conducted with 15 Stanford students in the spring of 1972. These students, some of whom were participating in calculus courses, and some of whom were simply interested in sharpening their integrating skills, interacted with the tutor over a monitored three week period. The students worked a total of 284 problems (19 each) of which 258 (91%) were selected by command of the students from the tutor's problem archive. Of all the problems, 282 (99%) were terminated in the solved state, and the other two were unsolvable problems initiated by the students (e.g.

integrand $= e^{x^2}$). The guessing technique was used 45 times with a success rate of 89%. The students asked the tutor for direct help in 90 of the problems. Typically, once help was requested, it was requested repeatedly. In the 90 "helped" problems, the students asked for approach choosing assistance 173 times, and approach application assistance 65 times. The students entered identifiable failure states (where application of the trial approach failed to yield a new transformation that they would accept) 98 times on 65 different problems. The probability that the student would enter a failure state was 0·29 if he had not previously entered a failure state on that problem and 0·40 if he had already entered a failure state on that problem. The probability that the student would ask for help was 0·32 if he had not entered a failure state and 0·54 if he had entered a failure state.

A major assumption in Section 4 was that learning occurred suddenly and at unpredictable intervals. This assumption allowed us to separate neatly the information updating and student learning processes. We assumed furthermore that we could identify the occurrences of student learning processes. We assumed furthermore that we could identify the occurrences of student learning unambiguously, thus knowing when to apply the student learning model. We shall now present an analysis of the student's responses that makes our assumptions of the existence and properties of learning discontinuities credible.

Consider an experiment in which we, the observers, have only the power to observe responses made by the participants. We are to assume nothing about the purpose of the experiment or the meaning of the responses. The responses themselves are sequences of positive integers which we assume arise from a multinomial distribution. We are told by the designers of the experiment that at certain designated points in the sequences it is likely that the participants altered their rationale for responding. The designers' suspicion of uniqueness of these points arises from observations that we are not permitted to see. We are asked to analyze the response data to (a) support or reject the hypothesis that the suspicious points separate differing response regimes; and (b) test the inclusiveness of the experimenter's criterion for selecting suspicious points by trying to find additional points that are significant statistically as regime separators. In this hypothetical experiment we have purposely obscured the underlying rationale for "suspecting" a given point so as not to allow the observer any bias in deciding that such a point indeed ought to separate response regimes.

In order to answer question (a), we propose to consider the sequence of responses s_1 before each suspicious point and the sequence of responses s_2 following each point. Using these sequences we calculate the chi-square statistic for the particular suspicious point. The chi-square statistic is chosen since it is the natural comparison for independent samples from two multinomial distributions. Since the magnitude of the chi-square statistic depends on the sample size, each candidate pair of sequences will be compared to 1,000 sequences randomly generated with the same overall response probabilities. We shall take as the null hypothesis the event that the subsequences s_1 and s_2 do not arise from different multinominal distributions. Thus if sequence s_2 really does represent a statistically significant change from s_1, the resulting chi-square statistic will be large in comparison with most of the 1,000 sequences generated under the null hypothesis. In practice, we shall accept only those suspicious points whose chi-square statistic has a significance of 90% or more (whose chi-square statistic is strictly greater than 90% of the chi-square values generated by the null hypothesis). Once we have identified a point successfully as separating two regimes of responses, we must ignore sequence s_1 in examining points further along the data since responses from sequence s_1 will contribute falsely to raising the chi-square values of subsequent points.

To answer question (b), we shall repeat the calculation of the chi-square statistic and the 1,000 null hypothesis trials at all of the non-suspicious points to see how many "non-suspicious" points are also regime separators. This is crucial as a test of the model predicting the occurrence of discontinuities.

Of course, this hypothetical experiment describes exactly the situation we face when trying to identify the learning points from the calculus students' response data. The suspicious points are those places where the student encountered a failure state and presumably had to consider whether or not his solution schemes were practical. As emphasized above, we did not make any assumptions about the student data other than assuming that between learning events each student's responses were derived from a multinominal distribution. This was felt to be a fair test of the existence of learning points since inclusion of extraneous student entries and ad hoc interpretation of each student protocol was avoided.

Several interesting facts were uncovered by this search. As a general rule, a minimum of eight responses were needed to establish a 90% certainty of the existence of a learning point, even with the most extreme data. For instance, the sequence 1 1 1 1 2 2 2 (consisting of only seven responses) does not possess any division into subsequences, even after the fourth response, that generates a chi-square statistic with 90% significance. In a similar vein, regardless of the total length of the sequence, the first two responses are incapable of indicating a learning point. For instance the sequence

$$1\,1\,2\,2\,2\,2\,2\,2\,2\,2\,2\,2\,2\,2\,2\,2\,2\,2\,2\,2\,2\,2\,2\,2\,2\,2\,2\,2$$

also does not possess any division in subsequences that generates a chi-square statistic with 90% significance. This result has the incidental effect of causing most of the changes in response probabilities due to "the start-up transient" not to be considered as significant learning points. (Nearly all the students made one or two anomalous responses at the outset before they became familiar with the tutor.)

The student responses were separated by state and the suspicious points were identified by looking at the complete protocols and marking all the times a student applied a transformation that failed to yield a new integrand (definition of the failure state). After response lists of fewer than eight responses and failure states occurring in the first two responses were eliminated, a total of 37 suspicious points remained. The chi-square analysis showed that 17 of the 37 points (45·9%) were indeed significant as response regime separators at the 90% level. The most important result of this analysis was that a complete scan of all the responses (461 in all) produced only three additional points significant as response regime separators at the 90% level. Thus although only 45·9% of the suspicious points seem to be genuine learning points, 85·0% of all possible learning points are identified by our model.

Why are half of the student failure rates obviously not learning points? A detailed examination of the student protocols for each of the insignificant points shows that the contributing causes are diverse. In three cases the failure state was "false" since the student subsequently reapplied the same technique successfully. In at least 10 cases the student encountered a succession of failure states in more than one problem type.

Since the tutor tended to choose archive problems from the most "critical" problem classification, some students did not return to all the troubled states frequently enough to produce a reasonably long run of failure free responses. Several short sequences of responses were encountered that were interspersed with two or more failure states and yielded inconclusive results. This, of course, should be viewed as a mild failure of the experiment since in this case it is not clear whether the student finished the experiment too soon or whether the tutor failed to teach the student effectively.

Returning to the original question of this section, what was the distribution of identified learning points in the student's responses? Examining 44 subsequences generated from the students' set of responses divided at each learning point, we find that the average number of responses generated between learning points is $461/44 = 10.47$, but the distribution of this number varies from 3 to 39 with 18 different values measured. We are now in a position to claim that the learning discontinuities occur *sporadically* since we have shown that the average number of responses between learning points is widely distributed. Furthermore, we can draw the conclusion that the learning discontinuities are *sudden* since our analysis showed that 85% of all the significant learning points agree with our model of the failure state as being the precise point where the responses change significantly. This completes the justification for separating the information updating and learning models, and in fact, for positing the independent existence of the learning model in the first place.

The most interesting question to ask about the calculus students is whether they became better problem solvers after their exposure to the tutor. In order to get a quantitative handle on measuring this improvement, we compared the length of the students' problem archive solutions to those of the tutor, as a function of the number of problems worked. Figure 2 shows the students' average number of additional steps

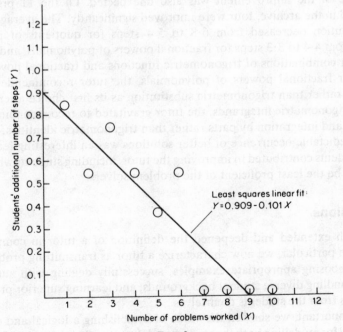

Least squares linear fit:
$Y = 0.909 - 0.101 X$

FIG. 2.

per problem worked as a function of the number of problems worked. Notice the general downward trend of the points, indicating that the students gradually learned how to solve problems in as few steps as the tutor. (No negative entries are recorded because each time the student solved a problem in fewer steps than the tutor, the tutor incorporated the student's solution into the archive.) A least squares linear fit of this data suggests that the average improvement amounted to $0 \cdot 101$ steps closer to the tutor for each problem worked.

A similar analysis shows that the student's probability of entering a failure state gradually reduces with the number of problems worked.

Since in this section we have shown that we can identify those moments when the student encounters learning discontinuities, we can deduce the actual values of the learning parameter α from the student's data. The average α measured in the student experiment was $\alpha = 0 \cdot 169$, which is a surprisingly powerful effect. This means that the student is only about 17% as likely to choose a failing technique in the next encounter with this problem state as he was before encountering the failure and its attendant learning discontinuity.

Before the integration experiment the author believed that only one or two of the students might be so adept that they would actually construct shorter solutions to some of the archive problems. Since the author had been involved in integral problem solving for at least two years prior to the experiment, and considered himself an expert integral problem solver, there seemed little chance that any improvements would actually occur. Upon examining the archive at the end of the experiment, it was found that no less than 25% of the original problem solutions had been shortened! From the detailed solution schemes, it was apparent that the tutor had acquired approach patterns never before used by the author. This was a lesson of the first magnitude.

The scope of the improvement was also unexpected. Of the 11 problem types respresented in the archive, four were improved significantly. The average number of steps to solution decreased from $6 \cdot 8$ to $5 \cdot 4$ steps for quotients of polynomials, decreased from $4 \cdot 4$ to $3 \cdot 3$ steps for fractional powers of polynomials, and from $3 \cdot 0$ to $2 \cdot 0$ steps for combinations of trigonometric functions and fractional powers of poly-nomials. For fractional powers of polynomials, the tutor recommended derivative substitution rather than trigonometric substitution as its first choice after the experi-ment. For trigonometric integrands, the tutor gravitated to recommending derivative substitution and integration by parts rather than trigonometric identities.

The unpredictable occurrence of better solutions was an interesting feature. Seven different students contributed to improving the tutor, including students who otherwise appeared to be the least proficient of the problem solvers.

8. Conclusions

This research extended and deepened the definition of a tutor in computer based education. In particular, we now characterize a tutor as transmitting problem solving heuristics, choosing appropriate examples, successfully dealing with student posed problems, handling diverse student backgrounds, and learning superior problem solv-ing heuristics from the students themselves.

Equally important, we showed the value of establishing a logical and quantitative methodology for modelling both the student and the tutor. This logical and quantitative base then allowed the tutorial strategy to be implemented with a reasonable foundation, rather than in an ad hoc manner.

The experimental results supported the view that learning discontinuities exist and can be identified. The experiment also allowed us to test the appropriateness of the various tutor thresholds, and to measure a number of student parameters, including the learning parameter in the learning model, the rate of learning, and the rate of reduction of failure to choose an effective approach.

Perhaps the most interesting result of the experiment was the unexpected scope of the improvement in the tutor wrought by the students. This suggests that tutorial systems with nothing but "hard-wired" heuristics may, in fact, be considerably less effective than their implementers think.

References

CARBONELL, J. R. (1970). AI in CAI: an artificial-intelligence approach to computer assisted instruction. *IEEE Transactions on Man–Machine Systems*, **MMS-11**, 190–201.

HEARN, A. C. (1970). *Reduce 2 User's Manual*. Stanford Artificial Intelligence Project Memo AIM-133, Stanford University.

HOWARD, R. (1971). *Dynamic Probabilistic Systems*. John Wiley, New York.

KIMBALL, R. (1973). *Self-Optimizing Computer-Assisted Tutoring: Theory and Practice*. Institute of Mathematical Studies in the Social Sciences, Psychology and Education Series, Technical Report # 206, June 25, 1973.

RISCH, R. (1969). The problem of integration in finite terms. *Transactions of the American Mathematical Society*, **139**, 167–189.

Appendix 1. The information updating and student learning models

$\{E|a\}$, the probability of observing the event E given a set of student approach probabilities, is given by the mutinomial distribution, where E is formally defined to be the event that in n independent selections from the state S_t, the student chose approach a_j a total of n_j times:

$$\{E|a_i\} = n!/(n_1!n_2! \cdots n_N!)a_{i1}^{n_1}a_{i2}^{n_2} \cdots a_{iN}^{n_N} \tag{A1}$$

The prior estimate of the student's approach probabilities for state S_i is given by a Dirichlet distribution (also known as the multi-dimensional beta distribution):

$$\{a_i\} = 1/\beta(m_1, m_2, \ldots, m_N)y_1^{m_1}y_2^{m_2} \cdots y_N^{m_N} \tag{A2}$$

where

$$\beta(m_1, m_2, \ldots, m_N) = m_1!m_2! \cdots m_N!/(m_1 + m_2 + \cdots + m_N)! \tag{A3}$$

and we have suppressed the index i on the right side of (A2).

We see that our model of the student's problem solving abilities (in state $S(i)$) is represented entirely by the set of integers $m_1, m_2, \ldots, m_N$, and in fact, the complete data structure required to represent the student is simply an M by N matrix, where M is the total number of problem solving states, and N is the total number of approaches. From (A2), the expected value of the approach probability a_{ij} is given by

$$\text{Exp}(a_{ij}) = m_j/(m_1 + m_2 + \cdots + m_N) \tag{A4}$$

i.e. the probabilities are just simple ratios.

The Dirichlet distribution possesses the *conjugacy property* relative to the multinomial distribution, so that the calculation of the posterior estimate has a very convenient form:

$$\{a|E\} = 1/\beta(m_1 + n_1, \ldots, m_N + n_N) y_1^{m_1 + n_1} \cdots y_N^{m_N + n_N} \tag{A5}$$

In other words, we can update the data structure representing the student simply by adding the observed frequency of use of approach 1 (namely n_1) to m_1, the observed frequency of use of approach 2 (namely n_2) to m_2, and so on, for each state. No complex calculations are required: we just add integers to the entries in the M by N approach probability matrix. In other words, all of the mathematics has only been the justification for this very simple approach!

It is worth making an important point here. We *might* have chosen by divine inspiration to represent information about the student in the very form given by this analysis, namely as a simple matrix of "hits", subsequently calculating probabilities by taking the ratio of observed hits for the approach desired to the total number of observed hits. The purpose of the careful preparatory analysis, therefore, has *not* been to develop a sophisticated computational technique for updating the information model, but rather to lay a proper logical foundation under a very simple technique.

The above analysis has been in terms of the approach probabilities a_{ij}. The same form of analysis can be carried out for the transition probabilities p_{ik} themselves, if desired. If this is done, then several interesting quantities can be calculated. By taking the M by N transition probability matrix T and eliding the rows and columns corresponding to the *trapping states* of the process (the states arrived at when a problem is finished and no further transformations can be made), we have the modified transition matrix T^*. We can then write

$$\tau = [I - T^*]^{-1} \tag{A6}$$

where I is the identity matrix and τ is the matrix of *expected delays before trapping*.

The matrix product

$$[\tau][1 \cdots 1]^{\text{transpose}} = [\nu] \tag{A7}$$

gives the column vector of the expected number of steps to a finished solution from each possible state. In other words, ν_i gives the *average absolute number of steps to solution* that the student will take in solving a problem in classification i.

Equation (A5) gives the form of the information updating model. The ad hoc learning model, which we have assumed must be applied after each problem solution where the student encounters unsuccessful approaches, simply hypothesizes that the effect of encountering an unsuccessful approach, followed by executing a successful approach, is given by the following equations:

$$a_{ij}, \text{posterior} = \alpha a_{ij}, \text{prior—for the unsuccessful approach} \tag{A8}$$

$$a_{ik}, \text{posterior} = \eta a_{ik}, \text{prior—for the successful approach} \tag{A9}$$

In other words, the unsuccessful approach is penalized by a constant multiplicative factor α, and the successful approach is rewarded by a factor η, where the value of η is chosen to maintain normalization of all the a_{ix}'s.

An advanced form of this theory would require that α itself vary with depth of student experience, since it stands to reason that a seasoned old "pro" is not going to alter his main-line problem solving judgement very much just because of a single failure of an approach. We thus expect that α would approach unity with increasing experience and α itself can be represented by an information updating model, much like the approach probabilities. This line of reasoning is explored to a degree in Kimball (1973).

13. A self-improving quadratic tutor

Tim O'Shea[†]

Computer Based Learning Project, Department of Computer Studies, University of Leeds, U.K.

A self-improving quadratic tutor comprising two principal components is described. One component is an adaptive teaching program where the teaching strategy is expressed as a set of production rules. The second component performs the self-improving function of the system by making experimental changes to the set of production rules. This component employs a deduction procedure which operates on a theory of instruction expressed as a set of modally qualified assertions. These assertions relate educational objectives to modifications which can be made to the teaching strategy. The cycle of operations proposed for the system is as follows—select an educational objective, make an experimental change in teaching strategy, statistically evaluate the resulting performance, and update both the set of production rules and set of assertions.

The tutor taught the solution of quadratic equations by the discovery method. The tutor was used by 51 students, and executed five experimental changes on its teaching strategy. This trial demonstrated that it was capable of improving its performance as a result of experimentation. Its limitations include a vulnerability to problems of local optima during "hill-climbing" and to a variant of the frame problem.

Introduction

Compared to human tutors, most Computer Assisted Instruction (CAI) programs which attempt to teach are severely limited. The limitations include:

(1) inability to conduct dialogues with the student in natural language;
(2) inability to understand the subject being taught, in the sense that the program cannot accept unanticipated responses;
(3) inability to understand the nature of the student's mistakes or misconceptions;
(4) inability to profit from experience with students or to experiment with the teaching strategy.

These limitations result in part from the way teaching and subject matter knowledge are represented and organized in CAI programs. As such, these shortcomings have been tackled as Artificial Intelligence (AI) (or "AI in CAI") problems by a number of workers (see, for example, Carbonell, 1970; Pask, 1972; Koffman and Blount, 1973). Perhaps the most successful CAI program with regard to problems (1) and (2) is Brown *et al.*'s (1976) SOPHIE. This program teaches electronic trouble shooting and employs a variety of alternative representations of the skill being taught for use in both interpreting the English input and demonstrating trouble-shooting strategies to the student. Other examples of programs that "know what they teach" are Goldberg's (1973) program, which teaches theorem-proving (and incorporates a heuristically programmed theorem-prover), and Sleeman's (1974) problem-solving monitor for

† Current address: Department of Artificial Intelligence, University of Edinburgh, Forrest Hill, Edinburgh EH1 2QL.

NMR spectroscopy. No really substantial contributions have been made to problem (3). In general the advances which have been achieved result from work in Educational Psychology rather than AI. Such advances have been derived from experiments in particular teaching domains such as the various arithmetic programs (e.g. Woods & Hartley, 1971).

Both Self (1974) and Stansfield (1974) have proposed that student models should be both explicit and represented as procedures. However, this application of the AI procedural embedding of knowledge thesis (see Hewitt, 1972) has not been generally applied to working CAI programs. For the most part the student models implicit in contemporary CAI programs are rudimentary.

The focus of this paper is problem (4)—the lack of learning capability in CAI programs. Only two CAI programs are reported in the literature which have a self-improving capability—that of Smallwood (1962) and that of Kimball (1973). In Smallwood's program, random local changes in branching decisions are made and evaluated. The teaching strategy, task analysis and student model are all implicit, and it is not possible to carry out and record the result of experiment on aspects of these components. In Kimball's program, sequences of integration transforms shorter than those which would be carried out by the program/tutor are learned from the student. So the program's ability to carry out integrations improves and hence its hints to the students may change, but its response-sensitivity as such (which depends on the "student trouble thresholds") remains fixed.

In the research described here, the aim was to express teaching strategies so that it would be possible to "prime" the system with general and specific hypotheses about alternative ways of teaching. The system should then carry out experiments to rest these hypotheses and amend the teaching strategy accordingly.

Teaching quadratic equations

The rationale for the discovery method (see Schulman & Keisler, 1977) style of teaching is that, if the student himself discovers solutions and methods of solution, this will deepen his understanding, promote his retention of the material and maintain his motivation.

For quadratic equations, a teaching session using the discovery method style of teaching usually proceeds as follows. The student is presented with the equations of the form:

$$\Box^2 + c = b \times \Box$$

and asked to guess the solutions, (x, y). Initially values of b and c are chosen such that the solutions are easy to guess and are easily seen to be true, for example, $c = 2$, $b = 3$, yields $x = 1$, $y = 2$. The problems are then made more difficult. The student is judged to have discovered how to solve this class of equations when he has demonstrated he is able to solve a range of problems which indicate that the appropriate rules have been discovered. These are that $x + y = b$, ("ADD" rule) and $x \times y = c$, ("TIMES" rule). Subsidiary rules which he may discover during the session and which can assist in the solution of the problem are that both x and y are factors of c, ("DIVIDE" rule) and that if $b = c + 1$, then $x = 1$ and $y = c$, ("ONE" rule).

The teaching strategy centres on giving the student carefully chosen examples which increase the likelihood of a student discovering a particular rule. Eventually, the student will appear to have mastered and be applying a particular rule. He is then presented with examples for which his rule is not sufficient, interspersed with examples for which his rule is adequate. This represents an attempt to discourage him from rejecting his rule, while at the same time encouraging him to try to discover other rules.

A preliminary experiment

A preliminary experiment was carried out in a primary school in Leeds with 20 ten-year old pupils. First the pupils were given an introductory session in which it was determined whether they could solve equations of the form:

$$\Box + 3 = 12$$

and

$$\Box^2 = 0$$

or a word problem isomorph of these equations; for example, "If a boy has a bag of marbles and adds three marbles to the bag and then tips out the bag and finds 12 marbles, how many marbles were in the bag initially?" In some cases a little practice and explanation was necessary, but eventually all the pupils could easily solve these pre-test equations.

While attempting to solve the quadratic equations, the pupils' motivation was affected by a number of factors. Some pupils had a very strong dislike of making mistakes and being told that a guess was wrong. They would guess rarely and reluctantly. When a pupil discovered one of the rules there would be a big upsurge in interest. Occasionally a pupil would become dispirited and start guessing lots of high numbers or in a series: 10, 11, 12, 13, . . . , etc. In this situation it seemed best to give him the solution and proceed with another "easier" example.

A number of features were observed to contribute to task difficulty for pupils who had not discovered the rules for solution. Most of the pupils had a fair idea of the reasonable range of values for their guesses. So increasing the value of b or c increased the difficulty. Holding b or c constant over successive examples made it easier for pupils to pick up the "ADD" rule or the "TIMES" rule, respectively. Where the factors of c were 2 and a prime (>5), this seemed to assist the acquisition of the "TIMES" or "DIVIDE" rule.

Pupil performance and strategies varied considerably. If they acquired a rule early in the session (particularly the "ONE" rule), they tended to apply it frequently. If they acquired a rule later on they would discard it easily. Some pupils were very systematic and would construct and test hypotheses. Others were without apparent method in their approach. A small number of pupils would persistently adhere to a rule despite obvious contradictions. One boy appeared to be making deliberate errors in his arithmetic to fit his incorrect rules.

Pupils would often find a first solution by guessing, either randomly or with the aid of the "DIVIDE" rule. The "DIVIDE" rule could be used to restrict guesses to factors of c. If they knew the "ADD" or "TIMES" rules, they could then apply one of them to the first solution to obtain the second.

After the pupils had mastered the rules they were asked to articulate them and, with one exception, could do this. The exception, who could solve difficult quadratic equations quickly, banged his head and pronounced: "It's in there, but I can't make it come out!"

Implications for teaching component of tutor

The tutor should be friendly ("No, have another go"), rather than stern ("Wrong"). Also, the program should intervene if a pupil has clearly given up (that is, lots of random, unlikely guesses).

The features which were judged to affect task difficulty are the size of b and c, the number of factors of c, whether b is prime, whether a solution is "1", and whether b or c are held constant over successive examples.

An important implication for the construction of the student model is that student guesses do not precisely reflect the student's state of knowledge. For example, a gap often occurs between getting the first solution and the second solution, even when the student has acquired a rule which should allow him to get the second solution directly after the first. Accordingly, the model will have to make estimates based on the student answers as to whether he has acquired or is testing a particular rule.

With respect to the tutorial strategy, it became apparent that the tutor must be very conservative, and in general should give students who appear to have acquired a rule a great deal of reinforcement (that is, lots of examples easy to solve with that rule). However, an excess of such reinforcement may make it harder for the pupil to eventually realize that his rule is useful but not adequate to solve every equation. This is the type of trade-off problem which must be resolved by the self-improving component of the tutor.

The teaching component

The four components of the teaching program proper are taken from Hartley's (1973) structure for CAI programs, namely: vocabulary of teaching operations (i.e. task administration); representation of task (i.e. task selection); model of the student (i.e. hypothesis tester) and means-end guidance rules (i.e. tutorial strategy). Although designed and implemented to run with the experimenting component, it could be, and was on a number of occasions, run independently as a non-self-improving tutor.

Task administration

This involves administering examples and general book-keeping. Administering examples includes presenting the examples, giving encouragement ("well done", "have another go", etc.), and responding to guesses ("nope", "that was a wild guess sunshine", etc.). These functions are best illustrated by the protocol in Fig. 1.

Example selection

The model of task difficulty derived from the preliminary experiment was expressed in terms of a task difficulty matrix which relates teaching goals and subgoals to example

CONSIDER THE EQUATION X TIMES X+18 = X TIMES 9 GUESS THE ANSWERS
STUDENT: WHAT HAPPENS IF I CANT
PLEASE TYPE IN A NUMBER OR TYPE STOP IF YOU WISH TO STOP
STUDENT: 1, 2
NOPE
STUDENT: 3
THATS RIGHT SEE IF YOU CAN GET THE OTHER ANSWER
STUDENT: 4, 5
NOPE
STUDENT: 6
WELL DONE YOU HAVE GOT BOTH THE ANSWERS
CONSIDER THE EQUATION X TIMES X+18 = X TIMES 19 GUESS THE ANSWERS
STUDENT: 3
NOPE KEEP TRYING
STUDENT: 6, 12, 2, 3
NOPE KEEP TRYING
STUDENT: 4, 5, 6, 7, 8, 9, 10
YOU ARE NOT TRYING TO THINK OF ANY RULES TO HELP YOU
WE WILL LOOK AT ANOTHER EXAMPLE
TRY TO FIND A RULE
THE RIGHT ANSWERS ARE IN FACT 1 AND 18
CONSIDER THE EQUATION X TIMES X+48 = X TIMES 19 GUESS THE ANSWERS
STUDENT: 1, 18, 12, 48, 19, 64, 9, 2
NOPE
STUDENT: 3
THATS RIGHT SEE IF YOU CAN GET THE OTHER ANSWER
STUDENT: 6
NOPE KEEP TRYING
STUDENT: 3
YES BUT YOU HAVE GUESSED THAT CORRECTLY BEFORE
STUDENT: 15, 18, 9, 1
NOPE
THAT WAS A LOT OF GUESSES
LETS TRY ANOTHER EXAMPLE
THE RIGHT ANSWERS ARE IN FACT 3 AND 16

FIG. 1. Extract from protocol of quadratic tutor in use.

features. These features are weighted as to how much they help or hinder the acquisition of the various subgoals.

The example selection procedure takes an input command of the form (GEN ((RULE1, HELP), (RULE2, HIN), PROPERTY)). This is interpreted as "generate an example which will help the student acquire or apply RULE1, which will hinder the application of RULE2 and for which PROPERTY is true". Using the task difficulty matrix, the example features are ordered with respect to their relation to the subgoals given in the command.

The features are then sorted according to two criteria. First, incompatible features are eliminated from the list. An example of a pair of incompatible features is "that one of the solutions to the problem be 1" and "that none of the solutions be 1". Then currently impossible features are eliminated. Consider the pair of features "that both solutions have numerical values less than 5". After a number of problems have been presented it may be impossible to find a new example with these features. The table of examples is then searched for the best fit to the remaining set of features. If no fit is found, the set of features is added to a list of sets of features now impossible to obtain. Then the feature with the smallest relative weight is dropped and the search repeated until an example is finally selected and administered.

The working and inter-relation of the various parts of the teaching component are illustrated in Fig. 2.

Tutorial strategy

The components of the tutorial strategy must be represented in a form amenable to automatic manipulation. The relevant features of systems of production rules are:

(a) they can be used to represent strategies;
(b) they can provide a clear, simple, transparent structure;
(c) they are amenable to automatic manipulation.

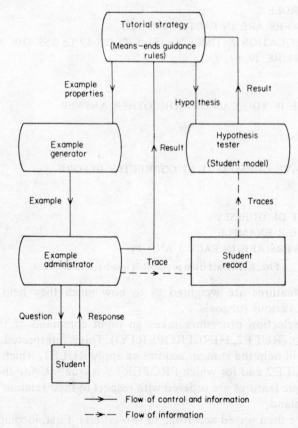

FIG. 2. Schematic diagram of the teaching component of the quadratic tutor.

The type of production systems employed in the tutor are based directly on Waterman's (1970) work. In the production rule systems employed here the mechanism used for conflict resolution (that is, which rule gets fired if more than one is potentially applicable) is rule order. The use of production rules for expressing tutorial strategies is discussed at length in O'Shea (1977).

In one sense the tutorial strategy may be said to encompass all the decisions taken during the implementation of a teaching program: decisions such as the format of the questions, the entries in the task difficulty matrix, the nature of the student model, and the order of examples generated. What is described here is the set of means-end guidance rules which relate the predictions from the student model to the process of task selection. These rules constitute a presentation strategy for the different example types, and co-ordinate the other components of the program, namely the task adminis- trator, task selector and student model (again see Fig. 2).

The presentation strategy is expressed as a set of production rules. The set is given in Appendix 1. The elements of the state-vector are variables associated with tutorial strategy such as the current teaching subgoal, the "reason" for the last tutorial action executed and estimates of the student's state of knowledge from the student model. In a complete cycle of operation the existing state-vector is first parsed (see Appendix 1) using the partitions. The left-hand sides of the rules are then searched for the first match with the parsed vector. The corresponding right-hand side, which in fact is a list of LISP function calls, is then executed and the state-vector is updated as a result.

The following functions are used on the right-hand side.

(a) (SETQ NAME X)—used to set parameters such as GUESSLIM: the maximum number of incorrect guesses permitted on any one example.
(b) (HYP RULE)—test the hypothesis that the student has mastered the rule in question (see section on Hypothesis Tester).
(c) (GEN ((RULE1, HELP), (RULE2, HIN)) (PROPERTY))—select, and administer example with appropriate features.
(d) (CONTINUE N)—generate and administer "N" more examples with the same properties as the previous one.
(e) (GOAL NAME)—sets a flag in the state-vector indicating the current subgoal.
(f) (DPRINTER NAME)—output the text labelled NAME.

The production rules can mostly be divided into those relating to the testing of hyotheses and those concerned with example selection. An example of the former is: ((1 A3 19 K1) ((HYP ONE))). This reads "if the program is in the hypothesis testing cycle and the current subgoal is the ONE rule, only test whether the student has acquired this rule". The rationale behind this rule is that testing the other hypotheses would be a waste of computer time. However, continual checking of all hypotheses would result in the program detecting incidental learning of other rules sooner. This is another kind of trade-off problem which the experimenting component will try to resolve.

The rules relating to example selection may be considered as describing a partially ordered set of goals. The goals fall into four classes, as follows.

(a) ADD, TIMES and ONE—get the student to master the rule named.
(b) ONETOADD, ONETOTIMES, ADDTOONE—get the student to master the second named rule without losing the first named rule.

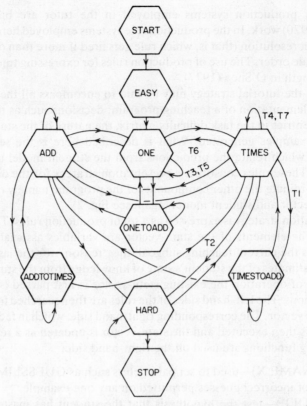

FIG. 3. Directed graph showing interrelation of tutorial goals and subgoals.

(c) EASY—give the student problem solvable by inspection.
(d) HARD—give the student examples only solvable with complete mastery of the task.

The interrelation of the goals is illustrated by the directed graph given in Fig. 3. Each node represents a goal, and the outgoing arcs correspond to the production rules associated with the goal. For example, GOAL TIMES may be left if conditions expressed by the right-hand sides of any of six rules labelled T1 through T6 are met. (See Appendix 1). The conditions these correspond to are:

(a) T1 "Has the student mastered and successfully applied both the ADD and TIMES rule for the last three examples?"
(b) T2 "Has the student mastered the TIMES rule but not the ADD rule?"
(c) T3 "Is incidental learning on the ADD rule greater than learning on the TIMES rule?"
(d) T4 "Is it 'very possible' or 'certain' that the student has mastered the TIMES rule?"
(e) T5, T6 Check for incidental learning on ADD and ONE rules respectively.

In the event of none of these conditions being fulfilled, rule T7 insures that example selection for the TIMES goal continues.

Hypothesis tester

While some assumptions about student learning are implicit in the tutorial strategy, estimates of the student's current state of knowledge are made by a hypothesis tester. This constitutes the explicit part of the student model.

The five hypotheses that may be tested are as follows:

(1) WORULE—that the student has no rule at all.
(2) WRULE—that the student has completely mastered all the rules.
(3) TIMES ⎫
(4) ADD   ⎬ that the student has mastered the particular rule in question.
(5) ONE   ⎭

As the discussion of the preliminary experiments indicates, evaluating these hypotheses presents certain difficulties. In particular, students often will appear to have completely mastered a rule and yet fail to apply it in appropriate situations, with the result that there is an occasional "gap" (that is, one or two incorrect guesses) between the first and second correct solutions. Also, phenomena such as temporary forgetting, lucky correct guesses and correct guesses which could have been achieved by more than one rule, make it very difficult for the hypothesis tester to definitely accept or reject a hypothesis. The hypothesis tester takes as input such factors as the size of the problem space (that is, the current number of legal guesses) and previous estimates of the student's state of knowledge, along with the student's guesses as he solves the current equation.

This difficulty in confirming or rejecting hypotheses is partly resolved by returning one of a range of values: CERTAIN, VERY POSSIBLE, POSSIBLE, DON'T KNOW, POSSIBLY NOT, CERTAINLY NOT.

Theory of instruction

For experiments to be evaluated, overall goals and measures associated with them must be identified. Four goals were selected for the tutor, namely:

(a) increase the number of students successfully completely the teaching session, (SS);
(b) increase the average score on a post-test, (PS);
(c) decrease the amount of student time used, (ST);
(d) decrease the amount of computer time used, (CT).

The theory of instruction consists of assertions relating general or highly specific changes in the tutorial strategy to the goals above. It would be possible to create such assertions about changes in the sets of production rules which constitute the student model. This was not done as it seemed unlikely that it would even be possible (because of time constraints) to examine all the possible changes on the tutorial strategy. The theory of instruction which was used for the experiments described below is given in full in Appendix 2.

The approach used here is a development of Black's (1968) natural deduction system. Two types of assertion are employed. Firstly causal assertions which relate actions (changes executable on the set of production rules embodying the teaching strategy) to effects (possible changes in teaching performance). Secondly, definitional assertions which group together classes of actions or effects. The set of causal assertions can be viewed as an action-driven production system (see Waterman, 1977), and is analogous to a collection of PLANNER consequent theorems (see Hewitt, 1972). The set of definitional assertions is essentially a list of associations used during the matching process to prevent endless deductions and facilitate generalizations.

CERT and POSS operators adapted from modal logic (see Hughes & Cresswell, 1972) are employed to distinguish consequences which will certainly follow actions from consequences which may follow actions. Some of the causal assertions are highly specific to the teaching component given above. For example, some refer to possible changes in parameters set in the tutorial strategy, e.g. (POSS (LOWER GUESSLIM) (DECREASE (STUDENT TIME))). This can be interpreted as "if the set of production rules constituting the tutorial strategy are changed so that the variable associated with task administration which sets a limit on the number of guesses per equation is lowered, then a decrease in student time may possibly result". [A list of parameters associated with task administration which may be reset by the tutorial strategy is given in Appendix 1, section (e).]

Other assertions refer to changes in the order of specific teaching subgoals, for example, (POSS (AND (AFTER (GOAL EASY)) (REPLACE (GOAL ONE) (GOAL TIMES))) (SHORTEN SESSIONS)). Other assertions are very general and could be reasonably found in any self-improving program with the same goals; for example:

```
(CERT (SHORTEN SESSIONS) (DECREASE TIMES))
(POSS (SHORTEN SESSIONS) (DECREASE SCORES))
(POSS (DECREASE (HYPOTHESIS TESTING))
     (OR (DECREASE (COMPUTER TIME))
         (INCREASE SCORES)
         (INCREASE (STUDENT TIME)) )   )
```

Note that some of the definitional assertions are also highly specific, e.g. (EQUIV (OR REPLIM SYSLIM GUESSLIM WILDLIM) EXLIMIT). In this case the class of parameters which assert the number of guesses permitted is being defined.

Other definitional assertions are completely general, e.g. (EQUIV CHANGE (OR INCREASE DECREASE)). All the specific assertions must clearly be written with reference to the existing set of production rules (or any form it might be amended to), and name elements which occur or might occur in it. General assertions are no use if the constructs they employ are not related by other assertions to changes in goal variables and changes in tutorial strategies. For example, the causal assertion: (CERT (KEEP BORED STUDENTS) (INCREASE TIMES)) would never be applied without assertions indicating how (KEEP BORED STUDENTS) might be achieved by changes in the tutorial strategy.

The deduction procedure

The deduction procedure operates as follows. Firstly, given a desired goal such as "decrease computer time", deduce the sets of actions (changes in tutorial strategy) which may achieve this goal.

Secondly, given a set of actions, deduce the possible consequences of these actions.

If alternative sets of actions are to be compared, then some measure of the likelihood of a consequence occurring is necessary. Here is a deduction procedure which computes possible consequences of different courses of action.

(1) Select a goal, for example (DECREASE (COMPUTER TIME)).

(2) Perform a search for matches on the right-hand sides of the causal assertions with this goal. The definitional assertions are used to check for matches, e.g. with the assertion (DEFEQUIV TIME (OR (STUDENT TIME) (COMPUTER TIME))) the goal of (DECREASE (COMPUTER TIME)) will match (CERT ACTION (DECREASE TIME)).

(3) The corresponding left-hand sides are detached, and Step 2 is repeated with any non-executable predicates as goals. Thus a list of executable predicates corresponding to function calls to the amender is built up.

(4) For the lists $\langle L_i \rangle$ of executable predicates thus obtained POSS(L_i), the number of causal assertions qualified by the POSS operator employed in the deduction of $\langle L_i \rangle$ is computed. Any list containing a non-executable predicate which cannot be matched on the right-hand side of some causal assertion is discarded. The a ($a \geq 2$) lists $\langle L_i \rangle$ with the smallest value of POSS(L_i) (i.e. the most likely) are taken as possible courses of action.

(5) For each list of executable predicates, $\langle L_i \rangle$ from $\langle L_i \rangle_a$ matches are made on the left-hand side of causal assertions. The corresponding right-hand sides are detached and again matched with left-hand sides. This process is repeated until no new matches can be made.

(6) From (5) all the predicates $\langle M_j \rangle$ where arguments are "goal" variables are identified. These are divided into those resulting in the achievement of goals $\langle G_k \rangle$ such as (INCREASE (STUDENT SCORE)), say, and those resulting in the deterioration of progress towards goals $\langle B \rangle_l$, such as (INCREASE (COMPUTER TIME)), say. A measure μ relating to the likelihood of the overall achievement of goals can then be computed for each L_i. For example:

$$\mu = \sum_{k=1}^{n} W_k \times P(G_k) - \sum_{l=1}^{m} W_l \times P(B_l)$$

where $P(M_j)$ is computed as $_\beta$POSS (M_j) $(0 < \beta < 1)$. Where POSS (M_j) is as above the number of causal assertions involving the POSS operator used in the deduction of M_j from $\langle L_i \rangle$, where W_j is the weight associated with the goal variable which is the argument of the predicate M_j.

(7) The list of executable predicates, $\langle L_i \rangle$ associated with maximum value of μ is then selected.

(8) The arguments of the executable predicates, $\langle L_i \rangle$, are then tested against a list of primitive arguments. These primitive arguments are the names of the variables of the state-vector and the names of the teaching operations which may be found on the right-hand side of the condition-action rules. Where a primitive argument is not found the definitional assertions are used to instantiate one. For example, if the executable predicate is (RAISE THRESHOLD) but no variable of the state-vector is called THRESHOLD then a definitional assertion such as (DEFEQUIV-THRESHOLD (OR TECHNIQUE-THRESHOLD PROBLEM-THRESHOLD)) can be employed to give (RAISE

TECHNIQUE-THRESHOLD), (assuming TECHNIQUE-THRESHOLD is the name of an element of the state-vector).
(9) The set of executable predicates can then be executed.

The amender

The operation of the amender involves the execution of two types of function. Firstly predicates which identify the production rules to be changed and secondly editing functions which execute the changes. The former can be used to identify rules in which named objects occur, or which fire under particular conditions or which set or change the correct tutorial subgoal. The latter functions can be used to change thresholds, parameters and partitions, add and delete actions, and to change the ordering of the tutorial subgoals.

The amender operates with an index listing the nineteen elements of the state-vector, identifying the elements which measured progress towards the tutorial subgoals, listing the primitive argument (e.g. $\equiv$MULT, $\equiv$EASY) and executable predicates (e.g. REMOVE, INSERT, etc.) and associating tutorial actions with goals. The latter was achieved simply by associating any action of the form (HYP $\equiv$X) or (GEN $\equiv$(((X HELP)...)) with the goal X. Actions not associated with any particular goal such as DPRINER, CONTINUE, HYPALL were indexed with all goals.

Statistical evaluations

A simple statistical program was implemented for the purposes of the experiment. It maintained records of all the students with respect to the four goal variables. The program carries out t-tests after each additional student has been taught. These t-tests are used to detect significant changes in the mean scores subsequent to the last experimental change in the set of production rules. If there is a significant change, using a 90% confidence interval, in any of the goal variables, the change is then evaluated to determine if it should be permanently incorporated in the set of production rules.

OI, the measure of overall improvement, was computed as a linear function of SS (student score), PS (post-test score), ST (student time) and CT (computer time). ST and CT were given negative coefficients, and the weights were chosen so that for the units in which SS, PS, ST and CT were measured a 5% increase in SS or PS score was "worth" roughly 20 additional student minutes at the terminal or 10 seconds of processor time. Otherwise the set of production rules prior to the change is restored. Small sample statistics and evaluation after each student were necessary in view of the small number of students on which it was expected to run the program.

Modifying the theory of instruction

A program for automatically modifying theories of instruction was implemented. This program creates causal assertions whenever a statistically significant relation is established during the evaluation of an experimental change to the tutorial strategy. It also creates causal assertions by applying all appropriate definitional assertions. These new assertions are "weak" (that is, modified by POSS operator) generalizations of the main result. Assertions may always be added or deleted by the experimenter if he

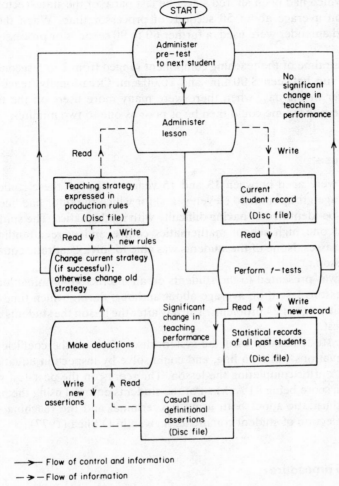

FIG. 4. Schematic diagram of operation of self-improving quadratic tutor.

wishes to give the program some "advice" or to "prime" it in some way. Examples of this program in practice are given in the next chapter.

Implementation notes

The final version of the program was implemented in LISP and ran interactively under Taurus, a time-sharing system on the CDC 6600/6400 at the University of Texas at Austin.

The system comprised five overlays each occupying 33 K and four disc resident files. The operation of the system is illustrated in Fig. 4. Wherever possible the LISP code had been compiled (see Greenawalt, 1974) for speed. An attempt was made to minimize the amount of evaluation in executing the production rules. For example, parsed symbolic state-vectors were stored, and the parsing only recomputed for those elements of the state-vector which had been altered since the last parse of the state-vector. An entire lesson used on average about 50 seconds of processor time. When the deduction procedure and amender were used, a further 60 to 90 seconds or processor time were used.

The response time of the teaching component ranged from 2 to 5 seconds when the program was run between 8.00 a.m. and 10.00 a.m. Occasionally, teaching sessions were held later in the day, when there were many more users on the time-sharing system. The response time could then be as poor as one to two minutes.

The tutor in use

The students were aged between 13 and 15 years. Although these students did not belong to the age group (nine to eleven years) for which the tutor had been designed, they could all be identified as having difficulty with mathematics. The students had all failed at least one high school mathematics course and were attending remedial mathematics classes. None of the students was able to solve quadratic equations at the start of the lesson.

The lesson was presented to the students on an interactive terminal located at the school. The lessons lasted on average about an hour, during which time the student attempted an average of 24 problems. The day after the lesson the students completed a written post-test.

74% of the students who used the system discovered all the coefficient rules for solving the equations while on line, and could solve by inspection equations such as $x^2 + 48 = x \times 19$ after completing the lesson. The scores on the post-test were mostly high, the mean score being 81%. Most of the students enjoyed using the program and were very enthusiastic about both using the terminal and the reaching style of the program. A selection of student comments is given in O'Shea (1977).

Experimental procedure

The tutor, without the self-improving component, was used to give lessons to the first twenty students. The students' records so collected provided the basis for evaluating the effects of subsequent changes in the teaching strategy on teaching performance. The self-improving component was initialized as follows.

(i) The magnitude of changes executed by the (RAISE X) and (LOWER X) function calls was set at 50% of the current values of X.

(ii) The confidence interval for the t-tests was set at 90%.

(iii) The maximum interval between changes in the teaching strategy was set at seven lessons. So if no statistically significant change had occurred after seven students had been run a new change was selected and executed. The previous change was to be incorporated if OI (the measure of overall improvement) had increased, otherwise it was to be removed.

(iv) β, the arbitrary "probability" assigned to possible assertions was set at 0·75. For a given goal, a, the maximum number of alternative possible courses of action was set at 2.

Had a much larger number of students been available it could have been possible to select a smaller magnitude of change in (i), a greater confidence interval in (ii) and greatly increase (iii). It would also have been possible to use a MYCIN-like weighting scheme (see Shortliffe *et al.*, 1975) with different values for β. For the purposes of the experiment, (i)–(iv) were set to insure that the self-improving program made a reasonable number of changes without being completely erratic.

After the program was initialized for the running of experiments it was employed to administer lessons to a further 31 students. The program operated as described by Fig. 4, with control initially at the deduction procedure. To illustrate the procedure employed, the cycle of operations used in the first experiment is described here.

The first goal the program adopted was to decrease the amount of student time. The deduction procedure was employed to deduce the best possible lists of changes in teaching strategy that might achieve this end and would possibly result in minimal deterioration of performance on the other goals. These changes were then executed by the production rule amender, on the set of production rules embodying the tutorial strategy. The modified set of rules were then employed by the pre-test administrator and tutorial strategy, to administer lessons to students. After each student completed his lesson a *t*-test was carried out by the statistical evaluator, to test for a significant change in teaching performance. This continued until seven lessons had been given. The change was incorporated into the teaching strategy as OI (the measure of overall improvement) had increased and control passed back to the deduction procedure, and the cycle of deduction, modification, statistical check continued for four further experiments. The five experiments are discussed in detail in the next section.

The tutor's experiments

The tutor carried out the following five experiments, selecting goals in turn from a "round robin" list.

1. The first goal adopted was to decrease the amount of time spent by students using the program, i.e. (DECREASE (STUDENT TIME)). (REMOVE MINOR) was deduced to be the course of action possibly facilitating this goal with minimum deterioration with respect to the other goals. As MINOR is not a "primitive argument" but defined as the name of a "class of goals", the appropriate definitional assertion was applied to give (REMOVE (GOAL ≡EASY)). This was then passed to the amender and executed.

The production rules that were identified to be changed were:

(a) ((2 B1) ((DPRINER START1) (GOAL ≡EASY)
            (GEN ≡((EASY HELP)) NIL) (CONTINUE 1)))
(b) ((19 K9) ((GOAL ≡ONE) (GEN ≡((ONE HELD) NIL
            (CONTINUE 1)))

(a) was identified by the "(GOAL ≡EASY)" on the right-hand side. (b) was identified by "K9", a partition associated with (GOAL ≡EASY). In rule (a) the REMOVE function deleted the action (GOAL ≡EASY) and the actions listed after it, (GEN ≡((EASY HELP)) NIL) and (CONTINUE 1), which are both associated with (GOAL ≡EASY) in the amender's index. The list of actions from the right-hand side of rule (b) was appended to the list of actions remaining in rule (a), and rule (b) was deleted. The net result of executing (REMOVE (GOAL ≡EASY)) was to leave the following rule in the position of rule (a):

$$((2 \ B1) \ ((DPRINER \ START \ 1) \ GOAL \ \equiv ONE)$$
$$(GEN \ \equiv ((ONE \ HELP)) \ NIL) \ (CONTINUE \ 1) \ ))$$

The result of this change was that the teaching program no longer presented two easy introductory problems. The changes in the mean score of goal variables was monitored after each additional student was taught. After the seventh student had been taught using the amended tutorial strategy, no significant (using the t-test with a 90% confidence interval) change in any of the goal variables had been detected. In fact the mean value of student time had increased. However, computer time had decreased and post-test scores had increased. The value of OI (overall improvement) had increased, so the change in the tutorial strategy was kept. The inconclusive result of this experiment illustrates the difficulties of running simple experiments on single variables where in fact the factors being examined for change are not independent. The changes in the various scores over the whole series of experiments are summarized in Table 1.

2. The goal of increasing the post-test score, (INCREASE (POST SCORE)) was next adopted. The deduced change in tutorial strategy was (REPLACE HYPS (HYPALL)), where HYPALL is the function which tests all the possible hypotheses. HYPS is not a primitive argument and is replaced by applying the definitional sssertion

$$((AND \ (HYP \ \equiv ONE) \ (HYP \ \equiv ADD) \ (HYP \ \equiv TIMES) \ (HYP \ \equiv WRULE)$$
$$(HYPALL)) \ HYPS).$$

The result is that the six production rules with instances of one or more of (HYP ≡ONE), (HYP ≡ADD) or (HYP ≡TIMES) have these instances replaced by (HYPALL).

This change affected teaching performance in that the program now tested all its hypotheses in situations where previously only the hypotheses directly related to a tutorial goal had been tested. Thus the program was experimenting with a trade-off between an increase in computer time against a possibly earlier detection of the occurrences of incidental learning.

After seven students had been taught a significant increase in mean post-test score and a significant decrease in mean computer time were detected. The former change possibly indicates that the quality of example selection had improved. The latter effect is accounted for by a large drop in the average number of examples administered. Another contributing factor is that the examples selected were possibly more appropriate. The assertions

$$(POSS \ (REPLACE \ HYPS \ (HYPALL)) \ (INCREASE \ (POST \ TEST)))$$

and

$$(POSS \ (REPLACE \ HYPS \ (HYPALL))$$
$$(DECREASE \ (COMPUTER \ TIME)))$$

were added to the set of assertions as a whole. As the value of OI had increased, the change in tutorial strategy was kept.

TABLE 1

Table of scores of goal variables from experiments with the quadratic tutor

	Comparison of means between	Result of experiment		Student time, ST (minutes)	Computer time—CT of CPU time	Student seconds score SS (%)	Post-test score, PS (%)	Overall improvement, OI
Initial Group (A) n = 20			M =	51·9	52·9	75	83	53·2
			S.D. =	15	8·85	44·4	22·1	
Experiment 1 Group (B) n = 7	A(n = 20) B(n = 7)	Inconclusive	M =	54·1	49·6	71·4	85·7	53·4
			S.D. =	5·98	6·43	48·8	29·9	
Experiment 2 Group (C) n = 7	A&B(n = 27) C(n = 7)	Success $t = 1\cdot99$ (CT) $t = 1\cdot76$ (PS)	M =	43·8	43·9*	71·4*	100*	83·7
			S.D. =	7·62	8·33	48·8	0	
Experiment 3 Group (D) n = 6	A&B&C(n = 34) D(n = 6)	Fail $t = 2\cdot73$ (PS)	M =	44·3	45·6	50	53·3*	13·3
			S.D. =	4·25	14·5	54·8	51·6	
Experiment 4 Group (E) n = 4	A&B&C(n = 34) E(n = 4)	Success $t = 2\cdot68$ (CT)	M =	39·3	38·5**	75	75	72·3
			S.D. =	2·5	8·58	50	37·9	
Experiment 5 Group (F) n = 6	A&B&C&E(n = 38) F(n = 6)	Success $t = 1\cdot85$ (CT)	M =	47·3	42*	83·3	90	84
			S.D. =	10	9·25	40·8	16·7	
Groups (E) & (F) n = 10	A(n = 20) E&F(n = 10)	$t = 3\cdot61$ (CT)	M =	44·1	40·6***	80	84	79·3
			S.D. =	8·67	8·68	42·2	20·6	

M, Group mean.
s.D., Standard deviation.
*, Significant at the 10% level (two tail test).
**, Significant at the 5% level (two tail test).
***, Significant at the 1% level (two tail test).

3. The next goal adopted was increasing the student score, i.e. (INCREASE (STUDENT SCORE)). The course of action deduced was (REPLACE HYPS (HYPALL)). However, as during the previous experiment exactly this change had already been executed it was not possible to execute this assertion, and the assertion (CERT (REPLACE HYPS (HYPASS)) IMPOSSIBLE) was created. In general in situations of this kind it would probably be more useful for the amender to delete assertions with the clause (REPLACE HYPS (HYPALL)). The deduction procedure was then invoked again and the action (RAISE ENCRATE) was executed. As ENCRATE did not occur on any action list, but was on the amender's index of changeable parameters, this was effected by directly increasing the parameter ENCRATE by 50%. If there had been an action (SETQ ENCRATE 2), say, this would have become (SETQ ENCRATE 3). The effect of this change on teaching performance was that students got more prompts of the form, "have another go". As a result of a bug in the program which gave encouragement, the amount of encouragement was increased by much more than 50% (in fact about 300%). The students were peppered with encouragement and as a result started guessing with complete abandon. After six students a significant decrease in post-test score was detected. The assertion

(POSS (RAISE ENCRATE) (DECREASE (POST SCORE)))

was added to the set of assertions. As OI had decreased the previous version of tutorial strategy was restored.

4. With the goal of decreasing computer time (LOWER HYPTIME) was deduced, and hence (LOWER TIMESCH) as an appropriate course of action. TIMESCH is the eleventh element of the state-vector and indicates the time and direction of the last change in hypothesized ability with the TIMES rule. It was employed in three production rules:

(a) ((1 A3 6 F1 11 G3 19 K3) ((HYPALL)))
(b) ((1 A2 6 F1 7 11 G3 12 G3) ((GOAL ≡HARD) (GEN
          ≡((WRULE HIN)) NIL)))
(c) ((1 A2 6 F1 11 G3 19 K3) ((GOAL ≡TIMESTOADD)
     (GEN ≡((TIMES HELP) (ADD HELP)) NIL))).

The eleventh element in each of these production rules is G3. G3 is given by the partition (G3 GREATERP ELEMENT 2). The change was executed by creating the partition (G6 GREATERP ELEMENT 1) and by rewriting 11 G3 as 11 G6 in the three rules above. This change was equivalent to giving less practice with the TIMES rule after it was judged (by the hypothesis tester) to be "certainly" mastered. After four students had used the program a significant decrease in computer time was detected. The two assertions

(POSS (LOWER HYPTIME) (DECREASE (COMPUTER TIME)))

and

(POSS (LOWER TIMESCH) (DECREASE (COMPUTER TIME)))

were added to the set of assertions. As OI had increased the change in tutorial strategy was kept.

5. Now with the goal of decreasing student time, i.e. (DECREASE (STUDENT TIME)), the action (LOWER HYPTIME) was again deduced. The assertion

(POSS (LOWER HYPTIME) (OR (DECREASE TIMES)
(DECREASE (POST SCORE))))

associates (LOWER HYPTIME) directly with the goal (DECREASE (STUDENT TIME)). The new assertions created after experiment 4 associate (LOWER HYPTIME) more strongly with the desirable side-effect of (DECREASE (COMPUTER TIME)). The result is that (LOWER HYPTIME) had become the strongest candidate (that is, it facilitates the achievement of the selected goal and has best side-effects) for execution.

The changes executed were similar to those in 4 with instances of "12 G3" being replaced by "12 G6". The effect was again a significant decrease in computer time, and new assertions created were

(POSS (LOWER HYPTIME) (DECREASE (STUDENT TIME)))

and

(POSS (LOWER TIMESCH) (DECREASE (STUDENT TIME))).

Summary of experiments

After being run with 30 students the system had carried out five experiments. One had no result, three had positive results, and one had a negative result. eight assertions had been added to the program's set of causal assertions. Comparing the performance of the program over the first 20 students (the initialization stage) and the last ten there was a decrease in mean computer time of 23%. This is significant at the 1% level using a two-tailed t-test. The mean student time, student score, and post-test score improved by 15%, 7% and 1%, respectively. None of these changes is significant at the 5% level using a two-tailed t-test (see Table 1).

The improvements in computer time and student time were not at the expense of deteriorations in student score or post-test score which were near their maximum values at the start of the experiment. It is harder to detect significant changes in student time than in computer time. For example, the larger standard deviation of the student time of the initial group of students was contributed to by broken air-conditioning in the terminal room. This prompted visits to the soft-drinks machine at the other side of the school. This sort of difficulty might be overcome by monitoring the frequency of student activity at the console and basing any measure of student time on this. Strictly the t-test should not have been employed with the variable student score. As a result of the way this score was determined it was in fact a binary variable (any individual student scoring either 100% or 0%). A non-parametric test such as the χ^2 would have been more appropriate.

Appraisal of program

In addition to the improvement in teaching performance the program's set of causal assertions had been added to. An incorrect assertion had been selected, evaluated and contradicted. Several other assertions incorporating the results of experiments had been created. As noted above, the fifth experiment was in fact partly carried out as a result of the assertions created after the fourth experiment. Given that the set of assertions had members of a general nature like:

(POSS (REPLACE MAIN MAIN) (CHANGE SOMEGOAL))

which reads "replacing some 'main' teaching operation by some other 'main' teaching operation may result in some effect on some goal", or

(CERT (SHORTEN SESSIONS) (DECREASE TIMES))

the program could have continued to execute experimental changes in the teaching strategy over a large number of students.

The results of the experiment should be approached with caution. Very small numbers of students were taught and a confidence interval of only 90% was used. A small number of experimental changes were carried out in practice. The only aspect of the teaching strategy experimented with was the tutorial strategy. However, the experiments do serve to illustrate how a self-improving tutor could operate in a practical CAI teaching role. To apply this system in other educational contexts or with other experimental designs it would almost certainly be necessary to extend the statistical evaluator so that it could perform other tests (such as analysis of variance and various non-parametric tests).

There is a hill-climbing problem in that the optimal sequence of experiments cannot be determined. There is also a "frame" problem (see McCarthy & Hayes, 1969); assertions are assumed to have a fixed probability of being true while in practice these probabilities will vary with the changes in the set of production rules. Another limitation is the assumption that the experimental changes are independent of each other. This results from the simple nature of the theories of instruction which can be expressed in the formalism put forward. In contrast a more complex theory would be an attempt to account for the interaction of different changes on the teaching strategy and might have some associated meta-theory related to the alternative experimental design associated with the testing of the theory.

The design becomes much more practical if we assume that in practice self-improving tutors would be used as tools by teachers and experimental psychologists to develop and test teaching strategies and theories of instruction. In that circumstance if the teaching performance of the tutor greatly deteriorated the human experimenter could intervene and change any suspect production rules. Similarly if an interesting experiment or class of experiment became apparent the educationalist could add appropriate particular or general assertions to the set of assertions which would initiate these experiments. In this way a self-improving tutor could be developed and extended in a similar synergistic mode to that successfully applied in MYCIN (Shortliffe et al., 1975). For the theory of instruction can be regarded as an action-driven production system (see Waterman, 1977) where the question to be answered by deductive inference on the assertions is "what change in teaching strategy will improve teaching performance with respect to educational objective x?".

Applicability of approach

The work described is particularly applicable to CAI programs intended to run under the very large multi-access systems such as PLATO (Dugdale & Kibbey, 1976) and TICCIT (Mitre, 1974). In such a computational environment decisions made in the construction of CAI programs affect very large numbers of students. These environments also give the possibility of collecting considerable amounts of performance data which should enable self-improving systems to make more reliable modifications. With respect to such use, self-improving tutors have the following desirable characteristics.

(a) They can run experiments and improve their own teaching performance.
(b) They can collect teaching program performance data in a goal-directed and selective manner.
(c) They have to be "transparent" with respect to their tutorial strategy. That is to say, to allow for self-improvement, the various functions of the program which affect the tutorial strategy must be made explicit. (For example, in the design presented such functions are modular and are expressed as sets of production rules. Such transparency allows flexibility and other desirable side-effects.)
(d) The overall educational objectives and any underlying theory of instruction must be made explicit.

In principle the approach presented could be employed to construct self-improving tutors for any domain where:

(1) a strategy of actions can be expressed as a set of condition-driven production rules;
(2) a theory of the possible utility of changing the actions can be expressed as a set of modally qualified propositional assertions.

It should be clear that in addition to the various limitations discussed above the potential for self-improvement depends on the initial set of production rules and on the initial set of assertions in the theory. It should also be clear that although the assertions can be very general or highly specific, the theory as a whole will represent not very much more than an economically expressed and partially ordered list or agenda of possibly useful experiments for "tuning" an existing tutorial strategy.

My principal debt is to my supervisor, Derek Sleeman, for the patient help, advice and encouragement he has so freely given. Roger Hartley and John Self have also generously spent much time helping me to clarify my ideas. I am grateful to Richard C. Anderson, Woody Bledsoe, Cornelia Boldyreff, Benedict du Boulay, John S. Brown, Ira Goldstein, Jim Howe, Gordon Plotkin, Martha Palmer, Don Waterman, Jon Wexler and Richard Young for helpful discussions at various stages of the research.

The preliminary experiments were conducted with the help and co-operation of the Headmaster, Staff and pupils of the Hunslet Moor Junior School, Leeds. The implementation of the program was made possible by the generous support of Robert Simmons. The experiments with the program were conducted with the kind permission and active assistance of the administrative officers (in particular Mr Schilab), the Mathematics Faculty (in particular Mrs Shelton, Mrs Waggoner and Mrs Conway) and the students of the Austin Independent School District.

I was financially supported by an SRC award while at Leeds University, and at the University of Texas my support came from NSF Grant GJ 509X.

References

BLACK, F. (1968). A deductive question-answering system. In MINSKY, M., Ed., *Semantic Information Processing*. M.I.T. Press.

BROWN, J. S., RUBINSTEIN, R. & BURTON, R. (1976). A reactive learning environment for computer assisted electronics instruction. *BBN Report No. 3314*. Bolt Beranek & Newman Inc., Cambridge, Mass.

CARBONELL, J. R. (1970). AI in CAI: An Artificial Intelligence approach to computer assisted instruction. *IEEE Transactions on Man–Machine Systems*, **MMS-11** (4).

DUGDALE, S. & KIBBEY, D. (1976). *Elementary Mathematics with Plato*. Urbana, Ill.: Computer-based Education Laboratory.

GOLDBERG, A. (1973). CAI: The application of theorem-proving to adaptive response analysis. *Technical Report 203*. Institute for Mathematical Studies in the Social Sciences, Stanford University.

GREENAWALT, M. (1973). *U.T. LISP Manual*. Computing Centre, University of Texas at Austin.

HARTLEY, J. R. (1973). The design and evaluation of an adaptive teaching system. *International Journal of Man–Machine Studies*, **5** (2).

HEWITT, C. (1972). Descriptions and theoretical analysis (using schemata) of PLANNER: A language for proving theorems and manipulating models in a robot. *Ph.D. Thesis*. Artificial Intelligence Laboratory, M.I.T. Cambridge, Mass.

HUGHES, C. E. & CRESSWELL, M. S. (1972). *Introduction of Modal Logic*. London: Methuen.

KIMBALL, R. B. (1973). Self-optimizing computer-assisted tutoring: theory and practice. *Technical Report No. 206 (Psychology and Education Series)*. Institute for Mathematical Studies in the Social Sciences, Stanford University.

KOFFMAN, E. & BLOUNT, S. E. (1973). AI and automatic programming in CAI. *Proceedings of Third International Joint Conference on Artificial Intelligence*, pp. 86–94.

MCCARTHY, J. & HAYES, P. (1969). Some philosophical problems from the standpoint of artificial intelligence. In MELTZER, B. & MICHIE, D., Eds, *Machine Intelligence*, **4**, 463–502. Edinburgh: Edinburgh University Press.

MITRE CORPORATION (1974). *An Overview of the TICCIT Program*. McLean, Virginia: Mitre.

O'SHEA, T. & SLEEMAN, D. H. (1973). A design for an adaptive self-improving teaching system. In ROSE, J., Ed., *Advances in Cybernetics*. London: Gordon & Breach.

O'SHEA, T. (1977). A self-improving teaching system. Unpublished *Ph.D. Thesis*. Department of Computer Studies, University of Leeds. To appear in Birkhauser ISR Series (1979).

PASK, G. (1972). *Anti-Hodmanship: A Report on the State and Prospects of CAI*. System Research Ltd., Richmond, Surrey.

SCHULMAN, L. S. & KEISLER, E. R. (1966). *Learning by Discovery*. Chicago: Rand McNally & Co.

SELF, J. (1974). Student models in CAI. *International Journal of Man–Machine Studies*, **6** (2).

SHORTLIFFE, E. H., DAVIS, R., BUCHANAN, B., AXLINE, B., GREEN, C. & COHEN, S. (1975). Computer-based consultations in clinical therapeutics: exploration and rule acquisition capabilities of the MYCIN system. *Computers and Biomedical Research*, **8**, 303–320.

SLEEMAN, D. H. (1974). A problem solving monitor for a deductive reasoning task. *International Journal of Man–Machine Studies*, **7** (2).

SMALLWOOD, R. D. (1962). *A Decision Structure for Teaching Machines*. Cambridge, Mass.: M.I.T. Press.

STANSFIELD, J. L. (1974). Programming a dialogue teaching system. *Bionics Research Report No. 25*. Bionics Research Laboratory, School of Artificial Intelligence, University of Edinburgh.

WATERMAN, D. A. (1970). Generalization learning techniques for automating the learning of heuristics. *Artificial Intelligence*, **1**, 121–170.

WATERMAN, D. A. (1977). An introduction to production systems. *AISB European Newsletter*, **25**, 7–10.

WOODS, P. & HARTLEY, J. R. (1971). Some learning models for arithmetic tasks and their use in computer-based learning. *British Journal of Educational Psychology*, **41** (1), 35–48.

Appendix 1: A set of production rules for the quadratic tutor

(a) *The elements of the state-vector*
  (i) CYCLE—The operation last performed by teaching program.
  (ii) TIME—The number of examples administered.
  (iii) NUMG—The number of guesses made by the student on the last example.
  (iv) EXDETAILS—A list of the features of the last example.
  (v) EXTYPE—A list of the parameters for GEN for the last example generated.
  (vi) TIMES—The hypothesized current ability of the student with the times rule.
  (vii)–(x) ADD, ONE, WRULE, WORULE—as in (vi) for the respective rules.
  (xi) TIMESCH—The time and direction of the last change in hypothesized ability with the TIMES rule.
  (xii)–(xv) ADDCH, ONECH, WRULECH, WORULECH—as in (xi) for the respective rules.
  (xvi) PRETEST—The student score on the pre-test.
  (xvii) REASON—The reason for termination of administration of last example.
  (xviii) GOALTIME—The amount of time since the selection of the current goal.
  (xix) GOAL—The current goal.

(b) *The set of condition-action rules*
  ((2 B1) ((DPRINER START1) (GOAL ≡ONE) (GEN ≡((ONE HELP)) NIL) (CONTINUE 1)))
  ((1 A3 17 I6) ((DPRINER TERM) (STOP)))
  ((1 A3 2 B3) ((DPRINER TIMETERM) (STOP)))
  ((1 A2 9 F1 18 J3 19 K8) ((DPRINER SUCCTERM) (STOP)))
  ((1 A2 18 J3 19 K8) ((GOAL ≡TIMES) (GEN ≡((TIMES HELP)) NIL)))
  ((1 A2 19 K8) ((CONTINUE 1)))
  ((1 A3 18 J4) (HYPALL)))
  ((1 A3 18 J3) ((HYPALL)))
  ((1 A3 6 F1 11 G3 19 K3) ((HYPALL)))
  ((1 A3 7 F1 12 G3 19 K2) ((HYPALL)))
  ((1 A3 8 F1 13 G3 19 K1) ((HYPALL)))
  ((1 A3 2 B2) ((HYPALL)))
  ((1 A2 2 B2 10 F8) ((DPRINER TIMETERM) (STOP)))
  ((1 A3 19 K1) ((HYP ≡ONE)))
  ((1 A3 19 K2) ((HYP ≡ADD)))
  ((1 A3 19 K3) ((HYP ≡TIMES)))
  T1: ((1 A2 6 F1 11 G3 12 G3) ((GOAL ≡HARD) (GEN ≡((WRULE HIN)) NIL)))
       ((1 A2 10 F7 19 K8) ((GOAL ≡TIMES) (GEN ≡((WRULE HELP) (TIMES HELP)) NIL)))
  T2: ((1 A2 6 F1 11 G3 19 K3) ((GOAL ≡TIMESTOADD) (GEN ≡((TIMES HELP) (ADD HELP)) NIL)))

T3: ((1 A2 6 F4 F7 18 J3 19 K3) ((GOAL ≡ADD) (GEN ≡((ADD HELP)) NIL)))

T4: ((1 A2 6 F8 19 K3) ((CONTINUE 1)))

T5: ((1 A2 7 (F8 F7) 19 K3) ((GOAL ≡ADD) (GEN ≡((ADD HELP)) NIL)))

T6: ((1 A2 8 (F8 F7) 19 K3) ((GOAL ≡ONE)(GEN ≡((ONE HELP)) NIL)))

((1 A2 7 F1 12 G3 19 K2) ((GOAL ≡ADDTOTIMES) (GEN ≡((ADD HELP) (TIMES HELP)) NIL)))

((1 A2 6 F7 7 F4 18 J4 19 K2) ((GOAL ≡TIMES) (GEN ≡((TIMES HELP) NIL)))

((1 A2 7 F8 19 K2) ((CONTINUE 1)))

((1 A2 6 (F8 F7) 19 K2) ((GOAL ≡TIMES) (GEN ≡(TIMES HELP)) NIL)))

((1 A2 8 (F8 F7) 19 K2) ((GOAL ≡ONE) (GEN ≡((ONE HELP)) NIL)))

((1 A2 8 F1 13 G3 19 K1) ((GOAL ≡ONETOADD) (GEN ≡((ADD HELP) (ONE HIN)) NIL)))

((1 A2 7 F7 18 J4 19 K1) ((GOAL ≡ADD) (GEN ≡((ADD HELP)) NIL)))

((1 A2 8 F8 19 K1) ((CONTINUE 1)))

((1 A2 6 (F8 F7) 19 K1) ((GOAL ≡TIMES) (GEN ≡((TIMES HELP)) NIL)))

((1 A2 7 (F8 F7) 19 K1) ((GOAL ≡ADD) (GEN ≡((ADD HELP)) NIL)))

((1 A2 7 F4 19 K6) ((GOAL ≡ADD) (GEN ≡((ADD HELP)) NIL)))

((1 A2 18 J3 19 K6) ((GOAL ≡TIMES) (GEN ≡((TIMES HELP) (ADD HIN)) NIL)))

((1 A2 19 K6) ((GEN ≡(TIMES HELP) (ADD HIN)) NIL) (HYP ≡TIMES)
      (GEN ≡(ADD HELP) (TIMES HIN)) NIL) (HYP ≡ADD)))

((1 A2 6 F4 19 K7) ((GOAL ≡TIMES) (GEN ≡((TIMES HELP)) NIL)))

((1 A2 18 J3 19 K7) ((GOAL ≡ADD) (GEN ≡((ADD HELP) (TIMES HIN)) NIL)))

((1 A2 19 K7) ((GEN ≡((ADD HELP) (TIMES HIN)) NIL) (HYP ≡ADD)
      (GEN ≡((TIMES HELP) (ADD HIN)) NIL) (HYP ≡TIMES)))

((1 A2 8 F4 19 K4) ((GOAL ≡ONE) (GEN ≡((ONE HELP)) NIL)))

((1 A2 18 J3 19 K4) ((GOAL ≡ADD) (GEN ≡((ADD HELP) (ONE HIN)) NIL)))

((1 A2 19 K4) ((GEN ≡((ONE HELP) (ADD HIN)) NIL) (HYP ≡ONE)
      (GEN ≡((ADD HELP) (ONE HIN)) NIL) (HYP ≡ADD)))

T7: ((1 A2) ((CONTINUE 1)))
      ((1 A3) ((HYPALL)))
      (() ((PRIN1 ≡FAIL)))

(c) *The set of partitions*
(PUT) ≡QUADPARTS ≡CYCLE ≡(
      (A1 EQUAL ELEMENT ≡GEN)
      (A2 EQUAL ELEMENT ≡HYP)
      (A3 EQUAL ELEMENT ≡ADMIN)))

```
(PUT ≡QUADPARTS ≡TIME ≡(
    (B1 EQUAL ELEMENT 0)
    (B2 EQUAL ELEMENT 10)
    (B3 GREATERP ELEMENT 30) ))
(PUT ≡QUADPARTS ≡NUMG ≡(
    (C1 EQUAL ELEMENT 2)
    (C2 BETWEEN ELEMENT 11 1)
    (C3 GREATERP ELEMENT 10) ))
(PUT ≡QUADPARTS ≡EXDETAILS ≡(
    (D1 MEMBER ≡NEW ELEMENT)
    (D2 MEMBER ≡OLD ELEMENT) ))
(PUT ≡QUADPARTS ≡EXTYPE ≡(
    (E1 MEMBER ≡(TIMES HELP ELEMENT)
    (E2 MEMBER ≡(ADD HELP) ELEMENT)
    (E3 MEMBER ≡(ONE HELP) ELEMENT)
    (E4 MEMBER ≡(WRULE HIN) ELEMENT) ))
(PUT ≡QUADPARTS ≡TIMES ≡(
    (F1 EQUAL ELEMENT ≡CERT)
    (F2 MEMBER ELEMENT ≡(CERT VPOSS POSS))
    (F3 EQUAL ELEMENT ≡DUNNO)
    (F4 MEMBER ELEMENT ≡(POSSNOT CERTNOT))
    (F5 EQUAL ELEMENT ≡CERTNOT)
    (F6 EQUAL ELEMENT ≡POSS)
    (F7 NEQ ELEMENT ≡CERT)
    (F8 MEMBER ELEMENT ≡(CERT VPOSS))
    (F9 EQUAL ELEMENT ≡NO CHECK) ))
(PUT ≡QUADPARTS ≡TIMESCH ≡(
    (G1 EQUAL ELEMENT 0)
    (G2 EQUAL ELEMENT 1)
    (G3 GREATERP ELEMENT 2)
    (G4 EQUAL ELEMENT −1)
    (G5 LESSP ELEMENT 2) ))
(PUT ≡QUADPARTS ≡PRETEST NIL)
(PUT ≡QUADPARTS ≡REASON ≡(
    (I1 EQUAL ELEMENT ≡CORRECT)
    (I2 EQUAL ELEMENT ≡GUESSLIM)
    (I3 EQUAL ELEMENT ≡SYSLIM)
    (I4 EQUAL ELEMENT ≡WILDLIM)
    (I5 EQUAL ELEMENT ≡REPLIM)
    (I6 EQUAL ELEMENT ≡STOP) ))
(PUT ≡QUADPARTS ≡GOALTIME ≡(
    (J1 EQUAL ELEMENT 1)
    (J2 BETWEEN ELEMENT 4 0)
    (J3 EQUAL ELEMENT 5)
    (J4 GREATERP ELEMENT 7) ))
(PUT ≡QUADPARTS ≡GOAL ≡(
    (K1 EQUAL ELEMENT ≡ONE)
```

        (K2 EQUAL ELEMENT ≡ADD)
        (K3 EQUAL ELEMENT ≡TIMES)
        (K4 EQUAL ELEMENT ≡ONETOADD)
        (K5 EQUAL ELEMENT ≡ADDTOTIMES)
        (K6 EQUAL ELEMENT ≡ADDTOTIMES)
        (K7 EQUAL ELEMENT ≡TIMESTOADD)
        (K8 EQUAL ELEMENT ≡HARD)
        (K9 EQUAL ELEMENT ≡EASY)))

Note: the initial partitions for ADD, ONE, WRULE, WORULE, are set the same as that for TIMES. Likewise the partitions for ADDCH, ONECH, WRULECH, WORULECH are the same as that for TIMESCH.

(d) *Example of cycle of operation for set of production rules*
The state-vector: (≡HYP, 17, 8, ≡(NEW, EQ1), ≡((ONE, HELP)), CERT, CERT, VPOSS, VPOSS, CERTNOT, 4, 3, 1, 2, 7, 10, ≡CORRECT, 5, ≡ADD) when parsed with the set of partitions gives the parsed vector: (A2, NIL, C2, D1, E3, (F1, F2, F8), (F1, F2, F8), (F2, F7, F8), (F2, F7, F8, (F4, F5), G3, G3, (G2, G5), NIL, G3, NIL, I1, J3, K2). This matches the rule labelled T1 and the right-hand side is executed.

(e) *Parameters associated with task administration which can be used*
    GUESSLIM—The maximum number of guesses which the student is permitted to make.
    ENCRATE—The intervals at which the student is given an encouraging remark.
    REPLIM—The maximum number of repeated identical guesses before the student is moved to a new example.
    SYSLIM—The maximum length of a sequence of systematic guesses before the student is given a comment on this.
    WILDLIM—The highest "wild guess" the student may make without comment.
    Notes: (i) The condition sides of the production rules have been written in an abbreviated form. So for example in the second rule of section (b), (1, A3, 17 I6) only matches if the first element of the state-vector is an "A3" and the seventeenth element is an "I6". (ii) The set of condition-action rules given here are those present in the system after the third experiment.

Appendix 2: Set of assertions used by the deduction system

(a) *Causal assertions*
    (POSS (DECREASE (HYPOTHESIS TESTING)) (OR(DECREASE
        (COMPUTER TIME)) (INCREASE SCORES) (INCREASE
        (STUDENT TIME))))
    (CERT (REMOVE HYPS) (DECREASE (HYPOTHESIS TESTING)))
    (CERT (AND(EQUAL (VAR CYCLE) ADMIN) (RAISE CONTINUE))
        (DECREASE (HYPOTHESIS TESTING)))
    (CERT (AND(EQUAL SUBRULES CERT) (REPLACE (HYPALL) ((HYP
        ≡ONE) (HYP ≡ADD) (HYP ≡TIMES)))) (DECREASE
        (HYPOTHESIS TESTING)))
    (POSS (INCREASE (HYPOTHESIS TESTING)) (OR(INCREASE

```
                    (COMPUTER TIME)) (INCREASE SCORES) (DECREASE
                    (STUDENT TIME)) ))
                    (CERT (REPLACE HYPS (HYPALL)) (INCREASE
                    HYPOTHESIS TESTING)) )
            (POSS (REPLACE MAIN MAIN) (CHANGE SOMEGOAL) )
            (POSS (REMOVE MINOR) (DECREASE (STUDENT TIME)) )
            (POSS (REMOVE (GOAL ≡EASY)) (DECREASE (COMPUTER TIME)) )
            (POSS (REMOVE (GOAL ≡HARD)) (DECREASE (POST SCORE)) )
            (POSS (AND(BEFORE (GOAL ≡TIMES)) (AFTER (GOAL ≡ONE))
                    (INSERT (GOAL ≡ADD))) (CHANGE SCORES) )
            (POSS (AND (REMOVE (GOAL ≡ONE)) (REMOVE (GOAL
                    ≡ONETOADD)) (REMOVE (GOAL ≡ONETOTIMES)))
                    (OR(DECREASE SCORES) (DECREASE TIMES)) )
            (POSS (LOWER EXLIMIT) (DECREASE (STUDENT TIME)) )
            (POSS (AND(AFTER (GOAL ≡EASY)) (REPLACE (GOAL ≡ONE)
                    (GOAL ≡TIMES))) (SHORTEN SESSIONS) )
            (POSS (AND(LOWER PROGLIMIT) (PRESENT (STOP))) (SHORTEN
                    SESSIONS) )
            (CERT (SHORTEN SESSIONS) (DECREASE TIMES) )
            (POSS (SHORTEN SESSIONS) (DECREASE SCORES) )
            (CERT (KEEP BORED STUDENTS) (INCREASE TIMES) )
            (POSS (KEEP BORED STUDENTS) (OR(DECREASE(POST SCORE))
                    (INCREASE (STUDENT SCORE))) )
            (CERT (AND(REPLACE (DPRINER TERM) (DPRINER ≡CONTINUE))
                    (REPLACE (STOP)
            (POSS (LOWER HYPTIME) (OR (DECREASE TIMES) (DECREASE
                    (POST SCORE))))
            (POSS (LOWER (VAR GOALTIME)) (OR (DECREASE TIMES)
             (DECREASE (POST SCORE))))
            (POSS (LOWER GUESSLIM) (DECREASE (STUDENT TIME)) )
            (POSS (LOWER EXLIMIT) (DECREASE SCORES) )
            (POSS (AND (LOWER GUESSLIM) (INSERT (ADMIN RIGHTANS)))
                    (CHANGE SCORES) )
            (POSS (RAISE ENCRATE) (DECREASE (POST SCORE)) )
            (POSS (DECREASE WILDLIM) (OR(DECREASE SCORES) (DECREASE
                    (STUDENT TIME))) )
            (POSS (RAISE SYSLIM) (INCREASE (STUDENT SCORE)) )


    (b) Definitional assertions
            (EQUIV AFTER (NOT BEFORE))
            (EQUIV ABSENT (NOT PRESENT))
            (EQUIV LOWER (NOT RAISE))
            (EQUIV INCREASE (NOT DECREASE))
            (EQUIV CHANGE (OR INCREASE DECREASE))
            (EQUIV (AND TIMES SCORES) ALLGOALS)
            (EQUIV (AND (STUDENT TIME) (COMPUTER TIME)) TIMES)
```

```
(EQUIV (AND (STUDENT SCORE) (POST SCORE)) SCORES)
(EQUIV (OR (COMPUTER TIME) (STUDENT TIME) (STUDENT
    SCORE) (POST SCORE) SCORES TIMES ALLGOALS) SOMEGOAL)
(EQUIV (OR REPLIM SYSLIM GUESSLIM WILDLIM) EXLIMIT)
(EQUIV (OR (VAR TIME) (VAR PRETEST)) PROGLIMIT)
(EQUIV (OR (GOAL ≡ONETOADD) (GOAL ≡ADDTOTIMES) (GOAL
    ≡TIMESTOADD)) SWITCH)
(EQUIV (OR (GOAL ≡ADD) (GOAL ≡TIMES) (GOAL ≡ONE)) MAIN)
(EQUIV (OR (GOAL ≡HARD) (GOAL ≡EASY)) MINOR)
(EQUIV (OR MAIN MINOR SWITCH) PROGGOALS)
(EQUIV (AND(HYP ≡ONE) (HYP ≡ADD) (HYP ≡TIMES) (HYP
    ≡WRULE) (HYP ≡WORULE) (HYPALL) ) HYPS)
(EQUIV (OR (VAR ADD) (VAR ONE) (VAR TIMES)) (SUBRULES)
(EQUIV (OR (VAR TIMESCH) (VAR ADDCH) (VAR ONECH)
    (VAR WRULECH) (VAR WORULECH)) HYPTIME)
```

Index